D1234661

COLD WAR
TRIUMPHALISM

COLD WAR TRIUMPHALISM

The Misuse of History After the Fall of Communism

EDITED BY ELLEN SCHRECKER

THE NEW PRESS

NEW YORK
LONDON

Compilation © 2004 by Ellen Schrecker
Individual essays © by each author

All rights reserved.
No part of this book may be reproduced,
in any form, without written permission
from the publisher.

Published in the United States by The New Press, New York, 2004
Distributed by W. W. Norton & Company, Inc., New York

LIBRARY OF CONGRESS CATALOGING-IN-PUBLICATION DATA
Cold War triumphalism : the misuse of history after the fall of communism /
    edited by Ellen Schrecker.
        p.   cm.
    Includes bibliographical references and index.
    ISBN 1-56584-899-3
    1. United States—Foreign relations—1989–   2. United States—Politics and
government—1989–   3. United States—Foreign relations—1945–1989—
Philosophy.   4. United States—History—1945—Philosophy.   5. World
Politics—1945–1989—Philosophy.   6. Cold War.   7. Cold War—Influence.
I. Schrecker, Ellen.
E840.C646   2004
327.73'009'049—dc22   2003061501

The New Press was established in 1990 as a not-for-profit alternative to the large,
commercial publishing houses currently dominating the book publishing industry. The New Press operates in the public interest rather than for private gain, and
is committed to publishing, in innovative ways, works of educational, cultural,
and community value that are often deemed insufficiently profitable.

The New Press
38 Greene Street, 4th floor
New York, NY 10013
www.thenewpress.com

In the United Kingdom:
6 Salem Road
London W2 4BU

Composition by dix!

Printed in the United States of America

10   9   8   7   6   5   4   3   2   1

CONTENTS

COLD WAR
TRIUMPHALISM

INTRODUCTION

Cold War Triumphalism and the Real Cold War

Ellen Schrecker

For more than forty years the Cold War loomed over the world, a bruising contest between two nuclear-armed superpowers and their allies in which the fate of the earth seemed to hang in the balance. At its height, each side viewed the struggle as an immutable clash between incompatible political and economic systems. Each, of course, claimed to be on the defensive—the Americans protecting Western civilization from an expansionist revolutionary power that had gobbled up Eastern Europe and was threatening the rest of the world, while the Soviets saw themselves as the beleaguered bastion of international socialism, fending off rapacious capitalists. During the course of the conflict, both sides built empires, developed weapons of mass destruction, and fought proxy wars that killed millions of people. Then, suddenly, it was over. Unwilling and unable to use force to keep its rickety imperium together, the Soviet Union simply fell apart. Within a few months, Communist governments had disappeared from the map of Europe and the Union of Soviet Socialist Republics was no more.

While the USSR's disintegration was largely caused by its own internal structural problems compounded by the doomed reforms of Mikhail Gorbachev, it was greeted by many in the West, conservatives in particular, as a great victory for the United States.[1] "The collapse of the Soviet Empire in Eastern Europe," hard-liner Richard Perle proclaimed, "is in large measure a result of the postwar strength and determination of the alliance of Western democracies."[2] Perle's formulation—and one could cite hundreds of similar ones—has become a truism in the world of politicians and talking heads. Communism's failure was America's success. That the denizens of Eastern Europe and the former Soviet Union might also have had a hand in the process rarely figures in the story. Instead, it was the strategic resourcefulness of the American government, the technological dynamism of the American economy, and the moral and cultural superiority of the American system that simply (but peacefully) overwhelmed the backward tyrants of Moscow. Our perseverance, *Commentary*'s Joshua Muravchik noted, won the day:

> After victory in World War I we turned inward and reaped unprecedented catastrophe. After World War II we assumed the burdens of international engagement and were rewarded by a triumph beyond our fondest dreams. We faced the most puissant enemy we or anyone had ever known, and we brought it down without having to fight a big war.[3]

Despite its massive distortion of the recent past, this interpretation dominates contemporary political discourse—at least within the United States. Outside of the left and a handful of academics, few even question the notion that America "won" the Cold War. Whether there actually was such a victory and what that victory entails are seemingly beyond debate. As a result, there has been no postwar reassessment of the U.S.-Soviet conflict, no final accounting of its impact on American society and the rest of the world, not even an attempt to explain why, given its anticlimactic outcome, it dragged on for so many years. Instead, an undemanding patriotic celebration prevails, glorifying Washington's past actions in order to justify its present ones. This triumphalism serves a partisan function as well: it supplies a supposedly irrefutable basis for disparaging left-wing critics of the Cold War, while it prepares the same historical dustbin for those who question current policies. The contributors to this volume, though differing among themselves about the wisdom and morality of the Bush administration's recent actions, are unanimous in rejecting its oversimplified view of the recent past. By presenting alternative interpretations of the Cold War, their essays complicate the standard narrative and thus challenge the uses to which it is being put.

The triumphalist history of the Cold War contains little nuance or ambiguity. It overlooks those aspects of the struggle that might spoil the victory bash, while it highlights those that bolster the status quo. Thus, the triumphalists see no problem with American militarism and the Pentagon's massive incursions against the federal budget, nor do they question the Manichaean approach to the rest of the world that lets policy-makers win public support for all manner of foreign adventures. Similarly, capitalism, no longer obscured by its Cold War euphemism "free enterprise," now reigns supreme in the triumphalists' increasingly Hobbesian economic universe. There is no room for victims (as opposed to losers) in this vision of the Cold War, nor any sense that the past might have taken a different turn or that the over-armed confrontation might have inflicted damages all on its own.

In fact, many triumphalists positively celebrate the militarization that marked the Cold War. Even though direct hostilities never broke out between the Soviet Union and the United States, American arms determined the outcome. "Our bloodless victory in the Cold War," Muravchik explained in 1992, "has just given eloquent answer to those who asked so insistently why we were 'wasting' so many billions on weapons 'that will never be used.' "[4] The arms race, in other words, was quite literally that—and not just a metaphor. Ronald Reagan brought us across the finish line. His Strategic Defense Initiative, a.k.a. Star Wars, was, in Margaret Thatcher's words, "the final straw for the Evil Empire."[5] The project conjured up the seemingly inexhaustible resources of the American military-industrial system and spent the already faltering Russians into submission.[6] "The Kremlin couldn't compete with the Reagan buildup," arch-conservative Ann Coulter declared.

> Contrary to cheery reports in the American media, the Soviet economy was a basket case. Reagan made it worse. . . . Reagan's unrelenting pressure on the Soviet economy forced the USSR to begin withdrawing its troops and largesse from aspiring Marxist dictatorships abroad.

Still, the Soviet Union could have stumbled along for a few more decades. . . . But Reagan wasn't going to let the USSR outlast him. The last great battle of the Cold War was fought in Reykjavik, Iceland, on October 13, 1986. That was the day Reagan refused to accede to Mikhail Gorbachev's demand that the United States abandon the Strategic Defense Initiative.[7]

All great epics need a hero, and, as Coulter's recounting implies, Ronald Reagan is the triumphalists' champion. "Were it not for President Reagan," presidential candidate Robert Dole told the Republican national convention in 1996, "the Soviet Union would still be standing today."[8] Disgusted by years of détente and containment, Reagan and his hawkish advisers decided to risk an all-out confrontation with the "Evil Empire." He pumped up the Cold War rhetoric, increased the U.S. defense budget, and aimed directly at the heart of the Soviet economy. "And when communism came down," Dole's running mate, Jack Kemp, explained, "it wasn't because it fell. It was because he pushed it."[9]

Triumphalists also frame the story as a moral parable. America won the Cold War because America deserved to win. Freedom, democracy, justice, courage, and the sheer grit and resolve of the American people triumphed over despotism and darkness. It was good vs. evil, black against white or, as Lynne Cheney put it, "the most salient fact" about the Cold War was "that the struggle was between the Communist totalitarianism of the Soviet Union, on the one hand, and the freedom offered by the United States, on the other."[10] It was a struggle, President Bush reminded the nation in his 2003 State of the Union address, against

> small groups of men [who] seized control of great nations, built armies and arsenals, and set out to dominate the weak and intimidate the world. In each case, their ambitions of cruelty and murder had no limit. In each case, the ambitions of Hitlerism, militarism, and communism were defeated by the will of free peoples, by the strength of great alliances, and by the might of the United States of America.[11]

Coulter gives the story a spiritual twist: "It wasn't just military might or a preference for the materialist bounty of capitalism that drove

Reagan's victory over communism. It was Americans choosing faith in God over faith in man."[12] Nor was she alone in seeing the hand of the Almighty in the undertaking. Treating the Cold War as a moral and even religious crusade was quite compatible with the traditional missionary thrust of American foreign relations.

And then there's the market. A big part of the celebration is the contention that the end of the Cold War was an economic as well as military and ideological victory. "It was," Francis Fukuyama, triumphalism's intellectual guru, explains, "in the highly complex and dynamic 'postindustrial' economic world that Marxism-Leninism as an economic system met its Waterloo."[13] For Fukuyama, as well as for his fellow market-oriented pundits, the fall of the Soviet Union demonstrates the superiority of Western capitalism—and in a way that transcends the material realm of economics. Just as winning the Cold War vindicated the West's military buildup, so too it conferred a similar legitimacy to the neoliberalism that came to dominate economic thought by the 1980s. Free markets were not just a mechanism, but a mantra and, like much of the ideological apparatus of the Cold War era, one that had an existence independent of the Cold War. If, as Nelson Lichtenstein claims in his contribution to this volume, market triumphalism is "the single greatest legacy of the end of the Cold War," it was a legacy that, Michael Bernstein shows in his essay here, had been developing ever since the 1970s if not before.[14] As early as the 1940s, it had become common to conflate free markets with democracy and to treat free enterprise as, in the words of one historian, "a fundamental freedom upon which all other freedoms ultimately depended."[15] Such a characterization gave a moralistic gloss to corporate behavior that might otherwise be viewed as self-serving. In any event, so the market triumphalists insisted, there was no alternative. Expanding upon the lesson supposedly provided by the Soviet system's collapse, they claimed that *any* government interference with the economy was doomed.[16]

Equally doomed was the political left—on both sides of the former Iron Curtain. Its prescriptions did not work and its hands were dirty, or so the triumphalists maintained. "The fall of the Berlin Wall, the collapse of communism behind the Iron Curtain, and the changing character of China," Milton Friedman announced in 1994, "have reduced the defenders of a Marxian-type collectivism to a small hardy band concentrated in western universities. Today there is wide agreement that socialism is a failure, and capitalism a success." So pervasive, in fact, is the notion that the left has lost all credibility that even critics of market fundamentalism declare the bankruptcy of the left.[17] For the right, especially for American neoconservatives, communism's fall brought only a partial victory; there was still a domestic Cold War to wage. Irving Kristol summed it up by lamenting that "There is no 'after the Cold War' for me. So far from having ended, my cold war has increased in intensity, as sector after sector of American life has been ruthlessly corrupted by the liberal ethos. . . . Now that the other 'Cold War,' is over, the real cold war has begun."[18] Kristol was, as usual, embroidering things a bit. He and his allies had been conducting their Kulturkampf against the left for years; the demise of the Soviet Union simply gave them new ammunition.

Some of that ammunition came from the former USSR itself. Its collapse opened some of its archives, releasing evidence (corroborated by some recent American disclosures) about Stalin's policies and Communist spying that reenergized traditional anticommunism. In our contribution to this volume, Maurice Isserman and I look at the way in which some triumphalists have used those new documents to vindicate the domestic Cold War against the left and, by implication, to disparage those who question its value today.

Finally, and most importantly, the triumphalist narrative now serves to justify what Chalmers Johnson here identifies as America's "other objectives," its "covert Cold War project to create a global capitalist order led by the United States."[19] As a consequence of its victory over communism, so the current wisdom goes, the United States has both the opportunity and responsibility for reshaping the global economy and supervising the international security arrangements that will allow free markets to flourish. Significantly, despite the defeat of its main enemy, Washington remains under arms. As the world's sole superpower, it cannot abandon the field. Accordingly, the military's post–Cold War vision, articulated by the Air Force chief of staff in 1996, is that of "Global Reach—Global Power," a strategy that "calls for our nation to be engaged around the world with the objective of enlarging the family of democratic nations."[20] In addition, the first Bush president reminded the nation, since the fall of the Soviet Union had not ushered in an era of peace and harmony, the U.S. had to remain on guard. Because "[t]he world is still dangerous," he announced as he prepared to invade Iraq, "there is no substitute for American leadership."[21] As Washington takes upon itself the mission of demonstrating that leadership and extending its power around the globe, it invokes many rationales: democracy, antiterrorism, economic development, nonproliferation, and even, it turns out, imperialism. But whatever the justification du jour, American policy-makers are constructing their current empire by mounting an updated version of the Cold War crusade that not only recycles past administrations' finest moments to legitimize today's unilateralist ones, but does so with the same Manichaean fervor.[22]

Nonetheless, even as we criticize its misrepresentations, it is important to note that much of the power of the triumphalist narrative comes from the kernels of reality embedded within it. Few observers would deny that the Soviet system was more *internally* repressive than the Western one or that American Communists spied for the Russians in the 1930s and 1940s or that Moscow's attempt to keep up in the arms race contributed to its collapse or that command economies rarely perform well. What is problematic, however, is the way in which the triumphalists' uncritical view of the American side elides other aspects of the Cold War to create an oversimplified and distorted version of its history that serves to justify Washington's past and present quest for hegemony.

We have put together this volume in the hope of correcting those distortions. While some contributors revisit selected aspects of the Cold War to uncover a more realistic version of the past, others are exploring the triumphalist interpretations themselves. Above all, this book seeks to hold the key assumptions of Cold War triumphalism up to critical scrutiny. Though the essays in this volume do that from different political and intellectual perspectives, they all demonstrate, in one way or another, how seriously the celebratory interpretation of the Cold War distorts our understanding of the recent past and thus provides a misleading and dangerous set of guideposts for the United States and the world in the twenty-first century.

Certain commonalities guide this endeavor. To begin with, it is clear that many of the phenomena so casually ascribed to the Cold War are independent of it. In fact, as the dean of American revisionist historians William Appleman Williams suggested, the Cold War needs to be "viewed as a confrontation that occurs throughout our history."[23] The United States would have promoted capitalism and pursued hegemony even without the struggle against the Soviet Union. And as so many historians have shown, the ideological and institutional machinery for that venture developed in the years before and during World War II, when an activist administration stressed preparedness, adopted a polarized worldview, and erected many of the economic and political structures that were to shape what would later become the national security state.[24] Even the virulent anticommunism of the McCarthy era, the Cold War's quintessential political pathology in the U.S., not only originated in earlier right-wing campaigns against the New Deal and its labor allies, but continued to serve a similar function long after American communism bit the dust.[25] Similarly, though Washington often tried to impose a Cold War grid on the conflicts that accompanied decolonization in the Third World, those conflicts had indigenous roots, even if the protagonists took advantage of the dueling superpowers for their own local ends.

The authors of this volume also recognize the importance of ideas. While it is clear that the economic interests, partisan considerations, and bureaucratic battles that helped to build the American Cold War polity still weigh heavily, the triumphalist narrative exerts its own power. History matters, not only in providing a set of metaphors to justify ongoing adventures, but also in shaping the contours of contemporary debates. The triumphalist version, by creating an aura of inevitability that proffers a flattened and oversimplified vision of the past, can close down that debate, just as a more nuanced interpretation opens it up by showing how individual decisions shaped policy, thus revealing the possibility of alternative paths to the present. In addition, the availability of prepackaged historical tropes short-circuits critical thinking, trivializing political discourse by substituting slogans and nostalgia for genuine engagement with real world issues while allowing policy-makers, in the words of Richard Neustadt and Ernest May, "to make the decisions they wanted to make with a minimum of fresh analysis."[26]

Even before the Cold War ended, misleading analogies and "lessons of history" pervaded the nation's political discourse; after it, they became ubiquitous. The icons of World War II are particularly popular. Was there any political commentator who did not mention Pearl Harbor when the World Trade Center came down? Or any American leader who did not cite Hitler and Munich when calling for military action? When Ronald Reagan began to devote ever larger portions of the federal budget to the Pentagon, he compared himself to Winston Churchill.[27] Even more to the point is the recent invocation of the early Cold War. Popular historians and politicians have elevated Harry Truman, in many respects a rather uninformed and often dangerously confrontational leader, into the veritable pantheon of American presidents, his allegedly crowning achievements—NATO and the Marshall Plan—transformed into templates for the projection of American power from Central America to the Persian Gulf.[28] The tensions and confusion of the late 1940s have now been transmogrified into what the Brookings Institution's Thomas E. Mann recently called "the most creative and productive period in American diplomatic history."[29] Small wonder, then, that contemporary policy-makers like Condoleezza Rice compare the present to that heroic era. "I really think," she confided to *The New Yorker* in 2002, "this period is analogous to 1945 to 1947."[30] The Cuban missile crisis conveys a similar aura—crisis, response, and America standing tall. That Kennedy's heroism also involved a refusal to unleash the Strategic Air Command gets conveniently forgotten.

So too do some of the less triumphant moments of American Cold War history. The Korean War has all but disappeared. Its fiftieth anniversary came and went without the martial hoopla that attended the festivities for World War II. Despite its association with the by now nearly-canonized Truman, there was no way to view Korea as an American success. In fact, the most newsworthy aspect of its commemoration occurred when the Associated Press ran an in-depth story about some overlooked American atrocities, sparking a brief controversy and a Defense Department investigation.[31] Vietnam, of course, was even more of an embarrassment. Though that conflict goes unremarked by the triumphalists, as Marilyn Young shows in her contribution to this volume, later policy-makers did learn something from it. They would try to minimize public discontent. In the quarter century since it left Vietnam, the American military has learned to clamp down on the media and avoid American casualties. Until recently, in fact, it has more often than not tried to stay out of war.[32]

But there may be other lessons that can be gleaned from the history of the Cold War. Scholars in the United States and elsewhere are still casting a trained and critical eye on the recent past. In the process, they are interrogating the triumphalists' basic assumptions and redefining the Cold War. Because they do not view that conflict as a morality play, but rather as a complex set of interconnections and power relationships, they are raising new questions about the means and objectives of the main protagonists, as well as about the costs to all sides. The following section will look briefly at some of these issues. Most of the attention will go to the United States, in part because of Washington's hegemonic role throughout the past half century and in part because of the academic specialities of the contributors to this volume. It goes without saying, however, that the Cold War was an international phenomenon and that an American perspective is, by necessity, somewhat limiting. For this reason, as well as many others, this survey cannot provide a definitive conceptualization of the nature of the Cold War or of its legacy. But it can start the conversation.

To begin with, it is clear that the Cold War served many functions. As Corey Robin suggests, not the least of those functions was to provide an ideologically and morally satisfying excuse for extending the American imperium.[33] Would American policy-makers have projected the nation's military and economic power throughout the world had there been no Cold War to justify it? Of course. American imperialism had been around for years—even if it was often cloaked by moralizing and euphemism. And at least some Cold War intellectuals, as Leo Ribuffo reminds us here, recognized the continuities that molded Washington's expansionist foreign policy.[34] Nonetheless, the anticommunist crusade did provide an ideological cover for the great power politics the United States has traditionally claimed to eschew. In most cases, the various proponents of American expansion simply grafted an anticommunist component onto their own agendas. The business-minded sought customers and investment opportunities, the missionary-minded spread American culture and ideals, the security-minded built weapons and alliances—and they all claimed to be fighting the Soviet menace. The diversity of these expansionist constituencies increased their overall clout as each group pressed for deals and policies that, sometimes consciously, sometimes not, created a vast and powerful empire.

The construction of that empire began before the end of World War II. The "Good War's" ideological mobilization fashioned a template that not only made it possible to demonize the German and Japanese enemies but also inculcated the polarizing mind-set that made it easier to justify the use of force against those and future antagonists.[35] Similarly, the war created the military and industrial infrastructure that shaped the embryonic national security state at home and then spread its dubious blessings abroad. Even as they were preparing to invade Germany and Japan in World War II, U.S. military planners were already designing what Bruce Cumings refers to as America's "archipelago of military bases around the world."[36] At the same time, economic experts at Bretton Woods and elsewhere were working out an international monetary system that in the name of stability would assure the domination of the dollar. The postwar world saw these initiatives implemented. That so many trappings of this empire were acquired by invitation, rather than outright conquest, does not conceal the accumulation of power.

No doubt the United States could have constructed its empire without mounting an ideological crusade to legitimize it. But the Cold War proved useful—and not just for Washington. It helped both sides maintain, as well as build, their empires. In that sense, it functioned as what Mary Kaldor called an "imaginary war," a bogus conflict that both the United States and the Soviet Union used to control the populations within their spheres. In retrospect, it is clear that nuclear warfare aside, neither power directly threatened the other's survival. In fact, the opposite may well have been the case, for the Cold War actually bolstered the positions of political elites on both sides. Positing a struggle against an implacable, expansionist enemy made it possible to build up a militarized economy and clamp down on dissent. Ideology was important here, especially in the West, which built its imperium upon consent rather than coercion. "[F]ar from threatening each other," Kaldor noted, "the two systems reinforced each other through their shared need for an imaginary war." There was no collusion; the mutual reinforcement that the Cold War provided was the product of a "fortuitous complementarity."[37]

The Cold War produced other ostensible benefits. As the Eastern bloc crumbled and ethnic conflict broke out in the Balkans, some observers, who otherwise had no shred of sympathy for communism, came to view the earlier struggle with nostalgia as a mechanism for the pacification of Europe. It was, in John L. Gaddis's now discarded term, "the long peace," four and a half decades of stability during which the two superpowers managed to contain their former enemies, Germany and Japan, while creating an enduring balance of power that eliminated the uncertainty and anarchy traditionally characteristic of international relations.[38] Moreover, once both sides possessed nuclear arms, war became too horrific to contemplate. It was the combination of the Soviet-American "bipolarity, an equal military balance, and nuclear weapons," that, John Mearsheimer, the most prominent academic exponent of this theory, believes, "fostered peace in Europe over the past forty-five years . . . transforming a historically violent region into a very peaceful place."[39] Such an interpretation does complicate a more simplistic triumphalism, for it portrays the Cold War, and not just its denouement, as a good in itself, especially if, as Mearsheimer and his fellow realists do, one posits stability as the most desirable element in any system of international relations.[40]

This is admittedly a Eurocentric assessment, one that gives primacy to a stable European order while ignoring violent conflicts elsewhere. But even in the Third World, the Cold War did provide some stability. The superpowers tended to rein in some interstate violence, ensuring that open warfare between India and Pakistan, for example, or the Israelis and the Arabs did not last too long or spin out of control. In addition, the Cold War conferred a measure of domestic stability throughout the Third World by letting smaller nations claim a role as members of a nonaligned movement that gave them an international identity as well as whatever rewards they could extract from the main antagonists.[41] Of course, since most of those rewards came in the form of military aid, it is unclear exactly what kind of long-term blessings they conferred.

Even within the United States, it is possible to list a few advantages that the Cold War bestowed upon American society. Thus, for example, official concern about the way in which the Soviet Union gathered propagandistic hay from the racism of the American South prodded the federal government to give more support to the struggle for civil rights than it might otherwise have done.[42] Scientific research and higher education also benefited directly from the Cold War. Invoking national security allowed Washington to circumvent congressional opposition to funding in areas like education that had formerly been considered too racially or religiously sensitive to touch. Similarly, the government managed to overcome traditional qualms about economic planning and implement an—albeit stunted—industrial research and development policy by disguising it as national defense.[43] None of these benefits, however, came free of charge. In order to take advantage of federal support for its crusade against segregation, the civil rights movement had to become respectably anticommunist and jettison its demands for economic equality, while academic cold warriors restructured the world of knowledge in ways that were not always intellectually or socially advantageous.[44] Of course, those developments might have occurred in any event. The real question is whether they were worth the price.[45]

Much of that price, we now know, came from the pockets and paychecks of ordinary Americans. For years, the nation's material wealth concealed the way in which the Cold War had deformed the economy, making it seem as if the United States could have both guns and butter—and, at least until the Vietnam War, ever bigger helpings of both. This is not to say that the nation's spiraling defense budgets did not cause concern about the economic and political consequences of diverting so many resources into the military. Even as he stepped up the confrontation with the Soviet Union and began to rearm, Truman fretted about creating an enlarged garrison state that would not only damage the economy, but also undermine democracy at home.[46] Eisenhower worried about the same thing. "Every gun that is made," he complained in 1953,

> every warship launched, every rocket fired, signifies, in the final sense, a theft from those who hunger and are not fed, those who are cold and not clothed. This world in arms is not spending money alone. It is spending the sweat of its laborers, the genius of its scientists, the hopes of its children.[47]

Both Truman and Ike were fiscal conservatives who saw the jousting over military appropriations as a struggle for the soul of America.

But, in the high tide of Cold War liberalism, when Keynesian economic advisers were providing a technical rationale for bigger military budgets, such concerns seemed positively retrograde. Still, it was clear that, even in prosperous times, defense spending did divert resources from social needs. And when the crisis of the welfare state hit the West in the 1970s and 1980s and Washington felt compelled to cut back, programs for the poor suffered much more heavily than they did in other industrialized countries that had not devoted such a disproportionate share of their national income to the military.[48] Within the Soviet bloc, the burdens of Cold War military spending were more equitably shared. Everybody's standard of living was lower.[49]

Not only did the arms race drain money from domestic budgets East and West, it also reconfigured the economic landscape within the United States. Just as the Pentagon established its "archipelago of military bases" by acquiring foreign outposts, so too it developed an archipelago of industry by siting defense plants and military installations in those favored sections of the nation that Ann Markusen and her collaborators have labeled the "gunbelt." Southern California, New England, Dallas–Fort Worth, the suburbs of Washington, D.C.—all owe much of their late twentieth-century prosperity to the nation's defense spending.[50] Again, the Cold War did not inaugurate these geographic shifts; World War II started the California boom and created the aerospace infrastructure that until recently dominated the Golden State's economy.[51] Still, the Cold War consolidated those developments. Furthermore, once established, the gunbelt became self-perpetuating, creating its own powerful constituencies that pressed for increased military spending and the confrontationist foreign policy that bolstered it.[52]

War is good for the economy—or so the traditional wisdom holds. Military Keynesianism, both during and after World War II, contributed mightily to the nation's prosperity, as did some of the technological innovations produced by the arms race. But such may no longer be the case. In fact, by the 1970s the defense industry had become a serious drag on the economy. Because of the Pentagon's reliance on what Mary Kaldor called a "baroque" style of arms procurement that focuses on performance rather than cost, many new weapons had become much too complicated and highly specialized for any conceivable civilian applications. They were wildly sophisticated, elaborate,

and hard to operate, while requiring enormous amounts of maintenance. And, of course, their price tags were astronomical; by the 1970s,
cost overruns for new weapons systems averaged 100 percent. Moreover, the military's insistence on ever narrower and more rarified applications diverted the nation's most highly trained scientists and
engineers away from more economically or technologically productive
research and development. Yet, such was the political clout of the main
defense contractors and their customers in the Pentagon that this ex-
travagant and inherently counterproductive system came to dominate
large sectors of the nation's economy—and not only in the United
States. The Soviet Union, determined to match the Pentagon missile
for missile and tank for tank, also adopted the same wasteful methods
of military production. So too did those Third World nations that received American military aid. And, as could be expected, the impact of
these "baroque" weapons systems on those less affluent societies could
often be pernicious, diverting resources needed for economic modernization and basic human needs into the essentially useless infrastructure these high-prestige items required, if not into the pockets of the
purchasers and suppliers.[53]

The Cold War hurt the U.S. economy in other ways as well. As Judith Stein among others has shown, Washington's preoccupation with
maintaining the allegiance of its East Asian and NATO allies abetted
the decline of American manufacturing industries. As the conflict
with the Soviet Union intensified in the aftermath of World War II,
U.S. policy-makers believed they had to restore the prosperity of Germany and Japan if those nations were to democratize and become reliable members of the Western bloc. Successive administrations,
therefore, promoted the economic resurgence of the nation's former
enemies as well as that of its other allies. In the process, Washington
blinked at the protectionist policies of those countries, while it encouraged investing abroad, refused to subsidize American industries, and
did nothing to stem the flow of imports that cut into the domestic markets of U.S. corporations. By the 1970s, those corporations were losing
out to their foreign competitors. The economy had become, in Stein's
words, "a handmaiden to the Cold War"—with disastrous results for
the nation's manufacturers and workers. Obviously, factors other than
Washington's desire to placate its allies also contributed to the decline
of the rust belt. Still, even when it had become devastatingly clear that

steel, for example, was suffering from the government's failure to protect it, Jimmy Carter refused to help the floundering industry. Among other things, he did not want to jeopardize European support for his anti-Soviet policy in Afghanistan.[54]

Burdensome as the Cold War has been economically, its other legacies have been equally, if not more, unfortunate. After all, while the Germans and Japanese were building and selling Toyotas and BMWs, the Americans and Russians were building and deploying nuclear weapons. By 1970 there were 39,700 of them. Today there are still over 20,000.[55] That the Cold War encouraged military planners on both sides to assume that they could enhance their own security by stockpiling weapons that could never be used offers further evidence of the underlying irrationality of that conflict. Though no atomic bombs have been dropped in warfare since Nagasaki, the nuclear arms race has contaminated everything from great power politics to children's nightmares. Nor did the end of the Cold War eliminate the danger. Accidental warfare remains a frightening possibility. As late as 1995, a NASA probe of the northern lights triggered a Russian false alarm that nearly brought Boris Yeltsin to the red phone. And there have been thousands of similar, if not quite so serious, Strangelovian moments over the past few decades.[56] Despite treaties to reduce the number of operational warheads, thousands of bombs are still in place, an omnipresent threat to the very existence of human civilization. Moreover, the new nuclear-war fighting strategies favored by the current Bush administration ensure that these stockpiles are not going to disappear any time soon.

Today, however, the main danger is not so much a nuclear exchange between the former Cold War rivals as it is nuclear proliferation and the acquisition of weapons of mass destruction by smaller states and independent actors. Again, the Cold War's legacy looms large, since each side used the dissemination of bomb-building materials and technology to consolidate alliances and woo unaligned nations, seemingly oblivious to the implications of putting nuclear weapons into the hands of governments that might actually use them. In almost every case, the prospects for immediate advantage trumped considerations about the dangers down the road. Thus, for example, during much of the Cold War, the Russians helped India build its bomb, while the Americans provided aid to Pakistan's; then, when the Soviet

Union invaded Afghanistan, the United States assisted both South Asian nations.[57] Yet neither superpower tried to defuse the conflict in Kashmir where the two nuclear-armed nations now confront each other in a conflict that could spin out of control at any moment. Similarly, when Washington was at odds with Iran in the 1980s, it overlooked the efforts of Iran's enemy, Iraq, to develop its nuclear program.[58]

The possible dispersal of the radioactive remnants of that program in the chaos accompanying the recent war in Iraq highlights an even more frightening scenario than the outright transfer of weapons and technology from one government to another: the so-called "nuclear leakage" of bomb materials into the hands of terrorists or other outlaw elements. While the prospect of North Korea or a similarly armed minor power peddling its radioactive wares on the open market is hardly reassuring, an equally grave threat comes from the stockpiles of the financially strapped former Soviet Union, which does not and perhaps cannot ensure that its scientists and weapons remain under tight control.[59] Though the American government presumably does have the resources to keep these dangerous items from falling into unfriendly hands, it has made only token gestures to do so. In fact, with the end of the Cold War, it even acquiesced in corporate demands to relax its own restraints on the export of nuclear technology and materials.[60]

Scary scenarios abound, many the unintended consequences of such earlier Cold War ventures as the CIA's support for Islamic warriors in Afghanistan. Yet even without Al Qaeda operatives detonating nuclear suitcases in New York harbor or spreading smallpox on the subways, the anticommunist crusade has already physically contaminated the United States. As one observer noted, "In preparing to fight a nuclear war with the former Soviet Union, America succeeded in 'nuking' itself," not only by exposing hundreds of thousands of ordinary citizens, workers, and soldiers to unacceptable levels of radiation, but also by allowing the toxic by-products of the arms race to pollute large sectors of the country. In 1994, the Department of Defense listed 10,439 suspected hazardous waste sites, with more than a hundred of them on the EPA's superfund list, including such notorious installations as Oak Ridge, Hanford, and Rocky Flats. Some of these places are so thoroughly polluted that they can never be cleaned up and have now been designated "national sacrifice zones." Nor are such noxious dumping grounds limited only to the United States. The problem is worldwide, as are the heightened cancer rates from nuclear tests and other lethal legacies of the Cold War nuclear arms race. And, given the astronomical price tag of the cleanup—simply disposing of the battery system for one Minuteman missile costs $3,500—these Cold War legacies will be around for years to come.[61]

The political fallout of the Cold War is every bit as deleterious as the physical. In the United States its main legacy is the national security state that produced and was produced by the militarization of American foreign policy. Over the years, as many of its earliest critics on both the left and the right predicted, that state has not only nibbled away at the rights of individuals, but also undermined the system of democratic governance itself. Not, of course, that the pre–Cold War polity was perfect or that all the nation's oppressive practices grew out of its conflict with the Soviet Union. Racism, sexism, and corporate greed shaped American institutions just as effectively as the Cold War; in fact, they often reinforced the negative consequences of the nation's growing militarization. Thus, for example, the geographical realignment of American politics that resulted in the so-called "southernization" of the Republican party can be traced in part to the spread of Cold War defense installations and industries to the South and West. As a consequence of that geographical shift, power leached out of traditional urban centers in the East and Midwest, moving to areas that harbored a more conservative antilabor and jingoistic political culture.[62] At the same time, those regions' accumulation of clout increased the national influence of the South's formerly segregationist politicians, further pushing American politics to the right.

Within the government itself, the Cold War contributed to the growth of what has come to be called the "imperial presidency." Naturally, there were precedents; Franklin Roosevelt was no slouch when it came to amassing power or concealing his actions from Congress and the rest of the country. World War II, like all wars, also strengthened the executive branch. Later administrations were thus building upon an earlier propensity to bureaucratize policy-making and insulate it from the democratic process. As early as the Berlin crisis of the late 1940s if not before, as Carolyn Eisenberg explains in her contribution to this volume, pivotal decisions came to be made by policy elites who did not believe that ordinary citizens could be trusted with the nation's foreign affairs. They consulted neither Congress nor the broader public, transforming decision-making into a bureaucratic function that lacked all political accountability.[63] Soon, in fact, the American people came to be seen as an obstacle to the conduct of the Cold War. Uninformed and unaware of the dangers the United States supposedly faced, they had to be induced to acquiesce in whatever measures the nation's leaders believed were necessary to protect national security. The process of doing so could be manipulative in the extreme. Thus, for example, as political scientist Andrew Grossman reveals, in order to gain credibility for the military's strategy of nuclear deterrence, citizens had to accept the bomb as a normal part of modern war. In order to obtain that acceptance, the government mounted a massive media campaign and civil defense program whose main purpose was to spread the (patently false) notion that a nuclear exchange could be survived.[64]

Most of the time, however, such elaborate machinations were unnecessary. It was enough to invoke an emergency and claim that an immediate crisis required presidential action unencumbered by constitutional niceties. Utilizing his official power as commander in chief, Truman skirted the requirement of a congressional declaration of war to send the military into action in Korea. He had, Michael Sherry pointed out, "conflated his authority to command forces *in* war with his right to commit them *to* war."[65] His successors did the same—in Vietnam, Central America, the Middle East, and elsewhere. Cold War exigencies provided cover for what was clearly an unprecedented expansion of presidential power, not to mention an obvious repudiation of the Founding Fathers' intent.

Adding to this lack of accountability was a growing insistence on secrecy, necessitated, so it was claimed, by the demands of national security. Not only did that secrecy further undermine the democratic polity by making it impossible for elected officials as well as ordinary citizens to keep tabs on their government—even if, as with Richard Nixon's secret bombing of Cambodia, the nation's adversaries knew perfectly well what was going on—but it also gave policy-makers extraordinary control over whole sectors of society. "Secrecy," Daniel Patrick Moynihan noted, "is a form of regulation," one that the Cold War significantly enhanced. Ironically, the stated function of the government's secrecy, its value in protecting American security, was not particularly well-served. Long before 9/11, the U.S. intelligence agencies' culture of suspicion and turf warfare distorted their operations. True, unlike the current situation, these agencies' main errors during the Cold War involved exaggerating, not ignoring, the power and malevolence of the enemy. Insulated from reality checks, these inbred organizations found themselves caught completely off guard when the supposedly mighty Soviet empire crumbled in a matter of months.[66]

Since the government seemed to be more concerned about keeping secrets from its own citizens than from its rivals, the function that secrecy performed is open to question. One could, of course, take a conspiratorial view of the situation and note that the imposition of such a counterproductive practice may well have been intentional. If nothing else, it shielded the individuals and organizations with a vested interest in preserving the political-military status quo from criticism, enabling them to continue spending money on weapons and other projects that they must have known were totally unnecessary. Moreover, as anyone who has filed a Freedom of Information Act request with the FBI knows, many of the Bureau's most tightly held secrets concerned its own unethical practices. Saving face may well have been more important than saving the nation.

Secrecy conceals injustice as well as ineptitude. From the unnamed informers of the McCarthy era's loyalty-security programs to the second Bush administration's refusal to release the names of the immigrants it incarcerated after 9/11, secrecy has always encouraged violations of individual rights. During the Cold War, national security provided a convenient fig leaf for political repression. Even anticommunist politicians like Moynihan recognized the irony of the situation. "The awful dilemma," he noted, "was that in order to preserve an open society, the U.S. government took measures that in significant ways closed it down."[67] That tendency toward political repression was worldwide. Almost every Cold War protagonist cracked down on dissenters in the name of protecting itself against an external enemy. In Russia and China heads rolled; in the United States screenwriters lost their jobs. And in Latin America, as Chalmers Johnson reminds us here, thousands of people just disappeared.[68]

Even when its perpetrators try to disguise it, political repression is hard to hide. But there were more subtle threats to American democracy that the Cold War encouraged. The spread of the military into so many sectors of society encouraged a hierarchical mind-set that prized "loyalty between superiors and subordinates, obedience to lawful commands, strict discipline and regimentation, and a willingness to sacrifice everything for the unit and the nation."[69] While such values may have been useful on the battlefield, they were, in many respects, antagonistic to the openness and respect for the individual that a vigorous democracy requires. Equally deleterious in its long-term impact was the polarizing habit of mind that accompanied the Cold War. In part the result of a conscious campaign to sell an expansive foreign policy to the American people, the demonization of the Communist enemy rendered that foreign policy far more rigid than necessary and created habits of mind that remain pervasive to this day. During the 1950s, for example, American policy-makers had so internalized the notion of the Soviet government as a power-mad dictatorship bent on enslaving the world that they were unable to envision conducting normal diplomatic relations with it.[70] Today, a similar mind-set demonizes so-called "rogue states" and makes it impossible to deal realistically with nations and subcultures deemed inimical to Western values. By labeling the current situation a "clash of civilizations" (in Samuel Huntington's terms), pundits and policy-makers do not even try to understand why the United States has become so unpopular throughout the world. Instead, they view their antagonists as beyond the pale and send in the marines.[71]

That many of these hostile forces developed in part because of great power meddling in the Third World is only another irony produced by the Cold War. The relationship between the rise of Al Qaeda and the CIA's support for the Mujahedin fighters in Afghanistan is well known. And we can trace similar developments in almost every area of the world where the Cold War protagonists armed and encouraged clients in the name of denying advantages to the other side. Most of the time, such interventions had little impact on the superpower rivalry. Instead they bolstered otherwise weak and repressive regimes, while encouraging the militarization that seriously deformed those nations' societies. Nor, despite the rhetoric both sides engaged in, did they encourage either democracy or socialism. America had a penchant for subsidizing dictators. Most of its military aid went to authoritarian governments like those in Egypt, South Korea, and Saudi Arabia, while the Russians and Chinese supported Kim II Sung. That assistance was both economically and politically counterproductive. Not only, as Chalmers Johnson shows, did it create militarized, hierarchical, and parasitic ruling elites, but it also diverted the client countries' economies into costly and unproductive expenditures on the training and infrastructures that the new armature required.[72] And, of course, it loaded them with foreign debts, making them increasingly vulnerable to the harsh and destabilizing demands of the international financial community.

At the same time, this military assistance often encouraged outright warfare and, by arming the protagonists, kept conflicts going long after they might otherwise have stopped. When the Cold War ended and both the United States and the Soviet Union withdrew their bounty, fighting in places like Ethiopia and El Salvador died down.[73] Whether the Cold War stabilized international relations, as theorists like John Mearsheimer believe, or whether it generated more conflict, it certainly did not make the world a more peaceful place. On the contrary, the Cold War weakened internationalism both institutionally and ideologically. Not only did it undermine the United Nations, depriving it of its effectiveness in dealing with international conflicts, but it also marginalized what had previously been a mainstream peace movement that had claimed the allegiance of a significant portion of the American elite.[74] As early as the late 1940s, as Carolyn Eisenberg notes here, the United States sabotaged the UN's attempts to broker a settlement of the Berlin crisis.[75] That sabotage continued throughout the Cold War as Washington either used the UN as a fig leaf for its own adventures or else simply ignored its existence. As a result, when the Cold War came to an end, terminating American and Russian interest in those parts of the globe where the two powers had once competed for influence, an international vacuum of power developed. A sturdy UN might have filled that vacuum (and, as Jessica Wang demonstrates in her contribution to this volume, it is beginning to move in that direction), but forty years of neglect had so stunted the organization that it could neither suppress ethnic conflicts nor allocate resources among rival claimants.[76] And, in any event, it may no longer be possible to erect any kind of strong supranational institution in the face of Washington's growing unilateralism. What is clear, however, is that the Cold War destroyed an earlier opportunity to build such an obviously needed institution.[77]

. . .

The list of opportunities squandered during the Cold War is long. In almost every part of the globe, in almost every human activity, we can trace the largely baneful impact of that forty-five-year conflict. Even for the winning side (and it is by no means obvious that an actual victory occurred), the Cold War's legacy offers few grounds for rejoicing. Concealing its deleterious effects only intensifies the damage. For that reason as well as out of a desire to set the record straight, we need to confront the uninformed and obfuscatory triumphalism that so seriously deforms American policy-making today.

This volume takes up that challenge; its contributors explore Cold War triumphalism from several different perspectives. Leo Ribuffo and Bruce Cumings, for example, look at its intellectual side. Ribuffo analyzes the work of three American thinkers who tried to grapple with the moral implications of the Cold War, while Cumings assesses that of some highly touted post–Cold War interpreters. Nelson Lichtenstein and Michael Bernstein explore the economic component of the triumphalist celebration: the ascendancy of neoliberalism. In explaining why the free-marketeers won such an easy victory, Lichtenstein looks at the ways in which mainstream thinkers downplayed traditional economic factors during the early Cold War. Bernstein describes how the neoliberal ideologists who came to power in the 1980s unraveled the Cold War Keynesian compact that had funded both a massive military machine and a growth-oriented welfare state, while professional economists, who should have known better, simply turned their backs.

By revisiting selected aspects of the Cold War itself, Carolyn Eisenberg, Jessica Wang, Maurice Isserman, and I raise questions about the inevitability of the conflict as well as explore some of the new materials that have emerged since the Soviet Union's demise. The most dramatic of those new materials revealed that dozens, perhaps hundreds, of American citizens spied for the USSR during the 1930s and 1940s, thus confirming Cold War–era charges and strengthening the triumphalists' case against the American left. In our essay, Isserman and I situate these revelations within the broader context of the Cold War and the history of American communism to provide a more complicated portrayal of Russia's spying than most conservatives are willing to concede. Carolyn Eisenberg does the same for the Berlin blockade, traditionally the most heroic chapter in the triumphalist saga. What she has found reveals a considerably less glorious account of a city that was not about to starve and a group of policy-makers so determined to assert American hegemony over Western Europe that they would divide a nation and risk a war. Jessica Wang's examination of the United Nations offers us yet another story of Washington torpedoing a pacific alternative to the tensions of the Cold War as it pursued its own increasingly militarized agenda.

Finally, we come to the present, and an exploration of how the Cold War's legacy plays itself out in the power politics of today. Marilyn Young looks at the aftermath of Vietnam, assessing the ways in which American policy-makers absorbed its so-called lessons in order to make later conflicts palatable enough to fight. As Chalmers Johnson sees it, those later conflicts are simply part of the ongoing Cold War, which may perhaps have ended in Europe, but still continues on its destructive trajectory throughout East Asia and Latin America. It is a trajectory, Corey Robin explains, propelled by the neoconservatives' muscular fantasies of empire. Rescued by 9/11 from what they bemoaned as the post–Cold War materialism of Clinton-era foreign policy, the Bush administration's neoconservatives are now living out those fantasies. What will happen when reality intrudes remains an open question.

One final note: As we first tried to conceptualize and then construct this volume, it was continually being updated to keep up with the seemingly ever-changing trajectory of American foreign policy. Perhaps it is an indication of the relevance of our project that almost every author kept having to make some kind of revision to keep his or her analysis current. Early drafts stressed the Cold War's contribution to the neoliberal vision of economic globalization. Later ones incorporated 9/11, and the final versions look to the conflict in Iraq. It is likely that the rush of events will overtake even these, our latest insights. Perhaps the violence in Iraq will subside. Perhaps it will turn out to be the quagmire so many have predicted. Certainly, it is hard to imagine that the current projection of American military power will be any more beneficial to the millions of ordinary men, women, and children in its path than it was during the Cold War.

Part I

Intellectuals

I

Moral Judgments and the Cold War: Reflections on Reinhold Niebuhr, William Appleman Williams, and John Lewis Gaddis

Leo P. Ribuffo

The Cold War was awash in moral judgments. From the outset, cold warriors joined President Harry S. Truman in discerning a conflict between "alternate ways of life" in which nearly every nation must choose. For cold warriors the choices lay between capitalist affluence and autarkic squalor, between religious faith and godless communism, between personal freedom and "totalitarianism." Most radical critics of the *basic premises* of United States foreign policy during the Cold War, many of whom were intellectual heirs to the Popular Front, did not question that alternate ways of life were at stake. Rather, they charged that the cold warriors' rhetoric obscured their acquiescence in and perhaps enthusiastic support of brutal dictatorships abroad as well as social inequality and suppression of dissent at home. Between these two poles, reflective cold warriors, reformist Communists, and freelance skeptics acknowledged that the United States and the Soviet Union respectively fell short of their high moral claims.

These conflicts still echo in American ideological and intellectual life with minimal rethinking among the combatants. Heirs to the Popular Front tradition continue to defend essentially the same ideological turf with a series of tactical maneuvers, for example, conceding that the Soviet Union spied on the United States while urging a level of historical empathy for the spies that they rarely accord even to the insightful noninterventionists in the America First Committee. Forsaking ambiguity as well as empathy, intellectuals in the cold warrior tradition find vindication in victory. The latest phase of this venerable controversy persists largely unperturbed by recent—or even old—research in foreign relations. Certainly George Will, William Kristol, Charles Krauthammer, and kindred Cold War triumphalist pundits show no sign of perusing the latest issues of the Cold War International History Project *Bulletin*. To be sure, though much of the "new international history of the Cold War" consists of routine empiricism, even routine empiricism can serve as a useful antidote to glib moralism and nostalgia.

Nonetheless, readers here need not dread yet another essay proclaiming that what "we now know" about the Cold War following the opening of some Soviet and Eastern bloc archives has settled or rendered irrelevant all previous scholarship, methodological issues, and ethical questions. Rather, I explore an aspect of Cold War intellectual history. Although the Cold War was awash in moral *judgments* from the White House to the neighborhood tavern, efforts to approach the subject via sustained and (ideally) consistent moral *arguments* were few and far between. In this article, I examine three writers who tried to do so: Reinhold Niebuhr, William Appleman Williams, and John Lewis Gaddis. Niebuhr was the most influential American theologian in the twenty years after World War II. Williams was the foremost "revisionist" interpreter of U.S. foreign policy from the early 1950s until his death in 1990. Gaddis remains the chief defender of Cold War containment strategy among contemporary diplomatic historians.

My perspective is, broadly speaking, a version of pragmatism. "Facts" and "values" do not dwell in separate spheres but interact, and we should be conscious of that interaction. Moral judgments should be based on the consequences of human actions at least as much as on the motives. Actions—or even notions about the right ways to act—are constrained by time, place, and circumstance. Consequences of human actions are often unpredictable and change over time, and these changes typically affect both our conceptualization of facts and our ethical judgments.

Historian Walter LaFeber has described Reinhold Niebuhr as the most influential American theologian since Jonathan Edwards in the eighteenth century. Although the accuracy of LaFeber's quip depends on whether or not we call Lyman and Henry Ward Beecher theologians, there is no doubt that Niebuhr was the preeminent theologian of Cold War liberalism as he was in a previous political incarnation the foremost theologian of Depression-era socialism.[1]

By the early 1930s Niebuhr had formulated an approach to God, humanity, and society that he called "Christian realism." According to Niebuhr, bourgeois secular liberals and Protestant social gospelers exaggerated humanity's capacity for virtue and wisdom. At most, altruistic behavior was possible only in small groups. Because men (as he put it) were inherently sinful, at least in a metaphorical sense, their social movements and governments were always morally tainted. Virtues turned into vices when they were pressed too zealously, and evil means were used to advance relatively noble ends. Nonetheless, men should not sink into cynicism but attempt to achieve ideals that were impossible to attain.

This "neo-orthodox" worldview was compatible with a wide range of political positions and Niebuhr himself held many of them during his life. When he first presented the essential features of Christian realism in *Moral Man and Immoral Society* in 1932, Niebuhr was a self-described socialist Christian convinced that the United States faced a choice between fascism and revolution. Among contending fallible social theories, Marxism was "essentially correct." Moreover, the revolution might require some evil means—violence—to survive. In the mid-1930s Niebuhr was still willing to cooperate with Communists in pursuing his goals. He was determined, however, "never" to support another international war as he had mistakenly supported World War I.[2]

By 1940, Niebuhr had shifted his politics to New Deal liberalism, endorsed convoys to supply Great Britain even at the risk of war with Nazi Germany, and opposed collaboration with Communists. In *The Children of Light and the Children of Darkness,* Niebuhr used Christian realist arguments to buttress a call for expanding the New Deal welfare state. Yet Marxists remained among the "children of light," and their claims to special virtue and wisdom looked not much worse than those of Roman Catholics. Sounding like Wendell Willkie in *One World,* Niebuhr compared the Soviet "new oligarchy" to Gilded Age "American 'go getters.' " In 1945–46, he still thought of the United

States and the Soviet Union as comparably adolescent nations in their pretensions.[3]

During the next three years Niebuhr joined famous and obscure Americans in becoming more critical and demanding of the Soviet Union. When he appeared on the cover of *Time* in 1948, the first of many "celebrity theologians" to emerge during the next decade, Niebuhr was a full-fledged representative of Cold War liberalism, a reputation that survives to this day. Even so, Cold War liberals were no more uniform in their beliefs than conservatives or Popular Front liberals. Niebuhr was more reflective than most, a disposition often obscured by his vitriolic attacks on domestic "anti-anti-Communists," a folkloric exaggeration of his influence on George F. Kennan, and his popularization by pundits and politicians who merely skimmed the surface of his ideas. Indeed, Niebuhr's growing fame was accompanied by the spread of what one biographer, Paul Merkley, aptly calls "adulterated Niebuhrianism." Yet as early as Niebuhr's publication of *The Irony of American History* in 1952, cold warrior boilerplate mixed uneasily with his serious effort to think through hard questions from a Christian realist point of view.[4]

Although Niebuhr often called "ironic" any actions or beliefs that struck him as incongruous, in this book he took great pains to distinguish his special conception of irony from pathos and tragedy. Pathos applied to those situations in which incongruities or absurdities resulted from "fortuitous cross purposes and confusions." Pathetic circumstances neither required repentance nor elicited admiration for those involved. Indeed, these situations might be comical. Tragedy required a "conscious choice of evil for the sake of good." Men or nations making such choices combined "nobility with guilt." Ironic situations differed from the tragic in that they derived from an "unconscious weakness" rather than a conscious choice. Nonetheless the men involved in them bore "some responsibility" for their decisions. While conceding that his readers might legitimately choose to view human flaws and failings as primarily tragic or absurdly pathetic, he believed that Christianity tended "to make the ironic view of human evil in history the normative one." Adam and Eve were expelled from Eden not because they consciously chose disobedience, but because they unconsciously misused the freedom God had given them. Biblical prophets warned repeatedly that such prideful "human pretensions" would provoke divine judgment.[5]

According to Niebuhr, all nations were marked by some form of "spiritual pride." In their own version, Americans thought that the United States had "turned its back upon the vices of Europe and made a new beginning." Both the New England Puritans and the Enlightenment founders of the republic believed in a special American destiny. In their most grandiose moments, Americans dreamed of "bringing the whole of human history under the control of human will." During the nineteenth century Americans proclaimed a mission to conquer a continent without acknowledging that they were moved partly by greed and ambition. As products of a commercial society, they deceived themselves into thinking that economic power, the chief engine of the United States's rise in the world, was more "covert"— and implicitly more virtuous—than the Europeans' overt exercise of political or military power. Nor did most of them see that expansion across the frontier and war with Spain in 1898 served as an evasion of domestic problems. On the contrary, buoyed by a successful imperialism, they acquired the "pride of power."[6]

Although Americans were "never as innocent as [they] pretended," Niebuhr saw no tragedy in what he candidly called "imperialism." Even in the nineteenth century there was no conscious choice of evil means to achieve virtuous ends, let alone a conscious choice of evil means to achieve evil ends. The United States, Niebuhr concluded with an innocence he often ascribed to others, had acquired more power than any nation in history "without particularly seeking it." Indeed, Americans had "no strong lust for power."[7]

Niebuhr became less critical when his sketch of diplomatic history reached the twentieth century. Following a standard liberal convention of the 1950s, he saw the United States as an almost passive entity "dragged protestingly and hesitantly into the world arena from the security of our continental cradle." Woodrow Wilson offered a "perfect expression of our original sense of mission" without acknowledging the country's "unconscious, hidden and tougher impulses." Then, during the 1920s and 1930s, the United States sank into isolationism and sought to "avoid its destiny as a world power." Indeed, as Nazism threatened civilization, the complex of "isolationist-nationalist-pacifist irresponsibility" reached almost "pathological proportions." So once again, under the leadership of Franklin D. Roosevelt, the United States needed to be dragged toward its destiny, a politically and culturally "hegemonic position" among nations.[8]

Twentieth-century "hegemony" looked more palatable to Niebuhr than nineteenth-century imperialism because the United States stood as a bulwark against Soviet communism. By 1952, he had long since demoted Marxists from the children of light. Yet communist "evils were distilled from illusions not generically different from our own" in that communism too developed ironically from "original dreams of justice and virtue." Nineteenth-century injustice made a "Marxist rebellion almost inevitable." Nevertheless, having assigned a "Messianic function in history to the poor," Soviet Communists had an "even simpler notion than we of finding an escape from the ambiguity of man's strength and weakness." The resulting "demonic religio-political creed" produced monstrous evils, as Niebuhr wrote repeatedly. Between passages of cold warrior boilerplate, however, the underlying affinities seemed to gnaw at him. For instance, both protagonists claimed innocence "according to their own official myths and collective memory."[9]

World hegemony would have been "morally precarious" under the best of circumstances, but the Cold War heightened the likelihood that the United States would claim—and suffer painful ironic consequences for claiming—excessive virtue and wisdom. Considering the domestic scene, Niebuhr came close to admitting that the delegitimation of Marxism had rendered private property almost "sacrosanct." As a cold war *liberal,* he ridiculed the pervasive denial of class tensions and, in a rare attempt at humorous wordplay, suggested that Americans were "rather more successful practitioners of materialism as a working creed than the Communists." Niebuhr was also disturbed by the arrogance that accompanied hegemonic foreign policy. The Marshall Plan was presented as an act of "generosity" when it represented "at best, a wise compound of concerns for the national interest with responsibility for a civilization of which we were a part." Such pretensions to greater virtue than was warranted occurred "again and again." Similarly, Niebuhr usually rejected simplistic invocations of the "socalled free world."[10]

International hegemony combined with innocent self-righteousness was dangerous as well as morally precarious. The United States might be "too secure in both our sense of power and our sense of virtue to be ready to engage in a patient chess game with the recalcitrant forces of destiny." The tragic threat, which Niebuhr endorsed in the early 1950s, to use nuclear weapons in order to preserve peace might lead instead to the worst war in history. No democracy could engage in preventive war but, he speculated a year after the Truman-MacArthur confrontation, the military might "heighten a crisis to the point where world war became inevitable." Or a "kind of apoplectic rigidity" among policy-makers might lead to war. "Constant proof is required that the foe is hated with sufficient vigor. Unfortunately, the only persuasive proof seems to be the disavowal of precisely those discriminate judgments which are so necessary for an effective conflict with the evil we are supposed to abhor." [11]

Niebuhr provided few specific recommendations for conducting foreign policy. When he did so, as his friend George F. Kennan observed, his opinions were unexceptional. The general Christian realist approach to the Cold War that Niebuhr presented in the early 1950s left enough wiggle room for him to become a relative dove within the context of Cold War liberalism. Until the mid-1960s, his evolving views were most affected by Soviet-American competition in the Third World, changes within international communism, and the increased power of nuclear and thermonuclear weapons. While exercising the "responsibilities" of an imperial power and hegemon of the anticommunist nations, the United States must adapt to these circumstances. In particular, he summarized in 1959, there needed to be a "less rigid and self-righteous attitude toward the world and a more hopeful attitude toward the possibilities of internal developments in the Russian despotism." [12]

Niebuhr never changed the basic conception of Marxism that he arrived at in the late 1940s. Communism, he insisted over and over again, was a secularized Hebraic and Christian messianism with a "holy nation" in the Soviet Union. He also savored developments that seemed to prove him right. He found tragedy in the fact that the Marxist alternative to capitalism "generated so much more terrible evils than capitalism itself." The doctrine of international worker solidarity was "nonsense." Similarly, the rejection of Soviet control by Polish and Hungarian Communists in 1956 as well as the subsequent Sino-Soviet split "refuted the utopianism of their common creed." The Soviet Union remained a "strange and formidable" adversary whose expansionism, Niebuhr wrote in a 1962 paraphrase of Kennan, must be "tamed by firm and patient resistance." Yet no one should talk "too simplistically or optimistically" of winning the Cold War. Rather, he wrote, consciously or unconsciously echoing President John F. Kennedy, the struggle might persist for decades or centuries without either "clear cut victory" or relief from the burdens of containment.[13]

Niebuhr became particularly concerned during the 1950s about competition to win favor among newly independent countries in Africa and Asia, which he atavistically called the "colored continents" and "dark continents." He stressed "one of the most vivid ironies of modern history," that both the United States and the Soviet Union, the hegemonic power in the communist bloc, "espoused the ideals of anti-imperialism." Unfortunately, the Soviets and the People's Republic of China (PRC) enjoyed "initial advantages" in the competition. Despite its record of brutality, and perhaps partly because of it, Soviet communism had brought rapid industrialization and impressive technological advancement to a poor country. Furthermore, the exaggerated Marxist argument that Western capitalist countries exploited their colonies "retained sufficient plausibility to impress the colored continents," Niebuhr conceded in 1959. In an "ironic historic coincidence," while the Soviet invasion of Hungary in 1956 delegitimized communism in Europe, the simultaneous Anglo-French invasion of Egypt helped to validate that ideology in the Third World. But the ideological struggle there "may nevertheless be won."[14]

No more than policy-makers in the Eisenhower and Kennedy administrations did Niebuhr come up with a consistent approach to the Third World in general or Africa and Asia in particular. While acknowledging that the Western record of imperialism harmed the anti-communist cause, he thought American leaders since the era of Woodrow Wilson were too quick to censure British and French imperialism. Britain's record of stewardship seemed superior to that of France, but Niebuhr showed no outrage over what he blandly called France's "stubborn problem" in Algeria. He doubted that newly independent countries in Africa and Asia would be hospitable to democracy or religious tolerance in the near future, and in the case of stable democracy he expected little better in Latin America. Inevitably "emerging nations" would "wrestle with various forms of pluralism." As Niebuhr wrote over and over again, Western Europe and the United States had struggled for centuries to reach the modicum of stability and justice finally achieved in the mid–twentieth century. Accordingly, one-party systems, whether in Tunisia, Ghana, or Mexico, should be viewed with "a certain sympathy" as long as they remained free of communism's "fanatic dogma." Even communist victories on the periphery might be tolerable. In 1962, for example, the United States could live with a communist regime in Laos "where the social patterns make Western democracy irrelevant." [15]

Niebuhr recognized important changes within the Soviet bloc. The upsurge of dissent that followed Stalin's death went further than communist oligarchs would allow. Under the leadership of Nikita Khrushchev, they forced a "re-Stalinization of the Russian empire." Nonetheless, Poland retained a "precarious semi-autonomy" after 1956. Even the Soviet Union showed a "measure of democracy." When the communist Presidium threatened his power, Khrushchev successfully appealed to the full central committee. Perhaps, Niebuhr speculated with a historical analogy, the central committee, like the Whig aristocrats in the eighteenth-century British Parliament, might serve to advance the cause of political pluralism. Other developments reminded Niebuhr of trends that had undermined absolute monarchies in the West, notably the Soviet reliance on scientific experts and an educational system "in some ways superior to our own." Communist inflexibility might, on the one hand, "hasten the disintegration of the system," or, on the other, produce renewed fanaticism and a threat to world peace, Niebuhr wrote in 1959.[16]

From the mid-1950s until his death in 1971, Niebuhr emphasized that American leaders needed to respond "with mature empiricism and realism," sometimes even "amused tolerance," to international changes generally and particularly to those within the communist sphere. He never made clear to what extent he thought American policy could affect developments in the Soviet Union. In prose murky even by Niebuhrian standards, he hinted at a strategy of engagement. "Every method of identifying our cause that will indicate some measure of community across the ideological chasm and that will beguile the adversary from his aberrations is a source of strength to us," he wrote in 1969. Notwithstanding his own lack of strategic clarity,

Niebuhr left no doubt that policy-makers typically fell short of his standards for diplomatic maturity. Rather, they reiterated glib comparisons of the Soviet Union and Nazi Germany, relied excessively on military alliances to implement containment, lagged behind the Soviets in understanding the Middle East, and to the perplexity of most of the world, dogmatically denied that the People's Republic of China was solidly established. The underlying problem transcended presidential administrations: "democratic utopianism." Niebuhr increasingly condemned the utopian insistence that the rest of the world should or could be made to embrace "our own kind of openness (including the alleged virtues of the 'free enterprise system') as the only basis for a free society."[17]

Flexibility was essential because the contest between communism and the West was taking place "on the edge of an abyss of nuclear catastrophe." Niebuhr's great fear of the nuclear abyss, already apparent in *Irony,* grew as the weapons themselves increased in "suicidal and lethal efficacy." Fortunately, an interest in survival had "over-ridden" the communist dogma that predicted an inevitable conflict with capitalism. The Soviets did not want war "any more than we do," Niebuhr concluded in 1959, but a nuclear catastrophe might come through "miscalculation or misadventure." In optimistic moments he discerned a "nascent partnership" between the United States and the Soviet Union dedicated to avoiding catastrophe. Taking the long view, Niebuhr compared this "competitive coexistence" to the truce that followed the wars between European Catholics and Protestants centuries earlier. That uneasy peace ultimately transformed Europe into a religiously pluralistic continent.[18]

When Niebuhr did turn his attention to day-to-day diplomacy, his capacity for such historical detachment and flexibility often yielded to Cold War orthodoxy—albeit an ambivalent version of Cold War orthodoxy. A partisan Democrat, he underrated President Dwight D. Eisenhower's intelligence. A mild enthusiast for the New Frontier, Niebuhr both celebrated the nuclear test-ban treaty as John F. Kennedy's greatest accomplishment and endorsed his defense of American "prestige" in Berlin (while rejecting the first use of nuclear weapons). On the one hand, Niebuhr opposed the economic embargo on Cuba and the invasion of 1961; on the other hand, he favored a blockade of Cuba when the Soviet-American partnership against nuclear war almost lapsed during the missile crisis of 1962.[19]

Escalation of the Vietnam War catalyzed Niebuhr's greatest reconsideration of American foreign policy since his embrace of Cold War liberalism during the late 1940s. Niebuhr had always felt uneasy about an American role in Indochina. In 1954 he opposed intervention to rescue the French troops besieged at Dienbienphu. France's loss of Indochina was rooted in a failure to "offer sufficient independence . . . to give moral dignity to the fight against Communists posing as nationalists." Of the three noncommunist countries created by 1956, only South Vietnam showed any capacity for nationhood or self-government. Even there, President Ngo Dinh Diem was an unreliable ally. Still, Niebuhr concluded in 1963 the United States could not stand aside and let Communists "over run" Southeast Asia. In 1964, after Diem was overthrown, Niebuhr felt even more conflicted. While supporting Lyndon Johnson's election, he criticized Johnson's Wilsonian fiction that American intervention was intended to protect the independence of a small country. The Communists exuded an "aura of nationalism" and most of the peasants were "probably indifferent" to the issue of communism vs. democracy. Rather, the United States was fulfilling its "responsibilities" as hegemon of the anticommunism bloc. Seeing no solution to the "baffling situation," Niebuhr fell back on muddling through by "continuing to support indefinitely" whatever military junta ruled in Saigon. He differed from the administration only in that he expressed in public many of the doubts Johnson and his advisers admitted in private. As late as February 1965 Niebuhr hesitated to criticize the administration for "failing to solve an impossible problem."[20]

What Niebuhr called the "phenomenal expansion" and "irrationality" of the Vietnam War moved him to action, anger, and a basic reexamination of the conflict. In 1966, he became a founding member of Clergy and Layman Concerned About Vietnam (CALCAV), the foremost religious coalition against the war. He praised divinity students who surrendered their draft deferments or burned their draft cards in protest. And he lamented to a friend, "For the first time I fear I am ashamed of our beloved nation."[21]

The transition was personally difficult not only because many of his friends, including Vice President Hubert Humphrey, supported the war, but also because Niebuhr remained intellectually, if no longer emotionally, a cold warrior. He considered the Vietcong the "fiercest of terrorists." Rather than viewing intervention as a logical consequence of containment, he believed that the United States had "inadvertently strayed" into a "civil war." He repudiated violence by the antiwar movement, never advocated unilateral withdrawal, and believed that the United States owed some sort of "debt" to South Vietnam.[22]

Deliberately remaining within the intellectual context of Christian realism and Cold War liberalism, Niebuhr mustered strong arguments against the war. President Johnson's invocations of Wilsonian self-determination failed to disguise a "venture to preserve imperial prestige." The "realist" arguments for the war were no more impressive than the idealist mythology. While the administration might be moved in part by "some vague residual fear" of communism, the communist monolith had "disintegrated." The domino theory—the notion that loss of an "obscure Asian nation" would lead to a series of defeats elsewhere—struck Niebuhr as "astounding." Instead of containing the People's Republic of China, as the Johnson administration contended, the war drove North Vietnam closer to the PRC. No irony was more poignant than the destruction of South Vietnam in order to save it. Furthermore, while spending "billions of dollars and thousands of precious young lives" to fulfill an amorphous debt to South Vietnam, the United States slighted the more significant debt owed to an African American community only recently granted full legal equality. The money wasted in Vietnam should be spent on domestic antipoverty programs.[23]

Even during the Vietnam War, Niebuhr never denied that communism retained a "more vivid mythical content" than the Cold War orthodoxy of the so-called free world. Yet he began to doubt that there were "radical differences" between the two worldviews. And in practice, both the United States and the Soviet Union betrayed "similar imperialist impulses."[24]

In the passage in *The Irony of American History* that teeters furthest from Cold War liberal orthodoxy, Niebuhr confessed the "uneasy feeling" that some of the American utopian dreams of "managing history" might have resulted in cruelties "similar" to those imposed by the Soviets if these had "flowered into action." William Appleman Williams both argued that such utopian dreams had flowered into action and also documented the cruel consequences.[25]

Unlike Niebuhr, Williams was never a cold warrior, preferred an Episcopalian social gospel to neo-orthodoxy, and considered a philosophy without a utopia "like the sky without stars." Niebuhr's "grand effort to revitalize the doctrine of Christian capitalism" failed, Williams wrote, not only because he misread Sigmund Freud to conclude that men could not be moral in society, but also because, by denying the possibility of achieving "great and noble goals," he repudiated the "very Utopia offered by Christianity." Williams's personal vision of utopia consisted of a community in which citizens engaged in honest dialogue about the issues they faced and, he hoped, decided on socialist solutions.[26]

Despite these differences—and despite the fact that he was a generation younger—Williams shared more common ground with Niebuhr than he acknowledged. First, he too struggled with three intellectual issues that concerned Niebuhr (along with most other serious thinkers) from the 1910s to the early 1950s. These decisively affected the ways in which he examined the Cold War. The first issue is usually called the problem of relativism. If, as seemed the case, there was no such thing as an objective standpoint, how can we conclude that one explanation is better than another?

Williams was atypical among historians of his generation in taking such epistemological issues seriously—and viscerally. Born in 1922, he graduated from the United States Naval Academy in 1944, served in the Pacific during World War II, and entered the University of Wisconsin graduate school in 1947. Along with many other combat veterans, he returned "really [wanting] to make some sense of what the hell is going on." The "central question" was "how one perceives the evidence and how one presents one's perceptions," Williams wrote later. To find answers, he drew on his scientific training at Annapolis as well as extensive reading in philosophy, psychology, and sociology. He also paid close attention to the ideas of Charles A. Beard, who had struggled with the problem of relativism during the previous generation. Williams ultimately joined Beard in concluding that there were ways to make "valid generalizations." The "citizen as historian" must try to transcend his own biases and do his best "to reconstruct what happened and to explain how and why it happened." More broadly, in consciously choosing between "conflicting theories of knowledge," Williams concluded that "seemingly separate parts are in reality always internally related to each other." Thus, in order to make sense of the world, it was necessary to view events from multiple "frames of reference" and to avoid harsh judgments on those whose perspectives differed from his own. "The only way forward is to make the effort to read with skepticism, compassion, and a readiness to recognize a truth we did not expect to find," Williams summarized in 1972.[27]

Furthermore, Williams like Niebuhr seriously confronted the ideas of Karl Marx. He did so, however, fifteen years later than Niebuhr, at a time when Marxist ideas were increasingly dismissed or stigmatized. Even intellectuals still sympathetic to socialism in the late 1940s viewed prevailing versions of Marxism as dogmatic and deterministic. While still in the navy, Williams worked with Communists in the civil rights and labor movements in Texas; he admired their courage but thought their approach to race relations insular and wrongheaded. But Marx himself was a "fellow Spinozan" who saw connections among seemingly separate parts of society. As Williams worked out his own idiosyncratic version of Marxism during the next three decades, he continued to view Marx as a master historian, economist, and psychologist of human alienation rather than as an "early computer offering the date of the birth of utopia."[28]

Finally, much as Niebuhr in the 1930s had reevaluated the pre–World War I Protestant social gospelers, Williams in the 1940s and 1950s questioned many of the interpretations and ideological assumptions of the "old progressive" historians. Williams found *much* more value in that scholarship, especially in the work of Beard and Frederick Jackson Turner, than did such contemporaries as Richard Hofstadter and Oscar Handlin. Yet he also found narrowness of vision and a tendency to reduce American history to a struggle between virtuous progressives and exploitative conservatives. As much as Niebuhr's writing, Williams's work overflowed with ironies. None was more significant or recurrent than this insistence that conservatives had been more effective reformers than liberals, not to mention radicals.

Although Williams is remembered above all as a Cold War "revisionist," he was not primarily a historian of the Cold War, especially as that specialty is currently defined. Indeed, Williams did not see himself only, or even primarily, as a diplomatic historian. He stressed repeatedly the reciprocal relationship between domestic and foreign affairs. He also believed that an understanding of the United States required a long view going back at least as far as British attitudes on the eve of settlement. In a sense, his most famous book, *The Tragedy of American Diplomacy,* an "essay" published in 1959, should be read as a supplement to his later, more ambitious book, *The Contours of American History.* For the Cold War to be understood, Williams summarized in 1972, it needed to be "decapitalized and viewed as a confrontation that occurs throughout our history" rather than as a Soviet-American conflict that began in 1944–45 or even 1918–20. As he explained in *Tragedy* (where the term *Cold War* was decapitalized), it was the "most recent phase of a more general conflict between the established system of western capitalism and its internal and external opposition."[29]

The American "traditional view of itself" in relation to the rest of the world consisted of three "classic" images. All were products of a long history and repeated misreading of that history. First, "the United States was isolationist until world power was 'thrust upon it' " to free Cuba from Spain in 1898, to protect democracy in 1917 and 1941, and "finally to prevent the Soviet Union and other Communist regimes from overwhelming the world." Second, "except for a brief and rapidly dispelled aberration" at the turn of the twentieth century, the United States had been "anti-imperialist throughout its history." Third, a "unique combination of economic power, intellectual and practical genius and moral rigor enables America to check the enemies of peace and progress—and build a better world—without erecting an empire in the process." Even Joseph Stalin did not maintain that the American record was "exactly the reverse of this common view," Williams conceded. Yet these three premises were much less right than wrong.[30]

Probably Williams's greatest contribution was to deny over and over and over again that the United States had ever been an isolationist nation. On the contrary, the "essence of American foreign policy" was the process of turning "one fragile settlement" into a "Global Empire." The founders of the republic were "militantly, even aggressively expansionist" and their goals lived on for more than two centuries.

While Williams acknowledged that imperialism enriched many capitalists, he did not maintain (Cold War liberal folklore to the contrary) that the survival of capitalism depended on expansionism. Rather, he stressed that Americans across class lines *believed* that their way of life depended on expansion even as they denied that their country was an imperial power. Long before Frederick Jackson Turner conceptualized his frontier thesis in the 1890s, they acted on the belief that prosperity and social peace depended on access to an allegedly empty land in the west. Accordingly, and to the exasperation of many readers, myself included, Williams used references to the "frontier-expansionist theory of history" to signal virtually every American exercise of power abroad. This term also served as shorthand for the prevalent American dream of utopia different from his own communal version. Beyond prosperity and a social "safety valve," the frontier seemed to promise personal freedom and a fulfilling sense of mission akin to what Niebuhr called "Messianism."[31]

Despite this persistent motif, Williams traced changes as well as continuity within what he ultimately called "empire as a way of life." The mercantilist founders and their political heirs down through the administration of John Quincy Adams formulated the rationale for expansion "so vigorously and advanced it so rigorously" that it became an "integral part" of the American "emotional and even psychological makeup." "The power and persistence of ideas in the face of changing reality was never more amply documented," Williams editorialized in a passage missed by critics who called him an economic determinist. Nonetheless, these mercantilists combined frontier expansionism with an attempt to build a national community of reciprocal obligation. Thus they also "provided many of the central ideas that later Americans turned to in an effort to restore some balance" to their way of life. John Quincy Adams, for example, warned against going abroad—meaning outside of what he considered the natural continental boundaries—"in search of monsters to destroy." Unfortunately, the social type that presented these views—responsible mercantilist conservatives—became less esteemed after the 1820s. The rise of mass democracy, incongruously symbolized by the election of Andrew Jackson, ushered in what Williams called the "age of laissez nous faire."[32]

Increasingly thereafter individualism and capitalism were less restrained by qualms about the primacy of property rights or a sense of mutual obligation. Increasingly too Americans of all classes favored expansion in hopes of jump-starting a stalled economy or improving their personal financial circumstances. Some at least acquiesced in imperialism in order to "strike a blow for freedom, either by blocking the expansion of European powers or by extending American activity as a world reformer." Many were just "caught up in the nationalist or patriotic support for the government that is common in all societies, or perhaps [were] sublimating their frustrations about life in America." The popularity of frontier expansionism beyond the elite had two significant consequences. Foreigners—including those living in North America who impeded the march westward—"were considered inferior and backward—proper subjects for education and reform in the American Way." And Americans were disposed to blame their own problems on the behavior of such recalcitrant foreigners. By the late nineteenth century, an "economic nationalism was defining various other nations as enemies on the basis of their response to overseas expansion."[33]

The late nineteenth century did bring an important tactical turn in empire as a way of life. After the United States reached its "natural limits" at the Pacific and Rio Grande, shrewd policy-makers concluded that overseas trade represented the new frontier. Borrowing from two British scholars, Williams applied to American foreign policy the concept of an "informal empire." The United States preferred to maximize economic and even evangelical influence without assuming the political, let alone military, responsibility for governing new territory. What Niebuhr regarded as the absence of a lust for power, Williams considered a craving for power without responsibility. Because even most opponents of acquiring Cuba and the Philippines after the Spanish-American War agreed with this broad strategy, they qualified, in Williams's phrase, as "imperial anti-colonialists." He nonetheless applauded opponents of the suppression of the Filipino independence movement, a barely remembered American war in which "people killed each other in every way which could be devised."[34]

Williams thought the Spanish-American War much less significant than the Open Door notes that followed in 1899 and 1900. In these diplomatic declarations circulated to the major powers, the United States sought "to establish the rules of the game, which would prevent the struggle in the marketplace from becoming a clash of arms." The metaphor of a door open to American access, influence, and economic pressure became Williams's favorite shorthand for the twentieth-century variant of frontier expansionism. Placed in one frame of reference, that of most policy-makers, the strategy "worked magnificently" for half a century, allowing the United States to maintain an informal empire with "but small amounts of force." From Williams's perspective, however, Open Door imperialism looked like "an attempt to exercise dominant power within a framework of 'freedom without responsibility.' "[35]

Although their terminologies differed, Williams's research-based history of American foreign policy intersected in places with Niebuhr's theologically oriented usable past. They agreed, for example, that the frontier served as a psychological escape, and looked askance at the American messianic mission. Yet their underlying differences were fundamental. Going beyond Niebuhr's complaint that Americans denied their country's imperial record, Williams insisted that the fact of empire was central to American ways of living. In addition, Williams showed that Americans had sought international power deliberately rather than unconsciously. "Nobody but Americans thrust world power on the United States." Far from thrusting world power on the United States, other countries and peoples, including those on this continent, tried to resist the advance.[36]

In the early twentieth century, the differences between President Woodrow Wilson and his first secretary of state, William Jennings Bryan, were particularly revealing. An opponent of acquiring the Philippines after the Spanish-American War and an "able critic of traditional colonial expansion," Bryan nonetheless wanted the United States "to uplift" the world while replacing Great Britain as "master of the international marketplace." In 1915, Bryan resigned as secretary of state when Wilson tilted toward the Allies during World War I. Philosophical and moral issues were also at stake. Bryan had come to understand that even an informal empire "might well supplant America's true claim to leadership" by moral example. His resignation marked the "high point of critical politics in the century after the Mexican war," Williams wrote in 1972.[37]

Wilson's "imperialism of idealism," in Latin America and elsewhere, was nonetheless imperialist. In attempting to undermine the revolutionary Soviet Union, Wilson illustrated the American inclination to apply the "principle of self-determination only to those societies that were willing to self-determine themselves within the framework of the status quo." Nor did imperial aspirations disappear after the defeat of the Treaty of Versailles. American leadership in naval disarmament and plans to bolster the German economy belied the "legend of isolationism" in the 1920s.[38]

No aspect of Williams's history of American foreign policy is more perplexing than his treatment of American entry into World War II. Paying slight attention to specific diplomatic developments during 1939–41, he offered the rote judgment that the "frontier-expansionist conception of history" made intervention inevitable. In most instances the Open Door strategy produced victory without war. In this case, however, when the United States tried to use economic power to force Japan out of China, the Japanese struck back. Williams repudiated the New Deal inclination "to reform the world" and implied that the Pacific war in which he had served was as unwise as other interventions. Here Williams stood apart not only from the "vital center" celebrations of President Franklin D. Roosevelt, but also from Popular Front celebrations of the Great Patriotic War. Rather, his skepticism echoed the arguments of Charles Beard, conservative "isolationists," and old progressive radicals whom both vital centrists and Popular Fronters, in a rare instance of agreement, cast into the dustbin of provincial ignorance.[39]

Yet Williams seemed to have had nagging doubts about subsuming the European theater of World War II under the bland rubric of the "war for the American frontier." Perhaps that is why he chose instead to focus on what might be called procedural issues. Roosevelt failed to "lead the country into a meaningful and necessary war against fascism." On the contrary, he invented the "credibility gap" in 1940–41 by lying about the undeclared naval war against Germany and likely consequences of aiding Great Britain. Williams left unclear whether this substitution of elitist manipulation for honest leadership made the war less necessary or meaningful. And he went so far as to put in a good word for the least thoughtful noninterventionist leader. Charles A. Lindbergh understood that the United States "was not powerful enough to control the forces which would be released (and created) by the war."[40]

Those forces made some sort of conflict between the United States and the Soviet Union inevitable, though not necessarily the Cold War as it developed. For Williams, the "problem of which side started" the Cold War was "neither a very intelligent nor a very rewarding way of approaching the central question about American foreign policy since 1941." The more subtle and important question was which side "hardened the natural and inherent tensions . . . into bitter antagonisms and inflexible positions." Here the United States bore primary responsibility for embarking on a strategy of containment. Furthermore, at least until 1962 the United States enjoyed a *vast preponderance of actual as well as potential power vis-à-vis the Soviet Union.*[41]

Williams toyed with a "fascinating 'iffy' question." Perhaps a balance of power "settlement" might have been achieved if American policy-makers had behaved like "proper imperial leaders." Acknowledging the Soviet Union's wartime sacrifices and fears for its future security, they might have acquiesced in a security sphere that included territory seized in 1939–41. Such concessions were unlikely, however, because the "philosophy and practice of open door expansion had become, in both its missionary and economic aspects, *the* view of the world." Perhaps, Williams conceded, the Soviets overreacted to the "grandiose" terms proposed by the United States. But he relegated that iffy question to a hypothetical book about the tragedy of Soviet diplomacy.[42]

Williams dismissed the notion advanced by his nemesis Arthur Schlesinger Jr. that the Cold War was inevitable because Stalin was paranoid. Policy-makers themselves had not dealt with the Soviet dictator as if he were mentally ill, Williams noted. How, then, could historians in retrospect render such a "flat-out" psychiatric opinion? He might reconsider if Robert Coles, Rollo May, and Abraham Maslow— three psychologists from different interpretive schools whose work he respected—weighed in on the question. Hardly anybody got the joke.[43]

Cold warriors who called Williams a Soviet apologist seemed almost willfully to ignore his recognition that communist revolutions entailed a "terrible price in terror and hardship." Nor did they understand his idiosyncratic patriotism. Nonetheless, Williams did not respond explicitly until 1973. It was easy to construct an academic or public career "by moralizing about the failures of other societies," but he saw no point beyond careerism and self-protection in such "perpetual outrage." Williams did not approve of imperialism by Russians or Israelis, and opposed repression in Brazil and France, he said, "but most of all I like them least by and in my own America."[44]

Unlike Niebuhr, however, Williams discerned "good as well as evil" in communist societies and insisted on their right to make their own mistakes. Equally important, while hailing the "great personal dedication and courage" of the Hungarian and Polish rebels of 1956, he inferred from these revolts that Communists themselves were the "most likely source" of improvements in their societies "short of war." Furthermore, among its many counterproductive consequences, the "callous" American strategy of containment made life harder for citizens of communist countries in the present and rendered reform less likely in the future.[45]

Although Williams opposed containment and its harsher offspring "liberation," he believed that the United States "need not abandon all efforts to influence" developments in the communist bloc. Paralleling Niebuhr, though with greater optimism and empathy, he discerned in the mid-1960s signs that the Soviet Union was "changing in ways that deny the American idea and image of it as a static and wholly evil society." American encouragement of the internal "positive forces" coupled with a soothing of continuing Soviet security fears might produce a "moderate degree of success." While leaving vague both the means and ultimate ends, Williams seems to have been advocating a generous version of detente as a way of enhancing freedom in Communist countries.[46]

While Niebuhr treated the Third World with condescension as a Cold War problem to be managed, Williams viewed poor nations not only as the primary victims of capitalist imperialism, but also as cultures worthy of respect. He paid particular attention to Latin America. There, as elsewhere, the imperialist impact involved more than economics. Instead of bringing widespread prosperity, imported capitalism simultaneously enriched an elite, disrupted rural life, and turned peasants into an urban underclass. Capitalism thus increased misery by destroying an "integrated culture" in which the peasants were "at least participating members, even if they were poor." The Alliance for Progress, which Niebuhr considered one of the Kennedy administration's great accomplishments, looked to Williams like a failure even from the perspective of patriotic Latin American capitalists. The Al-

liance would not even create "truly national and independent" capitalist systems such as had existed in the United States before the
Civil War.[47]

The Third World poor were not merely victims in Williams's
analysis. On the contrary, they could serve as an inspiration. "Billions
of people are beginning to control their own societies for the first time
in centuries," he wrote in 1964. If Americans could not bring themselves to be "exhilarated" by these efforts, they should at least "relax"
sufficiently so that "some of our blood might move out of our fright
glands back into our heart and our head." Americans might even learn
something from poor peoples whose day-to-day struggles offered a
"constant reminder of the idea and ideal of community."[48]

While persistently criticizing American imperialism, Williams
often wrote with empathy about policy-makers who created and tried
to manage the empire. True to his Beardian relativism, his own tem-
perament, and his commitment to "history as a way of learning"
through honest dialogue, he tried before rendering judgment to explore issues from within the policy-makers' frames of reference. For
example, from Woodrow Wilson's point of view an international
order based on the Fourteen Points looked "sound and noble."
Williams was especially generous to the modern "conservative heirs"
to John Quincy Adams whom he thought more likely to face the facts
that liberals or radicals ignored. His favorite conservative, Herbert
Hoover, was credited with trying "to build a community—a common-
wealth—based on private property without relying on imperial expansion." Dwight Eisenhower also understood that the "empire had
limits." Because there was so little candid and responsible commentary
from the contemporary right or center, Williams explained in 1980,
the left "must in truth honor if not indeed rehabilitate the best of our
conservative tradition in order to have a serious dialogue."[49]

Even an honest choice of the wrong road counted a lot for
Williams. No one should expect—let alone force—Americans to repudiate their three flawed "classic" premises about their country's foreign policy. Only rarely did human beings display the intelligence and
courage necessary to repudiate or modify their basic premises,
Williams believed. But Americans might begin to see or acknowledge
the consequences of their beliefs. Significantly, Williams named his
most popular book *The Tragedy of American Diplomacy* not *The De-*

pravity of American Diplomacy. The nation's tragic flaw was an inability to live up to its best ideals and thus to grant to others the freedom, democracy, and self-determination it claimed for itself. American motives were "not evil." Nor were all U.S. actions "wrong or fruitless." Aid programs like the Marshall Plan saved hundreds of thousands of lives. Yet many actions *were* counterproductive or evil. Frequently even benign intentions were undermined by an insistence on following the American example on "vital matters." But often the "American way of doing things simply does not work for other people." Or other people might prefer a different approach that produced "equally good results—perhaps better ones." Even in instances where the American way was the "*only* effective approach the act of forcing it upon others" contravened both American interests and ideals. Feeling coerced, other nations became less willing to evaluate American proposals on their merits.[50]

Williams viewed the 1960s as a test of "our very substance as Americans." The Vietnam War, the chief catalyst of that test, was not usefully understood as "Johnson's War." Lyndon Johnson "happened to be president" when the consequences of frontier expansionism worked themselves out "in front of our eyes—and with our lives." The tragedy Williams discerned in the American response to both the Cuban revolution and the Vietnamese civil war paralleled Niebuhr's ironic analysis. Once again, Williams wrote, the United States "invoked the principle of self-determination in order to disrupt coherent cultures and civilizations." In this context, the small, heterogeneous collection of liberal, conservative, and radical critics of basic Cold War premises finally won a hearing, and Americans had a "chance to break out of our traditional outlook."[51]

At his most utopian, Williams thought a social movement might be built to lead (rather than coerce) Americans away from empire as a way of life. He also elaborated on his utopian vision in a way that underscored his belief in self-determination as the most important ideal that the United States tragically failed to honor. He dreamed of replacing the imperial United States with a "federation of regional communities," preferably democratic socialist communities. Such a federation would not be "isolationist or indifferent to its own security"; it might even serve as a noncoercive model for other nations. But the new America would neither try to police "any part" of the world nor "attempt to expand the area of freedom by subverting the self-determination of other peoples."[52]

As early as 1969, Williams concluded that no movement on the left was strong enough to push through major reforms, "let alone structural change." Even so, he continued to hope that the Vietnam War and the economic slump of the 1970s might move ordinary Americans as well as some of their leaders to reconsider the consequences of empire as a way of life. As usual, he credited conservatives with greater realism. President Richard M. Nixon and Secretary of State Henry Kissinger understood that undermining the Soviet Union was "no longer conceivable" (though Kissinger presented the case for retrenchment in an amoral "wrong idiom" for Americans). On the other hand, President Jimmy Carter betrayed an "extremely weak understanding of strategy and tactics." At best, a sense of moral responsibility, perhaps a legacy from Carter's Annapolis training, bolstered his "concern for human rights and his inclination to allow other cultures to find their own way to Truth and Beauty."[53]

Beyond the White House, Williams speculated, Americans facing economic stagflation and the Iran hostage crisis in 1980 felt that the "crunch is here." Perhaps now they would admit that the United States "*is* an empire" and talk about it. Forthright imperialists could argue that the American empire was "good and healthy," a source of "psychic and material rewards." Perhaps citizens would settle for a restrained and "responsible empire" devoid of a "messianic global formulation" of national security—the direction in which Nixon and Kissinger had seemed to be moving. Even if his side could not convince Americans that the moral costs of empire outweighed the undeniable psychic and economic rewards, at least, Williams thought, issues would be honestly confronted and differences "clarified."[54]

By the time Williams died in 1990, the Cold War with the Soviets had ended, an event most Americans greeted with a sense of relief or triumph rather than historical or moral reflection. Beset by ill health and more pessimistic than ever about the country's direction during the 1980s, Williams increasingly practiced as well as preached his gospel of localism. He explored the maritime history of the Oregon coast, where he lived, and wrote columns for two newspapers in the state. While sympathizing with the antinuclear protestors of the early

1980s, he lamented that few citizens of the "Superpower" retained "even the dream of a common welfare."[55]

Perhaps because Williams sensed that empire as a way of life was stronger than ever in his own America, he wrote relatively little about Ronald Reagan's domestic or foreign policies. Most of what he wrote was formulaic. The president looked like the latest unreflective cold warrior in a line that stretched back to Truman; the culture that celebrated Reagan was "weary and nostalgic." Instead of trying to explain the president's domestic and international successes, Williams focused on the administration's deception, as he had when discussing the analogous painful issue of entry into World War II. He considered Iran-Contra much more serious than the Watergate scandal as a "fundamental threat to constitutional government." Williams was furious that fellow Naval Academy graduates who served as Reagan's national security advisers lacked the courage to disobey illegal orders. An equally angry but more detached Williams would have taken Reagan more seriously, perhaps placing him in the long line of underestimated conservatives who adapted sufficiently to preserve empire as a way of life.[56]

Occasionally Williams displayed his old eloquence. The responsible exercise of power had been a central concern of adult life. In 1986 he addressed the subject at Annapolis, where, he often said, he had first begun to think about the subject as a young man. "If you get too much power," he warned, "you are tempted to persuade or force other people to do things *that even you know are wrong*. You act against your own integrity, as well as against the public welfare and the public virtue. This is in truth the ultimate corruption. You begin to play at being God."[57]

During the early and mid-1990s, John Lewis Gaddis urged students of international relations to reexamine the recently ended Cold War with an eye to the moral dimension. He correctly discerned that Cold War debate contained few examples of sustained moral argument (as opposed to ad hoc moralism). In Gaddis's view, historians needed to focus on both the role of the United States in the collapse of communism and the ethical or unethical behavior of the contending parties. Unfortunately, historians hesitated to do so because they "allowed Williams's 'tragic' view of American diplomacy to obscure our vision." Revisionist criticism that might have fit particular policies at particular times and places had been transformed into "something approaching a universal frame of reference." Williams's heterodoxy had become morally flawed "conventional wisdom."[58]

Gaddis went on to end a 1993 essay on the "tragedy of Cold War history" with an assault on Williams's scholarly integrity as well as his favorite concepts and phrases:

> We need a clear sense of what real tragedy, in this less than perfect world, is all about. That means placing our concept of tragedy within an international context. It means comparing the American "tragedy" with the others that surrounded it. It means using history as a genuine way of learning, not simply as a convenient platform from which we hold forth, either in self-condemnation or congratulation. It means, in the most fundamental sense, meeting our obligations as historians, which involve being honest not only about ourselves but about the environment in which we have had to live. And it means according equal respect, as we have not yet done, to *all* of the survivors, and to *all* of the dead.[59]

Although Gaddis lamented inattention to the moral dimension of the Cold War, he was actually most distressed by the prevalence of moral judgments different from his own. He inferred from recent controversies over national history standards and an exhibition at the National Air and Space Museum about the bombing of Hiroshima and Nagasaki that historians in general were excessively critical of American moral failings. Particularly annoying was the ostensibly pervasive belief that the United States and the Soviet Union had been morally equivalent. Gaddis cited a 1986 debate between Secretary of Defense Caspar Weinberger and British historian E. P. Thompson in which Thompson defended the position that there was "no moral difference" between American and Soviet foreign policy. According to Gaddis, "watered-down versions" of this view were held by many American academics, none of whom he specified by name.[60]

The content if not the tone of Gaddis's attack on Williams and other unspecified revisionists was hardly surprising. On the contrary, a less strident and less moralistic version of the critique appeared in his first book, *The United States and the Origins of the Cold War,* which was published in 1972 when Gaddis was thirty-one. He acknowledged American mistakes and self-interest, and conceded that neither the United States nor the Soviet Union bore sole responsibility for the start of the Cold War. Even so, no actions by the Roosevelt or Truman administrations could have prevented the confrontation because of Soviet suspicion in general and Stalin's "paranoia" in particular. Gaddis did not engage in what Williams liked to call a "dialogue" with revisionists who argued otherwise. Rather, he dismissed them as practitioners of "economic determinism." Adhering to this "single-cause explanation of human behavior," they failed to understand that policymakers brought to their task a "variety of preconceptions, shaped by personality, ideology, political pressures, even ignorance and irrationality." In part, Gaddis attributed his own superior understanding of the origins of the Cold War (which he capitalized and saw beginning in the 1940s) to his greater methodological sophistication.[61]

Gaddis especially prized internal government documents as sources for understanding foreign policy. Despite this empiricist disposition, he paid much closer attention to methodological questions than did most diplomatic historians. As was the case with Niebuhr and Williams, his method affected his moral judgments about the Cold War.

Gaddis's practical response to the problem of relativism overlapped with that of most reflective historians. Like his (unacknowledged) fellow Spinozan Williams, Gaddis aspired to understand how "components interact to become systems." There was "no 'correct' interpretation of the past," he acknowledged. Historians were able to "represent" or "simulate" past reality. In so doing, they used their own imaginations "disciplined by sources." They needed to appreciate contingency and the ability of individuals to alter the course of events in historically fluid moments; they should never assume that "we're smarter now than they were then." Counterfactual simulations were useful for understanding the past as long as these mental experiments passed the "test of plausibility."[62]

Analogies helped too. Above all Gaddis liked analogies from what he called "evolutionary sciences," especially geology and geography. Geologists and geographers could not replicate in the laboratory the processes that created great mountain ranges, but they could "derive processes from structures" that survived to the present. Historians engaged in an analogous "mapping" of the "landscape" of the past. Moreover, Gaddis adapted from fractal geometry the concept of "self-similarity across scale." For instance, in dictatorships tyranny at the top was replicated in day-to-day cruelty at the bottom, and in democracies grassroots values ultimately affected the leaders.[63]

According to Gaddis, historians could not—and should not—avoid rendering moral judgments. Acknowledging that "times impose their morality upon lives," he hesitated to condemn ordinary men and women for behaving in ways that seemed normal in their day but repugnant in retrospect. Yet exceptions should be made for those whose cruelty cost millions of lives. In addition, Gaddis considered himself a Niebuhrian. Niebuhr was not only the "great master of irony," but also one of the twentieth century's "most profound thinkers on the connection between morality and reality."[64]

In 1982, Gaddis published *Strategies of Containment,* an interpretation of American foreign policy during the Cold War that combined diplomatic, economic, ideological, and military perspectives as an alternative to the "outbreak of revisionism." *Strategies* was characteristic of Gaddis's subsequent work in several respects. First, with the exception of Russian-American relations, he showed little interest in the substance of or recent scholarship about U.S. foreign policy before the start of the (capitalized) Cold War in the 1940s.[65] Accordingly, he accepted the hoary legend that world power was "thrust upon" the United States at various intervals during the twentieth century in the face of chronic "isolationism." The nineteenth-century American conquest of a continent was a given rather than an intellectual or ethical problem. Similarly, Central America and the Caribbean appeared as a "traditional sphere" of influence. In this respect, he differed from Niebuhr as well as Williams. Second, he showed scant interest in the Third World except for countries like Cuba and Vietnam whose actions catalyzed crises in American foreign policy. Much like Niebuhr, he viewed poor nations as problems to be managed.[66]

Third, in stark contrast to Williams, Gaddis rarely examined domestic influences on foreign policy. On the contrary, most of Gaddis's scholarship reflected his belief that American foreign policy depended "only to a limited degree upon mass perceptions." Therefore his occasional doubts about this postulate sound all the more striking. At the end of *Strategies* he wrote, "To a remarkable degree, containment has been the product, not so much of what the Russians have done, or of what has happened elsewhere in the world, but of internal forces operating in the United States." Moreover, what was "surprising is the *primacy* that has been accorded economic considerations in shaping strategies of containment, *to the exclusion of other considerations.*" Despite these qualms, Gaddis not only persisted in dismissing the revisionists as economic determinists instead of addressing their arguments and evidence, but also continued to view foreign policy almost entirely as the province of high-level officials and diplomats.[67]

Nevertheless, before the early 1990s, Gaddis's judgments sometimes coincided with those of the revisionists. The Open Door notes represented "as clear an example of the pursuit of self-interest through the proclamation of disinterest as we have in our history." During the Progressive era the United States "fell into the habit" of trying to reform authoritarian governments, a habit that persisted "at considerable cost and with little success." Without saying so explicitly, Gaddis implied that the United States bore some responsibility for the origin and duration of the Cold War. The revival of a "Wilsonian commitment to self-determination . . . did a great deal to alienate Americans from their Soviet allies" during World War II. In addition, policymakers mistakenly assumed that dictatorships were inherently expansionist. The "most egregious example" of this mistake came during the Cold War. American leaders repeatedly failed to understand that communism could be an "indigenous, popular, and quite independent force in certain parts of the world" and mistakenly viewed all victories by Communists or their allies as threats to the United States. Confusing Mao Zedong's concern for the security of his country's borders with "ideologically motivated aggression," Truman in 1950 "blundered into a disastrous conflict with China"; Gaddis also acknowledged that Mao led China because the "Chinese people chose to transfer their allegiance" to him. Subsequent American intervention in Indochina on the basis of the same assumptions "was even more disastrous." Although relations with the Soviet Union and China had improved by the late 1980s, the Reagan administration showed the same "curious myopia" when dealing with "Castro's Cuba and even Nicaragua under the Sandinistas."[68]

While maintaining that Stalin's paranoia made the Cold War inevitable, Gaddis recognized that even within the Soviet Union some

Communists and some versions of communism were better than others. The Reagan administration's effort to distinguish between, on the one hand, "non-Marxist autocracies" subject to change, and, on the other hand, ostensibly permanent Marxist dictatorships seemed a "tenuous semantic distinction." From time to time, Gaddis put the term "totalitarian" between skeptical quotation marks. Soviet policy changed "dramatically" after Stalin's death in 1953 and the new leadership made "surprisingly conciliatory gestures" toward the United States, he noted.[69]

As late as 1987 Gaddis took contrarian pleasure in describing the post–World War II era as the "long peace." Despite proxy wars and considerable bloodshed on the periphery, "Soviet-American hegemonic 'management' "—something akin to what Niebuhr called a "nascent partnership"—successfully prevented crises from escalating into world war as almost certainly would have been the case under earlier international systems. The prospect of thermonuclear apocalypse was the chief restraining factor, but Gaddis also credited "statesmen" in both superpowers with an "impressive capacity to subordinate antagonistic ideological interests to a common goal of preserving international order." With the Cuban missile crisis in mind, Gaddis was at his most eloquent when he wrote in 1978 that the "cause of peace" was well served by Kennedy and Khrushchev, leaders who proved capable of "perceiving shared interests through the distractions created by ideological differences, unwieldy bureaucracies, dissimilar backgrounds, and the allurements of pride and prestige." In the end, they managed to reverse, "in however a limited fashion, the lockstep process of escalation and counter escalation that had characterized the first two decades of the postwar era."[70]

Although Gaddis did not refer to Niebuhr in his conceptualization of a long peace, he discerned a genuinely Niebuhrian irony. While the carefully constructed international order created at the Versailles conference collapsed into world war within twenty years, the jerry-rigged Cold War order prevented such a catastrophe for two generations. As of 1987, the Cold War system showed "no perceptible signs of disintegration."[71]

The Cold War international system, the Soviet Union, and the worldwide communist movement collapsed within four years. Gaddis quickly concluded that documents now available from the Soviet

Union and East bloc gave a "renewed vitality" to the orthodox interpretation of the Cold War. Indeed, this new information discredited
both the revisionist historiography associated with Williams and
"post-revisionist" efforts to mix orthodoxy and revisionism. In 1996
Gaddis explicitly recanted his youthful flirtation with the "rather
mushy" post-revisionist approach.[72]

Although Gaddis appears to have been craving an opportunity to
affirm Cold War orthodoxy for years, the effect of this recantation on
his work varied from place to place. In *The United States and the End of
the Cold War,* a collection of essays published in 1992, unrevised "post-
revisionist" pieces appeared side by side with orthodox celebrations of
the American victory. In his 1997 synthesis of what "we now know,"
Gaddis often wrote cautiously about the conclusions that could be
drawn from Soviet and Eastern bloc sources. Still, the general direction of his thought was clear. Gaddis celebrated not only the American
victory over the Soviet Union in the Cold War, but also the victory of
orthodox diplomatic historians over realists and revisionists. In the
process, he embraced many of the Wilsonian beliefs he had earlier criticized.

Gaddis's turn was clearest in his essays dealing explicitly with
morality and Cold War foreign policy. The tragedy of Soviet foreign
policy—"tragedy, if not in a classical sense, then in an all too modern
one"—was that Joseph Stalin ruled the country, he wrote in 1993.
Gaddis paired Stalin and Adolph Hitler as "brutal romantics" afflicted
with "narcissism and paranoia." Far from a "hard-nosed realist" in international relations, Stalin was "incapable of functioning within the
framework of mutual cooperation." Gaddis offered no list of his favorite psychologists to sustain his now more strident presentation of
Stalin as a narcissistic paranoid. Rather, invoking the principle of self-
similarity across scale, he proposed a "fractal geometry of terror."
Stalin was so gratuitously cruel in personal relations that he drove his
wife to suicide and imprisoned a peasant whose dog annoyed him. It
was hardly surprising, then, that he sentenced millions of innocents to
death and caused millions more to die during agricultural collectiviza-
tion.[73]

On a larger scale, a Stalinist regime that killed millions of Soviet citizens was "likely to act similarly toward the outside world." While
American soldiers usually behaved themselves, Soviet soldiers in 1945

raped tens of thousands of German women, thus illustrating the mores of a "culture of brutality unparalled in modern times." Furthermore, Stalin's "*system*" and its "emotionally based ideological romanticism" in foreign relations survived "not only his own demise but his successors' fitful and half-hearted efforts at 'de-Stalinization.' " No Soviet leader until Mikhail Gorbachev in the 1980s was "fully prepared to dismantle Stalin's structural legacy."[74]

Here Gaddis joined the Wilsonians he had earlier criticized in concluding that a dangerous foreign policy could be inferred from a country's brutal domestic polity. Simply put, a vicious ideological dictatorship was almost certainly an expansionist dictatorship. Gaddis lamented that practitioners of the "old history" of the Cold War had unduly minimized the ideological aspects of the Cold War—an assertion that would have surprised Arthur Schlesinger Jr. as well as Williams. Perhaps, Gaddis speculated further, they did so for fear of sounding like Senator Joseph McCarthy and other leaders of the second red scare.[75]

Facing Stalin and Soviet totalitarianism (a term no longer placed in quotation marks), American policy-makers after World War II addressed a dilemma that Gaddis framed in explicitly Niebuhrian terms: "How much evil did we have to put up with . . . in order to accomplish good?" Containment combined practical self-defense with essentially sound ethics. Along with 1917 and 1940, 1947 was "one of those moments when national interest and national morality seemed to coincide." In a very general way Gaddis joined Niebuhr in acknowledging some moral costs. The "principle of candor" suffered when the Truman administration exaggerated the Soviet threat to win support for aid to Greece and Turkey and the Marshall Plan. Gaddis conceded too that the principle of nonintervention in the affairs of other states was violated in frequent covert operations and occasional invasions.[76]

Gaddis regarded NSC 68 as the "most morally self-conscious state paper of the era." In this document, Paul Nitze and his fellow foreign-policy analysts described three strategic options—isolationism, preventive war, or a massive military—and especially nuclear—buildup combined with an ideological offensive at home and abroad. They recommended the third alternative which, following a classic American convention, they framed as the prudent middle course. When the premises of NSC 68 were incorporated into official containment strategy in 1950, the United States in effect answered the Niebuhrian question about the Cold War. As Gaddis summarized, American officials embraced "one evil in order to forestall what seemed to be the greater one," the advance of communism. Curiously, however, Gaddis called this choice "moral relativism," a term more appropriate for the view (exemplified, for example, by Henry Wallace) that Soviet behavior in its own sphere was no concern to the United States.[77]

Gaddis cited but was little affected by material from Soviet and East bloc archives that undermined the orthodox picture of the Soviets as expansionist ideologues. We now know, for example, that Lavrenty Beria, the monstrous chief of the secret police, favored what Gaddis earlier had called "surprisingly conciliatory" gestures toward the United States after Stalin's death. We also know that the Soviets invaded Hungary three years later with considerable reluctance. In light of such material, Gaddis's changing treatment of the 1950s is particularly revealing of his shift to triumphalism. His discussion of that decade's lost opportunities was one of the strongest and longest parts of *Strategies*. If the Eisenhower administration had been more flexible, Gaddis suggested, the Cold War might at least have been ameliorated. In the triumphalist 1990s, Gaddis showed much less interest in those might-have-beens. And Stalin's less repressive successors no longer qualified as "statesmen" and co-managers of a "long peace" (a term Gaddis repudiated in 1997 as "not so much wrong as shortsighted").[78]

According to Gaddis, the Vietnam War provoked the "most serious debate about the relationship of morality to foreign policy . . . since the earliest days of the Cold War." On the one hand, "realists" such as George Kennan and Hans Morgenthau did not deny that "in situations of mortal peril, all means are justified to secure desired ends," but they doubted that the fall of South Vietnam would constitute a mortal peril. On the other hand, radical critics claimed that behaving in foreign policy in ways considered unacceptable in "personal or in domestic affairs" was "inconsistent, hypocritical, and ultimately immoral regardless of the justification." Once again Gaddis named no radical scholars who adhered to this position.[79]

If Gaddis had Williams in mind, he missed Williams's tough side. Unlike self-designated realists, many revisionists wanted the United States not only to behave better than it had behaved, but also to behave better than other countries would under similar circumstances. For instance, while critics of the bombing of Hiroshima and Nagasaki typically conceded that Germany, Japan, or the Soviet Union would have used nuclear weapons in 1945, they nevertheless lamented that the United States did so. There was this side to Williams, the idiosyncratic patriot who repeatedly urged his country to live up to its highest ideals. Yet idiosyncratic patriotism coexisted in his worldview with what is usually called realism. Williams understood that international politics is often brutal. He warned against trying to police "any part" of the world both to protect the United States from brutality *and* also to prevent the United States from adding to the supply of it. He was willing to concede a Japanese sphere in China and a Soviet sphere in Eastern Europe in order to avoid, respectively, the worse horrors of World War II in Asia and the Cold War. Archival evidence proving that the Soviet Union spied on the United States would not have surprised or shocked Williams into altering his worldview.

Gaddis's treatment of the post–Vietnam-era presidencies of Carter and Reagan highlighted his 1990s affirmation of Cold War orthodoxy. Carter appeared as a kind of Cold War revisionist in the White House, a man whose "primary" commitment to international human rights "overwhelmed the 'realist' approach." Carter admired Reinhold Niebuhr's theology but in Gaddis's view never learned from Niebuhr that "order was a prerequisite for justice." Ironically, the commitment to human rights by this misguided Niebuhrian probably worsened relations with the Soviet Union, Gaddis speculated. In Iran and Nicaragua, Carter's mild pressures "backfired" in helping to bring "anti-American regimes" to power.[80]

Using a favorite geological analogy, Gaddis entertained the possibility that the "tectonic" forces of history brought the Cold War to what he considered a happy ending. Perhaps the Communists who succeeded or emulated Stalin and Mao Zedong were unable to adapt to a postindustrial world of consumer goods and instant communication. If the outcome was "prefigured all along," then the "real tragedy of Cold War history was all the wasted efforts the opponents of authoritarianism put into trying to bring about what was going to happen anyway." Yet Gaddis ultimately believed that "resistance made a difference." Indeed, he gave much credit to Ronald Reagan for launching a rhetorical offensive against communism and sponsoring both a military buildup and covert operations to weaken the Soviet "evil empire."

Reagan challenged the Soviets during the early 1980s "in a manner unprecedented since the early Cold War." The president's failure to recognize that Castro and the Sandinistas represented indigenous radicalism no longer seemed significant to Gaddis. By the end of the Reagan administration, he concluded, "there was a closer correspondence between the traditional American ideals and the actual conduct of American diplomacy than at any point since the Marshall Plan. The country did once again have a foreign policy it could be proud of." [81]

While urging other historians to join him in addressing the ethical issues raised by the Cold War, Gaddis acknowledged the venerable historicist argument against making retrospective moral judgments. Because "times impose their morality upon lives," there might be "no point in condemning individuals for the circumstances in which they find themselves." At minimum, however, exceptions could be made for men and women powerful enough to impose "their morality on times." During the twentieth century, three Communists—Lenin, Stalin, and Mao—joined Hitler in passing this test. But the "body count" of Communist evil was enlarged further by the "little Stalins and Maos," a list on which Gaddis now included Fidel Castro and Ho Chi Minh as well as Kim II Sung and Pol Pot. [82]

When Gaddis posed his Niebuhrian question about Cold War means and ends, he vaguely conceded that the United States sometimes chose "evil means." Yet he passed no critical moral judgments on any specific policy-makers. Rather, he pointed to their occasional "feckless stupidity," frequently cited extenuating circumstances, and found silver linings. The silver lining in the mushroom clouds over Hiroshima and Nagasaki was the net saving of American and Japanese lives that would have been lost in an American invasion of Japan. The overthrow of Prime Minister Mohammad Mossadegh of Iran in 1953 and President Jacobo Arbenz of Guatemala the next year were unfortunate overreactions. So was Richard Nixon's covert program to destabilize the Marxist government of Salvador Allende in Chile. In 1971, Nixon continued to support President Yahya Khan of Pakistan despite his regime's atrocities in East Pakistan; Gaddis acknowledged the "slaughter" but doubted that withdrawal of U.S. support would have made a difference. Military intervention in the Vietnam War was the "single greatest error" made by the United States during the Cold War; it was "both foolish and tragic." Unlike Williams, Gaddis did not see the war as a logical and likely result of the strategy of containment. And unlike Niebuhr, who could barely contain his moral outrage, he went no further than to quote Secretary of Defense Robert McNamara's bland regrets, "We were wrong, terribly wrong." Consistent with his lack of interest in domestic affairs, Gaddis ignored the costs to American society of McCarthyism and what Niebuhr called the embrace of private property as almost "sacrosanct."[83]

Despite his call to study the Cold War as an ideological conflict, Gaddis made no connection between feckless foreign policy mistakes and the beliefs held by Americans in general and their leaders in particular. Whereas communism caused the Soviets to "lose touch with reality," Americans in his writings had no ideology, even in the neutral sense of the term as a coherent framework for understanding how things work—what Williams called a worldview. What Americans had instead was immense goodwill and a nonideological democracy. Accordingly, while recognizing that the United States created an empire after World War II, Gaddis discerned a benign and even beneficial imperialism. Here Gaddis joined the Wilsonians he had earlier criticized in concluding that a country's benevolent foreign policy could be inferred from its fundamentally sound domestic polity. This Wilsonian premise is partly true. So is the view that Americans typically thought they are acting generously abroad and sometimes did act generously, as Williams acknowledged. Yet neither point is true always and everywhere. Especially outside of Europe, the American empire was hardly benevolent. In his newfound Wilsonianism, Gaddis inadvertently highlighted how little he had learned from Niebuhr. As Niebuhr insisted over and over again, relatively moral behavior is more easily achieved within one's own group, including one's own country, than when dealing with outsiders, and even virtues, like aspirations to spread democracy, ironically turned into vices if pushed too zealously.[84]

That life requires hard choices was true long before the point became an adulterated Niebuhrian cliché. Perhaps the Cold War elicited so little systematic moral argument because the choices were so hard, the results so brutal, and the worst possible outcome, thermonuclear world war, beyond comprehension. In retrospect, no methodological or ethical questions should be off-limits. Newly released information *and* as yet unforeseen consequences of the conflict will reinforce some dearly held opinions and undermine others. Thus far, there is sound evidence to distress revisionists and orthodox scholars alike: that espionage advanced Soviet production of the atomic bomb by a year or two, and therefore emboldened Stalin to support the North Korean invasion of South Korea; that Stalin in his international dealings was often a hard-nosed realist who might have accepted the spheres of influence settlement Williams thought plausible; that the Cold War might have ended earlier and in better circumstances for all concerned if Stalin's and Truman's successors had shown greater vision during the 1950s and 1960s; and that the collapse of the Soviet Union brought declining living standards to millions of men and women in Russia and other successor states.[85]

As Gaddis argued, the "body count" should weigh heavily in our retrospective evaluations of international morality and immorality. Three questions stand out in addressing this issue. First, when should the body count begin? Confronting the problem that "times impose their morality on lives," as Gaddis put it, modern thinkers with little in common beyond a belief in progress, variously defined, have responded with differing versions of historicist ethical relativism. For example, Marxists have viewed history as a series of stages in which the bourgeoisie changes from a progressive to a reactionary force, premillennial Protestants have discerned in the Bible different covenants between God and humanity during a series of "dispensations" over thousands of years, and philosophical liberals have believed (to paraphrase Gaddis) that "we" can be more moral now than "they" were then. On a less theoretical level, practicing historians do not lament George Washington's failure to establish national health insurance. Nor do they usually portray Oliver Cromwell as one of history's monsters even though his effort to remove Catholics from their land in Ireland prefigured the brutal practice now blandly called "ethnic cleansing." Rather, historians typically reserve such higher, "modern" ethical standards for men and women living during later, better times.

In evaluating international morality, when should we declare the start of later, better times? Like most cold warriors since the early days of the conflict, Gaddis began the international moral calculus after World War I with Lenin, Stalin, Hitler, and Mao. Conversely, despite their contrasting opinions about the Cold War and the Soviet Union, both Niebuhr and Williams included in the body count men and women killed during the creation of the American and other empires. The different moral accounting reflects more than their deeper perspective on history. Even more important, neither Niebuhr nor Williams was a Wilsonian.

For Wilsonians, the post–World War I era was supposed to usher in a new dispensation based on international law, self-determination, democratic decision-making and, where necessary, collective military action against aggressors. As Williams emphasized, neither the defeat of the Versailles Treaty in the United States nor the world's inexorable movement in the opposite direction destroyed Wilsonianism as an ideal. Even critics of the Wilsonian international vision accepted the new dispensation in the sense that they too wanted to start a fresh moral balance sheet that left uncounted the bodies buried during the recent era of empire building. Nor was this disposition uniquely American. Belgians, for example, preferred to think of themselves as progressive victims of German imperialism during World War I rather than as creators of a terrible empire in the Congo. Furthermore, neither the leaders of Western governments nor the scholars who sympathized with them wanted a serious moral accounting for the ten million lost between 1914 and 1918 when rival empires clashed in what conservative historian John Keegan rightly called a "tragic and unnecessary conflict." [86]

In short, Gaddis in the triumphalist 1990s was applying to the Cold War a formula of international moral accounting that had been used for seven decades. Although comforting to citizens of Western democracies, this formula rests on a self-serving periodization of history. The horrors of World War I occurred less than a generation before Stalin and Hitler consolidated power, the brutal conquest of Africa and the American suppression of the Philippine insurrection less than two generations earlier. Indeed, the period from the 1890s through World War I represented the formative years for the Americans and Western Europeans who were later "present at the creation" of the Cold War. Thus it is particularly odd to exonerate the Western leaders of the early twentieth century as if they were contemporaries of Oliver Cromwell. If all of the bodies are to be counted, as Gaddis wrote, then the fatal decisions made, for example, by William McKinley, Woodrow Wilson, and the World War I general staffs should not be forgotten.

Second, to what extent should the personal character of national leaders count in judging their life-and-death decisions? For Gaddis it counted a great deal. Whereas Soviet or Chinese foreign policy could be explained primarily through the "fractal geometry of terror," in which the personal brutality of tyrants at the top was writ large in foreign policy, American leaders always appeared in his work as decent men who, in Robert McNamara's phrase, might be at worst "terribly wrong." Even in the absence of a tyrant at the top, however, nonchalant and gratuitous cruelty was not absent from the American record. Indeed, the self-conscious cult of toughness that accompanied the Cold War helped policy-makers to look away or walk away from the cruel consequences of their actions. The victims included not only foes, but also friends and neutrals caught in the cross fire. A man as decent as Eisenhower paid slight attention to the victims of the right-wing regimes that followed the overthrow of Arbenz in Guatemala, and showed no remorse that the United States had urged Hungarians to rise up in a hopeless revolt against Soviet tanks in 1956. The Nixon administration continued to support the murderous Pakistani Yahya Khan in 1971 partly because the president loathed Indian Prime Minister Indira Gandhi. If communism bears the moral burden of its "little Stalins and Maos," the United States bears some responsibility for the actions of its Cold War clients. Given the choice and a seat on a time machine traveling back to the 1970s, even Gaddis might prefer to be a dissident in Poland, Czechoslovakia, or the Soviet Union itself rather than Argentina, Chile, or El Salvador.

Although we need to remember the nonchalant and gratuitous cruelty inflicted by the United States and its allies, Williams rightly warned against the glib assumption that cruel policies were typically created by "evil men"—a fractal geometry of terror applied to the United States. By and large, as Williams concluded, they "believed deeply in the ideals they proclaimed." Williams understood that McKinley, for instance, was a model Christian gentleman (a term used here without sarcasm) who *nonetheless* presided over the brutal suppression of the Philippine insurrection. Along with the fractal geometry of terror, we need to confront what might be called the Niebuhrian paradox of terror: the capacity of decent men and women to perpetrate evil in what they consider a good cause. In the end, policy-makers must be judged less by their personal character or the purity of their motives than by the consequences of their actions.[87]

Third, should we expect a higher standard of international behavior from the United States *because* it is a rich, democratic, and secure country that suffered almost no civilian casualties, and relatively few military casualties, during the wars of the twentieth century? At minimum less self-congratulation is appropriate. Probably, as Gaddis wrote, American soldiers marching into Nazi Germany in 1945 behaved much better than their Soviet counterparts because they came from a liberal democratic society. Probably too their behavior would not have been so different if Germans had killed millions of American civilians. More generally, it is not much of a moral claim to say that Truman and Eisenhower were morally superior to Stalin and Mao.

In one of his glib digs at revisionists for harshly criticizing American policy-makers, Gaddis recalled Marx's quip that while human beings make their own history, they do not make it under circumstances of their own choosing. He forgot this advice in his own post–Cold War discussion of Soviet developments following Stalin's death. Nikita Khrushchev and his immediate successors tried to make their system less cruel while preserving communism at home and keeping control of the Soviet empire in Eastern Europe. Perhaps, as Gaddis suggested, the tragedy of post-Stalinist Soviet diplomacy was that no Soviet leader could bring himself to go further until Mikhail Gorbachev came to power in 1985. Yet was Khrushchev morally inferior to Lyndon Johnson, Richard Nixon, Robert McNamara, and Henry Kissinger? Their ability to rethink inherited assumptions was no greater than Khrushchev's, their personal risks in changing direction were much less perilous, and their combined "body count" in Indochina was far greater than his in Hungary and the Soviet Union. Moreover, while Khrushchev tried to improve a rigid and cruel dictatorship, the architects of intervention in Indochina corrupted an essentially sound and flexible American polity.

In short, it is neither "watered-down" nor industrial-strength moral equivalency to say that at some times and in some places the United States acted as brutally as the Soviet Union. The point is not to absolve Lenin, Stalin, Mao, or other communist dictators but rather to extend the list of evildoers to Americans whose cruelty is conveniently forgotten or casually forgiven, and who, in some cases, continue to influence foreign policy.

· · ·

Throughout this article I have followed the current standard practice of referring to the Cold War in the past tense. But this convention is misleading. Much as the contemporary bloodshed in the Balkans and the Middle East can be viewed in part as delayed consequences of World War I and World War II, the legacies of the (capitalized) Cold War will long outlive those present at its formal conclusion. In addition, the (decapitalized) cold war essentially as Williams defined it—a conflict between Western capitalism, led by the United States, and opponents in quite different (if not necessarily integrated) cultures—shows no sign of ending. The most visible result of post–Cold War triumphalism has been a willingness by three administrations to intervene militarily outside of this hemisphere on an almost routine basis. President George H.W. Bush mobilized an international coalition to roll back Iraq's invasion of Kuwait in 1991. With less international support and more qualms, Bill Clinton sent peacekeepers to Bosnia and ordered the bombing of Serbia because the Serbs, led by Slobodan Milosevic, murdered tens of thousands of Muslims in Kosovo. After Al Qaeda killed almost three thousand men and women on American soil on September 11, 2001, George W. Bush retaliated against this international guerilla network and its hosts in Afghanistan; in 2003, with minimal international support but much less domestic dissent than in 1991, he prosecuted a second Gulf War to overthrow Saddam Hussein's Iraqi regime. The geopolitical and moral merits of these actions varied considerably and, unlike many contributors to this anthology, I favored one of them, retaliation against Al Qaeda (for non-Wilsonian reasons). Nonetheless, the prevailing mood that facilitated military intervention in all of these cases calls to mind Niebuhr's complaints about the early Cold War: a messianic pride of power, an unreflective enthusiasm for "free markets," and an insistence on demonizing the enemy of the moment, even if he was a former ally. The main difference is that nobody in the 1950s doubted that the Soviet Union would fight well and perhaps kill millions of Americans. Thus in practice the Soviets were treated with greater caution than the compulsory Cold War rhetoric implied.[88]

Following the Afghanistan war some conservative and liberal interventionist pundits not only admitted that the United States had an empire (though they, like Gaddis, thought it a recent acquisition), but also endorsed an overt, ostensibly benevolent imperialism as a general policy. A few of these candid imperialists recommended emulation of the nineteenth-century British Empire, which, in their view, had enforced world order and brought a modicum of humanitarianism to places that otherwise would have been worse off. Other commentators agreed in principle but feared that the contemporary United States lacked the will to occupy foreign lands for a long time. They had a point—an old point. As Niebuhr emphasized, ordinary Americans built an empire while feeling uneasy about building one. And as Williams stressed, shrewd policy-makers at the top always preferred an informal, unnamed, and irresponsible empire in which the United States could spread its way of life and pursue its economic interests without bearing the burdens of explicit political control, not to mention long-term military occupation. At this writing, the Bush administration's approach to both Afghanistan and Iraq fits Williams's description of an informal and irresponsible empire almost perfectly.

Although no one within the Bush administration speaks openly of sustaining an empire, informal or otherwise, some of them do adhere to messianic aspirations that might have amazed Wilson and Dulles, let alone Eisenhower, Kennedy, and Nixon. The influence of this group can be seen in *The National Security Strategy of the United States,* which was released in September 2002 as the country engaged in a desultory and ritualistic debate about overthrowing Saddam Hussein. Most public discussion centered on the report's elaboration of the Bush Doctrine, the claimed right to launch preemptive strikes against anyone deemed a threat to national security. The Bush Doctrine was novel only in the openness with which the president proclaimed it. Decades ago, many cold warriors favored a preemptive nuclear attack if the Soviets appeared to be mobilizing to invade Western Europe, and the CIA in Iran and Guatemala covertly overthrew decent, representative governments that were no threat at all. Much more important was the *National Security Strategy*'s assertion that American ideals and interests required the spread of democracy and free markets everywhere. This notion, though novel only in its grandiosity, was nonetheless stunning.[89]

With a nod toward NSC 68, Gaddis called the *National Security Strategy* the "most important formulation of grand strategy in over half a century." More Wilsonian than ever, he saw grandiosity as a virtue rather than hubris. The Bush administration's goal of bringing the

Middle East "once and for all, into the modern world" reminded him in "boldness, sweep, and vision" of the Cold War–era transformation of Germany and Japan. But, at variance with *some* of what he had written, Gaddis suggested that the "new circumstances" faced by the United States after the attacks of September 11 were more dangerous than the Cold War had been. It had been "sufficient" to contain communist states without seeking to reform them. Now the "intersection of radicalism with technology" meant that the "persistence of authoritarianism anywhere can breed resentments that can provoke terrorism that can do us grievous harm." Accordingly, there were "compellingly realistic reasons to complete the idealistic task Woodrow Wilson began more than eight decades ago: the world must be made safe for democracy, because otherwise democracy will not be safe in the world." Absent from the *National Security Strategy,* and not much more evident in Gaddis's gloss, is the likelihood that the spread of American ways of doing things—especially by force of arms—will itself breed resentment and retaliation.[90]

Despite increasingly prominent defenses of an American empire, in fact if not by name, there has not been much of a national dialogue about the issue. On the whole the response by liberals and the residual community of radicals has been intellectually unimpressive. Many of them need to learn the fundamental Niebuhrian lesson that foreign policy *does* involve hard choices that cannot be resolved on the basis of reflexive denunciations of American imperialism, earnest pleas to give peace a chance (when war is opposed), or equally earnest pleas for "humanitarian intervention" (when war is favored). Selective interventionists on the left, such as those who favored the bombing of Serbia during the Clinton administration, may not have shared Williams's view that "there is a broad area in which every people is an island unto itself." But in choosing which people to rescue with American arms they need to recognize that the adjective *humanitarian* does not render war less brutal or less prone to unanticipated consequences. On the other hand, too much of the left opposition to the two Iraqi wars was marked by crude economic interpretations in which access to petroleum was seen as the only relevant consideration. Despite his own emphasis on economic factors, broadly conceived, Williams worked hard to teach the left that Americans have also tried to impose their way of doing things because they wanted to escape domestic problems, because they felt a psychic thrill, or because they were routinely patriotic. Or even because they honestly hoped to reform the world. Cold warriors typically viewed their interventions as humanitarian too. And opponents of George W. Bush's interventions may have to face the fact that, garbled syntax and all, the president may be yet another in the long line of flexible and effective conservatives.[91]

In sum, the post–Cold War era is awash in moral judgments. But we still lack sustained and consistent moral arguments that might help us to resolve—or at least clarify—difficult and painful foreign policy questions.

2

Time of Illusion: Post–Cold War Visions of the World

Bruce Cumings

T he vocation of the intellectual is to be a critic: that is also the very definition of an intellectual. The intellectual takes on a particular burden in the United States, however, because Americans are relatively less understanding and accepting of the social function of criticism, as compared with people in other advanced industrial states. But if the intellectuals are not the critics, who will perform this necessary task? No one, as Russell Jacoby was early to remind us,[1] and certainly not the scholars. The leading intellectual journal today remains the *New York Review of Books,* which had its birth and its early flourishing in the dissenting milieu of the 1960s, when it played a seminal role in intellectual debate regarding the civil rights, antiwar, and counterculture movements. It soon became an establishment journal, however, open primarily to safe opinion. Likewise, once the Vietnam War ended in the mid-1970s many intellectuals merged again with the broad middle, the liberal and (neo-) conservative mainstream, taking any number of journals of opinion with them (*The New Republic* and *Dissent* come to mind). After a long period of ferment that raised important and continuous challenges to the powers-that-be in all walks of American life, intellectuals now took upon themselves a task that was easy and largely without cost (the critique of communism), instead of continuing to do what was difficult and frequently might jeopardize careers and livelihoods (the critique of one's own society, and the consequences of American power abroad).

In the 1980s a period of critical quietism ensued when things should have been at their loudest, during the Indian summer of the Cold War and the deregulated market of the Reagan years. Neoconservatives were the intellectuals of the era, but few were more than uncritical celebrants of conservative Republicanism. The American labor movement seemed to wither, just as Margaret Thatcher was smashing labor in the United Kingdom. The American left, to the extent that one could still speak of such a thing, merely illustrated the trend with its increasing interest in post-structuralism and postmodernism, another form of quietism, however interesting it might be.[2]

Many intellectuals traded access to the best-read journals for an ideological discourse in which they dispensed with the homegrown critique that emerged in the 1950s and 1960s, and instead began to measure the strengths and weaknesses of American society against the standard of the Stalin-imposed regimes of Eastern Europe (and of course the USSR itself). They breathed a sigh of relief at our freedoms, and identified with the opponents of communist rule. This identification was, of course, all for the good if it carried with it an equally critical eye cast on one's own (very different) society, or that of American client states around the world. But it did not, in the writings of many of our leading lights who came to champion the dissidents of the communist world: all the neoconservatives, of course, but also fine thinkers like Susan Sontag and Philip Roth, many of those who write for *New York Review,* and all of those who write for *Commentary.*

Through these writings we learned of the moral collapse of actually-existing socialism, the stultifying and stupefying behavior of the party-hack politicians, the degradation of civic life, the cowardice of the academics, the crumbling infrastructure, the polluted waters, the industrial rustbelts, the decaying cities (good thing we didn't have any of that in America in the 1980s). People's movements in Eastern Europe, preeminently Solidarity, took advantage of the moral and political torpor of their leaders to build sufficient momentum finally to breach the Iron Curtain and dare Soviet leaders once again to mobilize their occupying armies against them.

Along came the utterly unexpected fall of the Berlin Wall and the collapse of the Soviet Union, and with it came a further, more general collapse of the critical function. These watershed events might have been seen as one among many people's movements against dictatorship throughout the world, linking Europe with Latin America and East Asia—this is the way that Mary Kaldor, for example, saw them at the time.[3] Instead, as Western communism came unstuck, the prevailing one-eyed bias leaped forth as a celebration of liberalism and the market. Overnight a complicated, highly contested history from the 1848 revolutions onward to the end of the Cold War became a morality play: electoral democracy and capitalism had won out on a world scale, and which hoodwinked dupe could not see this victory for what it was? Overnight, the Marxist critique of capitalism, taken to a high level in the 1970s and 1980s in journals such as the *New Left Review*, was consigned to the dustbin of history. Often it seemed that because Western communism collapsed, there was no longer space or legitimacy for a left critique (even though the New Left had been anti-Stalinist from its inception). This experience also highlighted the absence of any visible political alternatives to Reaganism and Thatcherism in America and England, and predictably both countries soon ended up with politicians who split the new difference to their benefit, so-called neoliberals and "Third Way" aficionados like Bill Clinton and Tony Blair.

The exception to my generalizations came mostly from intellectuals of the Catholic left, like Roberto Mangabiera Unger[4] and especially Alasdaire MacIntyre. Quite unlike Allan Bloom, who publicly celebrated an American politics for which he had a complete and absolute private contempt, MacIntyre sought the sources of moral decay and closed American minds precisely in liberal epistemology and the philosophy of market calculation, utilitarianism. At one point MacIntyre discussed our frequent debates between "individualism and collectivism, each appearing in a variety of doctrinal forms:"[5]

> On the one side there appear the self-defined protagonists of individual liberty, on the other side the self-defined protagonists of planning and regulation. . . . But in fact what is crucial is that on which the contending parties agree, namely, that there are only two alternative modes of social life open to us, one in which the free and arbitrary choices of individuals are sovereign and one in which the bureaucracy is sovereign. . . . Given this deep cultural agreement, it is unsurprising that the politics of modern societies oscillates between a freedom which is nothing but a lack of regulation of individual behavior and forms of collectivist control designed only to limit the anarchy of self-interest.

"Both ways of life," MacIntyre concluded, "are in the long run intolerable."

In this judgment MacIntyre showed his hand as a person marked by the 1960s New Left judgment that Soviet mass society and American mass society were both examples of an inhumane modernity. Earlier, Barrington Moore had also hinted at "the historical obsolescence" of both Western liberalism and Soviet socialism. "Industrialism, as it continues to spread," he wrote, "may in some distant future still these voices forever and make revolutionary radicalism [or libertarianism] as anachronistic as cuneiform writing."[6] Moore reminded us that market-driven liberalism carried a radical antipathy to all previous ways of human life, and that its liberal presuppositions about politics could easily give way to technocratic justifications for system maintenance and the exercise of power.

Perhaps the towering figure here, though, was Michel Foucault, who had begun articulating the "plague on both modern houses" decades earlier, really as World War II came to an end, and thereafter devoted his scholarly life to a prolonged critique of actually-existing Western society. For American intellectuals of the 1980s, though, it had appeared that only one form of modernism was intolerable—bureaucratic collectivism. Thus the events of 1989–91 might have done us a great favor in clearing the Erich Honeckers and Nicolae Ceausescu from our vision, and recentering debate on our own society. Instead we got a prolonged blowing of the triumphalist horn.

ILLUSIONS OF THE INTELLECTUALS

In the upheavals of 1989–91 the peoples of Eastern Europe and the Soviet Union recaptured themselves as masters of their own destiny, and in so doing demolished one argument after another about the totalitarian permanence of the regimes under which they lived, and the presumed extinction of their own individuality, their own autonomy, and their own capacity to act historically. The revolt was, in part, against a past that seemed immutable even to them: thus it had been for sixty years, thus it would be for eternity, the experience of Stalinism suggested. Instead, courageous acts of will predicated on rejecting a superficially totalitarian reality liberated people to act in the present. Daring acts of protest and witness, with monumental help from a friend in the

Kremlin named Mikhail Gorbachev of course, and the Stalinist systems with their illusory power collapsed.

This collapse called forth its own illusions, however, especially in the United States. One purpose of history, as some people write it, is to tell us what we cannot do. If our system is totalitarian, we cannot be free: we are condemned for eternity to be totalitarian. The right-wing theory was that totalitarian systems cannot evolve (Jeane Kirkpatrick and her "doctrine"), but right-wing dictatorships can. But on a world scale, they have nearly all evolved, whether we speak of the Western communist regimes or of authoritarian states in Latin America and East and Southeast Asia. And one of the most unexpected things in the whole process was that, for the most part, people acted in *evolutionary* ways: a simple rejection of official lying, recurrent peaceful petitions and protests, dogged persistence in the face of official repression and violence.

There are many ways by which we might come to understand the demise of authoritarian regimes, but in the U.S. the dominant tendency was to turn these events into a celebration of ourselves. A major study of "Revolutionary 1989," participated in by about sixty prominent scholars, government officials, and East European émigrés, concluded that as soon as Eastern European peoples were done with communism, they "turned immediately to liberal democracy and the free market as the way of their future."[7] The American illusion is that all is for the best in the best of all possible worlds in a liberal polity that also functions as the model for mankind: truths held self-evident here are, or ought to be, self-evident everywhere else. My position (you can call it an illusion if you like) is also Louis Hartz's, that the American polity is a fragment of the European liberal tradition, knowing something but by no means all of what it means to maintain that tradition over time.[8]

In his classic book *The Liberal Tradition in America,* Hartz understood Americans to be a born-free people lacking knowledge of the sources of their freedom and especially the long struggles that over many centuries finally realized basic guarantees of democratic rights elsewhere in the world. In his first chapter in *The Founding of New Societies,* dealing with the "fragments" of liberalism in North and South America,[9] Hartz presents a liberalism never fully known or realized, spinning out its telos in a vacuum otherwise known as the North American continent, finding few if any of the "collisions" with non-liberal forms that mark European history or that formed the Latin American amalgam (except in the slaveholding South, and from that we got the grandest American collision, the Civil War). Or as he put it, "A part detaches itself from the whole, the whole fails to renew itself, and the part develops without inhibition ... a North America where the bourgeoisie, having escaped both past and future, unfolds according to interior laws."[10] In the fragment is also a strong propensity toward a total politics: if our truths *are* self-evident, what reason would any human being have for believing differently? When Attorney General John Ashcroft spoke recently at the annual gathering of global elites in Davos, Switzerland, he reacted to accusations of racial profiling of Muslims in his Justice Department by saying that he does not distinguish people according to their race, but according to their values.[11] That is, I am not a racist: I accept all people who value *the same things I do.* I am incapable of discrimination *unless* we are talking about people who do not value modern liberalism. Martin Luther King wanted people to be judged by the content of their character, not the color of their skin. But he did not think character was molded in one crucible.

From this standpoint, in 1989–91 the worst happened: the American people were vindicated precisely in their instinctive liberalism, the tip of an iceberg of unexamined eighteenth-century assumptions that may have little relevance to the United States in the twenty-first century, but carry on nonetheless as the signs of our politics. The end of the Cold War thus prompted a spate of melodramatic literature seeking to give meaning to this evidently cataclysmic event, a genre which we might label "the end of the Cold War and me." The dramatic events of 1989 encouraged a host of people to say "I told you so," rushing into print with musty prognostications about the bankruptcy of communism written back in 1955, or various triumphalist claims about the West's future. This tendency was perhaps most pronounced in John Lukacs's fatuously self-important 1993 book entitled *The End of the Twentieth Century and the End of the Modern Age,* but he was by no means alone. The end of the Cold War occasioned a hailstorm of commentary, in which analysts found it easy to see their own illusions confirmed, precisely because of their distance (in Hartz's sense) from the events that actually brought about the end of Western communism. Each illusion carried its own diagnosis and prognosis, its own set of "I told you so's," and its own time-bound subjectivity: we won't know who's right until years from now, or maybe we'll never know.[12] But we do know who was wrong.

Jeane Kirkpatrick can conveniently forget her "doctrine" and find in the collapse of the East European system a vindication for Cold War anticommunism going back to the Truman Doctrine. Christopher Hitchens can claim to find in the same events an end to neoconservatism in American politics, with his own well-put collection of I-told-you-so's, thus arriving at a conclusion that the past decade has rendered preposterous.[13] Mainly, though, the dominant tendency was to see in the events of 1989–91 every reason to celebrate the American experiment (a surprising turn after a decade in which the intellectuals declared America to be in abject decline, punctuated by President Jimmy Carter's politically fatal concerns about an "American malaise."). An instantly reconfigured history became the last refuge of every self-congratulatory platitude.

Three views, however, came to dominate American discussions about global affairs in the 1990s, which we can summarize with three names: Francis Fukuyama, John Mearsheimer, and Samuel Huntington. Each of them drew on a broader discourse through which Americans have historically defined their global purpose: realism and idealism. Mearsheimer was the frank realist, arguing that we will learn to love the Cold War when we experience the instability of power politics and national rivalries long held in check by the structure of bipolar confrontation. The so-called "long peace" of the bipolar rivalry between Moscow and Washington would soon give way to sharp rivalry among the big powers, analogous to the nineteenth century or the 1930s. Fukuyama was the idealist, if one not fully in the American mold, drawing as he did on an obscure strain of Hegelian theory identified with the Hungarian philosopher Alexandre Kojève. But he arrived at his general theme through a critique of realism, and that theme could not have been more American: not only was liberal democracy triumphant over communism, it was the best (or "most just") system. This stunning success, however, would perhaps have an uncomfortable result: the conclusion to the contested history that had marked the modern world, as liberalism dissolved all its opponents. Huntington is even less clearly an American idealist, but his "clash of civilizations" rested on the assumption that seven or eight civilizations exit in our world (although one was better than all the others), and that as they coalesced in coming decades the new axis of global politics would spring forth.[14]

The most formidable of these arguments was to be found in *The End of History and the Last Man*. One day in 1989 I saw a notice for a lecture on Hegel, by a man named Fukuyama. I thought he might be one of the venerable Japanese scholars of Hegel, since Hegel's organic worldview resonated so deeply in modern Japan. The venue was conveniently located on the first floor of the building where I work, so I walked in, sat down, and waited expectantly. Presently Allan Bloom, fresh from penning his bestseller *The Closing of the American Mind*, introduced a State Department functionary young enough to be one of our students, with claims that he had produced the definitive text on the deep meaning of the end of the Cold War. Mr. Fukuyama proceeded to discuss Alexandre Kojève and Hegel's notion of the "end of History." Only at the University of Chicago, I thought to myself, could intellectuals be so deluded; one of the enduring, and perhaps endearing, continuities of this university is to be standing in a lunch line listening to an undergraduate declaiming loudly on the true meaning of Hegel's dialectic. Only within these cloistered walls could someone be so unremittingly solipsistic as to find in the fall of the Berlin Wall the proof that Hegel was right after all. And so I departed after twenty minutes—thinking that this line of argument would go nowhere.

Little did I know that this lecture would soon appear to great acclaim in the *National Interest*, and later form the basis of a bestseller. "Fukuyama's bold and brilliant article," according to Allan Bloom, who sponsored Fukuyama and published the article in the *National Interest*, "is the first word in a discussion imperative for us, we faithful defenders of the Western Alliance . . . [for Fukuyama] it is the ideas of freedom and equality that have animated the West and have won [sic] by convincing almost all nations that they are true . . ." (for Fukuyama, unbelievers exist only in "Managua, Pyongyang, or Cambridge, Massachusetts.")[15] But it wasn't just extinct-volcano organic reactionaries like Bloom who hailed Fukuyama; he was hailed everywhere. In a laudatory article on Fukuyama in the *New York Times Magazine*,[16] Cambridge, Massachusetts, was again described (seriously) as a "citadel of 1960s subversion," but the author also pointed out that Fukuyama was a latecomer to his position: in fact, Charles Krauthammer had written some months earlier that the burning question going back to Plato, "what is the best form of governance?," had been answered:

> After a few millennia of trying every form of political system, we close this millennium with the sure knowledge that in liberal, pluralist, capitalist democracy we have found what we have been looking for.

(Well, that settles it.) The *Times* continued this uncritical celebration for more than a decade: in a feature article in 2002 on another book by Fukuyama, a *Times* reporter wrote that "*The End of History* was too powerful and hopeful a guide to the post-Communist world to be ignored." The reporter went on to quote Fukuyama from a recent interview: "the Western modernizing package gives access to a standard of living everyone wants," and that is the source of its "universal" appeal.[17] Today there still seems to be little resistance to Fukuyama's program.

In the triumphalist literature *The End of History* had an unquestionable difference: like others Fukuyama viewed the end of the Cold War as a millennial transition, but few would have imagined doing so through a reprise of the thought of Georg W.F. Hegel—and perhaps least of all the great philosopher himself, who would flip in his grave to see his dialectic grinding to a halt in the Valhalla of George H.W. Bush, Bill Clinton, and George W. Bush's 's philistine United States. Hegel gave us history with a purpose, with a telos, with a capital *H,* an unfolding with a beginning, a middle, and an end: behold, all the past as prehistory, as mere prelude to the manifest world-historical spirit of the present age. Fukuyama's argument had an unquestionable ingenuity, taking the thinker perhaps most alien to the pragmatic and unphilosophical American soul, Hegel, and using his thought to proclaim something quintessentially American: that the pot of gold at the end of History's rainbow is free-market liberalism. History just happened to culminate in the reigning orthodoxy of our era, the neoliberalism of Thatcher and Reagan.

In the book Fukuyama adopted the perspective of a particular Hegel scholar, Alexandre Kojève. Not a household word in America, perhaps, but Kojève has been taught for decades at Chicago, mainly within the confines of the philosophy department or the Committee on Social Thought, where Bloom resided for many years. (When William

McNeill, who inhabited the history department for decades, reviewed *The End of History* for the *New York Times,* he caused much mirth at the university by declaring that he had never heard of Kojève.) Kojève established his reputation in France during the 1930s by leading many French philosophers (who naturally had looked to Rousseau and Baudelaire) to understand that Hegel was in many ways both the culmination of traditional philosophy and the first great philosopher of the modern age.

Nearly as important as Hegel to Fukuyama's argument was another German philosopher: Friedrich Nietzsche, who, the author says, gave us "the last man" as the likely culmination of Western liberalism, and counterposed to that figure the type he preferred, the *übermensch,* a difficult term usually mistranslated as *superman.* According to Fukuyama's rendering, "the last man" is a comfortable slave, with physical security and material plenty, a person who believes in nothing (or everything); a sunny disposition and a polite willingness to listen to all views masks an inner emptiness; to the extent that "the last man" has any culture at all, he is a cultural relativist. The *übermensch* is the opposite: a "man with a chest," whose will to power triumphs over the herdlike conformity of modern democracies: "Nietzsche believed that no true human excellence, greatness, or nobility was possible except in aristocratic societies,"[18] Fukuyama opined.

Nietzsche had radicalized Hegel's argument that people are motivated by *thymos,* a striving for recognition that Hegel regarded as the most basic human need, and which can be compared to Rousseau's *amour-propre,* Alexander Hamilton's "love of fame," James Madison's ambition, and Nietzsche's conception of man as the "beast with red cheeks."[19] Believers in liberal democracy might cheerfully follow the others, but they can't follow Nietzsche "very far down the road" because his *megalothymia* made him "an open opponent of democracy and of the rationality on which it rested." (Indeed, Fukuyama sees Nietzsche as a precursor of Nazism.) Kojève, on the other hand, is acceptable because even if he agreed with Nietzsche that Western man was going to hell in a handbasket, unlike Nietzsche he "did not rage at the return to animality at the end of history," but merely quit teaching and took a job in a bureaucracy "meant to supervise construction of the final home for the last man." The reader might expect this to be the architectural firm responsible for *Animal Farm,* but it was in fact the European Commission.[20]

Fukuyama's theory does not go beyond this level of abstraction, however much he may repeat it throughout the book, but he does seek to relate the march of History, the need for *thymos,* and the perils of *megalothymia* to the current age. The good guys are "the most free and therefore the most human of beings," people like "the revolutionaries who battled with Ceausescu's *Securitate* in Romania, the brave Chinese students who stood up to tanks in Tinananmen Square, the Lithuanians who fought Moscow for their national independence, [and] the Russians who defended their parliament and president." The bad guys are of course communists and fascists, but also "cultural relativists" and those who "struggle for the sake of struggle," like the protesting French students of 1968 "who had no 'rational' reason to rebel, for they were for the most part pampered offspring of one of the freest and most prosperous societies on earth."

Fukuyama sprinkles criticisms of American liberalism throughout his text, especially the inability to come to agreement on moral issues, the failures of our leaders (but usually just the ones from the Democratic Party), and the perils of community in a time of atomized individualism. But he still argues that "a contemporary liberal democracy like the United States permits considerable scope for those who desire to be recognized as greater than others" (*thymos* again), and "the first and foremost of these outlets in a liberal society is entrepreneurship."[21] He ends the book with his hope that the unfolding events of the past few decades mean that "the idea of a universal and directional history leading up to liberal democracy may become more plausible to people, and that the relativist impasse of modern thought will in a sense solve itself"; mankind will come to seem like "a long wagon train" that finally reaches the end of its journey, which is of course free-market liberalism.

It isn't just the average American who would need a scorecard to follow the tortured logic of Fukuyama's argument, but also philosophers knee-deep in Hegel and Nietzsche. Can it be that the antithesis of "the last man" is Ronald Reagan, a person whom Washington insider and fixer Clark Clifford once called "an amiable dunce"? Is the thymotic entrepreneur-*cum*-monopolist Bill Gates the ideal American? Can Daniel Cohn-Bendit of Paris '68, whose red hair once added to his "Red" reputation, really be the "beast with red cheeks"? Did the march of History and *thymos* culminate with *Time* magazine in that amazing year, 1998, having essentially no honest choice but to make Monica Lewinsky the "man of the year"? (the editors chickened out, of course). And does this make of the former president the real *megalothymatic* "last man"? (Clinton does have red cheeks.)

An endless list of similar puns crowd the mind, but these are easy points to make. Furthermore in regard to our "relativist impasse," Fukuyama is unquestionably right. The characteristic of leadership in our time is that there is none: in all the world only one political leader calls up our admiration for his courage, his witness, his teaching, and his example, in the manner of a Martin Luther King or a Gandhi: Nelson Mandela, the product of aristocratic upbringing and long, lonely decades of anticolonial struggle. Our recent and unlamented two-term president was by contrast an adolescent, still trying to find himself, still seeking the approval of everyone, still thinking that he could fool the authorities. The moral and ethical debates of our time, as Alasdaire MacIntyre has argued, proffer an unresolvable choice between politicized alternatives: pro-life *vs.* pro-choice, affirmative action *vs.* white rights to equal access, whether our kids should be protected from smut on the Internet or whether smut is protected under the strictures of "free speech." It is not the debates that are characteristic, so much as the inability to form a principled moral position that would resolve them—and even to see that very thing as a form of oppression. To have a strong, self-confident point of view is almost to appear as a totalitarian. The more common response is to settle down amid an uncomfortable anarchy of viewpoints, dismissing each as the incommensurable product of our visceral feelings rather than our rational thought, yielding the common practice of being contented with one's own feelings, conceived (by ourselves) as mere prejudices—but pleasant and even precious nonetheless, because they are *my* prejudices. But Fukuyama merely highlights these dilemmas, without the slightest indication how we might go about resolving them, short of becoming Hegelians.

Fukuyama's book delineates much of what passes for debate in American intellectual life. Like many celebrants of liberalism and "the West" (for example his mentor Allan Bloom), Fukuyama substitutes for actually-existing liberalism an ideal version, drawn from the fine words and high-minded phrases of iconic figures like John Locke, John Stuart Mill, and Alexis de Tocqueville—and even then, with a highly selective reading. In the leading intellectual journals these days it often seems sufficient to settle an argument just to quote Locke or Tocqueville or Jefferson, or to derisively dismiss a "modern" like Marx or a "postmodern" like Jacques Derrida. Fukuyama soon became sufficiently centrist or mainstream to get called upon by *Foreign Affairs* or the *New York Times* for commentary, just as most mainstream publications accepted without comment his treatment of Hegel and Nietzsche, whereas anything that can be deemed left-leaning or "postmodern" is continuously subjected to ridicule and calumny—especially in the flagship intellectual magazine, the *New York Review of Books*. What would a critique look like that took Fukuyama to task on his own terms? It would begin with his treatment of Hegel and Nietzsche, whose thought is caricatured almost beyond recognition in this book.

Fukuyama is wrong to assume a deep difference between Hegel and Nietzsche over the nature of modernity. It is true that no one was more critical than Nietzsche of Hegel's abstracted notions of "the idea" or "the spirit," but as Keith Ansell-Pearson has shown, he shared with Hegel an aversion to the anomie of modern society, with its narrow, economistic notions of individualism, and both thinkers hoped to restore an ethical basis to citizenship, or to the idea of being human. The major agenda of modernity, in Hegel's view, was to found a new form of ethical life (*Sittlichkeit*), in the face of the war of all against all brought forth by modernity. Likewise Nietzche offers his *übermensch* as the way to overcome the quiet nihilism of "the last man," a person without passion or commitment pursuing an empty relativism; Nietzsche's great interpreter and translator in the U.S., Walter Kaufmann, saw in the term *über* a meaning of going across, or over, or beyond, the idea being that man is a bridge and not an end point, a bridge to one's best self, with self-overcoming as the law of life itself. For Kaufmann, therefore, the *übermensch* connotes "a notion of noble human agency," the devotion of one's life to great deeds, to going beyond the conforming and confining morality of the herd[22]—something not far from Allan Bloom's teaching in *The Closing of the American Mind*. Such a person lives, however, without the comfort of God or religion, and must be the lawgiver for himself—or as Nietzsche put it in *Beyond*

Good and Evil, an individual who is "obliged to give himself laws and to develop his own arts and wiles for self-preservation, self-enhancement, self-redemption."[23]

The name "Michel Foucault" is enough to make some people terminate a discussion, and that name does not appear in Fukuyama's book—in spite of Foucault famously saying in 1967, "All philosophical reflection today is a dialogue with Hegel."[24] But if there is one person who was clearly Nietzsche's disciple in our time, it was Foucault; for him, Nietzsche was the first philosopher to think creatively about power outside the confines of political theory. Foucault's absence is doubly interesting because Kojève's analysis of Hegel was among the greatest influences on Foucault's thought, at a time when concerns about "the end of History" gripped a generation of young French intellectuals, and, moreover, at a time that made it all seem plausible: 1945. The defeat of fascism, the collapse of European empires, and the substitution of American for British global leadership appeared to signal the end of the prehistory of the modern: but then the modern took two forms, liberal America and the socialist Soviet Union, each providing a stark alternative to the other, and thus an occasion for philosophers like Jean-Paul Sartre, Maurice Merleau-Ponty, and Raymond Aron to mount the deepest inquiry into the meaning of the bipolar rivalry that came to dominate the postwar world.[25] To this debate Foucault eventually provided a radical alternative, a highly sophisticated body of thought that was nonetheless consonant with the global emergence of a "new Left": the U.S. and the USSR were two sides of the same modern coin; for each their pretensions to new forms of freedom were less important than their joint acceptance of the modern project to discipline, mold, and punish their citizens.

Foucault grounded his thought in the schemes of another icon of modern liberalism, Jeremy Bentham—an original celebrant of English liberalism and the author of the modern era's definition of "the Good": the greatest good for the greatest number, an idea that propelled the extension of democratic rights and equality and caught the aspirations of masses of people to rise into the middle class. But Bentham was also a social engineer, indeed it was to this that he gave over "his boundless imaginative faculties," in the words of Karl Polanyi. Poorhouses converted to armaments manufacture, decennial population censuses, "frigidariums" for fruits and vegetables, convict-run textile factories, "Chrestomathic Day Schools" for the upper middle class, contraceptives to keep the poor rate down, and so on.[26] As Nietzsche noted, there was always "a touch of *Tartuffe*" about Bentham's idea of "the happiness of the greatest number";[27] far more representative of modernity were new power grids and techniques of surveillance and control by which the rational, "modern" individual, understanding himself as the only important subject, held sway over the object: the irrational, the premodern, the colonized, the feminine, the heterodox. Heterodox human objects got defined, constituted, and controlled by "rational" human subjects, their interaction being purely instrumental rather than interactive and intersubjective.

The Panopticon was the logical outcome of Bentham's brand of modern rationality; once called a "mill to grind rogues honest, and idle men industrious,"[28] it was in fact a prison in which the individual cells surround a watchtower, arrayed in circles that admit light and thereby silhouette every single inmate for the guard in the center. The guard, however, cannot be seen by the inmates, creating an image of continuous and omniscient surveillance, and thus the prisoners police themselves. Bentham's ingenious device thus became a metaphor for Foucault, whose lasting contribution was to redefine power for our (modern or postmodern) time by looking not at its central fount (e.g., sovereign state power) but at its distant sources, in the rivulets and eddies where power affects everyone—"those points where it becomes capillary," in his words.[29] These include the production of effective instruments for the formation and accumulation of knowledge, and thus power—methods of observation, techniques of registration, procedures for investigation and research, apparatuses of control and surveillance, taken to their logical conclusion in the ubiquitous closed-circuit television cameras that monitor so much of daily life in America. Foucault used these insights to draw attention to the abuses of human dignity by various modern systems of power (schools, prisons, mental asylums), thus founding a radical critique of all of modernity, whether here, in Moscow, or in Tokyo.

Fukuyama, on the other hand, develops a tortured logic leading to a deeply conservative argument in favor of the status quo, and to a kind of iron cage in which every person is presumptively free and every interest is represented. *The End of History* creates a discourse of power that says in essence, you've never had it so good, so what are you complaining about? Anyone who protests infringements on his or her rights in today's America gets little help from the author, because he thinks Americans have too many "rights" as it is: rights to "recreation, sexual preference, abortion, childhood, and so on." Fukuyama attributes this mad extension of frivolous "rights" and the inability of people to agree on the true nature of human dignity to the denial of "the possibility of autonomous moral choice," which in his view has been "the entire thrust of modern natural science and philosophy since the time of Kant and Hegel." Once again Nietzsche gets his due load of abuse: "modern man now sees that there is a continuum from the 'living slime,' as Nietzsche put it, all the way up to himself," thereby ending up in "the justification for man's dominion over nature," an ineluctable logic leading to "the animal rights movement."[30] Fukuyama thus overlays caricatures of Hegel and Nietzsche upon an argument about contemporary politics in America (when it isn't just contemporary foolishness), with "philosophy" brought in to buttress, say, "family values" and right-wing Republicanism, with every calumny laid against the pervasive changes in American democracy since the civil rights movement, the student protests of the 1960s, and the rise of the women's movement and multiculturalism.

The essence of Nietzsche's teaching about modern life is that we are told we are free individuals, thus to deprive us of our real freedom; we are told that the people rule, so we won't notice how we are ruled, and who really rules; we are told to be moral, just as our religious, corporate, and government leaders squander the moral capital they inherited from exemplary forebears; we are told that we live in the best of all possible worlds, so that we do not think about other possible worlds. Fukuyama encourages us to think that "History" has brought us to a state of grace, to the only conceivable system, whereas Nietzsche taught that "man should above all learn to live and should employ history only in the service of the life he has learned to live."[31]

If the question is "the last man" *vs.* the real freedom of the individual, Nietzsche might be the great philosopher of America. If the last man finds comfort in the herd, individualism is the great promise of American liberalism—and Nietzsche is the champion individualist, celebrating in his *Untimely Meditations* the "plastic power of a man, a people, a culture," in "the capacity to develop out of oneself in one's own way, to transform and incorporate into oneself what is past and foreign," and to realize the full panoply of positive powers that constitute a human being at his or her best. This would begin with the ahistorical disposition that Nietzsche thought essential to freedom in the present and that so distinguishes Americans from Europeans, but would develop toward the "suprahistorical vantage point" that is that of the *übermensch,* an oceanic feeling of knowing all that has happened and accepting it, while being strengthened by and overcoming that heritage in a manifold freedom of the present—"to employ history for the purpose of life!"[32]

This central element in Nietzsche's philosophy has resonance with Hegel's desire to find a higher unity in the "spirit" or "idea" that would overcome the discontinuities and fragmentation of modern life. For Nietzsche, however, Hegel's philosophy was the most elaborate justification imaginable for a self-satisfied complacency about the present, as if all history were merely the prelude to the age one happened to inhabit: as he wrote in *Untimely Meditations,* "for Hegel the climax and terminus of the world-process coincided with his own existence in Berlin. Indeed, he ought to have said that everything that came after him was properly to be considered merely as a musical coda to the world-historical rondo or, even more properly, as superfluous." (Elsewhere he was even less reverential toward Hegel: "Heirs of the world-process! Summit and target of the world-process! Meaning and solution of all riddles of evolution come to light in modern man, the ripest fruit of the tree of knowledge!. . . . Overproud European of the nineteenth century, you are raving!")[33]

If Fukuyama's philosophical learning is disappointingly one-sided, his broader argument cannot be dismissed by pointing out that history did not end in 1989—for example, in the immediate recrudescence of non-liberal politics, as in Islamic fundamentalism, Balkan collisions, or skinhead fascism in Germany. These he would see as atavisms making his point that there is no longer a significant alternative to liberalism that can excite men's minds or organize masses of people; there is no longer any force that offers a top-to-bottom alternative to the liberal organization of modern life. In that he is right, if for the wrong reasons; it is not the absence of the Soviet alternative, but the absence or diminution of a variety of humane palliatives to an untrammeled capitalism that marks our time. Today there is no serious alternative to neoliberal orthodoxy, anywhere, even if there has been much protest about it around the world. Beginning around 1980 and pioneered by Margaret Thatcher and Ronald Reagan, neoliberal demands for unfettered markets, massive deregulation, and a pox on the house of labor carried before it not just the Western communist states, but threatened the entire postwar domestic compact by which peoples the world over evolved some form of social market or safety net to protect large sectors of the population against the worst effects of the capitalist business cycle. Whether it is Germany's social market, Japan's egalitarian lifetime employment, France's admirable health care, vacation, and retirement system, the American New Deal, or the manifold economic gains of the "Asian tigers," the ruthless efficiencies of neoliberalism have placed their political economies under the global jurisdiction of multinational corporations and their administrative allies, like the International Monetary Fund.

It is a scandal that the end of the Cold War should have given us a book that flatters us to such unseemly degree, that plays up to the famed complacency and optimistic spirit of Americans, couched in the thoughts of a nineteenth-century German philosopher of legendary stuffed-shirt pretensions whom most college-educated Americans can be counted on never to have comprehended even if they chanced to read him, a philosopher whose relation to political power was also celebratory and complacent but about whom our author is gullibly idolatrous, an author who likewise moves seamlessly between political power (the State Department, the RAND Corporation) and ersatz punditry—and that this same book would not just become a bestseller, but be applauded by conservative and liberal alike, providing a vocabulary and a grammar to understand the post–Cold War era. This in a country where it is now an art form to buy a book or see a film without giving your money to a global mega-corporation, something only marginally harder than finding a book or a film that does not insult your intelligence. The World-Historical Process culminating in Rupert Murdoch, Dreamworks, and Disney? To make a pun on something Nietzsche once said about God, the best thing that can be said on behalf of the "the end of History" is that it does not exist.

The megalomaniacal (or *megalothymotic*?) attempt to claim for the American defeat of Soviet communism an "end of History," a conclusion to the struggles of the modern world, flatters us and fools us into thinking that we triumphed over a worthy adversary, rather than a defensive and brittle movement that aspired to essentially the same things as "the last man" of contemporary American couch-potatodom. Both World War II and the Cold War were contests of unequals, not in the sense that the U.S. towered over its antagonists—Germany, Japan, the USSR—in the sinews of national power (even though it did), but in the incommensurability of the enemy: to pit Hitler against Roosevelt, Truman against Stalin, or Brezhnev against Reagan and then tell us we must choose "freedom," is to completely trivialize the meaning of freedom; assuming the freedom to choose, who could possibly choose otherwise? In this sense, however, we have indeed moved into a new realm of freedom, because if we fail now, there will be no Hitler or Stalin, no alien "ism," to blame it on. History is now up to us, it is no longer a matter of vanquishing monsters and demons (even if George W. Bush thought it was): we are alone with ourselves and our fate.

DEMOCRACIES DO FIGHT EACH OTHER — AND EVERYBODY ELSE TOO

Another new literature emerged since the end of the Cold War, arguing that the proliferation of democratic governments during and since the 1980s, whether in formerly communist nations or in those run by right-wing authoritarian systems, holds out the hope of a long peace in our time owing to the propensity of democracies not to fight each other. In this growing literature, Spencer Weart contributed the best book:[34] it is comprehensive, surveying all of recorded human history in search of roughly three dozen cases that he thinks prove the virtues of his theory; it is theoretically informed, thoughtful and, well-written— all in all, an important and absorbing book. It also happens to be the best book in a literature that is fundamentally flawed, because the proof of the pudding is in the definition of "democracy" used in this literature. One could just as easily argue that communist states didn't fight each other either (the exception being China's brief 1979 border war with Vietnam). The "democratic peace" literature has been interesting primarily to scholars, only penetrating the public domain now and then since 1989. Far more important has been the argument of "realists" that every nation-state fights for power with every other state, democracy yielding no difference in this national pastime, and we will soon learn to love the Cold War when we see what comes after it.

John Mearsheimer's "Back to the Future" essay in *The Atlantic* foreshadowed this argument and the book that he later produced, *The Tragedy of Great Power Politics*. If you thought the twentieth century was cruel, with upwards of 100 million people killed in warfare, wait until you experience the twenty-first: "This cycle of violence will continue far into the new millennium," Mearsheimer writes, and hopes for peace "will probably not be realized," because great-power competition is the natural state of affairs—making for a world of sharp conflict that is nasty, brutish, and eternal.[35] Dr. Mearsheimer presents his theory of "offensive realism" in "a handful of simple propositions" that come at the reader like staccato machine-gun fire. Great powers are those that can field a conventional army capable of conducting all-out war, and that have a survivable nuclear deterrent; they perpetually seek to maximize their share of world power in a zero-sum struggle with other powers doing the same thing; and their ultimate aim is to be the hegemon—"the only great power in the system." This state of affairs is tragic, according to Mearsheimer, precisely because it is unavoidable and ineluctable; it is neither designed nor intended by human beings, yet we are all caught up in it, inescapably and forever.[36]

This book does not have a tragic tone, however, because Prof. Mearsheimer has too much fun explaining why we're all going to hell in a handbasket of our own (unconscious) design. His treatise is a milestone in the literature of realpolitik for its simplicity and directness, its unswerving commitment to a single handful of pithy, tried-and-true realist propositions, and its unalloyed, straightforward shoot-'em-up style. Bullets seem to whiz by as Mearsheimer tells us that anarchy reigns in the international system, that the guy with the biggest weapon wins ("the strongest power is the state with the strongest army"), it's a dog-eat-dog world and when you get into trouble there's no 911 to call, going democratic won't help either because regime type makes no difference (democracies fight each other too, contrary to liberal opinion), and a cruel fate awaits us all because for every human neck "there are two hands to choke it."[37] Maybe so, but this book is also a throwback to what C. Wright Mills once called "crackpot realism," and it might also be the urtext for the unilateralism of the Bush administration.

Mearsheimer gives us the Clint Eastwood theory of international affairs. The big powers, being big powers, have the biggest guns and are always on the march. If they aren't, well, they're just biding their time and building up their armies, looking for a chance to strike. The French will delight in Mearsheimer's account of modern German history, the Germans being on the aggressive onslaught every day of the week from Bismarck through Hitler, just as Koreans can savor his depiction of Japan's expansionist bent from 1868 to 1945. Even pasta- and wine-loving modern Italy was constantly seeking "opportunities to expand," its "hostile aims were ever-present"; if Italy nonetheless wasn't going anywhere, it's because "its army was ill-equipped for expansion." You would think that the spectacle of the world's second-ranking superpower closing up shop and turning itself into fifteen squabbling nations in 1991 would be a bit of a stretch for the tenets of "offensive realism," but no—the USSR's self-liquidation was another instance of realism in action. Now realism tells us that the great clash of the new century will be between the U.S. and China. But at least we don't need to worry about Japan and Germany: they may be the second and third largest economies in the world, but they haven't been great powers since 1945: why? Because the U.S. keeps its troops on their soil. And if the troops should leave? Then they're great powers after all and all bets are off.[38] It's nice to have a parsimonious theory that explains everything.

For writers in this tradition, there are only two theories, realism and liberalism (or idealism). Mearsheimer tells us that today, just as George Kennan told us half a century ago in his classic little book, *American Diplomacy*. The liberals are irremediably deluded, of course, but the only realists that capture Mearsheimer's attentions are his contemporaries in American political science like Kenneth Waltz, Stephen Krasner, and Stephen Walt, or renowned predecessors like E.H. Carr and Hans Morgenthau; by and large the realists write for each other—and applaud each other's sagacity about the hard truths of human behavior—or is it animal behavior? On a Pacific beach north of Santa Cruz, two-ton elephant seals wallow about in the sand while waiting for the winter weather to clear. A mammoth alpha male maintains a harem against all the other males, who spend their waking hours trying to slither in for a dalliance with one of the females, only to be beaten back by the ever-vigilant (and indeed sleepless and exhausted) alpha male. Prof. Mearsheimer perfectly captures this world with his theories, just as the administration of George W. Bush seems to mimic the alpha male's indefatigable unilateralism. But as a more subtle realist named E.H. Carr once taught us, shrewd leaders act like realists while talking like idealists—they are "masters in the art of concealing their selfish national interests in the guise of the general good."[39] Now there's a definition of what effective human power actually sounds like—and no bullets whizzed by.

A CLASH OF CIVILIZATIONS?

Samuel Huntington's influential attempt to recast world politics in cultural and civilizational terms seemed to explain more about the nature of post–Cold War conflict, because of the reappearance of old ethnic conflicts between Serbs, Croats, and Muslims in the former Yugoslavia, along a presumed East-West divide going all the way back to the division of the Roman Empire into Western and Eastern branches, and to the subsequent split between Western Christianity and Eastern orthodoxy.[40] September 11 appeared to bring this theory to life; one would be hard put to find in those terrorist attacks an end to history or an example of "realism" in action, but they did seem to portend a new and darkening horizon for the "clash of civilizations."

Huntington's theory rests on the assumption that several distinct bodies of inherited ideas and practices exist in our world, and that they either already have or soon will constitute themselves in opposition to each other; as they do so, the new axis of global politics will spring forth. Unlike Fukuyama's celebration of the victory of "the West," Huntington finds an Atlanticist civilization in decline, embracing Western Europe and North America (but not Latin America, which he splits off into a separate "corporatist, authoritarian" civilization[41]), finding its primary competition from a rising East Asia, which Huntington finds useful to divide into two: China and Japan, he says, represent separate and distinct non-Western civilizations. This bifurcation would not occur to East Asian specialists, but it serves Huntington's purposes. Like Mearsheimer's book, Huntington's comes to an end with a scenario for "civilizational war" between the U.S. and China.[42] (China looms large on the American radar screen, regardless of one's perspective.) The main thing Huntington wants to do in this book, however, is to replace George Kennan's containment doctrine with a new paradigm. Kennan's 1940s-era realpolitik, as we will see, ob-

scured a similar preference for Western civilization and a correspon-
ding disdain for all other cultures; Huntington's civilizational discourse masks a new realpolitik for the twenty-first century, in which
the West as he conceives it will husband its remaining strength for a
coming global confrontation.

East Asia and the United States—utterly different civilizations to
Huntington—in fact share much in common, and there is much similarity in their modern experience (in part because so much of that experience has been generated by a strong American presence in the
region since 1945). If we take Japan and the U.S., for example, we find
that both nations look at the world with a bifurcated stare, yielding in
both nations a dialectic of to-the-world or away-from-the-world.
Hartz, in his *Liberal Tradition in America,* located this as the primary
pattern in the American relationship to the world, launching out to
transform the world in the American image, followed by a predictable
failure and a retreat into some form of isolation. Hartz (and Tocqueville) understood that this was not a back-and-forth orientation to the
geographic external world, but an oscillation about the European
world: center of civilization, Americans ran toward it (Anglophilia,
Atlanticism, and "Europe-first") or away from it (Anglophobia, the
New Order for the Ages,[43] the frontier, and "Asia first"). For the leaders of American foreign policy roughly since the War of 1812, however, the Atlanticist gaze did not avert, spots did not grow on the eyes;
instead the gaze was soothing (if shaded by the British navy), like
watching a setting sun sink into the horizon on a lazy August evening
(it is an old world; we are the new; patience is our virtue). This is the
Atlantic world Huntington wants to revive, and preserve; for him it is
the only civilization truly worthy of his respect.

Huntington's book is not triumphalist, but it is still a celebration of
"the West" as against the rest. What distinguishes Atlantic civilization
is "its values and institutions"—which he lists in the following order:
"Christianity, pluralism, individualism, and rule of law," attributes
that "made it possible for the West to invent modernity." He approvingly quotes Arthur Schlesinger Jr. on Europe as "the source—the
unique source" of these fundamental attributes, and argues that the responsibility of Western leaders is "to preserve, protect, and renew the
unique qualities of Western civilization."[44] But he does not believe
that the West should impose its ways on other civilizations, or expect

that when they "modernize" they will become more like us. Huntington is a classical conservative, not a liberal or a neoconservative, interested in husbanding the flagging resources of an Atlantic civilization that he considers superior to all the rest, at home and abroad. The home struggle, predictably, is against "multiculturalism" and the "culture wars" that raged in the 1990s.[45] The book thus becomes a long lament for a lost or declining Atlanticism, an America defined originally and primarily by New England (Huntington comes from an old-line Boston family), and a "West" led by white men—and hopefully Protestant ones. Huntington is honest and straightforward about his preferences, and lacks any concern for partisan advantage (unlike Fukuyama's transparent appeals to the neo-right). But the majority of Americans of color, class, and gender difference from Boston Brahmins will not find their views and interests represented in this book.

The main problem with Huntington, however, is his failure to understand the very Western liberalism that he wants to privilege. As Robert Latham has shown,[46] the Atlanticist order built in the late 1940s was a complex and problematic episode in the history of a modern practice that had defined as liberal an England that had a sharply inegalitarian class society, a highly restricted franchise (even after the reform act of 1867, only 30 percent of the adult population could vote), and an empire—one that included not just a host of disenfranchised colonial populations, but through its trading relations, cotton production by millions of slaves and sharecroppers in the American South. The liberal state would also include a United States that in 1945 was a democracy for the adult white population and an apartheid-like southern autocracy for the black population. And during the Cold War, a liberal world order led by the United States included Trujillo's Dominican Republic, Tito's Yugoslavia, Suharto's Indonesia, Park Chung Hee's South Korea, and Mobutu's Zaire.

This liberal order was (and is) a complex, heterogeneous historical system that could not be categorized simply as market driven or democratically governed. But there is still something distinct about what Latham calls liberal modernity: if for Karl Polanyi the self-regulating market had an inherent tendency to transcend national boundaries, for Latham the same is true about the emergence and ordering logic of liberalism. One logic is indeed that of the market: liberal modernity is closely associated with open exchange, at home and abroad. But there is also the logic of individual rights, representative government, and collective self-determination. Then there is the historical recognition that so much of this was brand spanking new in the 1940s: most of those practices associated with liberalism—free trade, basic civil and political rights, universal suffrage, and national self-determination—can only be dated from the mid-nineteenth century as doctrine and (limited) practice, and only achieved global dominion after 1945. That states could be liberal but not democratic was a commonplace before that time.

This is why Latham rightly emphasizes the "historicity, contingency, and mutability" of liberal modernism, as well as its heterogeneity: a dictatorship like Trujillo's was obviously not liberal, but its partial incorporation into the American organized world order (connoted as the "free world") was a commonplace aspect of a plural and diverse order that, as a whole, remained a central part of liberal modernity. The partial inclusion of a sordid tyrant like Trujillo reflected an essential element of liberal hegemony: the demarcation of boundaries, of limits to the realm, most often expressed negatively. The best thing one could say about Trujillo was that he was not a Communist, and Washington would only support his overthrow if it were assured that the Dominican Republic would not go communist as a result.

Huntington's Atlanticist "West" suddenly looks very different: is not a Martin Luther King or a Malcom X a central part of American liberalism, and thus its contemporary civilization? Can he explain how the presumably "Confucian" civilization of South Korea produced one of the world's strongest labor movements in the past two decades, or a civil society that in 1997 and 2002 elected two former dissidents to the presidency? Are the "blue states" and "red states" of the 2000 election an example of the clash of civilizations (or "Atlantic culture" *vs.* multiculturalism), or further testimony to the deeply contested nature of American liberalism? These questions answer themselves, and suggest that the attributes of liberalism that Huntington holds dear manifest themselves around the world in a heterogeneous democratic civilization that is available to all peoples, and grows stronger all the time.

CONTAINMENT IN PERPETUITY

The ostensible conflict in the years of the Cold War was a global struggle between communism and capitalism, with frightening military formations arrayed along the central front in Europe. Others argue that this was an imaginary conflict, a shadow obscuring the real history of the four decades of the Cold War. Hardly any lives were lost along the central axis of conflict, in Europe, occasioning two verdicts on the Cold War: Mary Kaldor has argued in effect that containment worked because there wasn't anything seriously to contain; the Soviets had no intention of invading Western Europe or Japan, and the bipolar conflict had its main use in disciplining the allies of Moscow and Washington. Still others, like John Lewis Gaddis, use the same evidence to argue for "a long peace" in our time, caused by the effective implementation of George Kennan's containment doctrine.

Kennan's strategy had a curiosity mostly missed in the literature, however, based on an unspoken premise: the doctrine was meant both to contain the enemy, the USSR, *and* the allies—mainly West Germany and Japan. Kennan was the engineer of a strategy in which West Germany and Japan were shorn of their previous military and political clout, but their industrial economies were encouraged to revive, and they were posted as engines of growth in the world economy. Meanwhile the U.S. kept both countries on defense dependencies and shaped the flow of essential resources to each (especially cheap energy from the Middle East), thus to accumulate a diffuse leverage over all their policies and to retain an outer-limit veto on their global orientation. It still does so today, long after the Cold War ended; indeed, if there is one common thread running from 1945 to the present, it is the ever-widening sphere of American containment of an unruly world, with no end in sight.

The postwar order took shape through positive policy and through the establishment of distinct outer limits, the transgression of which was rare or even inconceivable, provoking immediate crisis—the orientation of West Berlin toward the Soviet bloc, for example. The typical experience of American hegemony, however, was a mundane, benign, and mostly unremarked daily life of subtle constraint, in which the United States kept allied states on defense, resource, and, for many years, financial dependencies. Latham calls this structure the

American "external state" and views it as a central element of liberal world-order building. A vast global militarization underpinned this order, which during the Cold War came to encompass 1.5 million American troops stationed in hundreds of bases in thirty-five countries, formal security commitments to forty-three countries, the training and equipping of military forces in seventy countries—a phenomenon often treated as an unwitting or unfortunate result of the bipolar confrontation.

Today "containment of communism" seems rather a joke. There are decidedly few Communists to contain, and those few are so defensive and vulnerable that the expansive force of their system is just a memory. But the domestic interests that formed around the containment system are still dominant, and still find utility in interventions now directed against assorted "rogue states." And win, lose, or draw, the troops never come home: World War II was the clearest kind of military victory, but U.S. troops remain on the territory of their defeated enemies, Japan and Germany, and exercise a lingering constraint on their autonomy. However many justifications come and go for that remarkable and unprecedented situation (in that the leading global power stations its forces on the territory of the second and third largest economies), the fact remains that it has persisted for well over half a century, and shows no signs of ending.

American combat troops first landed in Korea not in 1950, but on a pristine September day five years earlier. On another beautiful September day in 2001, the eleventh day, 37,000 of them were still in South Korea. Korea is the best example in modern history of how easy it is to get into a war, and how hard it is to get out. Vietnam would have been the same, and indeed was essentially the same from the mid-1950s when Washington committed its prestige to the Saigon government, to the mid-1970s when the war concluded with an American defeat— because the U.S. could sustain neither a stable Saigon regime nor a divided Vietnam. If it could have done so, we would still be there, stuck in the aspic of another Korea. The Gulf War came to an end when George H.W. Bush and his advisers, preeminently Brent Scowcroft, kicked on the brakes well short of Baghdad and thus spawned another containment system, leaving upwards of 9,000 U.S. troops in Saudi Arabia and various new military bases there and elsewhere in the Middle East. Now the primary effect of the war in Afghanistan appears to be a permanent American commitment to try to stabilize the most unstable region in the world: the belt of populous and mostly Muslim countries stretching westward from Indonesia all the way to Algeria, and northward to Central Asia, into the former Soviet republics and the Muslim populations of China's western reaches.

In early 2002 the Pentagon announced a new commitment to lay down "a long-term footprint in Central Asia," as reporters put it: an air base near Bishkek, the capital of Krgyzstan, that would hold up to 3,000 troops; massive upgrading of existing military bases and facilities in Uzbekistan (like the former Soviet base at Khanabad) and Pakistan (where several bases now house American forces, with next to no media access or scrutiny); creation and expansion of remnant military bases in Afghanistan; and the replacement of marine expeditionary forces sent into Afghanistan during the war with Army regulars settling in for the long haul ("Army units tend to establish more permanent bases," reporters said with considerable understatement). The spokesman for the U.S. Central Command told reporters that in the future the U.S. will find great value

> in continuing to build airfields in a variety of locations on the perimeter of Afghanistan that over time can do a variety of functions, like combat operations, medical evacuation and delivering humanitarian assistance.[47]

A year later, a looming war with Iraq suggested yet another American venture in garrisoning a key Middle Eastern state. And if past is prelude, American forces will remain in these places for decades.

After 1989, advocates of realpolitik like Mearsheimer were quick to argue that "West-West" conflicts would quickly replace the East-West conflict, that soon the French and the Germans would again be at each other's throats, or to worry that Germany and Japan had not fully learned the lessons of their defeat in World War II, or that intercapitalist rivalry would only be deepened by the end of the Cold War, or that a "reemergent threat" (in Pentagonese) would take over Russia. More than a decade later, however, we cannot say that West-West conflict has deepened since 1989; rather it has lessened. Germany and Japan have given little evidence that their postwar democratic revolutions are in jeopardy, and the French and Germans were positively cozy in the face of Bush's extremism. Above all, the United States found itself in the best of all possible worlds in 1991, having won the Cold War but still retaining its leverage vis-à-vis Germany and Japan, with upwards of 70,000 soldiers stationed on the soil of each country.

Long after the Berlin Wall fell and in spite of all kinds of predictions to the contrary, unified Germany does not dominate Europe, Japan has not gone nuclear, China discovered the market, France has a world-historical predicament of national identity, and the American Century continues apace. Huntington's "West" remains today a citadel of comfortable and peaceable modern civilization, and that disparity no doubt animates the nihilism of those who have no way of joining this world, and so try to demolish it. But it is hard to see, in the absence of any believable political alternatives, a West or an America in decline. Instead the U.S. has vastly expanded its archipelago of military bases around the world, while retaining most of its Cold War leverage over its allies; it still holds the linchpins of political and military stability among the advanced industrial countries.

This far-flung structure gives us the best explanation for the extraordinary continuing weight of this singular superpower in world affairs—that, and its remarkable economic productivity compared to anyone else (China's growth is rapid, but its productivity is still Third World). And here is the answer to why various "realists" like Mearsheimer, not to mention Samuel Huntington and Francis Fukuyama, all got it wrong: realpolitik does not govern the contemporary actions of the big powers; regional clashes of older civilizations in places like former Yugoslavia or Central Asia mask the burgeoning triumph of modern civilization (to which they are also—and ineffectively—reactive); and the triumph of the Western liberal program does not mean "the end of history" because modern liberalism is itself a heterogeneous, contested, and deeply unfinished business.

Part II

Economics

3

Market Triumphalism and the Wishful Liberals

Nelson Lichtenstein

A triumphalism of the free market is today the single greatest legacy of the end of the Cold War. The idea that capitalist markets are essential to, even define, the democratic idea has always been present in the West, but the idea achieved a majoritarian weight in the 1970s, and a near hegemonic power after the fall of the Berlin Wall. "Let us celebrate an American triumph," thundered Mort Zuckerman in *US News* late in the 1990s, "a triumph" based on the rock of an unfettered capitalism: "privatize, deregulate, and do not interfere with the market."[1]

Americans are now told to believe that democracy and the free market are identical, that wealth itself, especially that attached to the technology of the global market, can itself have a liberating impact. Tom Frank has labeled this the "new market populism" that has generated a stunning reversal in the way many think about democracy and the market. Old-fashioned populists held that laissez-faire capitalism presented the gravest danger to freedom, democracy, equality, and the material well-being of most citizens. The new market triumphalism turns that skepticism inside out, offering up the free market as the gateway to universal liberation. Capitalist markets do not distort or subvert social harmony, they are the key to the resolution of all social and political problems, both at home and abroad. As Thomas Friedman of the *New York Times* put it: "International finance has turned the whole world into a parliamentary system" that allows people to "vote every hour, every day through their mutual funds, their pension funds, their brokers, and, more and more, from their own basements via the Internet." Thus markets are not just mediums of exchange, but mediums of consent.[2]

And in a maddening piece of ideological larceny, market triumphalists invoke that ultimate sanction—once the principal asset of the left—the stamp of historic inevitability. Francis Fukuyama put this most famously in his essay "The End of History," written just before the fall of the Berlin Wall: "Liberal democracy combined with open market economics has become the only model a state could follow." Shortly afterwards futurist George Gilder offered a characteristic bit of eschatological certainty. "It is the entrepreneurs who know the rules of the world and the laws of God."[3]

American stateswomen have been no less modest in their rhetoric. When U.S. bombs first fell on Yugoslavia in April 1999, Madeleine Albright asserted, "The movement toward more open economic systems has been a powerful contributor to the democratic trend. We see this everywhere from Central Europe to Central America." The 2002 *National Security Strategy of the United States of America,* prepared under the authority of National Security Advisor Condoleezza Rice, seemed to put the power of the American state behind the Fukuyama-Gilder thesis, to wit: "The great struggles of the twentieth century between liberty and totalitarianism ended with a decisive victory for the forces of freedom—and a single sustainable model for national success: freedom, democracy, and free enterprise."[4]

Today, words like *reform* and *liberalization,* and sometimes even *revolution* denote the process whereby an open market in labor and capital replaces the regulatory regimes, either social democratic or autocratic, that were erected earlier in the century. In effect, Woodrow Wilson—or a rather distorted version of Wilsonian liberalism—has won the great debate, not only with V. I. Lenin but with Edward Bernstein and John Strachy. "For years socialists used to argue among themselves about what kind of socialism they wanted," comments Denis MacShane, a former official of the International Metal Workers Federation, now a Tony Blair Labour MP, "but today, the choice of the left is no longer what kind of socialism it wants, but what kind of capitalism it can support."[5]

Of course, such market triumphalism is not just for foreign consumption. Although given much energy by the fall of communism and the various "shock treatments" foisted upon Poland, Russia, Chile,

Czechoslovakia, Indonesia, and other nations, the remedy is urged upon the U.S. itself. *Forbes* columnist Peter Huber argued that it was "market forces and the information age" that had beaten the Soviets and would soon force the dissolution of America's largest economic organizations. "If you have grown accustomed to a sheltered life inside a really large corporation," he advised, take care: "The next Kremlin to fall may be your own."[6] Indeed, Anders Lewis, a freshly minted Ph.D. in history, stirred up a listserv hornet's nest when he lectured an older generation of labor historians: "The ideas of Adam Smith, Friedrich Hayek, Ludwig von Mises, and Milton Friedman have triumphed, and workers are better off because of this."[7]

Such sentiments have not been appreciably modified in the world that came to exist after September 11, 2001. "The sort of people who work in financial markets are not merely symbols but also practitioners of liberty," wrote Michael Lewis in the *New York Times Magazine*. "They do not suffer constraints on their private ambitions, and they work hard, if unintentionally, to free others from constraints. . . . It tells you something about the worldview of the terrorists that they crashed half their arsenal into the World Trade Center. They believed that the bond traders are as critical as the U.S. generals and the politicians to extending liberty's influence in the world. They may be right. And that should make you feel proud."[8]

How to explain this ebullience, this moralistic triumphalism of our time? The most obvious explanation is that we live at a moment in which an American brand of political capitalism has in fact proven itself the most internationally potent and economically successful on the planet. The American Century, first declared in 1941, has hardly run its course. As Michael Cox has pointed out, the U.S. model of global capitalism has proven supremely attractive because its gravitational pull is now almost entirely unimpeded by the attractive power of any other competing body. Not only did the Soviet Union collapse during the early 1990s, but so too did competition, both economic and ideological, from a Japan-centered Pacific Rim. From an ideological and model-building perspective, the collapse of the Soviet Union had been discounted long before it took place. Few critics of American capitalism looked east of the Elbe for inspiration or advice. Still, the demise of this empire, and the increasing marketization of the Chinese economy that preceded it, seemed to demonstrate that any organization of society that substituted economic planning for a market mechanism was bound to lead to a disaster of the first order, both political and social.[9] Indeed, the elimination of this world-historic rival devalued the ideological role played by those Keynesian, social-democratic programs and compacts that in the early Cold War years had been a vital component of the claim that in the world of "actually existing" capitalism the sharp elbows had been tucked and the market forces tamed. The collapse of the Soviet Union thus made possible the celebration of a globalized capitalism with nary a backward glance, especially when all this was accompanied by the eclipse of organized labor in the Atlantic world, the corrosive impact of America's uniquely bitter racial divide on social and economic policy, and the élan with which Ronald Reagan and Margaret Thatcher mobilized elements of the working class on behalf of laissez-faire principles.[10]

The demise of a Japanese-centered "Pacific Century" has been equally dramatic and perhaps even more potent in advancing the idea that there no longer exists any alternative to a distinctively American version of global markets and capitalist social mores. Japan has been the world's second largest economy for more than thirty years, and in the 1970s and 1980s the entire East Asian model for advanced capitalism, with its quasi-planning from the top, its innovative and seemingly cooperative labor relations, and its technological prowess, represented the real challenge, both economic and ideological, to American theorists of a new laissez-faire. But the collapse of that nation's real estate, banking, and technology bubble in 1990 inaugurated more than a decade of stagnation and crisis. The stock market dropped 80 percent, economic growth evaporated, and American technology companies ran away from their once fearsome Japanese rivals. Despite the manipulation of every fiscal and monetary lever at its command, the Tokyo planning ministries and the highly politicized Japanese banks, which had once been given such credit for shaping the entire economic miracle, have found their recovery efforts repeatedly frustrated. To Paul Krugman, the Japanese experience has exemplified a deflationary, confidence-destroying "return of depression economics."[11]

The collapse of the Soviet Union, the stagnation of the Japanese economy, and the return of a modest degree of growth to the American economy, at least during most of the 1990s, are the kind of facts that cannot be ignored. But they don't tell the whole story or explain the ease with which a triumphal mood had begun to ferment among an important slice of the American intelligentsia even in the years before 1990. This is a story that Godfrey Hodgson has told so well in *The World Turned Right Side Up: A History of the Conservative Ascendancy in America*.[12] It is not necessary to repeat the story told in that book; instead this essay explores a question that has been almost invisible in the presumptive triumph of market economics and market morals. Why has the success of such market populism, this species of capitalist utopianism, been so effortless, so uncontested, and so unexpected?

Well, of course it has not. Liberals and the left have protested all the way, and there have been many others, among both the Keynesian liberals and the Burkian conservatives, who have entered a dissent. But since the 1970s market-oriented conservatives have been on the offensive; while liberals have been living off the capital of the New Deal for more than two generations. That was and is a large reservoir of ideas, but it has not been enough to stem the right-wing tide when in the 1980s it became clear that capitalist markets, both petty and grand, foreign and domestic, did in fact undermine Eastern Europe's communist regimes. At that point conservative intellectuals took this undeniable phenomenon and made of it a global, near meta-historical generalization, applying it not only to nations with command economies, but to every region and every regulation in the world.

The ideological success of the laissez-faire triumphalists has been eased because many of the most respected liberals and system-analyzing radicals have been so wrong about the trajectory of postwar capitalism, and well before the demise of the Soviet Union. Indeed, the current rhetoric declaring the global triumph of the market has obscured a salient fact of the postwar era: For most of those decades many liberal intellectuals, even some radical ones, chose not to focus debate on the virtues or faults of capitalism. They were silent on this question, not because they were themselves cheerleaders for corporate power, but because they felt the very phrase *market capitalism* no longer adequately described key traits of social life in the industrial West. They thought that capitalism itself was in the midst of a great transformation, one which gradually and inevitably substituted a socialized planning ethos for the outmoded anarchy of the market.

This was not only the perspective of the left, mind you, but of that once impressive species of liberal ideology that held hegemonic sway during the quarter century after the end of World War II. As historian Howard Brick has argued, left-liberal intellectuals were entrapped by a sort of "wishful thinking" in which an unheralded victory, a kind of "silent revolution," promised the effective suppression of the market and the subordination of economic affairs to social regulation. Through this prism, the devaluation of economic institutions in the postwar liberal agenda represented an imaginative, even a utopian, leap beyond the present toward a postcapitalist, or postindustrial, order where social needs might be addressed independently of pure economic forces. They hoped for and sought a progressive evolution of political society, in which purposeful planning and democratic decision-making rendered market forces increasingly ineffectual.[13]

Both postwar liberals and those who stood on their left too readily assumed the hegemony of the New Deal order, the bureaucratization of industrial conflict, and the increasing interpenetration of political and economic structures. They postulated the existence of a postwar social compact, of a labor-management accord, of a corporate liberalism, of a military-industrial complex whose social and ideological consequence was one of claustrophobic inertia, not market fragmentation.[14] From Robert Taft to Barry Goldwater to Ronald Reagan, the left has rarely accorded conservative ideologues of the market the respect due a powerful adversary. John Kenneth Galbraith thought the right wing of the GOP "the stupid party," while a generation of postwar social scientists psychologized the right in order to marginalize it. In *The End of Ideology,* the urtext of postwar liberalism, Daniel Bell focused his considerable intellect exclusively upon the *left-wing* exhaustion of political ideas. He took no notice of the ideological revival on the *right,* which was about to launch the Goldwater insurgency.[15] Liberals and radicals alike were therefore left utterly unprepared for the social stress caused by the return of capitalist economic crisis in the 1970s and the revival of a laissez-faire right wing in the 1980s and 1990s.[16]

Of course, it is important to understand that such unpreparedness was not simply a product of left-wing myopia, or Cold War wishfulness. The crisis of transatlantic capitalism during the first half of the twentieth century had seemed to teach both policy liberals and social conservatives that free-market capitalism was an increasingly obsolete system at variance with the social, political, and psychological realities that structured economic life. Such was the worldview of Adolf Berle and Joseph Schumpeter, who were among the most influential theorists of capitalist transmutation during the first half of the twentieth century. Both were accomplished students of corporate finance and macroeconomic policy, both served at the highest levels of their respective governments during moments of acute crisis (post–World War I Austria, Depression-era America), and both wrote books of remarkable staying power, sustaining a coterie of academics and activist intellectuals well into the postwar era. Schumpeter, who came out of the great pre–World War I tradition of Austrian political economy, was undoubtedly the more profound intellectual, but his ideas about the trajectory of Western capitalism also sustained the more policy–oriented thinking generated by Adolf Berle, whose upper-class, Protestant progressive education gave him rapid entry to the highest New Deal–New Frontier circles.

With economist Gardiner Means, Adolf Berle wrote *The Modern Corporation and Private Property* in 1932. The book provided an ideological rationale for New Deal planning, consumer activism, labor organizing, and state regulation of the large corporation. America's huge corporations, which then controlled one-third of the national wealth, had themselves abridged the fundamentals of liberal capitalism. Not only had oligarchy replaced competition, but of even more consequence, management usurped the prerogatives of traditional ownership. If the shareholders had therefore lost control of the corporation to a set of unelected, self-perpetuating managers, then the modern corporation could best be understood not in terms of "the traditional logic of property and profits . . . not in terms of business enterprise but in terms of social organization." And like the church, the military, and the state, such power had to be either regulated or democratized if a republican government were to exist.[17] "Whatever the authors' original intent," wrote historian Richard Pells half a century later, "their ideas were continually cited as evidence that capitalism had to be replaced by a more collectivist economic system." Indeed, as late as 1982, Hoover Institution conservatives offered the book a backhanded compliment when they organized a conference largely designed to denounce its pernicious influence.[18]

Although Berle himself made his peace with a hawkish brand of postwar liberalism, he remained enough of an old progressive to believe that corporate power and capitalist markets had to be self-consciously fought and tamed. By the 1950s and 1960s he was an opponent of the left, especially in Latin America, but Berle saw a vigorous brand of New Deal–style statecraft as essential to a well-regulated capitalism. As chair of the Twentieth Century Fund for two decades after 1950, Berle fully endorsed a mission statement that declared "the Fund's approach is that of the social engineer who assembles and considers all the available information on a problem and then makes the best possible plan for action. . . ." [19] And as late as 1968 he retained much hope for social reform, arguing for the continuing growth of an American state, "partly as an administer of wealth distribution, partly as a direct distributor of certain products. In notable areas *production for use rather than production for profit* is emerging as the norm." This was a viewpoint that would soon lose its edge, and not only among liberals grown skeptical of such administrative hubris. [20]

Joseph Schumpeter was not a liberal. He was an Austrian conservative who venerated the values and lifestyle of the *haute-bourgeoisie* from which he had sprung. Transplanted to the U.S. in the 1930s, he was instinctively hostile to the New Deal, to brain trust planning, and to left-wing intellectuals in general. Unlike Berle, he did not welcome the demise of the entrepreneur or the autonomous corporation, but in his famous *Capitalism, Socialism and Democracy,* published in 1942, he forecast the inevitable decay and collectivist transmutation of laissez-faire into a rationalized and nationalized system, what he calls "socialism." [21]

Like Berle, Schumpeter thought the entrepreneurial function was inevitably and necessarily becoming bureaucratized. But unlike the New Deal brain truster, whose big book was published at the very depth of the Depression, Schumpeter is important to our story because his highly influential theory of market demise depends not on a crisis of capitalism, but upon the cultural contradictions inherent in capitalism's very success. Like Daniel Bell, who would write the *Cultural Contradictions of Capitalism* a quarter century on, Schumpeter saw a distinction between capitalism as an economic system, which he thought stable and successful, and the "civilization of capitalism," which he thought subverted by prosperity, inflation, and empowerment of the masses, in short by all those modern values that destroyed deference, loyalty, and tradition. "Capitalism," he argued at the onset of World War II, "creates a critical frame of mind which, after having destroyed the moral authority of so many other institutions, in the end turns against its own; the bourgeois finds to his amazement that the rationalist attitude does not stop at the credentials of kings and popes, but goes on to attack private property and the whole scheme of bourgeois values. The bourgeois fortress thus becomes politically defenseless." [22]

This sense of an inevitable, politicized transmutation of the market into something more systematic and more purposefully totalizing is very much a product of the early postwar years. The great collective effort put forth in World War II was in part responsible, but we can also see this kind of "big think" generalized and carried well into the early Cold War era when ideological combat between two conflicting social systems had such a profound impact on Western social thought. It is important to remember that as late as 1960 the word *capitalism* had a distasteful odor in Europe, Asia, and even within the U.S., where *free enterprise* was the preferred nomenclature. In Western Europe the State Department and the CIA supported the "non-Communist left," which enabled a generation of ex-socialist, but anticommunist intellectuals the freedom to define the West in terms that marginalized existing market relationships and looked forward to a long era of progressive social reform. [23]

The management theorist Peter Drucker shared much of this same vision, even as he sought to put the idea of a planning order and a politicized capitalism at the service of corporate America. Like Schumpeter, Drucker was a theorist of capitalist stability. Indeed, he was the youngest member of an Austrian generation that also included Friedrich Hayek and Ludwig von Mises. But Drucker had a far more engaged, practical relationship to actually existing capitalism. After witnessing the Nazi rise to power he emigrated to the U.S., where he became one of the founding fathers of management science and one of the great tribunes of American capitalist civilization. Drucker was convinced that "nothing could induce the overwhelming majority of the American people to give up the belief in a free-enterprise economic system except a major catastrophe such as a new total war or a new total depression." But in 1946, when he wrote his pathbreaking *Con-*

cept of the Corporation, he understood that such views were not universally endorsed. Thus he titled the first chapter of his study of General Motors, "Capitalism in One Country." [24]

Like some twenty-first-century advocates of the universal market, Drucker often cast his mid-twentieth-century prescriptions in metahistorical terms. The modern corporation, he asserted, is the paradigmatic institution of the modern world, "the representative social actuality." Big business, he wrote in the *Concept of the Corporation,* is "the general condition of modern industrial society irrespective of the forms of social organization or the political beliefs adopted in particular countries. . . . The emergence of Big Business as a social reality during the past fifty years is the most important event in the recent social history of the Western world." [25]

But if Drucker was a herald of corporate America, he was equally determined to divorce such views from any taint of the old laissez-faire. To Drucker and to a generation of societal savants who would follow, the corporation was essentially a planning mechanism, a Weberian rationalization of industrial society. "The problem of the political, social and economic organization of Big Business is not unique to one country but common to the entire western world. And this means that there is a wide area where it makes little difference whether we discuss conditions in the United States or in Russia, whether we assume a free-enterprise society, Communism or Nazism . . . the entire realm of social engineering is an objective realm." [26]

This effort to marginalize questions of economic organization and motivation is characteristic of the way Western intellectuals sought to wage the Cold War. In this schema markets, profitability, and capitalism are but second-rate questions: the key issue is that of organization, planning, and technique. Management theorists like Drucker assumed that the primacy of market exchange had given way to new principles of corporate organization as social development came to depend on the encouragement of "social goods" like science and education. Since productivity gains now relied so heavily on such scientifically trained workers, public funding of research and education became the central motive force of economic development. In effect Max Weber would increasingly trump the economic forces identified either by Adam Smith or Karl Marx. [27]

On the left, liberals and radicals took the kind of thinking that went into Drucker's rather sanguine prognostication about the role that corporations and the state would play in a new regulatory planning regime and deployed it at the service of their social imagination. Unlike Drucker, Arthur Schlesinger Jr. was a liberal Democrat. When he published *The Vital Center* in 1949, Schlesinger declared himself a part of the "non-Communist left." He was a militant New Dealer who thought the pivot of American history turned upon the conflict between the business community, often in alliance with a not-so-democratic state, and the plebeian movements and their intellectual allies, who sought to rebalance the social scales. "Class conflict," wrote Schlesinger in *The Vital Center,* "is essential if freedom is to be preserved, because it is the only barrier against class domination." [28]

But Schlesinger shared with Drucker a conviction that neither class nor economics stood at the fulcrum of social choice. Like so many others who had witnessed the rise of Stalinism and fascism and experienced the power of the warfare state, he was transfixed by the specter of an organizational revolution that transcended property relations and business interests. In the democratic West this augured well. "Britain has already submitted itself to social democracy," wrote Schlesinger in *The Vital Center,* and "the United States will very likely advance in that direction through a series of New Deals and the advance will be accelerated if the country fails to keep out of a depression." But Schlesinger expected no dramatic conflict, because in a post–New Deal America the differences among classes "are much less impassible than the differences between capitalist democracy and authoritarianism; and sometimes in the heat of battle the warring classes tend to forget their family relationship." [29]

We can see how some of these mid-century ideas were deployed at the service of a specific set of Cold War policy prescriptions, both foreign and domestic, when we consider the influential work of the first postwar generation of industrial relations scholar-activists. In 1951 when Clark Kerr, John Dunlop, Frederick Harbison, and Charles A. Myers proposed that the new and immensely rich Ford Foundation fund a worldwide study of "Labor Relations and Democratic Policy," echoes of a Depression-era set of radical, anticapitalist assumptions could still be found beneath the Cold War overlay that justified their ambitious research design. Drafted by Lloyd Fisher, a former Longshoremen's Union staffer who was now Kerr's aide-de-camp, the initial grant application argued that the "condition, character, and beliefs of the working classes will be among the decisive influences upon the political structure of modern nations . . . and world peace." But the Ford Foundation rejected the application, along with other international, labor-focused research proposals by Adolph Strumthal, Summer Slichter, and Margaret Catherwood.[30]

Paul Hoffman, the former head of the Marshall Plan in Europe, was then president of the Ford Foundation. Richard Bissell, who had also served with the European Cooperation Administration, was a key adviser, responsible for screening research proposals, among them that of Kerr and his associates. Bissell would soon move on to the Central Intelligence Agency, where he helped plan the coup in Guatemala, develop the U-2 spy plane, and organize the Bay of Pigs invasion. Indeed, even as he worked as a program officer at Ford in 1951 and 1952, Bissell was part of a high-level group of well-connected consultants who met regularly with Director Allen Dulles and key CIA officers. Like the Ford Foundation itself, Bissell thought of himself as an internationalist and a thoughtful liberal. He was a Keynesian economist, and an economic planner during World War II and in the postwar ECA. Bissell was opposed to the militarization of the Marshall Plan after 1950 because he was convinced that the essential ingredients to an effective anticommunist foreign policy revolved around the encouragement of economic growth, social stability, high levels of education, and a culture of cosmopolitan exchange. He was therefore instrumental in funding MIT's Center for International Studies, where "modernization" studies under the direction of Walt W. Rostow proved so influential during the remainder of the 1950s.[31]

We don't know precisely what role Bissell played in the Ford Foundation's initial rejection of the Kerr-Fisher grant proposal, but it is clear that when Kerr resubmitted the application in early 1952, it had a very different character. Now entitled "Utilization of Human Resources: a Comparative Analysis," the multi-university, multinational research design eliminated all mention of the phrase *working class,* and in its stead adopted in more explicit fashion the emerging discourse of modernization, industrialization, and human resources. This project fit in well with the Ford Foundation's funding priorities of the 1950s and 1960s: education, managerial expertise, economic development in the newly independent nations, and an orientation toward U.S. foreign policy that differed little from that of the Eisenhower Republicans. Indeed, throughout the 1950s the research project was guided through the Ford bureaucracy by Thomas Carroll, a Harvard Business School product, who encouraged Kerr and Dunlop to put the development of the managerial strata at the center of any theory of transnational industrialism.[32]

With a budget that eventually reached well into the millions, this remarkably influential, two-decade research effort funded at least ninety scholars (mainly at MIT, Berkeley, Harvard, and Princeton), and generated dozens of books, scores of articles, and numerous high-profile conferences. The "Inter-University Study," as it came to be called, was an engine of ideological reconfiguration, in which an entire generation of left-of-center academic intellectuals became invested in a set of ideas that marginalized both class conflict and the business enterprise, capitalism and its ideological opponents. In their place the Kerr-Dunlop study put at the center of the postwar universe the inexorable growth of an increasingly hegemonic set of rule-making bureaucracies that structured labor, capital, and government in all industrial societies. A technically sophisticated, highly educated managerial stratum was central to this process, in both the West and the East, and as the driving force behind economic development in Africa, Latin America, the Middle East, and the Indian subcontinent.[33]

By the time Clark Kerr, John Dunlop, and their associates published *Industrialism and Industrial Man* in 1960, they had reached the conclusion that the process of "industrialization" had replaced the dialectics of capitalism as a worldwide principle framing the evolution of society. As Kerr put with characteristic bravado, "In our times it is no longer the specter of Communism which is haunting Europe, but rather emerging industrialization in many forms that is confronting the whole world. The giant of industrialization is stalking the earth, transforming almost all features of older and traditional societies." Classes would still exist in such a society, and unions remained important institutions that represented the interests of lower-skilled manual workers. However, the resultant "conflict will take place in a system of pluralistic industrialism . . . it will take less the form of the open strife or the revolt and more the form of the bureaucratic contest. Persuasion, pressure, and manipulation will take the place of the face-to-face combat of an earlier age." But whatever the nature of the conflict, the stakes were far lower than those once imagined in earlier decades. Regardless of the form of industrialization, Soviet, Western, or in the underdeveloped world, a universal "web of rules" was intrinsic to industrialism's Weberian universe. These technocratic and rationalist constraints devalued collective action, marginalized the role of government, and heightened the centrality of the managerial elite as the "initiator" and "manipulator" of the industrial system.[34] So powerful was this bureaucratic, rule-making impulse that Kerr, who became president of the University of California in 1960, not only forecast a long-range convergence between the social structures of the Soviet Union and the United States, but even more famously, in his 1963 manifesto, *The Uses of the University,* argued that in the growth of a knowledge economy, business would necessarily accommodate itself to the disinterested standards, the social mores, and the planning values characteristic of the nation's burgeoning set of institutions of higher education.[35]

The New Left had a far more critical vision of the United States than did Schlesinger, Kerr, and so many other organizational liberals. The Berkeley radical Mario Savio would soon denounce Kerr's vision of business-university convergence, but Savio's generation shared this in common with University of California President Clark Kerr: both thought that market capitalism had been bureaucratized in a society that had become increasingly subject to the rule of a managerial elite. If Kerr and Drucker saw this planning regime as one of progress, pluralism, and rationality—indeed if Kerr thought that the corporations themselves were taking on some of the characteristics of the science-driven university—then most on the left found Kerr's vision a nightmare, sometimes denoted by the phrase *garrison state.*

On the emergent New Left, no figure was more influential in propagating this dark, claustrophobic vision than C. Wright Mills, who was, and remains, one of the most trenchant and popular critics of postwar American capitalism. At the core of Mills's analysis was a theory of capitalist development that foresaw economic instability leading not to radical reform, but to the rule of a new, statist power elite. In its twentieth-century form, capitalism was inherently unstable, prone to a recurrent cycle of depression, war, and hothouse boom. In the 1940s, when his amazingly prolific writing career began, Mills expected another slump in just a few short years, and according to his analysis, so too did the most sophisticated representatives of big business, who therefore backed an administratively guided political economy, a sort of postwar New Deal, but with a much more authoritarian, business-oriented elite firmly in command. Under this regime corporatist decision-making would replace parliamentary democracy, while the market would become but a nostalgic small-town fiction under a regime of price, wage, and production controls. Mills called this "a corporate form of garrison state" or "a state capitalism with many corporate features," but whatever the nomenclature, it is "the main drift" that leads eventually to what Franz Neumann, that most influential student of fascism, had called "totalitarian-monopolistic-capitalism."[36]

As late as 1948, however, Mills's outlook was not one of despair, because he looked to the labor movement, "the chief social power upon which a genuine democracy can rest today," as the social formation that might well avert such a garrison state. He feared for organized labor, not because of its destruction at the hands of individual capitalists, even as the state looked on approvingly, but rather Mills foresaw labor's claustrophobic incorporation into a suffocating, authoritarian, politically charged political-military regime, a devolution he sometimes labeled, "the main drift." *The Power Elite,* his 1955 masterwork, elaborated upon this idea, and it became something of a bible for the early New Left, sharing shelf space with Herbert Marcuse's *One Dimensional Man,* which also forecast a fat and sloppy working-class incorporation into the capitalist embrace.[37]

Mills was right about a lot, but this particular nightmare proved unfounded. Labor's fate was not incorporation but fragmentation, marginalization, and a growing incapacity to make any sort of impress on the capitalist market, in either labor or goods. When Barry Goldwater began to denounce "monopoly unionism" in the late 1950s, he was not interested in construction of a regime that the New Left would later denote as "corporate liberalism." Representing a growing, self-confident ideological element that had never accepted either the New Deal or the managerial state, the Goldwater New Right wanted the market to reign supreme, in race relations as well as in business affairs and industrial relations. Goldwater, and his growing list of allies in the middle rank of the Republican Party, never bought into any version of a post–World War II labor-management accord, nor did they countenance the growth of federal power over against that of the southern oligarchy or individual business units, which is why Goldwater's vote against the 1964 Civil Rights Act foreshadowed so accurately conservative priorities on race, market, and the constraint of state power.[38]

This was a trajectory that neither American liberals nor their left-wing critics understood. In the 1960s most thought that the Goldwaterite vision was a complete dead end. Instead, the United States was entering a world in which society would be organized according to some new, trans-economic principle. If you reread the Port Huron Statement, published by the Students for a Democratic Society in 1962, one finds much criticism of American business, of social inequality, and especially of the "military-industrial complex." The latter phrase was taken from the farewell speech of no one of less stature than President Dwight D. Eisenhower, who in effect now endorsed the dark analysis found in Mills's *The Power Elite*. Thus, if earlier generations of radicals had derided capitalism as an anarchic, irrational system, the New Left scorned American capitalism because it was too rational, based on a soul-destroying set of technological and bureaucratic imperatives that stifled individual expression.[39] "Do not fold, spindle, or staple." Thus did the New Leftists adopt as their individualistic credo the punch-card admonition of the early mainframes.

In the 1940s and 1950s liberal theorists of capitalist transmutation had thought that interest-group pluralism now constituted the only real basis for a well-constrained democracy. Schumpeter was an elitist who feared mass politics, and Berle thought "an equipoise of strong organizations" necessary to balance managerial power with labor and consumer interests. Robert Dahl, the foremost theoretician of postwar political pluralism, defined twentieth-century democracy as a "polyarchy,"[40] in which a kind of consensual democracy survives, but only as competing elites bargain, compromise, and govern. To all this the New Left counterpoised participatory democracy and a new era of citizen activism. But the youthful SDSers who met at Port Huron could not figure out what to say about the shape of American capitalism. Indeed, after Paul Potter asked his New Left followers to "name the system" at a 1965 antiwar protest, he later reflected that "capitalism was for me and my generation an inadequate description of the evils of America."[41]

John Kenneth Galbraith, who was America's most celebrated and well-connected liberal economist in this era, codified such skittishness in his magnum opus of 1967, *The New Industrial State*. For liberals about to confront the 1970s and 1980s, no handbook could have been more disastrous. The corporations had once been regulated by the market and therefore independent of the state, argued Galbraith, who was here following the lead of fellow New Dealer Adolf Berle. But under contemporary conditions, "the mature corporation, as part of a comprehensive structure of planning, has no similar independence. It identifies itself with social goals, and adapts these to its needs. . . . More specifically, if the state is effectively to manage demand, the public sector of the economy . . . must be relatively large. That means that the state is an important customer, and it is especially needed in developing advanced technology which would otherwise be beyond the scope of industrial planning. Under these circumstances the independence of the mature corporation is further circumscribed. . . . There is no chance . . . of a solid front by mature corporations against the state." [42]

Market triumphalists have not let such views pass unnoticed. When President Clinton awarded Galbraith a Presidential Medal of Freedom in September 2000, Virginia Postrel, author of *The Future and Its Enemies,* gave him the dustbin of history boot. "Galbraith has spent his career peddling nonsense," charged Postrel, a frequent contributor to the *Wall Street Journal* and to the libertarian magazine *Reason*. His argument for a planning technostructure, in both the U.S. and the old Soviet Union, has been "utterly discredited by the experience of the past several decades." [43]

Indeed, those liberal intellectuals who devalued the pervasiveness and anarchic power of the capitalist market and instead projected a sociological convergence between the market-taming corporations of the industrial West and the planning bureaucracies of the statist East gave away much of the ideological ground that would soon be exploited by neoconservative intellectuals in the 1970s and 1980s. The latter preached a virtuous marriage between civil society, democracy, and untamed markets. As Seymour Martin Lipset put it in a 1978 symposium, "Capitalism, Socialism, and Democracy," sponsored by the neoconservative magazine *Commentary,* "The chief value of capitalism is not really its unequaled record of production and distribution of goods, but rather its guarantee of a private sector, a sector of society based upon property and income that is clearly distinguishable . . . from the power of the national state."[44]

Daniel Bell was as wishfully mistaken as Galbraith about the evolution of capitalist planning and the withering away of the market. But whereas no one today reads *The New Industrial State,* Bell's *The Coming of Post-Industrial Society* (1973) is still widely respected. A new edition appeared in 1999, and more importantly, Bell's concept of postindustrialism, which one can also read as post-market capitalism, is taken as a given by much of both left and right. To Bell, market exchange will atrophy in the new world of superabundant information and autonomous knowledge workers. This serves as useful camouflage for market triumphalists because it deflects attention from the unprecedented concentration and mobility of capital, devalues the autonomy and power of corporate managers, and ignores the very real growth of wage and wealth inequality. But Daniel Bell could make the idea of a postindustrial transformation wondrously seductive to left-of-center futurists. As he put it in *The Coming of Post-Industrial Society:*

> It seems clear to me that, today, we in America are moving away from a society based on a private-enterprise market system toward one in which the most important economic decisions will be made at the political level, in terms of consciously defined "goals" and "priorities." . . . No social or economic order has a writ of immortality, and the consumer-oriented free-enterprise society no longer satisfies the citizenry, as once it did.
>
> This is a society that has rested on the premises of individualism and market rationality, in which the varied ends desired by individuals would be maximized by free exchange. We now move to a communal ethic, without the community being, as yet, wholly defined. In a sense, the movement away from governance by political economy to governance by political philosophy—for that is the meaning of the shift—is a turn to non-capitalist modes of social thought. And this is the long-run historical tendency in Western society.[45]

In contrast to the pillorying taken by Galbraith, Daniel Bell got a warm embrace from those same triumphalist quarters. Francis Fukuyama declared that the appearance of a third edition of Bell's *The*

Coming of Post-Industrial Society made him "realize just how right Bell was in his social forecasting." Fukuyama gave this old Social Democrat a pass because he was willing to ignore chapters with headings such as "The Subordination of the Corporation" or "Social Choice and Social Planning." Bell's argument for a regulatory capitalism in a postindustrial world was simply shoved aside, out of mind and out of place. Instead, Fukuyama hailed what the post–Cold War conservatives found so affirming to their worldview: the breathless proclamation of a transformed techno-social era, the evisceration of all the industrial-age political and organizational categories, the demise of class antagonism, and even Bell's concern with the cultural tensions—and especially the threat to bourgeois values—generated by such rapid social change.[46] And unlike Galbraith, who chose to ignore rather than argue with those to his left, Bell picked many a fight over the years, often against the New Left and its postmodern offspring.

But there is another reason that Reaganite conservatives from George Gilder to Newt Gingrich embraced Bell's idea of a postindustrial world. It devalues all that was or is characteristic of the old order, including the production of things in actual factories, various forms of routine service work, and the existence of a labor movement, either as a defender of a dying class of manual laborers or as an institution necessary to defend the interests of those who still worked for their bread in the postindustrial wonderland. Indeed, the failure of the trade unions to organize white collar and professional workers, which was becoming well noted as the 1950s turned into the 1960s, seemed to confirm that these workers had an interest and outlook inherently hostile to the unions, the welfare state, and the planning impulse. House Speaker Newt Gingrich, for example, was a New South conservative whose ideological aversion to trade unionism and the welfare state came larded with a set of facile, techno-social imperatives derived from the most deterministic brand of postindustrial theory. He celebrated the writings of ex-leftists Alvin and Heidi Toffler, whose popular prognostications, including *Future Shock* (1970) and *The Third Wave* (1980), had much in common with the work of Daniel Bell and Peter Drucker. Indeed, Gingrich also had a theory of history that saw the technologically sophisticated corporation as the culmination of America's democratic heritage.[47]

This bundle of techno-social ideas actually began on the center-left, when a generation of hopeful savants sought to transform and devalue the meaning of work itself. In a burst of optimistic prognostication, public intellectuals of the 1950s, men like Norbert Wiener, William Foote White, David Riesman, and Clark Kerr, argued that first, a new world of postwar consumption would replace work and production as the social and moral foci of life, and that second, the decline in the hours of work and the growth in leisure-time activities would further marginalize the work experience. In their classic studies of mid-century blue-collar life, sociologists Eli Chinoy and Robert Dublin found that factory workers just wanted to get out of the factory, not make life there better. "If this finding holds generally," wrote Dublin, "the role and significance of work in American society has departed from its presumed historical position." Indeed, whatever the valuation of traditional work, the days of the factory were numbered. Just as tractors, reapers, and other forms of mechanization had slashed the farm population, so too would automation generate such an increase in factory productivity that blue-collar work would practically vanish. And as for the growing world of the salaried, white-collar employees emplaced within the bureaucratic corporation, both David Riesman and C. Wright Mills affirmed their alienation and psychological disengagement, a judgement available in the influential white-collar novels of that era, including Saul Bellow's *Adventures of Augie March* and Sloan Wilson's *The Man in the Gray Flannel Suit*.[48]

This mood was advanced in the late 1950s and early 1960s when a new era of factory "automation" seemed to burst upon the scene. There was a large trade in reports and conferences about how the working class would soon deal with all its newfound leisure. A 1964 manifesto, "the Triple Revolution" signed by, among others, Robert Heilbroner, Irving Howe, Gunnar Myrdal, and Tom Hayden, foresaw in automation and cybernation "a new era of production" sparked by gains in productivity so large that one could cope with the disruptive effects only by severing the link between employment and income, a linchpin of the old capitalist, industrial order. Trade unionists like Walter Reuther, who argued that such prognostications were rather premature, were thought unimaginative, if not somewhat conservative.[49]

The contemporary heirs to this kind of thinking have been those who have seen the late-twentieth-century economy based on a "post-Fordist" production regime. In what they have called a "second industrial divide," MIT's Charles Sabel and Michael Piore held that cyber-world high technology, greater international competition, and a cultural differentiation of product markets had undermined Fordist, mass production methods and the consumption patterns upon which they rested. Capital-intensive mass production, which both Henry Ford and Walter Reuther once thought the key to a general abundance, has now become an economic albatross whose very rigidities have exacerbated periodic recessions and rendered U.S. products less competitive. The nineteenth-century victory of mass production over a supple, creative craftism was hardly inevitable, held Piore and Sabel; it was in fact a "blind decision" whose techno-social debilities are only now becoming clear. Who wants to buy another Chevy when craftsmen at the Bavarian Motor Works can build a dozen different models that all feel custom-made?[50] And when millions of Americans hook up to thousands of Web-based narrowcasts, the mass-consumer audience that used to watch *I Love Lucy* on Wednesday night has been forever fragmented.

Workers and corporations must therefore accommodate themselves to a new world of "flexible specialization," which requires a more highly educated workforce, rapid shifts in production technology, smaller firms serving specialized markets, and the creative deployment of skilled labor. In the 1970s and 1980s Germany, Austria, and northern Italy were held the exemplars of this kind of productive system, while Japan's capacity to penetrate U.S. markets seemed to demonstrate the virtues of a nonadversarial, highly flexible work regime.[51]

Elements of this perspective have been present in the viewpoint of Robert Reich, Bill Clinton's first secretary of labor, whose celebration of a powerful new class of "symbolic analysts" left little place for class politics in the new order. "Symbolic analysis involves processes of thought and communication," wrote Reich, "rather than tangible production." According to his *The Next American Frontier,* a Reichian bestseller of 1983:

> This new organization of work necessarily will be more collaborative, participatory, and egalitarian than is high-volume, standardized production, for the simple reason that initiative, responsibility, and discretion must be so much more widely exercised within it. Since its

success depends on quickly identifying and responding to opportunities in its rapidly changing environment, the flexible-system enterprise cannot afford rigidly hierarchical chains of authority.[52]

Such techno-social forecasting seemed to open up a new era of democratic producerism, a hopeful, even inevitable world not altogether different from that once projected by Berle, Bell, and Galbraith. Indeed, in *The Second Industrial Divide,* Piore and Sabel argued that computerized craftsmanship would propagate a new world production order amenable to a revitalized Jeffersonian democracy. Instead of acting as adjuncts to machines, post-Fordian skilled workers might become sturdy industrial yeomen. The computer, wrote Piore and Sabel, is a "machine that meets Marx's definition of an artisan's tool: it is an instrument that responds to and extends the productive capacities of the user."[53] In this schema, post-Fordism or post-industrialism—by the 1990s the two had merged into a somewhat gauzy construct—resolved the gritty conflicts of the old industrial order by simply leaving them behind. If a new era of technological innovation were empowering ordinary workers, then all those issues of power, equality, and distribution that had once made the labor question so intractable had now been transcended.

But the stark fact is that in the twenty-first century more people on this planet work in factories than at any other moment in world history. There are more assembly-line workers now than ever before, even if the production facilities are in Malaysia rather than Milwaukee, Sumatra rather than Saginaw. Likewise, the proletarianization of office and service work proceeds apace, even if the new telecommunication and call-processing centers are located in Bangalore rather than Boston, or North Dakota rather than northern California. The goods and services thus produced still require bosses, banks, and bourses to commodify labor, turn a profit, and reproduce a capitalist social order. In its 1996 report, even the World Bank took note of this phenomenon by appropriating *The Communist Manifesto* for its own free-trade purposes: "The need of a constantly expanding market for its products chases the bourgeoisie over the whole surface of the globe," wrote Marx in 1848. "It must nestle everywhere, settle everywhere, establish connections everywhere."[54]

This understanding of capitalism's trajectory, in the twenty-first century as well as the nineteenth, returns us to the propositions advanced by the market triumphalists of our own time. Their conflation of the capitalist market with the democratic impulse has been highly influential, not only because it has been backed by the increasingly overt use of American power, but because they have succeeded in returning us to a definition of liberal democracy that Marx himself would have recognized: a world of free trade, weak government, unregulated wealth, and corporate cultural hegemony. The wishful intellectuals identified in this essay recognized the inequity and instability inherent in the world of nineteenth-century liberal capitalism, and to transform it they advanced a far more ambitious agenda, derived in large measure from the social democratic aspirations that were so common on both sides of the Atlantic during the early twentieth century. Indeed, many of these theorists staked their optimistic prognostications upon the socializing dynamic that the Marxist tradition itself had understood to be a feature of capitalist development, especially in its late corporatist-militarist phase. They were anticapitalists insofar as they expected this system to transmute itself into a more harmonious and humane set of social and institutional arrangements. But these intellectuals forgot that capitalism is above all a system not just of production but of power, of classes and not just culture. Without politics, ideology, and human agency, it will not transform itself into another system or another stage of history. If the end of the Cold War, and the wars that have followed, serves to remind us of this immutable circumstance, then the capitalist triumphalism of our time need not go unchallenged.

4

Cold War Triumphalism and the Deformation of the American Economy[1]

Michael A. Bernstein

Having been one superpower during the Cold War, the United States now stands alone as a "hyperpower." In the prosecution of an allegedly preemptive war against Iraq, and with an ensuing occupation and reconstruction of that nation that will clearly take years, the U.S. has powerfully demonstrated its military, economic, and political hegemony to the wider world. There is no more vivid contemporary symbol of America's triumph over the Soviet Union during the Cold War, nor more transparent representation of its current imperial aspirations, than this. Yet the extent to which the destruction of the Iraqi regime of Saddam Hussein gives eloquent testimony to unilateral American power today, it also contributes to the completion of a multi-decade process by which the Cold War and its aftermath have transformed, indeed deformed, the American political economy itself.

The prosecution of the Cold War involved the forging of a unique link between international objectives and domestic policy goals in the United States. Maintaining large military deployments around the world and pursuing an aggressive strategy of containment against Soviet and Chinese interests posed significant political and economic challenges for the federal government. The resultant bipartisan pursuit of unprecedented amounts of peacetime public spending was the essential economic ingredient not only of the military success of the Cold War but also of the rise of the "mixed private/public economy" of the post–World War II era. On the one side, massive allocations of public resources to military-industrial procurement and force-deployments played a key role in driving the Soviet economy (and military) into oblivion. On the other, Cold War spending became the central political integument supporting an increasingly active commitment by Washington to economic and social programs at home that fostered full-employment growth and business-cycle stabilization.

Indeed, from the start of the Korean conflict in 1950 to the first presidential election of Ronald Reagan in 1980, American politics were distinguished by the degree to which major political parties and actors were all committed to the pursuit of a Cold War spending strategy at home and abroad. This is not to say that dissent did not exist, nor is it to ignore the wholesale repression of that dissent (especially in the McCarthy period of the 1950s). But the fact remains that Democratic and Republican presidents alike, during these three decades, found consistently common ground between the fiscal demands of waging Cold War abroad and securing social and economic melioration at home.

In fact, in the early 1980s, when President Ronald Reagan denounced the Soviet Union as an "evil empire" and predicted its timely demise, there ensued a flurry of predictions about the eventual accumulation of a peace dividend, the availability of even larger sums of federal monies that, released from the pressures of Cold War confrontation, could now be deployed by government away from military purposes toward civilian needs. The president's prognostications, and the eventual collapse of the Soviet regime under the leadership of Mikhail Gorbachev, appropriately signaled, at least in a rhetorical sense, the high tide of Cold War triumphalism in recent United States history. And yet, the material benefits of the peace dividend, despite the ideological smugness occasioned by Reagan's declarations and the devolution of the Soviet Union itself, never materialized.

On the one side, the evisceration of the peace dividend had everything to do with the geopolitical goals of the Reagan administration and the determination to maintain enormous amounts of military power to secure them. On the other, it had even more to do with the impact of a broader set of economic policies, and ideas, that had defined not simply the Reagan presidency but also the contradictions of Cold War political economy from the start. Indeed, Reaganomics, a core part of the reaction against Cold War liberalism, ultimately played a key role in a systematic reconfiguration of the national economy as a whole. This is all to say that the "victory" of the United States in the Cold War with the Soviet Union actually heralded a stunning defeat for an economy that had once grown prosperous and secure on an altogether different system of public spending, monetary management, and industrial regulation. It is one of the great ironies of contemporary American history that the Cold War, when viewed in a political-economic context, is a seemingly appropriate object of nostalgic longing.

Today, in the wake of the war with Iraq, the debris accumulated from the implosion of the Cold War economy is everywhere to be seen. The links once forged between high military spending, aggressive foreign policy initiatives against the nation's "enemies," and domestic social welfare commitments have been shattered. At the same time that a major war effort has been undertaken, requiring (by current estimates) more than $80 billion to bring U.S. troops to Baghdad, the federal government now seeks to substantially reduce domestic spending commitments across the board. In May 2003, the Bush administration pushed a major tax-cut bill through the Congress, calling for approximately $1.6 trillion in revenue reductions—the vast majority of the tax breaks thus incurred will accrue to the wealthiest Americans (those earning $1 million or more per year). For the first time in modern American history, a president has radically cut taxes while waging war.

The domestic implications of the altogether extraordinary financial architecture of the Iraq war were (and are) profound. With no plan to absorb the cost of this foreign adventure, the fiscal policies of the current Bush administration have created enormous problems for the federal balance sheet. The estimated budget deficit for fiscal 2003 stood upwards of $400 billion (at the time of this writing). As a consequence, an unprecedented array of reductions in domestic spending programs were envisioned, totaling out to approximately $265 billion in so-called entitlement programs over the next decade. These cuts included $92 billion in Medicaid disbursements, $12.5 billion in food stamps allocations, and $14 billion in veterans' benefits. Another $244 billion in reductions were contemplated for discretionary spending categories such as federal health clinics, environmental protection initiatives, and the Head Start program for preschool children.

President Bush's contemporary destruction of the Cold War political economy of the past half century actually completed a process that began decades earlier; one that found its most important roots in the economic policies of the Reagan administration. It is safe to say that some of the most compelling evidence concerning the perverse impacts of Reaganomics is found in the national statistics on the distribution of wealth and incomes. Throughout the 1980s and 1990s, there obtained a stunning deterioration in distributional equity in the American economy. Specifically, between 1983 and 1998, almost all of the increase in accumulated wealth, nationwide, engrossed only the top 20 percent of households. Paralleling this arresting symptom of distorted expansion was the reality of an increasing share of households sustaining zero or negative growth in their net worth in the same time period. Income statistics tell a similarly distressing story. The top 20 percent of American households, during the 1980s and 1990s, garnered almost 90 percent of the total rise in incomes. To say that national economic growth, at the end of the Cold War, became increasingly uneven and unfair, is a gross understatement.[2]

Distributional income and wealth data portray only the most generalized aspects of the distortions generated in the American economy in the wake of the Cold War. A close consideration of the formulation and implementation of the conservative economic policies that emerged as the Cold War came to a close offers more vivid evidence in this regard. Indeed, within the elaboration of Reaganomics in the realm of fiscal and monetary policy, and with reference to a unique political offensive to dismantle the regulatory apparatuses that had originally emerged at the height of the Cold War to sustain and balance economic expansion, it is possible to discern the details of a process of retrenchment that has become one of the defining characteristics of the late twentieth- and early twenty-first-century American experience. The Cold War had once been a crucial part of the engine by which the federal government stimulated rapid and equitable growth in incomes, wealth, and employment. A powerful political reaction was occasioned by its conclusion, one that, in economic terms, worked dramatically to reverse all of the gains in welfare, distributional equity, and stability that had been realized decades earlier.

Ronald Reagan's stunning landslide victory over Jimmy Carter in the 1980 presidential election formally signaled the transition from

Keynesian-style demand management in Washington to the allegedly new strategies of supply-side economics. Believing that the fundamental source of the problems facing the contemporary American economy had to do with supply problems rather than with demand fluctuations, the supply-side theorists focused their policy proposals on the means by which macroeconomic supply conditions might be improved. Increasing the output of goods and services, the new administration presumed, would alleviate the twin problems of stagnation and inflation that had troubled the economy since the late 1960s.

Supply-side theory drew attention to what were believed to be the distortions created by high levels of government spending, high taxation of income, and extensive governmental regulation of economic affairs. Excessive income taxation, Reagan's advisers argued, stifled productive effort, for example, by discouraging overtime work. It robbed individuals of the fruits of enterprise and risk-bearing. Finally, it distorted economic decision-making so as to slow growth and create the very fiscal pressures that contributed to the problems of "stagflation" in the first instance. The purported solution involved a radical reduction in taxes, a systematic shrinking of government spending programs and, thus, federal agency budgets, and the elimination of what were claimed to be costly regulatory measures. In this respect, Reaganomics involved, among other things, the systematic dismantling of the Cold War political economy of the United States.

During the 1980 presidential campaign, Ronald Reagan had asked the American electorate if they were "better off now than they were four years ago." For a vast majority, this had been a most persuasive rhetorical quip as the rates of inflation and unemployment had remained quite high throughout the Carter presidency itself. Yet ironically enough, the passionate response that Reagan's interrogatory evoked expressed itself almost entirely in an anti-statist fashion. In the highly charged political environment of the 1980 campaign, tax reduction became not an instrument of countercyclical policy but rather a symbol of relief for a populace hard-pressed by economic instability itself. Far from being a measured response to unemployment and excess capacity, as had been the case with the "Kennedy round" of tax cuts in 1964, the downward revision of the revenue schedules undertaken in 1981 was a crude sop in an election year. No doubt Keynes himself would have been appalled at this opportunistic manipulation of what he had believed to be one of the finer achievements of a "general theory" of economics. That the Reagan tax cuts were disproportionately favorable to the wealthiest segments of society, and thus so at variance with the progressively redistributive objectives of Keynesian practice, was simply a harsh yet accurate manifestation of their genuine intent.[3]

That supply-side economics was less a new wisdom brought to bear on matters of public policy than a catechism devised by those with other, more blatantly political fish to fry was made strikingly clear in the fiscal policy choices it ostensibly encouraged. Chief among these, of course, was the scheme for income tax reduction; unlike the arguments derived from applied macroeconomics that had militated in favor of the use of revenue policy as a means to stabilize consumption spending over the cycle, those used to justify this linchpin of Reaganomics were premised on assertions rather than econometric evidence.

Exactly just what symptoms the supply-side therapies were in fact capable of alleviating was never made clear. At the same time that the first round of Reagan tax cuts were implemented, the largest peacetime increase of American armed forces and weapons systems began. Indeed, the stimulatory impacts of so unrestrained an indulgence in federal spending prompted many supply-side advocates to claim (erroneously) that the tax-cut strategy had done its job. So dramatic was President Reagan's military buildup, a strategy epitomized by his determination to create an unprecedentedly large 600-ship Navy, that by the end of the 1980s the national economy allocated close to $300 billion annually to the Pentagon—an increase of approximately 120 percent since 1980. The fiscal consequences of defense spending in the 1980s were such that the purported budgetary benefits of supply-side economics could never be measured. During the first Reagan term, the annual federal deficit grew from 2.7 percent to 5.2 percent of gross domestic product. If fiscal balance had been the central promise of the new departures in policy practice undertaken in 1981, the federal ledger became, by 1983, an indelible record of failure. By 1989, the total national debt stood at some $2 trillion; in this regard, Ronald Reagan stood alone as one of the most profligate peacetime spenders in the history of the republic.[4]

Perhaps it was quite fitting that supply-side theory had painted itself into the corner of federal deficits much as the high tide of Cold War spending during the Vietnam War had done. After all, the entire idea of peacetime military expansion after World War II had been sold in part to the Congress and local public officials on the basis of all the resources and funding that would flow their way. Military bases brought jobs to local communities and profits to local businesses. Defense spending in general created better-paying jobs that provided higher purchasing power for the other products of domestic industry. Fiscal policy had, in fact, counted in its bag of tools the potentially stabilizing influence of Pentagon procurement (not to mention of other public goods disbursements) in the face of the business cycle. Seven successive post–New Deal presidential administrations had also embraced that logic. The exigencies of the Cold War had combined with the domestic politics of the "mixed economy" in forging that kind of bipartisan commitment to public spending. Why should Reaganomics have been any different?

Yet it was, indeed in ways that were quite profound. Keynesian-style demand management had always grounded itself on the assumption that budget deficits incurred in bad times would be redeemed with higher tax receipts in the boom. Moreover, as a surging economy approached its capacity ceiling, the reimposition of higher tax rates would be justified as an instrument of further stability. In stark contrast, Reaganomics made no such claim upon the future. Tax reduction as a political strategy, especially when coupled with increased spending on federal operations such as defense, carried no guarantees of subsequent restoration. Quite the contrary. To the extent that revenue cuts became fixed by a kind of political inertia, the very tools of Keynesian fiscal policy were blunted. Thus it was, in an exquisite historical irony, that Ronald Reagan's immediate successors in the White House—the first George Bush and Bill Clinton—faced the sheer impossibility of implementing countercyclical fiscal measures even had they wished to do so. In this sense, although the Reagan administration practiced a kind of Keynesianism in its dramatic expansion of military spending while at the same time reducing federal taxes, supply-side economics did unambiguously achieve one particular policy objective—it made the future use of Keynesian spending policies seemingly problematic if not impossible.[5]

Cutting the tax lifeline of federal economic policy practice during the 1980s was as effective a conservative strategy of political retrenchment as it was manipulative of public sentiment. It also utilized a supreme conceit—that victory in the Cold War somehow proved that a traditional capitalism was the best of all possible worlds—indifferent to the fact that it was a uniquely nontraditional capitalist system that had made the nation so prosperous after World War II. In place of the Keynesian argument that more equitably distributed incomes and wealth, effected by the tax system itself, would generate higher aggregate consumption and thus more robust economic growth, a "new classical" economics, one of the heady ideological products of Cold War triumphalism itself, posed a simpler view of the market system. Tax cuts, which would necessarily place proportionately more discretionary income in the hands of the wealthiest portions of the population, conservatives claimed, would encourage investment that in turn would enhance employment. Thus would the benefits of fiscal austerity "trickle down" through the income distribution. That greater tax savings for the rich would stimulate investment was a proposition that directly contravened Keynes's claim that it was investment, through its impact on employment and production (and thus incomes), which ultimately garnered rises in savings. Overall, taxes could thus be condemned as the mortal enemy of incentives to work and to invest. Lost from view was the Keynesian rejoinder—that judicious tax policy, through the enhancement of the consumption and investment it would stimulate, could serve to guarantee the profits of enterprise and thereby the prosperity of the whole.[6]

So widely shared was the passion for tax cuts as a kind of Holy Grail of a new classical economics that even the major political parties, toward the end of Ronald Reagan's second presidential term, could find little on that score about which to disagree. All that was left was political pandering to targeted constituencies. For the Republicans that meant emphasizing the usefulness of tax reduction for upper-income groups and the broadening of the argument to include proposals for reductions in the prevailing levy on capital gains and stock dividends. For the Democrats the riposte was to focus on what was so beguilingly labeled "middle-class tax relief." Both parties flirted with radical suggestions to eliminate the entire structure of income taxation itself—usually toying with half-baked ideas concerning the implementation of a single- (or "flat") rate income tax or a national sales (or "value added") tax. With genuine justification, an observer new to the scene might have concluded, during the 1988 presidential campaign especially, that John Maynard Keynes had never published a word.[7]

Like most nostrums, tax reduction created more problems than it solved. Federal spending, whether engrossed by military initiatives such as those undertaken during the Reagan presidency, or propelled by transfer-payment programs long on the books (like Medicare, Social Security, and Aid to Families with Dependent Children), rose in both absolute terms and on a per-capita basis throughout the 1980s and early 1990s. A rising national debt only seemed to make more obvious the failures (and the failings) of supply-side economics and its attendant pieties. It was hardly surprising, therefore, that conservatives increasingly focused their attention on disbursements themselves. Within this context arose the next offensive against economic statecraft, the second prong of the attack originally launched by the Reagan tax cuts—the proposal for a balanced budget amendment to the United States Constitution.[8]

A hardy perennial in the garden of conservative economic ideas, the balanced budget amendment became decidedly fashionable in 1985 when the National Governors Association passed a resolution favoring its adoption. It became the catalyst for a great deal of campaign posturing and a consistent addition to the list of bills pending before each Congress. While it consistently failed of passage, it remained a talisman of the right, appropriately so given the fact that it would, by statute, eliminate the essential instrument of Keynesian fiscal policy from use by the Treasury, a kind of final nail in the Keynesian coffin. No wonder then that it was (and is) an object of great admiration among conservatives, equally loathsome to liberals.

For fairly obvious political reasons, critics of Keynesian-style spending techniques focused their attacks on absolute levels of indebtedness. Large numbers, especially those rendered in red, were impressive instruments of persuasion in the dismantling of the Cold War economy. Yet as any banker knew, let alone economic specialists, debt burden could only be meaningfully evaluated with reference to the ultimate ability to pay. In this context, the national debt, representing a claim on the wealth and income streams of future generations, necessarily had to be measured with reference to the gross domestic product (GDP) itself. As a share of annual income, debt reveals its true burden. By this measure, American public finance, while obviously deranged in the wake of the Vietnam era, had since the early 1980s shown tangible improvement—not surprisingly because the ratio of annual deficits to the GDP had steadily fallen from a high of 6.3 percent in 1983 to 1.4 percent in 1996. Looking at the debt as a whole, in 1995 the national shortfall stood at $3.6 trillion, just over half of a $7 trillion GDP. This compared quite favorably with a debt-GDP proportion of over 100 percent at the end of World War II—interestingly enough, the beginning of a period of growth and expansion in the national economy that was historically unprecedented. In this context, the central target variable would be one linking the rate of growth in the debt to the rate of growth of the macro-economy—a notion altogether obscured in the public debates surrounding a balanced budget amendment.

In point of fact, the transformation of the nation's political landscape in the wake of the Vietnam era had subverted the very foundations of a liberalism that had once made sense out of the economics of the Cold War. An emphasis on political-economic issues that had framed the high tide of activist government since the New Deal had provided a bipartisan coalition with the economic means and the ideological ends to maintain itself. So soon as social issues concerning opportunity and equality occupied center stage, most vividly in the formulation of a "war on poverty," American liberalism ran headlong into the abiding national puzzle of race, ethnicity, and class. A backlash was the inevitable result, one that shifted a dynamic emphasis on productivity and plenty during the 1950s and 1960s to a static refrain concerning the costs and benefits, the winners and losers in market outcomes during the 1980s and 1990s. So dependent had Cold War liberalism been on sustained growth as a vehicle of redistributive betterment and justice that the first signs of macroeconomic instability, with its inevitable stoking of racial and class divisions in American society, robbed it of its voice and authority.

Perhaps it was predictable, given the rightward turn of American politics in the late twentieth century, that professional economics would itself regress and retrench. A kind of naïveté coupled with an unbridled enthusiasm had propelled the discipline's leading lights to make claims on its behalf it could not redeem. Once events, and the ideological shifts they provoked, overtook the statecraft economists had so painstakingly fashioned, their flanks were wholly exposed to an unrelenting and unparalleled assault. Reversion to classical principles, a rejection of heterodox notions, an insistence on a professional deportment unable and unwilling to join with the ideological issues in dispute, and a contentment with a return to scholarly detachment were understandable if pathetically timid reactions.[9]

It has long been a conviction of those who study the history of the sciences that moribund intellectual traditions may only be overcome by the effective articulation of alternatives. For modern American economics the possibilities for such a restructuring were by the late 1990s, precisely because of the effectiveness of the professionalizing processes that had obtained since the turn of the century, few and far between. A select few at leading colleges and universities continued to wield enormous influence over the distribution of research grants, their own ranks replenished from a hiring process disproportionately focused on the graduates of a small number of highly regarded training programs, including their own. Any examination of publication practices in the field would serve to demonstrate as well that the dissemination of research results remained powerfully concentrated in the hands of an elite few. It is a striking yet hardly surprising finding that, at the height of the economic instability occasioned by the Vietnam war, the OPEC oil price shocks, and the downward trends in productivity enhancement experienced throughout the 1970s, alumni of only seven graduate programs in the discipline authored well over half the scholarly articles published in the nation's three leading economics journals. Such disciplinary inbreeding was hardly conducive to the elaboration of alternative paradigms.[10]

If, by the 1990s, economics was a social scientific discipline fast retreating from a public role it had sought for decades, it was clearly not the case that the influence of all of its practitioners was on the wane. Supply-side theorists, in ways far out of proportion with their achievements, continued to enjoy a prominence and an authority in economic debate that was virtually hegemonic. Anti-Keynesian rhetoric became ever more fashionable; calls for parsimony in governmental expenditure policy, often phrased in ways approximating a morality play, went virtually unchallenged. No better signal of the sea change that had taken place could be found than the news, broadcast in the fall of 1997, that a young Harvard University professor (and now a key economic adviser to the second Bush administration), N. Gregory Mankiw, would receive a $1.25 million advance from a major textbook publisher to produce a new volume in which Keynes's name barely appeared once. As advance copies of the text made their way into the hands of reviewers, even *Business Week* magazine could express alarm at the widening popularity of what it derisively called "Feel-Good Economics."[11]

Over three decades ago, the eminent historian William Appleman Williams, reflecting upon the entire span of the nation's past, noted that policy appeals based on the principle of laissez-faire were, more often than not, actually premised on a slightly different conviction— that of *laissez-nous-faire*. Arguments militating in favor of reduced government involvement in economic life usually reduced themselves to strategies, on the part of particular elites, to secure opportunities with which to exercise greater control over resources, the workforce, and households. Williams's thesis had particular relevance with respect to the transformations in political practice and economic thinking that prevailed in the United States after the early 1970s. As the Cold War consensus of the postwar era dissolved, it was replaced by an increasingly detached political economic ideology that actively condemned governmental activism in the marketplace.[12]

Since the economic turmoil of the early 1970s, indicting government for the nation's material woes had become an ever more expansive enterprise. Dismantling the Keynesian apparatus of the federal government had been only part of this project. Eager to ferret out any plausible cause of inefficiency and inflated costs in the national economy, analysts, political leaders, policy advocates, and pundits became increasingly preoccupied with the perceived burdens of governmental regulation in the marketplace. New elites within the business community also played a significant role in this regard—deploying the rhetoric of deregulation to gain access to markets from which they had previously been excluded by explicit government control. Deconstructing a variety of federal statutes and agencies, along the lines specified by an offensive against such statist intervention in economic affairs, became a significant parallel strategy in the eradication of Keynesian practice. Proponents of what was dubbed "privatization" argued that such reforms in the ways government did business would lead to greater efficiency and care in the allocation of scarce resources. By leaving decisions to businesspeople and other expertly trained individuals in the private sector, the "privateers" claimed, an appropriate system of incentives and capabilities would yield a more optimal distribution of services and a more inspired utilization of scarce public monies.[13]

Deregulation had a bipartisan gestation, its birth facilitated by the anti-taxation attitudes fostered during the economic uncertainties of the 1970s. It was Jimmy Carter's presidential administration, building upon some initial and tentative steps taken by Gerald Ford's White House, that launched the first systematic efforts to reassess and ultimately eliminate to whatever extent possible federal oversight in the finance, telecommunications, and transportation sectors. The initial forays were predominantly focused in the aviation industry, culminating in the closure of the Civil Aeronautics Administration when Congress passed the 1978 Airline Deregulation Act. Fast on the heels of that landmark legislative decision came the 1982 settlement between the antitrust division of the Department of Justice and the American Telephone and Telegraph Corporation (AT&T), an agreement that began the systematic deregulation of the nation's telecommunications infrastructure. Shortly thereafter, the Reagan administration began reconfiguring the government's role in the nation's banking industry, an effort that had profound and exceedingly costly consequences in the savings-and-loan sector for years to come. By the time the first George Bush took office, the momentum of the deregulatory process had grown very large indeed. Declaring a moratorium on all new federal regulations early in 1992, the president also asked Vice President Dan Quayle to chair a new Council on Competitiveness as an informal "super-arbiter" of national regulatory issues.[14]

While the Quayle Council lasted only a year, liquidated in its infancy by Democrat Bill Clinton in one of his first acts as president, the political movement of which it stood as a striking exemplar continued. So irresistible was the appeal of deregulation rhetoric that policy initiatives were proposed and often enacted without due consideration of either their justification or their consequences. Increasingly, mainstream American economists made themselves part of this process—often eager to formulate techniques for its implementation, rarely willing to confront many baseless assertions deployed on its behalf.

. . .

The legacies of Cold War triumphalism reveal themselves in almost every aspect of American social and political life: in an uncritical celebration of major events in the history of the Cold War; in a virtual amnesia that surrounds discussion of the great political purges of the 1950s and 1960s, and a resultant acceptance of the quite narrow range of acceptable political discussion that passes for debate in the present; in the hegemonic swagger of the American government on the world scene and the linked indifference with which the State Department conducts its affairs with other nations and regions; and in the wrongheaded self-assurance that a nation torn by racial bigotry and class prejudice need not trouble itself with further projects of social reform.

Yet nowhere are the unfortunate and corrosive impacts of Cold War triumphalism more vivid than in the recent economic history of the United States. By the early 1990s, a dramatic boom began in American stock and allied financial markets that continued, in almost uninterrupted fashion, until the terrorist attacks of September 2001. The presumption that the boom would last forever infected the sensibilities of Americans drawn from all walks of life. In 1995 alone, more than $100 billion was invested in the stock market—and investment in speculative capital simply increased from there. Many working people placed their entire retirement nest eggs into 401(k) plans and Investment Retirement Accounts. "Day-trading," a highly volatile enterprise in which literally millions could be lost in seconds, became a fad. With the proliferation of virtual, electronic marketplaces, many individuals tried their hands at such gambling—while often lacking the time, training, and financial security to underwrite their excessive risk-taking. Meanwhile, electronic commerce took off, with spectacular run-ups in the stock values of firms that existed solely online, most of which had never executed a genuine transaction nor met a formal delivery date for their output. By the early months of 2001, the Dow Jones Industrials had broken 10,000—an unimagined plateau. Seemingly, the American economy had indeed reaped the benefits of the peace dividend.

Economic booms never last forever, and that which had defined the American economy's prospects from the end of the Cold War to the turn of the twenty-first century was no different. By the early summer months of 2001, warning signs marred virtually every market horizon.

Energy prices accelerated upward; stock-market values softened, as profit-seekers cashed in on the high values generated in the boom; manufacturing output slowed; and layoffs began to rise. Then, with the September 11 attacks in New York and Washington, D.C., the upper turning point was clearly reached.

In the midst of the economic slide after 9/11, it became increasingly obvious that the national economy, working in a dramatically unregulated environment in which the federal government's capacity for countercyclical management had been decisively curtailed, had become quite fragile indeed. Strikingly enough, the very timidity of the fiscal spending proposals brought before the Congress to deal with the downturn gave ample testimony to that fact. Even the most aggressive pump-priming bills, debated on Capitol Hill, embraced spending targets that approximated a mere one to two percent of gross domestic product. The fragile nature of the national infrastructure, in the face of the terrorist attacks, was also demonstrated by the inability of the Federal Aviation Administration to make rapid adjustments to the disarray occasioned in airline operations by the attacks themselves, and they were further portrayed by the chaotic response of an enervated public health apparatus in the face of a series of horrifying, yet unexplained contaminations of the national postal system by letters laced with anthrax.

As if the recession after 9/11 and related economic dislocations were not enough, by early 2002, yet another dramatic incident further evidenced the fragility of the national marketplace in the wake of deregulation and the application of supply-side economics. Enron Corporation, one of the largest firms in the country with major interests in energy trading and distribution networks, filed for bankruptcy early in January of the new year. As liquidation proceedings documented, it rapidly became clear that the company had run up its stock values through a wide array of manipulations, falsified accounting records, and outright deceit. The accounting giant Arthur Andersen Company became implicated in the debacle when it was revealed that its auditors not only participated in the subterfuge but also began the systematic shredding of documents once it became clear that the end was near.

At the time of this writing, the course of the current recession remains in doubt. A growing scandal around the Enron bankruptcy,

with allegations of federal government involvement in the conceal-
ment of the firm's sharp-dealing, often threatened to push news of the
sustained military operations against the alleged perpetrators of the
September 11 attacks from the front pages of the nation's news dailies.
Indeed, a torrent of new allegations have emerged regarding potentially criminal conduct with respect to accounting practices at World-
Com, Tyco International, Harken Energy Corporation, and Peregrine
Systems—to name just a few of the major corporations now caught up
in ever-widening investigations of enterprise misconduct. Amidst this
economic uncertainty, one thing remains quite clear. The dismantling
of Keynesian-style fiscal management (the policy hallmark of the Cold
War era) and the deregulation of the nation's marketplaces that began
during the high tide of the Reagan presidency has had an enduring impact on the ability of the government both to maintain cyclical stability
in the face of economic shocks and to sustain regulatory vigilance and
control of financial and other related practices. As a consequence, especially since the September 11 attacks, the federal government finds
itself incapable of taking matters decisively in hand.

Making war against Iraq, the culmination of a Cold War triumphalism that now propels the American government to pursue a
strategy of absolute domination in the Middle East (and elsewhere),
strangely enough only further interfered with Washington's ability to
manage the nation's economic affairs. The conservative constituency
brought to power in the closely contested (and deeply controversial)
2000 presidential election has insisted on pursuing a reactionary
agenda in domestic affairs that conflicts decisively with the fiscal realities of imperial ambitions abroad. Throughout most of the Cold War
era, successive presidential administrations (drawn from both major
political parties) had yoked high levels of public spending for military
and diplomatic initiatives overseas with measured countercyclical
policies directed toward balanced and fair economic growth at home.
Yet the very "victory" in the Cold War with the Soviet Union that the
triumphalist rhetoric of these conservatives celebrates severed this link
between imperial splendor in the world and socioeconomic progress at
home. While the imperial ambitions remain, the progressive domestic
agenda does not.

In many respects, the collapse of the Cold War coalition that
brought conservatives determined to confront Soviet influence in the

wider world together with liberals focused on social needs at home was the direct result of the "success" of the Cold War itself. Liberals themselves, ironically enough, contributed to this remarkable script of political economic deconstruction. Eager to criticize the errors of American foreign policy in the wake of the debacle of the Vietnam war, the left nonetheless neglected to explore, in a thorough and rigorous fashion, the close economic and political connections between military-industrial spending, anticommunist containment strategy, and social welfare initiatives that had defined the "New Deal order" since the end of World War II. As a result, the primary mechanisms of fiscal and monetary control that had fostered the progressive social agendas of the Cold War era were ripe pickings for a conservative insurgency determined to destroy the vestiges of the New Deal while remaining committed to the anticommunist containment goals of the past.

Of course, since the collapse of the Soviet Union and the devolution of its satellite states, the global containment strategies of the United States are no longer focused on the activities of a (now crippled and bankrupt) Red Army and Navy. Indeed, containment today is all about the pursuit of pro-capitalist policies throughout the world. Whether anti-Soviet containment had been an aggressive or a defensive foreign policy posture in the post–World War II era has long been a subject of debate among historians and political scientists; today, by contrast, containment of the world's regions on behalf of capitalist American interests is an unambiguously aggressive stance fashioned by an ultraconservative U.S. government indistinguishable from the economic elite that it serves. It is this unabashed (and truculent) smugness about the privilege, superiority, and entitlement of American capital in the international arena today that is one of the central products of the Cold War triumphalism of the past two to three decades.

To be sure, since the end of the war in Iraq, there have emerged some rather crude examples of the ways in which a new conservative coalition seeks to tie foreign policy to domestic concerns. The award of reconstruction contracts to individual corporations, most of which have as their primary retainers major leaders in the American government (most notably and notoriously Vice President Dick Cheney), gives concrete testimony to the derangement of the Cold War–era consensus regarding public spending strategies and anticommunist containment. Over a half a billion dollars will engross the Bechtel Corporation as it executes a contract to rebuild Iraqi infrastructure for which it never had to bid; similarly Vice President Cheney's former employer, the Halliburton Corporation, will earn as much as $7 billion to restore Iraqi oil fields to full production. These singular examples of political economic corruption stand in sharp contrast to Cold War projects like the Marshall Plan that had sought to benefit an entire national economy in the project of postwar reconstruction in Western Europe.

Needless to say, the postwar reconstruction of Iraq will take place on a world stage markedly different from that of 1948. Over a half-century ago, the U.S. economy stood alone among the major industrialized nations as the source of manufacturing output and skilled labor. Today, U.S. policy is oriented no longer toward containing (a nonexistent) communist influence but rather the influence of foreign capital in its competition with American wealth in world markets. When, in May 2003, WorldCom Corporation, one of the disgraced entities in the accounting scandals that have plagued the American economy since 2000, won a contract to build Iraq's first cell phone network, the effort was born as much of a determination to bring the money for the project home to a U.S. firm as it was to exclude prime foreign competitors from reaping any benefits at all. Part of the legislation passed in the Congress to frame the disbursement of public monies for postwar reconstruction in Iraq included stipulations that any new telecommunications networks utilize technological standards developed by American, rather than European, firms.

The contemporary disjunction between American foreign policy and domestic management of economic needs has placed the second Bush administration in the grips of a profound dilemma. While it pursues its aggressive foreign strategies, tied as they are to exceedingly conservative fiscal and monetary policies at home, the American government struggles to control an economy that shows increasing weakness over time. Unemployment stubbornly rises, rates of capital formation have stagnated, the international value of the dollar steadily weakens as global financial markets become increasingly concerned about insipid economic performance in the U.S. as a whole. Where earlier Cold War presidential administrations had consistently found ways to stimulate economic growth and employment at home while containing Soviet and Chinese influence overseas, the Bush government, uncritically accepting the political products of a Cold War triumphalism born decades before, struggles to reconcile its divergent and contradictory policy impulses.

Nevertheless, in one way the Bush administration, by the time of the decision to invade Iraq, had at last found an apparent way to link its aggressive goals in foreign affairs with domestic political needs. By falsely and perversely suggesting a connection between the terrorist attacks of September 11, 2001, and the Iraqi regime, Washington mobilized public sentiment and squelched dissent (while browbeating and threatening other nations in the Security Council of the UN) in order to justify the overthrow of Saddam Hussein. In the wake of this deft yet sly manipulation of opinion, much political hay was made in forecasting the "shock and awe" the American armed forces would provoke in Iraq on their way to rapid and inevitable victory on the battlefield. Yet, ironically enough, it was not the Iraqi but rather the American people who were, in the end, truly "shocked and awed"— first, after the horrors of September 11, into accepting the government's insistence that the suppression of genuine political debate, and the dragnet arrests of countless numbers of immigrants and foreigners within U.S. borders, were necessary components of enhanced national security; and second, as a result of the mean-spirited and conniving way in which government officials exploited the high feeling unleashed by the September 11 attacks, into supporting a war against Iraq, the goals of which remain unclear and confused.

Cold War triumphalism had once celebrated not only the victory of American interests over the despotism and hostility of Soviet and Chinese communism in the wider world but also the unique ability (and mission) of the federal government to pursue social and economic progress at home while defending national interests abroad. It nevertheless rapidly became a crucial ideological and political instrument, in the hands of conservatives, to justify the transformation of the containment doctrine, from an ostensibly defensive foundation to an increasingly aggressive effort to secure the fortunes of the world for American capital. At the same time, this triumphalism was also adroitly utilized in the systematic dismantling of a political-economic coalition determined to preserve high levels of growth and employment for the vast majority of the nation's population. In this sense, as American troops raced toward Baghdad in March 2003, the crowning offensive of a political-economic war at home was also well under way. The Cold War deformation of the American economy was now at last complete.

Part III

The Past

5

"Papers of a Dangerous Tendency": From Major Andre's Boot to the VENONA Files

Maurice Isserman and Ellen Schrecker

[T]he left's sentimentality about itself and nastiness about this nation suffered another wound last week, when the Yale University press published *The Secret World of American Communism,* a selection of documents from the archives of the former Soviet Union. . . . The American left's dislike of America is not news, but it still strongly colors the teaching of history, so discrediting the left is still important.

—George Will[1]

Nothing so effectively shores up the American predilection for moral certainty as a good batch of incriminating documents.

In the introduction to *The Fear of Conspiracy,* an anthology of writings cataloguing "images of un-American subversion from the Revolution to the present," David Brion Davis contended that "Americans have been curiously obsessed with the contingency of their experiment with freedom."[2] In two and a quarter centuries of national independence, peril has been conceived of by fearful Americans as coming in a variety of forms, from the selfish scheming of effete aristocrats to the sullen resentments of brutish laborers. But the most potent images of the "un-American," from those to be found in the literature of the nativist crusades of the nineteenth century through the red scares of the twentieth century, have involved domestic conspiracies in league with hostile foreign powers, the homegrown traitors who, in Michael Rogin's words, are thought to act as "the instrument of an alien order."[3]

One of the recurring themes in this anti–un-American scenario (or what Rogin calls the "countersubversive tradition") is the notion that the conspirators themselves can be expected to reveal their hand through their own words, set deviously or carelessly to paper; that there will be, in the popular phrase, a "smoking gun," hidden away in some dark recess, and that when it is found, justice will prevail.

Perhaps this preoccupation with the uncovering of self-indicting documents is a result of the central role that the written word played in defining America's early national history, setting the American experience largely apart from that of nations tracing their origins to misty preliterate pasts.[4] Many of the earliest settlers of British North America, and certainly of the New England colonies, were drawn from a population of Puritans, devoted followers of a vernacular liturgical tradition, apt to keep a copy of John Bunyan's *Pilgrim's Progress* alongside the family Bible, and, notwithstanding the scarcity and expense of paper on their side of the Atlantic, anxiously engaged in tracking their own spiritual pilgrimage through daily journal entries. From the first days of settlement, sometimes even before their feet touched American soil, there were colonists who were also busily and solemnly scribbling away on documents of a more public nature, affirming and refining received notions of natural law as well as sacred truth as they contemplated the meaning of their individual and collective "errand into the wilderness."[5]

Over time, this prodigious outpouring of compacts, covenants, and charters shaped a powerful sense of providential and national mission, culminating in the writing of the Declaration of Independence, and state and federal Constitutions. The American foundation myth revolves in significant measure around the self-conscious belief that new words could make new worlds. "You and I, my dear friend," John Adams commented in 1776 to Richard Henry Lee, a fellow signer of the Declaration of Independence, "have been sent into life when the greatest lawgivers of antiquity would have wished to have lived. How few of the human race have ever enjoyed an opportunity of making an election of government . . . for themselves or their children?"[6]

But where there are "lawgivers" there will also be lawbreakers. Words can betray as well as affirm; if snakes could write there would have been deceit inscribed on the page even before Adam and Eve were expelled from Paradise. Documents from the American revolutionary era would bear witness not only to open proclamations of faith, but also to surreptitious acts of treachery, for the Founding Fathers harbored in their midst a Founding Traitor. Words carelessly committed to paper revealed his presence in 1780 to his fellow revolutionaries and to posterity. It was then that British Major John Andre, traveling incognito behind American lines in northern New York, was apprehended by rebel patrollers. The patrollers, who may well have contented themselves with simply robbing Andre if he had carried nothing but money on his person, instead discovered hidden in his boot a cache of papers that included detailed descriptions and sketches of the fortifications at West Point, a key American stronghold on the Hudson River. So they turned him and his papers over to local patriot authorities.

That Andre was up to no good was apparent; he was heading towards British lines with valuable military secrets. He was, however, only the courier. And although his captors did not realize it at first, the documents hidden in his boot harbored an even darker secret, for they were in the handwriting of West Point's commander, Maj. Gen. Benedict Arnold of the Continental Army. That Arnold's hand in the affair went temporarily unrecognized proved his salvation. Col. John Jameson, the American colonel who took Andre into custody in Westchester, sent a message to the commander of West Point to notify him of the breach of the fort's security; his captive, he wrote, "had a parcel of papers taken from under stockings which I think of a very dangerous tendency."[7] On receipt of Jameson's dispatch, Arnold hastened downriver to make his escape aboard the British armed sloop *Vulture*. Andre was hung soon afterwards, while Arnold survived to die in bed. But he lived forever after in American memory in infamy, his name a virtual synonym for disloyalty.

"[T]here *are* conspiratorial acts in history," as Richard Hofstadter noted in his famous essay on the paranoid style in American politics, "and there is nothing paranoid in taking note of them."[8] Arnold, who would have sold out his country for a promised payment of 20,000 pounds, well deserved the scorn of subsequent generations; the documents in Major Andre's boots revealed him as a man, in George Washington's phrase, stained by "treason of the blackest dye."[9] But there were to be other accusations of treason in the years to come, supposedly supported by the discovery of still more damning documents that, at least in retrospect, leave more of a stain upon the accuser than the accused. Thus the Reverend Jedidiah Morse, a prominent Boston minister and Federalist stalwart, warned his congregation in 1799 that the "Illuminati," a secret society alleged to be sponsored by revolutionary France, and seeking to subvert both "our holy religion and our free and excellent government," was spreading its influence in the United States with the aid of Thomas Jefferson and his supporters.

How did Rev. Morse know all this? He had, he maintained, come upon "an official, authenticated list" of its officers and members in the United States, a list contained in a letter, "an authentic copy of which I also possess. . . ."[10] The free and excellent government of the United States survived unscathed, even though Jefferson himself became president the next year; the only lasting damage was to Morse's reputation. His sermon, an early offering in David Brion Davis's collection, is also a textbook example of the paranoid style of politics. Morse was not content with merely passing on rumors or reports of subversive behavior and intent; he had to brandish written proof (even if it was likely of his own manufacture). "One of the impressive things about paranoid literature," Hofstadter suggested, "is precisely the elaborate concern with demonstration it almost invariably shows. . . . The very fantastic character of its conclusions leads to heroic strivings for 'evidence' to prove that the unbelievable is the only thing that can be believed."[11]

The collapse of the Soviet Union in 1991 led to the discovery by historians, as well as by a broader public in the United States, of many new "documents of a dangerous tendency" revealing the existence of what some choose to regard as scores, perhaps hundreds, of Red Benedict Arnolds. New archival sources have confirmed the guilt of individuals previously accused of espionage on behalf of the Soviet Union, including Julius Rosenberg and some of the Washington bureaucrats identified by "blonde spy queen" Elizabeth Bentley, and have revealed the names of other American Communists who were either active participants in such efforts or at least compromised by their contacts with Soviet agents in the 1930s and 1940s. It is also now clear that not merely were individual Communists like Rosenberg drawn into spying on behalf of the Soviet Union, but that top leaders of the Communist Party of the United States (CPUSA) in the 1930s and 1940s were well aware of these activities and actually helped to recruit agents and coordinate their efforts.

The documents bearing these revelations came from several sources. The first were the archives of the CPUSA and the Comintern, stored for decades for safekeeping in Moscow, and opened to foreign researchers in 1991. It was from these archives (some now on microfilm at the Library of Congress) that John Haynes and Harvey Klehr (along with their various Russian collaborators) drew the materials contained in two important documentary collections published by Yale University Press, *The Secret World of American Communism* (1995), and *The Soviet World of American Communism* (1998), with more volumes under Haynes and Klehr's editorship forthcoming. A second Moscow resource consisted of the newly opened foreign intelligence files of the KGB, the chief Soviet security agency, known in the 1930s and 1940s as the NKVD. These files, which unfortunately have only been shown intermittently, selectively, and for a price to researchers, provide the basis for Allen Weinstein and his Russian collaborator Aleksandr Vassiliev's *The Haunted Wood: Soviet Espionage in America—the Stalin Era* (1999). And, finally, there are the VENONA Project files, released in Washington by the U.S. National Security Agency in 1995.[12] (*VENONA* was the code name of a top-secret Cold War intelligence project designed to decipher thousands of cables between Moscow and its embassy and consulates in the United States that had been intercepted by the United States Army's Signal Intelligence Service during and immediately after World War II.) After Senator Daniel Patrick Moynihan spurred the release of the VENONA documents, Haynes and Klehr brought out their study, *Venona: Decoding Soviet Espionage in America* (1999), which was followed a year later by Eric Breindel and Herbert Romerstein's *The Venona Secrets*.[13]

Political differences should not prevent historians from giving credit where it is due. We are indebted to Klehr, Haynes, and Weinstein, and their collaborators, for their pioneering work in uncovering new documentary sources. We agree with commentators who, drawing upon the newly available evidence, believe that these documents should prompt historians of the Cold War (and especially those on the left) to reconsider significant and troubling issues regarding the relationship between American communism and Soviet espionage.[14] Thomas Powers was absolutely right when he concluded in an influential review-essay of new books on espionage for the *New York Review of Books* in 2000, "Not all the victims of McCarthyism were harmless idealists on the left."[15] However, we do not believe that the meaning of the new sources can be interpreted as simply, confidently, and politically one-sidedly as some commentators on the political right would have them read, that is to prove, as George Will would have it, that it confirms, once and for all, left-wing "nastiness." The new sources do not represent a long-delayed vindication of McCarthyism, either as practiced by the junior senator from Wisconsin in 1950–1954 or as the much broader, institutionalized forms of anticommunist political repression that marred American democracy from the late 1940s through the mid-1960s.

Most of all, we should be wary of reading into these "dangerous documents" more dangers than they truly reveal. "The distinguishing thing about the paranoid style," Hofstadter argued, "is not that its exponents see conspiracies or plots here and there in history, but that they regard a 'vast' or 'gigantic' conspiracy as *the motive force* in historical events. History *is* a conspiracy. . . ."[16] The "communist conspiracy" was not all-pervasive in the 1930s and 1940s, nor was communism in those years all conspiracy. While the revelations in the VENONA/Moscow archives are of genuine historical significance, a distinct whiff of Hofstadter's "paranoid style" has unfortunately hovered over their early reception. Genuine evidence of the complicity of some Americans in Soviet espionage has fueled reckless speculation, partisan slander, and an unwillingness to tolerate nuance and ambiguity in historical interpretation. *Espionage* is one of those words, along with *treason* and *disloyalty,* that summon up powerful emotions—understandably so—but also make it difficult to draw the distinctions necessary for exploring historical complexities.

The new historical sources certainly reinforce the image of American Communists as conspirators operating on behalf of a hostile foreign power. That is, they show that at least a hundred (and possibly as many as three hundred if we adopt Haynes and Klehr's accounting) men and women passed political and military secrets on to the Soviet Union. Most of these spies were either members of the Communist Party or close (if often deeply closeted) "fellow travelers."

The names that emerge from the new documents are, in the main, familiar; Theodore Hall, a young Harvard-trained physicist working for the Manhattan Project in 1945, may well be the only major new spy outed by the opening of VENONA. What the sources released in

Moscow and Washington have more often provided is confirmation of earlier espionage suspicions and charges. In the process, they have re-habilitated the tarnished reputation of Elizabeth Bentley, the Vassar graduate whose revelations helped to unravel the Kremlin's main espi-onage network in Washington. Because she was such an unstable, self-dramatizing character—traits ruefully noted by both her Russian handlers and by FBI agents—Bentley's credibility had long been doubted. Lacking confessions from most of the men and women she had identified and unwilling to let on that it had cracked the Kremlin's code (though the decryption project harbored a Soviet spy), the gov-ernment could not produce enough other evidence to prosecute them for espionage. The release of the VENONA cables and the Moscow files shows that Bentley, to whom the Russians had given the cover name "Good Girl," had been telling the truth. She figures prominently in these documents, as do most of the people she named when she de-fected to the FBI in the fall of 1945.[17]

The significance of the documents go well beyond questions of guilt, for they help us re-create the world in which the men and women who became spies made their choices. They also give us a glimpse into the attitudes of Soviet handlers towards their American collaborators—a relationship often defined by cynical pragmatism, but occasionally displaying an odd strain of sentimentality. Julius Rosenberg, for example, alternately identified as "Liberal" or "An-tenna" in VENONA, comes through in the Soviet cables (as well as in the memoirs of his handler, Alexander Feklisov) as an ardent true be-liever who, in Feklisov's words "saw his collaboration with Soviet in-telligence as a kind of religious calling."[18] He became so wrapped up in espionage activities that his Soviet superiors worried about him put-ting himself "out of action with overwork."[19]

Another energetic operative who surfaces in VENONA and the Moscow files had also been named before. He was Nathan Gregory Sil-vermaster, a government economist who had been Elizabeth Bentley's main contact in wartime Washington, D.C. Silvermaster, code-named "Pel" and "Robert," was an enthusiast on the Rosenberg model, who elicited warm praise from Soviet intelligence as "a man sincerely de-voted to the party and the Soviet Union . . . politically literate, knows Marxism, a deeply Russian man . . . known in Washington as a pro-gressive liberal . . . [and] understands perfectly that he works for us."[20]

(That last clause, by the way, is worth noting, for it suggests that there were a number of people whose names show up in VENONA and other sources who lacked a perfect understanding of who exactly they were working for when they passed on confidential information.)

In popular imagination, spying is usually linked with attempts to learn military secrets. The KGB's main wartime coup was, of course, unearthing the existence and design of the atomic bomb. Klaus Fuchs, a German refugee who belonged to the British contingent at Los Alamos, turned over the information that, along with Ted Hall's materials, enabled Soviet scientists to replicate the plutonium weapon that destroyed Nagasaki. Julius Rosenberg's connection with atomic espionage was largely serendipitous, the product of the U.S. Army's decision to assign his brother-in-law, David Greenglass, to the Los Alamos machine shop. Other than recruiting Greenglass, and passing along the crude mechanical drawings he supplied, Rosenberg had little involvement with atomic espionage. He was busy facilitating the efforts of his left-wing City College classmates to transmit information from the defense plants and laboratories where they worked. His operations yielded thousands of pages of what the KGB considered "valuable materials" that dealt primarily with electronics and weapons systems. At one point he even handed over a fully assembled proximity fuse for an antiaircraft shell that he had managed to smuggle out of the factory wrapped as a Christmas gift.[21]

Most of the agents whose names crop up in the new sources were not, however, involved in military espionage. They worked in the Treasury and War Departments, including the Office of Strategic Services, or OSS, the precursor of the CIA, and passed along political and economic information—assessments of German industrial output, reports on loan negotiations, and plans for the postwar reorganization of Europe. Yet despite the wealth of information they were receiving, the Russians complained that they lacked sufficient contacts among top policy-makers and they continually pressed their sources for more, and more high-level, material. "We are interested," an April 1942 dispatch explained,

> in the [U.S.] government's plans for the country's foreign and domestic policy, all machinations, backstage negotiations, intrigues, all that is done before this or that decision of the government becomes known

to everybody. . . . . The task is to penetrate into those places where policy is born and developed, where discussions and debates take place,
where policy is completed.[22]

Among the most remarkable revelations that emerged from the new
releases was the extent to which the Communist Party USA was itself
embroiled in Soviet espionage. That individual spies like Julius Rosenberg were Communists is not exactly news. But that the party helped
on a regular basis to recruit spies and vet their political reliability did
come as a surprise, as did the indication that some of its top leaders, including the wartime general secretary, Earl Browder, actually ran espionage operations. Such an arrangement may well have been useful
for convincing timid or politically fastidious recruits that their information was destined for party, not Kremlin, eyes. It also shows that
there were few, if any, services that the leadership of the CPUSA was
not prepared to offer upon demand from Moscow.

The new documents have drawn renewed scholarly and public attention to a long-standing debate among historians about the essential
nature of American communism. On one side of that debate, to use the
language suggested by John Haynes, have been the "traditionalists,"
like Haynes himself and his colleague Harvey Klehr. In books like
Klehr's *The Heyday of American Communism* (1984), and Haynes and
Klehr's *The American Communist Movement: Storming Heaven Itself*
(1992), traditionalists followed the lead of Theodore Draper's top-
down studies of the CPUSA's first decade to argue that whatever local
causes the party may have embraced, "American Communists always
strove to do what Moscow wanted, no more, no less."[23] On the other
side of the debate stood a grouping referred to variously as the "new"
or "revisionist" historians of American communism. In such works as
Mark Naison's *Communists in Harlem During the Depression* (1983),
Robin D.G. Kelley's *Hammer and Hoe: Alabama Communists During
the Great Depression* (1990), and Maurice Isserman's *Which Side Were
You On? The American Communist Party During the Second World War*
(1982), the authors acknowledged Moscow's control of the CPUSA,
but sought as well to explore how tensions between the demands of
foreign-imposed ideological dictates and homegrown political experiences combined to shape a generation of American Communists from
the 1930s through the 1950s.[24]

The conflict between these two camps had been going on for over a decade before the fall of the Soviet Union and the subsequent availability of the new archival sources. It was a fruitful debate and one that was of intense interest to partisans on both sides, but rarely attracted much attention outside the precincts populated by members of the Historians of American Communism. One of the few occasions when it drew a wider audience was the publication of Theodore Draper's two-part series on the "new history of American communism" in the *New York Review of Books* in 1985. Draper mocked those who were then in the process of fashioning new interpretations of the history of the CPUSA as a "minor academic industry," whose practitioners were "a little-noted academic subdivision of the 'Yuppie' social stratum," pining for the salad days of their radical youth in the 1960s, and projecting their nostalgia backwards into a rose-colored view of popular-front communism.[25]

As Draper's acerbic tone suggests, little love was lost between the competing sides in this debate. Ironically, one of the few things that traditionalists and revisionists seemed to agree upon was the irrelevance of espionage in the history of the CPUSA. The word *espionage* did not appear in Theodore Draper's 1985 *New York Review of Books* series, nor did it surface when he returned to the subject with a lengthy review essay in the same magazine in 1994. Irving Howe and Lewis Coser devoted exactly two sentences to espionage in the 600-plus resolutely anti-Stalinist pages of their 1957 study *The American Communist Party: A Critical History;* they concluded that while reports of spying American Communists were not without some basis, they were on the whole "exaggerated." And in 1992, in their book *The American Communist Movement,* Haynes and Klehr concluded that "espionage was not a regular activity of the American C. P."[26]

VENONA and the Moscow documents both revived and recast the debate between traditionalists and revisionists. The previously neglected issue of communist spying was now center stage, an 800-pound gorilla that nobody could ignore. Haynes and Klehr now happily reversed themselves, declaring that "espionage *was* a regular activity of the American Communist party [italics added.]"[27] Traditionalists not only felt that their viewpoint was vindicated by the new documents, but they believed that they in effect owned the VENONA/Moscow archives. The end of the Cold War not only saw the demise of a foreign enemy; for the traditionalists it also demolished the standing of the foe closer to home, and they sounded alternately baffled and scornful when confronting continued disagreement. "One suspects," Haynes would write in *The Journal of Cold War Studies* in 2000, that "revisionist complaints about [Cold War] triumphalism stem mainly from an unwillingness to confront the damning evidence that has emerged from the long-closed Soviet and East European archives. Having invested so much emotion and intellectual effort in portraying the [American Communist Party] as a loyal opposition that sought only social justice and 'a better world for the masses,' revisionists want nothing more than to avoid discussing the new documents that undermine their cherished vision." [28]

For the traditionalists, VENONA and the Moscow archives ended any need for further debate: according to Haynes and Klehr, "the CPUSA was indeed a fifth column working inside and against the United States in the Cold War." [29] Such a conception had, of course, been the standard refrain of anticommunists of all stripes in the late 1940s and 1950s, and the conventional wisdom of the earlier era took on a new life in the VENONA era. As Herbert Romerstein and Eric Breindel sweepingly assert in *The Venona Secrets:* "[A]ny American Communist would have been proud to be chosen to spy for the Soviet Union." [30]

But the VENONA files/Moscow archives can be read in a variety of ways. Spying and Communist Party membership were not, in fact, identical categories in the 1930s and 1940s. Of the approximately 50,000 party members in World War II, 49,700 were uninvolved in espionage, even taking the highest estimate of communist participation in the KGB's network. The average Communist in 1944 was far more likely to be a fur worker or a public school teacher than a policy maker in the Treasury Department, and thus an unlikely candidate for a Soviet operative to approach for workplace gossip. And even among the tiny minority of Communists and their fellow travelers who did occupy sensitive posts, not all were necessarily approached or agreed to spy on behalf of the Soviet Union. Owen Lattimore, the East Asian scholar and State Department consultant pilloried by Joe McCarthy as Moscow's "top spy" and "Alger Hiss's boss," is conspicuously absent from the new sources.

VENONA and the Moscow archives thus bear less resemblance to a smoking gun than to a double-edged sword, which is to say that they can cut in more than one way, suggesting innocence as well as guilt. The new sources raise as many questions as they answer. Fragmentary and far from transparent, they need to be handled with the kind of informed skepticism that historians have traditionally applied to sources drawn from police and intelligence records. Using the same set of documents from VENONA, Klehr and Haynes exonerate while Breindel and Romerstein indict J. Robert Oppenheimer on charges of serving as a Soviet agent while directing the Manhattan Project. In a more recent book, *Sacred Secrets: How Soviet Intelligence Operations Changed American History,* Jerrold and Leona Schecter produce a memo to KGB chief Lavrenty Beria that seems to suggest Oppenheimer's complicity in espionage efforts at Los Alamos, but fail to account for the apparent contradiction between this new piece of evidence, and the material already available in the VENONA files.[31]

A similarly vexing issue—and one that we cannot answer with the currently available materials—concerns the actual impact of Soviet intelligence operations. In a court of law, it would be sufficient to prove that spying took place to achieve a conviction. But historians are not prosecuting attorneys, and questions of guilt or innocence are not the only ones that need to concern them. They have a responsibility to ask broader questions—commonsense questions—including what difference Soviet spying actually made.

This is easier in the realm of military espionage. The materials transmitted from Los Alamos by Klaus Fuchs and Ted Hall sped up the Soviet acquisition of nuclear weapons by several years and may well have contributed to Stalin's decision to give Kim Il Sung a green light to invade South Korea.[32]

But the picture blurs when we turn to political intrigue. The Schecters boldly state in the subtitle of their book that Soviet spies "Changed American History." As an example, they argue that Harry Dexter White of the Treasury Department, acting on Soviet orders, played a major role in policy decisions that worsened Japanese-American relations in the years leading up to World War II, and that led ultimately to an unnecessary war in the Pacific. This assertion echoes ancient charges from the far right that Roosevelt, or those around him, somehow connived in the Japanese attack on Pearl Harbor. Their argument borders on what Hofstadter described as the "paranoid style" in American politics, in which all history becomes the product of conspiracy. Some conservative historians uncritically embraced the Schechters' argument; Harvey Klehr, to his credit did not, and in a review in the *Weekly Standard,* called the book "confusing and not entirely persuasive," at least insofar as it vastly overstated White's influence over the Roosevelt administration's diplomatic and military policy.[33] One could also argue that the Schecters' argument absolves the Japanese military and government from a pattern of aggression in Asia, which long preceded Harry Dexter White's appearance in policy-making circles in Washington.

None of this, of course, vindicates White's involvement in Soviet intelligence operations. But it does suggest a useful counterfactual question: If there had been no Harry Dexter White, no Nathan Gregory Silvermaster, or no Alger Hiss, would the history of the world really have been all that different between the 1930s and 1950s? Would the Soviet Union have collapsed, or Stalin have moderated his policies, or the United States have gained the upper hand in determining the postwar fate of Eastern Europe or China? Nothing revealed thus far in the new sources available in Washington or Moscow establish any credible basis for making such an argument.

Stripped of the elements of paranoia and hyperbole that the Schecters and some others have brought to the discussion, there is still much to be learned from VENONA and the Moscow archives. For historians of the left, they provide a starting point for deciphering the mixture of estrangement and faith that created a romance of the clandestine among American Communists in the 1930s and 1940s, and led some to become involved in Soviet espionage efforts.

Before we can understand what made people become spies for the Soviet Union, we need to understand what made them become Communists. And to understand that requires a feeling for historical tragedy, for the ways in which honorable aspirations can lead to dishonorable outcomes, a capacity all too rarely displayed in triumphalist readings of the history of the Cold War. Though ultimately they must be judged by their record and not their intentions, the early Bolsheviks themselves did not foresee the circumstances that would lead them to become the architects of a new totalitarian order in the Soviet Union. Nor were the grimmer aspects of Stalin's rule the source of attraction the "Soviet experiment" held for millions of people around the world who joined and sometimes risked their lives on behalf of the communist movement. The old socialist aspirations of fraternity and equality flowed into the movement that from the 1920s through the 1940s seemed to many on the left in the United States, as elsewhere, the best and often the only available vehicle for their realization.

When the Communist International, or Comintern, as it was called, was founded in Moscow in 1919, at a moment of revolutionary fervor and illusion, it promised to set the world ablaze. The Bolshevik revolution was a year and a half old; a spirit of working-class unrest was abroad from Seattle to Budapest; revolutionary socialists, syndicalists, and anarchists everywhere looked hopefully to Moscow for guidance in what appeared to be the imminent final conflict with capitalism. Then, within a year or so, it became apparent that the prospects for revolution in the industrialized West were either fast receding or had been vastly exaggerated. There would be no Soviet Germany, Britain, or United States ready to link arms with its Russian brother. Socialism, it seemed, by grim necessity would have to first be built in only one country. With their own revolutions postponed, the Bolsheviks' foreign admirers clung all the more tightly to the inspiration provided by the lone outpost of proletarian power. The Russians, first among equals in the early days of the Comintern, became the unquestionable source of doctrinal authority.

One of the chief lessons the Bolshevik revolution taught its adherents was the necessity for a strictly disciplined, secretive party in the struggle against capitalism—a lesson that was proclaimed from Moscow to represent the essence of "Leninism." Wherever Communists organized, be it under an autocracy or in a "bourgeois democracy," the same set of organizational principles were thought to apply. And there was more. At its second congress, held in Petrograd and Moscow in 1920, the Communist International adopted twenty-one conditions for admission as member parties. Third on the list was the condition that parties must establish an "illegal apparatus . . . to assist the revolution."[34] This inflammatory language did not necessarily mean the commission of crimes such as terrorism, sabotage, or espionage. Rather, taken in original context, it meant that Communists everywhere had to be prepared to carry on the party's activities under the kind of difficult or repressive political conditions that the Bolsheviks had faced under the tsar. In the early years of American communism in the United States, this condition translated not so much into illegal action of any sort as into an obedient, formulaic gibberish, strikingly illustrated by the decision of the CPUSA's newspaper, the *Daily Worker,* to print a resolution in 1929 calling for "all necessary preparations for illegal functioning of the leading organs of the Party."[35] Real conspirators do not reveal their intentions to "function illegally" in press releases; that is a gesture for romantic amateurs.

"Illegal functioning" did, however, roughly describe the kind of quasi-underground existence forced upon Communists in much of the United States for much of the CPUSA's history. If the Communists were overly skeptical of the virtues of bourgeois democracy, this skepticism was not entirely the product of having pored over the pages of *What Is to Be Done?* too many times. When the party came into existence in 1919–1920, all left-wing organizations—communist, socialist, and anarchist alike—were being treated by the authorities as illegal conspiracies. The first red scare was at its height. Immigration officials were rounding up foreign-born radicals for deportation, and the New York State Legislature's Lusk Committee was raiding Socialist Party headquarters. In 1919 the U.S. Congress refused to seat the moderate Socialist Victor Berger though he had been duly elected by the voters of Milwaukee; the following year the New York State Legislature gave the same treatment to six legally elected socialist assemblymen. In such an atmosphere, it seemed to make perfect sense for the just-hatched communist movement to scorn conventional politics and embrace an underground existence. Ironically, when local police and federal agents swooped down on the CP's 1922 convention to arrest the delegates, the party was just authorizing its return to legality. Even during much of the so-called "red decade" of the 1930s, it was still hard for Communists to function openly outside of a few big cities. Local authorities would break up meetings, arrest the speakers, and run party organizers out of town. Immigrants could be deported, civil servants could lose their jobs, and demonstrators could be beaten and jailed by the police.[36]

The penalties were especially severe for party members in the labor movement, the magnet for so many of the CP's most dedicated and energetic cadres. Much of industrial America remained a police state as far as labor unions were concerned. Long after the first red scare had faded from the headlines, union organizers, even those with impeccably non- or anti-Leninist political credentials, had to operate secretly if they were to recruit workers in the automobile plants of Flint, Michigan, the steel mills along the Monongahela River, or the farming communities in California's Imperial Valley. Especially for those party members who tried to set up industrial unions or work with sharecroppers in the deep South, physical violence and the threat of death was an ever-present reality. Thus most Communists in the labor movement outside of the New York garment district kept their affiliation secret.

The party's commitment to internationalism also drew its adherents into the shadowy networks of the antifascist underground in Europe and the anticolonial revolutions in Asia, Africa, and elsewhere, where conspiratorial tactics were a sign of neither romantic affectation nor ideological dogmatism, but a simple matter of stark necessity. The American Communists who fought in the International Brigades during the Spanish Civil War often traveled with false names and papers before being delivered to the battlefield by a well-organized recruiting operation. Party leaders received additional exposure to this clandestine world when they went overseas to work with the Comintern or study at the Lenin School in Moscow. Steve Nelson, a Lenin School graduate, went to Berlin in 1933 carrying instructions from Moscow to the German communist underground. Later he smuggled funds to Chinese Communists in Shanghai before going off to service in the International Brigades in Spain.[37] Others worked more directly with Soviet intelligence agencies in underground operations abroad. In a 1938 letter to Georgi Dimitrov that Haynes, Klehr, and Firsov discovered in the Moscow archives and reprinted in *The Secret World*, CPUSA leader Earl Browder noted that his own sister, Marguerite Browder, had for the past seven years "been working for the foreign department of the NKVD, in various European countries." (It is worth noting, incidentally, that Browder's purpose in writing was to ask for his sister's release from her intelligence duties and her return to the U.S. Browder feared what "hostile circles" in the U.S. would do with the information if Marguerite's activities ever became public.[38])

In the 1930s a spirit of left-wing cosmopolitanism was in the air. One did not have to be a seasoned revolutionary to feel its pull. "Everything in the outside world seemed to be moving toward some final decision," American literary critic Alfred Kazin recalled in his memoir *Growing Up in the Thirties.* Kazin, who came of age in a socialist immigrant household in New York City, did not in the end become a Communist, but remembered well the appeal of the movement to himself and his contemporaries:

> There seemed to be no division between my effort at personal liberation and the apparent effort of humanity to deliver itself. Reading Silone and Malraux, discovering the Beethoven string quartets and having love affairs were part of the great pattern in Spain, in Nazi concentration camps, in Fontemara and in the Valley of the Ebro, in the Salinas Valley of California that Steinbeck was describing with love for the oppressed, in the boilers of Chinese locomotives where Chiang Kai-shek was burning the brave and sacrificial militants of the Chinese Communists. Wherever I went now, I felt the moral contagion of a single idea.[39]

For those in Kazin's generation who took what then may have seemed the next logical step and joined the party, the choice did not require any deep soul-searching about potential conflict between domestic and international loyalties. American Communist Party recruits in the 1930s believed they were signing onto a worldwide class and antifascist struggle, not enlisting on one side in a superpower conflict. Unfortunately, the "great pattern" in humanity's struggle for emancipation—that "moral contagion of a single idea"—did not leave much room for ambiguities; if the Soviet Union was sending arms to Loyalist Spain while the Western democracies appeased Hitler, it didn't necessarily mean (as it seemed at the time to many) that the Soviet system itself should be celebrated as a higher, truer form of democracy than that prevailing in the West. Communists remained deeply, willfully, and, yes, tragically, blind to the true nature of Stalin's regime. British historian E.P. Thompson, writing in 1957 in a journal called *New Reasoner* (better known in a later incarnation as *New Left Review*), described the process through which some of the communist movement's greatest strengths were transformed into its most appalling defects:

In storm and defeat, in concentration camp and partisan detachment, there grew up that intensity of self-abnegation, that sense of acting as the instrument of historical necessity, above all, that intense loyalty to the Party. . . . [Stalinism] turned these virtues into instruments of destruction. The centre of moral authority was removed from the community or the conscience of the individual and entrusted to the Party.[40]

Even more than others in the communist movement, one might assume that those who agreed to serve as spies were likely to have surrendered the center of moral authority to the party. Here too VENONA and the Moscow archives hold some surprises for the careful investigator. Though some of the KGB's American collaborators threw themselves immediately and enthusiastically into espionage activities, Soviet spymasters often had to go to elaborate lengths to draw even the most committed Communists into cooperation, and then, after documents had begun to exchange hands, they would often maintain elaborate fictions about the final destination and purpose of the purloined materials. Elizabeth Bentley and Jacob Golos, her lover-*cum*-handler, struggled constantly to isolate their KGB superiors from their Washington operatives, fearing that direct contact with the Russians would alert their more skittish sources that their materials were going to Soviet intelligence agencies instead of party headquarters in New York. As one KGB agent reported to Moscow about a potential espionage recruit in 1937: "He has very little experience and sometimes behaves like a child in his romanticism. He thinks he is working for the Comintern and he must be left in this delusion for a while."[41]

Even after recruitment, Soviet spymasters had to constantly worry whether their informants would stay recruited. In the 1930s, when the groundwork was being laid for the Soviet espionage network in the United States, the worst of the Stalin-era purges were taking place. The spectacle of the self-devouring Soviet elite was not good for the morale of the men and women who had risked so much in agreeing to spy on their behalf. On the whole, ironically, those Americans who had crossed over into the communist espionage underground in the 1930s seemed to pay closer attention to the dark side of the "Soviet experiment" than their peers in the aboveground movement. Whittaker Chambers is the best-known example, but there were others as well. Laurence Duggan badgered his KGB controller, Itzak Akhmerov, with his doubts. "He claims he cannot digest events in the Soviet Union," Akhmerov cabled Moscow in early 1938. "He thinks something is fundamentally wrong, since there cannot be so many members of the Right and Left opposition [within the Soviet Communist Party] who become traitors."[42]

Though some interpreters of VENONA have argued that any Communist would have been thrilled to be asked to spy on behalf of the Soviet Union, the evidence suggests otherwise. Rarely did the Russians send even the most eager recruits after really big secrets until they had gotten them used to the idea of handing over materials of considerably less consequence, with little or no obvious harm to the security interests of the United States. Harry Gold, later to gain notoriety as the courier who carried data on the atomic bomb from Los Alamos to his Soviet controller in New York, got his start in industrial espionage in the 1930s by stealing the secret of minor chemical processing procedures from his employer, the Pennsylvania Sugar Company, and that (according to Ronald Radosh and Joyce Milton) was only after much soul-searching and delay.[43] Another important figure in the Kremlin's espionage operations, Morris Cohen, accepted as his first KGB assignment the task of keeping tabs on the pro-Nazi German-American Bund in New York City, while Elizabeth Bentley did the same for Italian fascist sympathizers.

Even those individuals who began their espionage careers passing along official government secrets could sometimes persuade themselves that their actions were harmless, or even beneficial for American interests, properly understood. They were internationalists whose political allegiances transcended national boundaries, but they also believed that all nations' true interests were essentially bound up with those of the USSR, and what they thought of as the Soviets' peaceful, progressive agenda. Helping the Soviet Union build its own bomb was, Ted Hall explained, "developing a pathway towards a better, more harmonious world."[44]

These were delusions, and it is easy in retrospect to feel morally superior to those who could hold them. Easy, but not sufficient. To see the world as American Communists did in 1944 requires a leap of imagination that in the era of Cold War triumphalism becomes an ever greater challenge, but worth the effort if our purpose is historical understanding. In 1944 the U.S. and the USSR were allied against a supremely evil and aggressive Nazi Germany. The Soviet Union was doing most of the fighting and sacrificing in the common war effort. As Elizabeth Bentley explained to her FBI interlocutors in 1945, her contacts in Washington "felt that the information they obtained was to help an ally, Russia, who up to the time the U.S. entered the war was having great difficulty in fighting their war against Germany."[45] Her chief contact, Treasury Department official Nathan Gregory Silvermaster, passed along U.S. military intelligence estimates of the Wehrmacht's strength and deployment to his Soviet handlers in the summer of 1941; if such information wasn't already being made available to America's new ally in the war against the Nazis, it must have seemed to Silvermaster that it should be freely shared. Even as late as 1949, when the Truman administration's Loyalty Review Board cleared Bentley's agent, William Remington, it did so in part on the grounds that "our government's attitude toward Russia in 1942 was such that giving the Russians information with respect to the progress of our war effort wouldn't necessarily spell disloyalty."[46]

The 1930s were the seedtime for Soviet espionage in the United States, and the first half of the 1940s were harvest time. However spectacular its wartime record, KGB successes within the United States were short-lived. In the fall of 1945, the defection of Soviet code clerk Igor Gouzenko in Canada and that of Elizabeth Bentley in New York crippled Soviet intelligence-gathering in Washington. The Russians immediately broke off their contacts; and when they tried to restart their apparatus, most of their earlier sources had long since resigned or been purged from their government jobs. The subsequent decoding of espionage reports in the VENONA project led in a few years' time to the detection and arrest of most of those involved in the theft of atomic secrets during World War II. By the time Joe McCarthy came on the scene with his charges that hundreds of Soviet agents and spies remained in positions of influence within the American government, the reality was quite different.

The VENONA/Moscow documents are now playing into the triumphalism spawned by the end of the Cold War, reinforcing the demand that, as Haynes puts it, historians of the era "celebrate the West's moral victory over the Soviet Union."[47] The loser's archives are thrown open, and selectively picked over for the most sensational and damning documents; the winner's archives, in contrast, remain largely off-limits but are selectively opened to provide materials that celebrate its Cold War triumphs (such as the American penetration of the mysteries of the VENONA code.) The sheer mass of new materials threatens to obscure the need for critical perspective on their selectivity. The temptation is to conclude, as one leading diplomatic historian did in the title of a book devoted to "rethinking Cold War history," that "We Now Know" who was to blame for the Cold War, and that was Joseph Stalin and his successors. End of story.[48]

If the essential righteousness of the American Cold War effort is now beyond serious debate, what about the domestic Cold War? Were the domestic red-hunters on the right track all along after all? A penitent Nicholas von Hoffman, usually a stalwart supporter of liberalism, confessed in a column in the *Washington Post* in April 1996 that he now understood that "The Age of McCarthyism . . . was not the simple witch hunt of the innocent by the malevolent as two generations of high school and college students have been taught." (A Google search on "Nicholas von Hoffman and Joe McCarthy" turns up scores of right-wing Web sites citing that phrase as the ultimate vindication of McCarthyism.) "McCarthy may have exaggerated the problem, but not by much. The government was the workplace of perhaps 100 communist agents in 1943–1945. He just didn't know their names."[49] Here too apparently, We Now Know.

But when McCarthy made his charges in February 1950, he wasn't talking about Communist agents in 1943–45; he was talking about *current* employees of the U.S. State Department. He was not simply "exaggerating" a problem—he was making it up.[50] That is one thing we do know now, thanks to a 1951 memorandum found in the Moscow archives in which KGB officials acknowledged to their superiors that they no longer had any significant inside sources within the American government: "the most serious drawback in organizing intelligence in the U.S. is . . . the lack of agents in the State Department, intelligence service, counterintelligence service, and other most important U.S. governmental institutions."[51] We also now know that by 1953, the year of the Rosenbergs' execution, the FBI had quietly written off the American Communist Party as a serious espionage threat.[52]

The real danger here is not that Joe McCarthy's reputation will undergo historical rehabilitation; the rather strange work of hagiography published by Arthur Herman in 2000 has found few admirers among historians, save in the conservative journal *Continuity* (the most critical thing that *Continuity*'s reviewer Kevin Smant could bring himself to say about Senator McCarthy was that he "inspired, in a negative way, radical historians to engage in revisionist work on the historiography of the Cold War.").[53] Nor, perhaps, is the damage to the reputation of this or that long-deceased federal employee mentioned in VENONA all that important, save to surviving family or friends. The passionate debates that have filled pages and pages of letters columns in *The Nation,* like those of rival Civil War buffs or grassy-knoll aficionados in other publications, may seem increasingly besides the point in coming years to the more complicated business of coming to terms with the history of America's rise to world power.

What future historians may find of most interest in the release and reception of the VENONA/Moscow documents is not so much the revelations they contain about the covert doings of left-wing subversives in the mid–twentieth century, but rather the use the documents found in the hands of right-wing counter-subversives at the end of the twentieth and beginning of the twenty-first century. "The unveiling of Venona," Ann Coulter pronounced in her bestselling 2003 screed *Treason,* "was as close to Judgment Day for liberals as we'll ever get in this life."[54] As George Will candidly noted in 1995, conservatives welcomed the arrival of volumes like Klehr and Haynes's *Secret World of American Communism* not so much as a scholarly achievement, but as a weapon to be wielded in the "important" political task of "discrediting" the left.

And one of the things that future historians may find puzzling is just who and what this late-twentieth- and early twenty-first-century "left" was thought to consist of by its opponents, and why its discrediting seemed of such momentous import to them. The Soviet Union was gone and its memory discredited. American communism survived only as a decrepit sect. Never in its entire historical existence had American capitalism enjoyed greater prestige, or confronted fewer ideological challenges at home or abroad from the political left. (Obviously the United States still had enemies in the world, but the Al Qaeda network did not target the World Trade Center because of anything its adherents encountered in the collected works of Marx and Lenin; Osama bin Laden got his start in the jihad business as an anti-

Soviet warrior in Afghanistan, backed by the largest covert operation in the history of American intelligence.)

Those future historians will have to come to their own conclusion. But to us it seems as if turn-of-the-century conservatives could not bring themselves to let go of a former adversary who had served so well and so long to stoke the fires of their purifyingly self-righteous anger. Thus it somehow came about that academic historians who dissent from the current triumphalist mood—of all powerless species of political beings—have found themselves substituted in recent conservative demonology for earlier and more formidable "un-American" ancestors. In the mid-1990s, during the controversy over the Smithsonian's *Enola Gay* exhibit, it was diplomatic historians who were denounced as "revisionists" (as if that were a derogatory term within a profession that is constantly rewriting the past to account for new information and interpretations) for arguing that ending the "Good War" may not have required the incineration of Hiroshima and Nagasaki. At the same time, and increasingly, it has been historians who have failed to toe the conservative line on the history of American communism, and the related topic of Soviet espionage, who have been pilloried as the enemy within. John Haynes, in a relatively mild recent example of this substitution process, explained to readers of the *Journal of Cold War Studies* in 2000 that "most" of the historians who read the VENONA/Moscow archives differently than he did "shared a hostility to capitalism, anticommunism, and the American constitutional order." Haynes went on to argue that revisionist historians regarded "American Communists, whatever their faults, as kindred spirits in the fight against capitalism and established American institutions."[55]

Though regarding the revisionists as politically errant, Haynes at least did not exaggerate their power to warp the minds of fellow Americans (in that he followed the lead of Theodore Draper, who back in the 1980s dismissed the new historians of communism as just so many "yuppies"—less a dangerous political adversary and more a fit topic for derision). The same cannot be said of some of those who have taken up Haynes and Klehr's side in the debate over the meaning of the VENONA/Moscow documents. In the pages of the *Washington Times,* the *Wall Street Journal,* and on various right-wing Web sites and talk shows, the "paranoid style" reasserted itself time and again. If left-wing conspiracy was not necessarily the motive force of history, it was certainly the motive force behind the writing and teaching of the subject in the nation's institutions of higher learning. In the words of *Washington Times* columnist Arnold Beichman—who cited as his authority a talk that Haynes gave to the Heritage Foundation—the collected works of revisionist historians of American communism amounted to the "dominating orthodoxies in mainstream historiography today."[56] Similarly, for red-diaper baby-turned-conservative gadfly David Horowitz, the "genetic heirs" of the Stalinist left "dominate the liberal-arts faculties of the nation's elite universities and thus the historiography of the Cold War itself."[57] Roger Kimball, writing in the *Wall Street Journal,* offered no less alarming a portrayal of the vast powers of revisionist historians to spread sinister nonsense when he congratulated Haynes and Klehr for "having the courage to break with the 'prevailing academic consensus' " that the "CPUSA was merely an impatient version of American liberalism . . . an independent political organization, free from Soviet control."[58]

It must be a heady feeling to dictate the terms of the "prevailing academic consensus"; alas, it is not one that revisionist historians of American communism have experienced. To the extent that there is still something that can be called a mainstream in the profession, it is probably represented by the collection of thick narrative tomes in the Oxford History of the United States series that are written by leading American historians and designed for use in undergraduate survey courses. The volume for the period of the CPUSA's greatest strength, entitled *Freedom From Fear: The American People in Depression and War, 1929–1945,* garnered for its author, David M. Kennedy, the Pulitzer Prize for history in 1999. Kennedy barely mentions the Communist Party at all in *Freedom from Fear,* and then usually disparagingly. The only two sources for CPUSA history he cites in his otherwise detailed bibliography are Harvey Klehr and John Haynes's *The American Communist Movement,* and Irving Howe and Lewis Coser's *The American Communist Party.*

The VENONA/Moscow archives have much to teach us. But they will prove "documents of a dangerous tendency" if all they do is reinforce simplistic readings of the past meant to serve current partisan purposes of a vindictive right: "Judgment Day for Liberals," in Ann Coulter's chilling phrase. We write at a moment when university faculties are being maligned as "the weak link in America's response to the attack" of September 11, when right-wing Web sites report on dissenting voices in the academy as a "fifth column," and when President George W. Bush has branded those who question his explanations for the U.S. invasion of Iraq as "revisionist historians."[59] We have seen this kind of thing happen before, and the precedents are not encouraging. The opening of closed archives is an important step forward in advancing our understanding of the complex and tragic history of communism in the United States; better still would be evidence of the opening of closed minds.

6

The Myth of the Berlin Blockade and the Early Cold War

Carolyn Eisenberg

As the Bush administration expands its "War on Terrorism," top officials eagerly invoke the heroic days of the early Cold War. Speaking at Johns Hopkins University, National Security Advisor Condoleezza Rice reflected that "an earthquake of the magnitude of 9/11 can shift the tectonic plates of international politics." The attacks on the Pentagon and World Trade Center were bringing to an end the time of transition, inaugurated by the fall of the Soviet Union. "Before the clay is dry again, America, . . . must take advantage of this new opportunity." This, she opined is "a period akin to 1945 to 1947, when American leadership expanded the number of free and democratic states—Japan and Germany among the great powers—to create a new balance of power that favored freedom." [1]

It is not surprising that the inception of a "containment" policy should be the positive reference point for the present crisis. For with the demise of the USSR and the ending of the Cold War, that early history has been enshrined in public memory as a time when great American leaders grasped the immense challenge that lay before them and responded brilliantly.

Despite decades of revisionist scholarship on the early Cold War, the findings never penetrated into the mainstream of American culture. Within the field of diplomatic history, critical historians have received substantial recognition for the quality of their work. However, the constraints of commercial publishing, book reviewing, and textbook writing, and the unwillingness of the mass media to incorporate dissenting perspectives has limited their access to audiences outside the colleges and universities.

When CNN produced its highly publicized, multipart series *Cold War,* it relied on the centrist historian John Gaddis as its chief consultant, and simply excluded alternative views. To this date, the most widely read book on the subject of the early Cold War remains David McCullough's Pulitzer Prize–winning biography of Harry Truman.[2] The work offers an inspiring portrait of the plainspoken man from Missouri, who rose unexpectedly to the pinnacle of world power and saved Western Europe from the Soviet hordes. Professional historians might object that McCullough did little work in the archives and relied almost entirely on other secondary works, interviews, and news articles from the period. Yet this much-promoted biography dovetailed with the conventional wisdom and captured the popular imagination.

If historical revisionism was marginal before the Cold War ended, the disintegration of the Soviet bloc has made it virtually invisible. For with the pulling down of the Berlin Wall, the routing of the communist regimes in Eastern Europe, and the final dissolution of the Soviet Union itself, the doctrine of "containment" seemed vindicated. Following George Kennan's 1947 advice, American leaders had pursued an "adroit and vigilant application of counter-force at a series of constantly shifting geographical and political points"[3] It had taken decades, but by assembling overwhelming political, economic, and military power, and confronting challenges across the globe, the "free world" had triumphed.

The self-congratulation inherent in this historical memory informed American foreign policy in the immediate aftermath of the Cold War. What had worked so well in the past against the USSR could be useful in the future. In particular, the first President Bush was loathe to dismantle the American military apparatus. As his subordinates (among them Condoleezza Rice) negotiated the reunification of Germany, they were careful to insist that it be brought into the NATO alliance. This was especially distressing to Soviet President Mikhail Gorbachev, who apprehended that such a step would undermine his standing at home. Yet his argument that a reknit Europe had no need for a western military alliance was discounted.

Moreover during the Clinton years, the administration insulted the

Russian leadership even more directly by choosing, together with its European allies, to expand NATO through the inclusion of three former nations of the Warsaw Pact: Poland, Hungary, and the Czech Republic. The occasion for that provocative decision was appropriately enough the fiftieth anniversary of the Berlin blockade and the western airlift.

In the traditionalist narratives of the early Cold War, the East-West confrontation in Berlin appears to be the defining moment. According to these accounts, Stalin had chosen to starve a city into submission but the courageous Western powers, spearheaded by the United States, had resisted fiercely. To overcome the harsh "blockade" of the city, Truman had sent the airplanes: huge C-54s landing on the outskirts of Berlin every two minutes. This action was immortalized in the still-distributed photos of hungry Berliners looking to the sky as the planes swooped into Tempelhof airport, carrying the food and fuel to get them through the winter.

As a way of celebrating this dramatic moment and heralding the plan to expand NATO, in May 1998 President Clinton spoke at a "remembrance ceremony" at Tempelhof airport.[4] He reminded the audience of how "the fate of free Berlin had hung by a thread." Except for "a few visionaries" nobody believed that it was possible to supply a city by air. But the planes were sent anyway and "as they came and went and came and went again, the airlift became a sharing of the soul—a story that tells people never to lose faith, adversity can be conquered, prayers can be answered, hopes realized, freedom is worth standing up for."

This vision of the past was meant to be inspirational, as the story of the airlift had always been. Yet the official account had always been inaccurate, as neatly demonstrated by U.S. military historian William Stivers in a little-noticed article appearing in *Diplomatic History* (1997).[5] Stivers convincingly proved that there never was a Berlin blockade in any ordinary usage of the term. He acknowledged that the Soviets shut down the access routes from the western zones of Germany into the city. However, "no effort was made . . . to seal off the western sectors from either East Berlin or the surrounding countryside. As a result, a flood of goods—roughly half a million tons . . . entered the western sectors from Soviet area sources." If the Berliners were saved from starvation in the winter of 1948–1949, they might well have thanked Stalin along with Harry Truman and British Prime Minister Clement Attlee.

Yet the misrepresentation of the Soviet "blockade" is tied to deeper misunderstandings about the nature of this first major crisis of the early Cold War. In the ensuing article, I suggest three propositions: First, the Berlin crisis was never about the freedom of the city, but about the Western decision to create a separate West German government in violation of Yalta and Potsdam. Second, that the American and British determination to push ahead with partition precluded a diplomatic solution and seriously undermined the United Nations. And third, that this antipathy to compromise created a necessity for overwhelming military power and a usable nuclear arsenal.

A more clearheaded view of this U.S.-Soviet confrontation points to some wider themes. For it challenges the assumption that the division of Berlin and the associated split of Germany and the European continent were simply artifacts of Stalin's avarice. And it undermines the conventional belief that forty years of political polarization and military face-off were unavoidable short of Soviet surrender.

The Bush ideologues may find their model in the grand designs of the past. But for those outside the circle, it is useful to explore what happened the last time a small group of officials turned danger into "enormous opportunity," and set out to remake the world. Did they, as Condoleezza Rice proclaims, create "a new balance of power that favored freedom"? Or was the effect of their handiwork an imbalance of power that spawned needless repression and war?

I.

The Soviets committed many sins in occupied Germany, but the promotion of schism was not one of them. Partition was an Anglo-American decision reached during the spring of 1947, and made final during the November Conference of Foreign Ministers.[6] Central to American and British thinking was the desire to incorporate the west German zones into the Marshall Plan and to deny the Soviets any voice in West European recovery. The prospective division of Germany was threatening to Russian interests because their zone had less people, less land, and less industrial wealth than those of the west. If Germany was cut in two, they would lose their access to the Ruhr and face the prospect of a rump state that in alliance with Western Europe could become economically and even militarily powerful.

By late 1947, the Americans were anticipating that, once they and the British began to create a separate West German state, the Soviets would retaliate in Berlin.[7] Western occupation rights in the city were based on a zonal agreement that had been approved at Yalta and presumed quadripartite governance of the country. Western forces had entered the city on July 25, 1945, as part of a general redeployment of national armies into the prescribed zones and a decision to activate the four-power Allied Control Council.[8] It was clear that the abandonment of the quadripartite project would undermine the basis for a Western presence in Berlin, given the city's location inside the Soviet zone. U.S. policy-makers briefly entertained the thought that by negotiating a unified currency reform, which would facilitate interzonal trade, Stalin would more easily accept a divided country. However by March 1948 the State Department had decided that the benefits of a quadripartite currency would not outweigh the disadvantage of continued Soviet involvement in the West German economy. Although the four powers were close to an accord, it instructed U.S. Military Governor Lucius Clay to scuttle the talks.[9]

Shutting out the Russians was one of many obstacles faced by the Americans and British. West European political leaders, most volubly the French, were reluctant to form a national German government, even one based on the western portion of the country. Their fear was that a politically independent albeit partitioned Germany would be a potential military threat if allowed to reconstruct its economy with large-scale American aid. Meanwhile, the West German politicians whose cooperation was indispensable were loathe to take responsibility for severing connections with the eastern zone.[10]

During March, the Six Power London Conference (comprised of the U.S., U.K., France, the Netherlands, Belgium, and Luxembourg) grudgingly authorized the three Western military governors to outline the principles for a West German state.[11] The Soviets reacted by walking out of the Allied Control Council and imposing restrictions on rail and highway traffic into Berlin. Their actions sent ripples of alarm through Washington and London, but did not produce any reconsideration of partition.[12] By late April the Russians had retreated, lifting most of their new regulations and signaling a desire for further talks on currency.

The shift was the opening phase of the May "peace scare" in which Moscow seemed to be bidding for negotiations on a wide spectrum of international issues.[13] U.S. policy-makers regarded the overtures skeptically, perceiving that fresh talks would aggravate Western differences over German reconstruction and partition.[14] The overriding priority for both the Americans and the British was to get the forthcoming session of the London Conference to authorize a West German constituent assembly that would draft a new constitution. Any prospect of a settlement with the Soviets would provide the West Europeans with an excuse to delay. It therefore seemed wiser to forgo further diplomacy.

When the London Conference reconvened, its proceedings were as fractious as anticipated. Whereas the Americans were prepared to ease security restrictions on western Germany in order to aid the formation of a new government, the West Europeans were less sanguine. The lenient American attitude on such issues as reparations, level of industry, supervision of the Ruhr, and a prospective disarmament treaty fanned their objections to a constituent assembly. By June 1948, congressional passage of the European recovery plan gave U.S. officials sufficient leverage to wrap up an agreement in London.[15]

However, no sooner was the agreement signed than a ferocious battle erupted in the French Assembly over its terms.[16] With American and British diplomats covertly lobbying the individual representatives, Foreign Minister Bidault was able to eke out a narrow victory over his opponents. Yet the publicity surrounding the French quarrel enhanced the fears of West German politicians,[17] who apprehended that the London Accords might give them fresh responsibilities without commensurate authority. And there was also the excruciating matter of the forfeited eastern zone. If a government was created for West Germany, what would be the impact on friends and relatives who lived under Soviet occupation? And would the West German public buy the explanation that the east had already been lost?

These rumbles notwithstanding, immediately following the decision of the French National Assembly, the Americans raced to effect partition. On June 18, U.S. Military Governor Lucius Clay informed

his Soviet counterpart, Marshal Vassily Sokolovsky, that a currency reform would be instituted within forty-eight hours for the western
zones. Sokolovsky replied furiously that "by your illegal decision you,
without the knowledge and agreement of the Control Council . . . effect a separate currency reform in Western Germany, whereby you liq-
uidate the unity of money and complete the split of Germany."[18] In
response, the Soviets instituted their own reform by affixing stickers to
the old currency and declaring this legal tender for both the zone and
Berlin.[19] When the Western powers retaliated by introducing their
new marks into the former German capital, the Russian military authorities cut off the electricity and stopped all railroads, barges, cars,
trucks, and pedestrians traveling between the western sectors of Berlin
and the western zones.

As the Americans understood, the western currency reform threatened to disrupt the economy of the eastern zone. However, the Soviet
"blockade" was not simply about currency. Rather it was the long-
expected Russian response to the impending formation of a West German government. For months, Moscow had signaled that if the
Western powers created a separate state and abandoned four-power
control of Germany, they would be effectively nullifying the provisions of Yalta that provided for a Western military presence in Berlin.[20]

From a tactical standpoint, the Russians were acutely aware that
West European and even West German support for partition was
quite fragile. By threatening Berlin, they were challenging that resolve. Their not-so-hidden message was that the split of Germany was
very hazardous and that the plight of the West Berliners could become
the plight of others.

2.

At first U.S. policy-makers could not see how to protect the western
sectors. Disorganized and divided, they argued intensely over a range
of tactical issues: the relative merits of an armed convoy vs. an airlift,
the number of planes that could be safely diverted to the German theater, the proper custodianship of atomic weapons, the form and character of Allied protest notes, and even the feasibility of using the new
Russian currency in Berlin.[21] Yet the most crucial decision was the one

that all the American participants took for granted: the refusal to consider German unification.

That refusal and the associated unwillingness to make any agreement that could jeopardize partition, restricted the possibility of a diplomatic solution. The Americans initially resorted to diplomacy because of strong pressure from their allies, and their own assumption that Berlin could not be long supplied. However, the Soviets made it clear that the real issue was the future of Germany. In a July 14 letter to the three Western governments, they emphasized that Berlin was "an inseparable component part" of the agreement for quadripartite administration for all Germany.[22] Deploring the "systematic violations" by the United States, Britain, and France of the wartime agreements, they insisted that negotiations on Berlin must encompass the entire German question.

The Americans were loathe to discuss that wider topic. Three weeks into the blockade and they were still quarreling with the West German minister-presidents (provincial governors), who under the London Accords were supposed to convene a constituent assembly. In an acrimonious meeting in Coblenz, the German leaders warned against measures that "would widen further the rift between west and east." They further resolved that "everything should be avoided that would give the character of a state" to the new organization. While yielding to their request that a new constitution be termed a "basic law," General Clay and his political adviser Robert Murphy insisted that they proceed with the project despite their many misgivings.

Against this background, the Americans wished to keep the discussions with the Soviets on the narrow topic of the Berlin crisis. However, neither the French nor the British thought that reasonable. When formal talks finally opened in Moscow on August 1, Stalin moved into the breach.[23] In meetings with the three Western ambassadors—Walter Bedell Smith (U.S.), Frank Roberts (U.K.), and M. Yves Chataigneau (France)—he assured them that his government had no desire to drive the Western powers out of Berlin, but stressed that Western juridical rights were linked to the city's status as the capital of a united country. The West German Parliamentary Council was scheduled to open on September 1. Once that body wrote a new constitution, there would be nothing left to discuss.

Stalin was willing to consider the arrangements for the Berlin currency. Over a period of weeks the ambassadors worked with Soviet Foreign Minister Vyacheslav Molotov to produce a directive to the military governors, authorizing them to complete arrangements for the use of the Soviet marks in the city.[24] For a moment it appeared as if the Russians might lift the blockade if this agreement was accompanied by a willingness to rapidly convene a new Council of Foreign Ministers conference on the larger question of Germany's future.

All of the Western ambassadors, including the normally hawkish Walter Bedell Smith, believed that this was an advantageous deal. Yet even this modest arrangement was unacceptable to American officials, including Charles ("Chip") Bohlen, who was then chairing the intra-departmental crisis committee on Berlin and U.S. Military Governor Lucius Clay.[25] Hoping to avoid another foreign ministers conference, the State Department instructed Smith to gain Soviet recognition of western "juridical rights" in Berlin as part of the agreement. This obvious act of sabotage enraged all three of the ambassadors. The British representative, Frank Roberts, cabled the Foreign Office that unless there was some way of keeping "Clay . . . and the State Department in check we shall find ourselves with agreement dashed from our lips, a thirsty public wondering why, and an even worse position than when we started these talks. . . ."[26]

The Americans ultimately backed down on this particular item, but the deal came apart in Berlin as the military governors haggled over the precise arrangements for the city's currency.[27] Underlying the tedious technical disputes was the American hesitation about doing anything that could disrupt the work of the West German Parliamentary Council. For the Soviets, the American reluctance to hold any discussion of the impending partition eliminated the incentive for a settlement.

By mid-September, the four powers had reached an impasse. The British and French preferred to continue negotiations, whereas the Americans wished to break them off. U.S. officials had found the Moscow talks to be very dangerous, as their allies, and even their own ambassador, seemed to constantly gravitate towards compromise.[28] Moreover, in the intervening months the supply situation in Berlin had markedly improved. Western airplanes were bringing in up to 5,500 tons a day, convincing General Clay that the airlift could succeed through the harsh winter months.[29] To the Americans, the success of the airlift obviated the need for further diplomacy.

Though unacknowledged, an important background factor was the continuing availability of food and supplies from the eastern zone. As early as July, Marshal Sokolovsky had promised to insure "the normal supply of essential goods" to Berlin—a pledge that was immediately followed by an offer of thousands of tons of wheat. Although American and British officials did not want West Berliners to register for Soviet provisions, 5 percent of the population did so anyway. Even if they did not register, the West Berliners were able to obtain goods by "black marketeering," by making Eastmark purchases in the "free shops" of East Berlin, or through barter arrangements in the eastern-zone countryside. As explained by U.S. military intelligence, while the airlift was "effectively supplementing other sources in supply of the most critical items, the vast majority of the needs of the population and industry . . . are still met through East-West trade, which is only slightly less necessary to the Soviet sector than to the western parts of the city."

As of October 1948, Secretary of State George Marshall had convinced his more timid colleagues, Ernest Bevin and Robert Schuman, to forgo direct negotiations with the Soviets and to turn the matter over to the United Nations.[30] He was therefore appalled to discover that President Truman had decided to reopen talks with Stalin through a personal emissary, Supreme Court Justice Fred Vinson. Busy with his reelection campaign, the president did not appreciate the tight connection between the plans for a West German state and the Soviet actions in Berlin. He had naively supposed that his subordinates were anxious for a settlement and would welcome his assistance.

To Marshall and his colleagues Truman's intervention was infuriating, jeopardizing their hard-won agreement with France and Britain to halt direct negotiations in Moscow. For public consumption they let it be known that the president was "playing politics" and had undermined United Nations diplomacy. Embarrassed by the leaks in the press, Truman quickly retreated from peacemaking. This abdication was consequential since the president was the one elected official in a position to shape the United States response to this most dangerous postwar crisis.[31]

In reality, the State Department was turning to the United Nations as a means of escaping the deliberations in Moscow and avoiding a diplomatic solution. To minimize international dissent, it preferred to work through the Security Council rather than the General Assembly. As explained by Dean Rusk, "In SC we could clearly isolate the USSR. Its only supporter would be Ukraine, which everyone would recognize as Uncle Joe talking out of the other side of his mouth."[32] Furthermore, "SC gives us maximum flexibility as we can control the parliamentary situation and either bring issue to head or extend consideration over longer period as we wish."

Yet even the Security Council was not so docile, as the representative from Nationalist China introduced a resolution calling for *all* the disputants to refrain from measures that would aggravate the Berlin situation. There was considerable sentiment in this body for restarting four-power discussions, using the Moscow directive on currency as a beginning step. An alarmed Chip Bohlen complained that the Western powers had approached the UN because Soviet actions "constitute a threat to peace." Now unfortunately France and other "neutral members" were construing this "as a request of the Council to use its conciliatory powers to bring the two parties of the dispute together." This could only result in "a great propaganda victory for the Russians."[33]

The "neutral members" to whom Bohlen was referring were the six nations of the Security Council that were not direct parties to the dispute—China, Argentina, Colombia, Belgium, Syria, and Canada. These rallied behind a British draft resolution, condemning the Soviet blockade and demanding its cessation.[34] While the resolution satisfied the American demand that there be no four-power discussions of German unity until the blockade was lifted, it put the subject back on the negotiating table. However, since the Soviets were disputing the Security Council's jurisdiction in the crisis, their approval was unlikely. Just to be sure, the American representative, Philip Jessup, was instructed to slow down U.S. consent until he knew for sure that the Soviet representative, Andrei Vyshinsky, would veto.[35]

On October 25, the Russians fulfilled expectations by rejecting the Security Council measure. Yet paradoxically the 9-2 vote, though an important moral victory for the Americans and British, generated new demands for compromise. UN Secretary-General Trygve Lie now wished to involve the Secretariat in the quest for solution, the Australian president of the General Assembly, Herbert Evatt, made similar claims for the General Assembly, while the "neutrals" on the Security Council continued unofficial talks with Vyshinsky on prospects for a currency deal.[36]

Given the choices, the Americans and British felt safest in the Security Council.[37] They regarded both Lie and Evatt as politically unreliable and too susceptible to Russian arguments. As explained by Jessup, the best way to prevent consideration in the General Assembly was "to encourage activity on the part of the Council, or at least not discourage it, provided it was kept within reasonable bounds." That way if there were any reports from the Secretariat, they would go to the six whom "we could hope to . . . keep straight through the influence of our friends, particularly Belgian and Canadian."[38]

The Americans and British therefore accepted a proposal by the Security Council president, Juan Bramuglia, for a "Committee of Financial Experts" to study the Berlin currency situation and make recommendations for using the Soviet marks under four-power supervision.[39] Yet having acceded to the Bramuglia proposal, the Americans then generated a variety of impediments, including pressure on their French and British colleagues to immediately use the western marks as the exclusive legal tender in their sectors.[40]

At the United Nations, there was widespread irritation with the Americans for undermining the peace process.[41] It was therefore especially uncomfortable for the U.S. delegate, Philip Jessup, to read in the *New York Herald Tribune* that General Clay was claiming that conditions in Berlin would make it impossible to utilize a single currency. He angrily wired Secretary of State Marshall that the Clay interview "has caused me major embarrassment" and "increased the suspicion surrounding US policy."[42] Apparently there "is not and never has been" a technical U.S. plan for quadripartite control of the Soviet mark in Berlin.

However, Clay's remarks pointed to a genuine problem. For by mid-November the Berlin city government was disintegrating. In their cables home, both General Clay and his political adviser Robert Murphy complained of Soviet interference with the administrative agencies. Yet the U.S. military government was itself promoting a breach by encouraging the City Assembly to hold municipal elections in defiance of the Soviet Kommandant. In practice, this would mean that the western sectors would become politically separate.[43]

In view of the UN mediation efforts, the obvious course was to hold off on the balloting, scheduled for December 5. This would give the Bramuglia group time to produce a plan on the currency and perhaps pave the way for the lifting of the blockade, which might in turn ease political tensions in the city. When the French pointed this out, Robert Murphy reacted furiously, insisting that to cancel the elections at this point "could only be interpreted by the Berlin population . . . as a weak-kneed if not cowardly surrender and retreat." This would be a "political defeat equivalent to the battle of Leipzig."[44]

At Clay's headquarters the determination to barrel ahead with elections had several sources, including the desire to tie the western sectors of Berlin to the new West German state. Despite its problematic location inside the Soviet zone, the Americans felt a burgeoning emotional affinity with the city's leadership. Not only was there gratitude for the courage and dignity displayed by this group, there was also a practical conviction that the Berlin politicians were the most vital force in western Germany, who could generate needed support for the impending partition. To the U.S. military government, the division of Berlin had become nearly as attractive as the division of Germany itself.

In fending off the international pressure to delay the Berlin elections, American diplomats were rescued by the impatient Russians. On November 30, a rump group of pro-Communist politicians gathered in the Berlin Opera House, proclaimed themselves the true City Assembly, and formed their own Magistrat. Much relieved, Chip Bohlen reflected that "by this stroke of luck for us the Soviets have split the city before the elections," allowing the Western powers to proceed with the Berlin balloting and to make the western marks exclusive legal tender. More important, it offered a convenient exit from the UN mediation. Instructing Jessup to seize the moment, Bohlen emphasized that "we have been given a better opportunity . . . to escape from the more dangerous consequences of Bramuglia's proposal and I think we should use it to the full."[45]

Not everyone in the administration was as cynical as Bohlen. Secretary of State Marshall swung back and forth on the desirability of a settlement. Yet the weight of opinion was with the hard-liners, who increasingly believed that the Berlin blockade was advancing their purposes. The spectacle of the airlift was boosting the American image across the western zones, creating popular momentum for the work of the Parliamentary Council. Over Soviet objections this body was continuing its deliberations, moving ever closer to a completed basic law.

Meanwhile the Russians were feeling the pinch as a western counterblockade of the eastern zone was depriving its factories of the coal, steel, and machine tools that they needed to operate. Textile, metalworking and electrical equipment plants were curtailing production and in some cases shutting down, creating desperate shortages of consumer goods.

In the political realm, Soviet popularity was at an all-time low. Discredited Communist Party leaders were known to be bitter and demoralized. Lest any proof be needed of how poorly the Soviets were faring, the December Berlin elections provided sustenance. Despite a Communist boycott, an impressive 83 percent of the registered voters came out to the polls, demonstrating their resentment of the blockade and contempt for the Russian occupiers.

The definitive split in the Berlin city government gave the U.S. negotiators an excuse to withdraw from the UN talks. However, the British and French representatives continued to work with the Bramuglia group on a currency plan that could be implemented, even in a divided city.[46] By late December, the proposal was completed and rumors were rife that the Soviet delegation would sign on. To stem the criticism by their Western colleagues, the Americans hastily put together a counterproposal, albeit one which seemed egregiously one-sided.[47] This exasperated British Foreign Minister Bevin, who wondered whether the United States preferred "to go on as at present in Berlin, or was it seeking a reasonable settlement? Frankly the impression made upon me by the United States counter-proposal as a whole was that the United States did not want a settlement at present."[48]

The Soviets did finally endorse the Bramuglia proposals,[49] but without American support the United Nations offer fell apart. By late January the UN economists were exhausted, disillusioned, and eager to go home. Their collective sentiment was expressed by Gunnar Myrdal, who believed that Stalin had been personally overseeing the UN discussions and was aiming for a solution.[50] If the blockade was now continuing, this was the responsibility of the Americans. Though the experts' final report carefully refrained from placing the blame on any one party, its substance suggested Western culpability. To the relief of the British, the Canadians successfully persuaded the Security Council president not to publish it.[51]

The failure of the Bramuglia plan removed the United Nations as a significant actor in the Berlin crisis. This was by far the most serious conflict that had faced the organization, and while it had never been the American intention to have it play a mediating role, an unforeseen assortment of participants gravitated to the task, among them the secretary-general, the president of the Security Council, the representatives of the six "neutrals," and finally the financial experts themselves. All had perceived legitimate grievances on both sides and all were seeking a means of reconciling competing interests.

United States policy-makers could see little value in such proceedings. Once the UN moved beyond a simple condemnation of the Soviets, its operations became a threat rather than an opportunity. By thus rejecting an independent role for the organization, the Americans helped to weaken one of the few remaining mechanisms for the peaceful solution of East-West problems. This had large implications for the future of the United Nations, for it was now clear that as the world's leading power, the United States would not recognize its authority.

3·

These failed diplomatic efforts provided the context for the American turn to militarism. A review of the Moscow discussions and the United Nations deliberations suggests that, contrary to the public's impression at the time, there were a number of ways to end the Berlin standoff without endangering the city.

The most certain route was to halt partition. As acknowledged by Ambassador Walter Bedell Smith, "we could have produced an agreement in fifteen minutes . . . by an offer to abandon London."[52] For U.S. policy-makers, such an interruption had become unthinkable, although they never shared this conviction with the American people. Moreover, in the summer of 1948 there was reason to think that more moderate measures would suffice: that a simple commitment to *discuss* German reunification and a compromise on the Berlin currency might induce a retraction of the blockade. These approaches were not tried because *Western* support for the German partition was too precarious. During subsequent months, as the Soviet position grew weaker, there were more indications that they would accept face-saving concessions. However, U.S. officials were reluctant to end the crisis until the West German state was safely launched.

It is significant that U.S. policy-makers chose to run the risk of war rather than incur the dangers of diplomacy. They certainly were not eager for armed conflict and did what they could to minimize outbreaks of violence. Yet their distinctive conception of national security led them to hazard a military encounter rather than compromise their plans for West European integration. It is true that over the ten-month period, the sense of emergency receded. But so long as the Soviet military was impeding access on the ground, and Western supply planes were filling up the air corridors, there was the potential for armed conflict. This nurtured a preference for building up a nuclear arsenal and for the establishment of a military alliance with Western Europe.

In the first stages of the crisis, the Americans' most daunting problem was how to provision Berlin without leaving the populace totally dependent on Soviet contributions. While resorting to an airlift, they did not believe it would be adequate to the task.[53] At whatever point the supplies became insufficient, the Western powers might have to quickly decide whether to leave or fight.

Secretary of the Army Kenneth Royall wanted the president to immediately address this underlying issue. At the June 28, 1948, meeting of the National Security Council, Truman was handed three option papers prepared by the State and Defense Departments.[54] The stated choices were: 1. to decide immediately to withdraw from Berlin and to concert with allies on plans for doing so, 2. to decide immediately to continue in Berlin by all possible means, including an armed convoy, or 3. to try to stay in Berlin without using force, while postponing the final decision on a military response. In the Truman folklore, it was at this session that the decisive leader faced down his timid subordinates with the stirring injunction: "we stay, period."[55] In actuality, the president was trying to short-circuit the kind of intricate discussion that he loathed by avoiding the question. When Royall took him to be endorsing option 2, Truman commented that "we would have to deal with the situation as it developed."[56]

Underlying the exchange was the Defense Department's concern that there be realistic plans for conducting a war, if the U.S. intended to hold the western sectors. The peril would become most acute if they had to use an armed convoy to supply the city. But there was also a possibility that the Soviets might interfere with the air corridors, causing a sudden outbreak of hostilities.

To reduce the likelihood that the Soviets would menace the airlift, the National Security Council decided to dispatch B-29 bombers to Europe.[57] It was this type of plane that had carried out the attack on Hiroshima. Since it was widely assumed that the B-29s were nuclear-capable, U.S. policy-makers hoped they would provide sufficient deterrence to the Russians. In fact, only a small fraction of B-29s were designed to carry atomic weapons and these were not the ones selected for Europe.[58] If the Soviets called the American bluff, there would still be the problem of how to respond.

This was precisely the question that Truman was trying to duck. However, the issue was resurrected in mid-July when General Clay began pushing for an armed convoy to challenge the blockade.[59] In the early stages of the crisis, the U.S. military governor wished to resolve matters quickly, believing that the Soviets were much weaker than his superiors imagined. In all likelihood they would retreat when confronted, although Clay acknowledged that having staked their prestige in Berlin, there was a one-in-four chance that they would fight.[60]

Such odds were not acceptable to other military officials, who still wanted to know how the United States could fight such a war. Secretary of Defense James Forrestal and the Joint Chiefs of Staff believed the Western powers had insufficient troop strength to prevent the Red Army from overrunning Europe.[61] This lent urgency to the question of atomic weapons. After a brief delay, the B-29 airplanes had arrived in England and Germany. But so far there had been no decision about whether atomic bombs could be used in the event of war.[62]

In an effort to reduce that ambiguity, Forrestal resumed a long-festering dispute with the Atomic Energy Commission over custody of the bomb.[63] For more than a year, the military had complained that civilian possession of America's atomic stockpile would hamper efficient deployment in a crisis. Now the crisis had arrived, and the Defense Department wanted Truman to change the policy. The president understood that by shifting custody, he would increase the possibility of use and he did not want some "dashing young colonel" to make the decision when would be "the proper time to drop one."[64]

The custody issue was the subject of a somber meeting at the White House in late July. All the participants were intensely aware that "even at that moment some terrible thing might be happening in Berlin" that would sweep away volition.[65] Yet Truman was obviously reluctant to employ the weapon. He emphasized that the bomb was "so terribly destructive, destructive beyond anything we have ever had."[66] It wasn't just "a military weapon." It would "wipe out women and children and unarmed people." So it had to be treated differently "from rifles and cannons and ordinary things like that." These ruminations disappointed Army Secretary Royall, who noted that "we have been spending ninety-eight percent of all the money for atomic energy on weapons . . . and if we weren't going to use them, that doesn't make any sense."

Coming at the height of the Berlin crisis, the exchange over atomic custody was profoundly disquieting to the Defense Department. Despite perfunctory disclaimers, its bid for possession was part of an effort to make the atomic arsenal more usable. In rejecting it,[67] the president had revealed his deep resistance to bringing the bombs into action. There had been intimations of this attitude during the spring, when the Joint Chiefs of Staff unveiled their nuclear war plan, "Grabber." The president had then indicated that he did not want to be dependent on atomic bombs to fight a war, and had asked for an alternative nonnuclear option.[68] It was one thing to proffer such an opinion when the international situation was calm. Yet here was Truman, with a blockade on in Berlin, C-54s crowding up the air lanes, and Russian troops surrounding the city, sounding so negative about America's main weapon.[69]

Having sustained a defeat on the custody issue, the Defense Department rejected Clay's request for an armed convoy. As explained by Secretary Royall, this proposal could not be adopted unless "we make preparations for fighter and bomber support, and at the same time have several A-bombs available (in England or elsewhere) for immediate use, and that use be left entirely to the military."[70]

During August, the military issues receded while negotiations proceeded in Moscow. However, once the Americans decided to terminate these talks, the need for a war-winning strategy was again urgent. As anxiety mounted, President Truman was briefed by top Defense Department officials on military strategy, bases, and bombs. In his diary he recorded "a terrible feeling . . . that we are very close to war."[71] His sentiments were amplified by Budget Director James Webb, who disclosed to Atomic Energy Commission Director David Lilienthal that

> The situation in Berlin is bad. . . . The Russians seem prepared to kick us in the teeth on every issue. Their planes are in the corridor today, and anything could happen. Anything—they might walk in tomorrow and shoot General Clay.[72]

Truman had always been "optimistic" about maintaining peace, but now "he is blue . . . mighty blue."

Within the administration, these apprehensions led the Joint Chiefs of Staff to accelerate their planning for a military emergency.[73] As arrangements were made to evacuate U.S. dependents and select German civilians from Berlin, the American commanders in Germany, Austria, and Trieste received their battle instructions. Because of the perceived weakness in conventional capability, the Defense Department focused on the availability of nuclear weapons. Lt. Gen. Lauris Norstad was sent to England to look into the construction of nuclear support facilities, while the chiefs examined other prospective bases for atomic aircraft. In a quiet sequel to the earlier imbroglio, the Air Force collaborated with the AEC on procedures for transferring nuclear custody should the bomb be needed.

But would permission to use the bomb be forthcoming? Truman's July ruminations had revealed a sharp distinction in his mind between threatening a nuclear attack (the aim of the B-29s) and carrying one out. In mid-September, the National Security Council concluded that "in the event of hostilities, the National Military establishment must be ready to utilize promptly and effectively all appropriate means available, including atomic weapons."[74] More directly now, Forrestal sought a presidential commitment to draw upon the atomic arsenal. To his great relief, Truman was willing to say that while "he prayed that he would never have to make such a decision . . . if it became necessary, no one need have a misgiving but what he would do so."[75]

As noted by historian David Rosenberg, at the inception of the Berlin blockade the American arsenal consisted of approximately fifty atomic bombs, none of which were completely assembled.[76] Nevertheless, the possession of these weapons had provided policy-makers with the confidence to confront the Soviets on a matter of vital interest and to refuse even marginal concessions. But the experience had been chastening. Having for the first time challenged the enemy to the brink of war, the whole administration—including the president—had learned a vital lesson: that international relations was different from poker, where one could bluff an opponent with relative impunity. In the affairs of nations, where stakes were much higher, the ability to intimidate an adversary implied a willingness and ability to implement threats. That realization created an imperative for better planes, additional bases, and a larger, more lethal stockpile.[77]

Once Truman had agreed that the bomb might be used, his subordinates were sanguine about a long crisis. The airlift had vastly exceeded everyone's expectations, and it now seemed much safer to use the nuclear threat to keep the Soviets out of the air lanes. This meant the German partition could go forward, without any need to accommodate the USSR's concerns.

On September 30 with formal responsibility for the crisis passing to the United Nations, Secretary of State Marshall sought Bevin and Schuman's assurance that there would be no direct negotiations with the Russians until the blockade had been lifted.[78] The secretary urged his colleagues to realize the strength of their position. The airlift was "buying time" while Western Europe rebuilt economically and militarily.[79] Meanwhile the atomic bomb was tying the USSR's hands. The Soviets may initially have believed that the "American public would never support the use of the bomb," but now they knew better. Obviously the Berlin situation was abnormal, but the West was "on the road to victory."

Although Bevin and Schuman acceded to the American agenda, they did so unhappily. The nuclear monopoly emboldened Washington officials but was less comforting to British and French partners who, at each stage of the Berlin crisis, seemed to suffer a failure of nerve. Such timidity irritated U.S. policy-makers, but ultimately led them to the formation of NATO.

In understanding how the blockade helped to militarize U.S. foreign policy, the backsliding of allies is a critical feature. For both the British and the French, the great danger of the Berlin confrontation was that the Red Army might overrun Western Europe.[80] Even if the United States used atomic weapons, this would not necessarily halt a Russian ground offensive. Because they felt militarily vulnerable, both countries were more inclined to conciliate the USSR. For Bevin, the cross-pressures were especially intense since he, like the Americans, was strongly committed to partition. But in contrast to the Americans, when hostilities seemed imminent he inclined towards diplomacy.

Observing the meekness of the West Europeans, U.S. officials were convinced that territorial defenses must be enhanced. Even before the Berlin crisis, the United States had been moving towards a military alliance with the West European states.[81] But in the spring of 1948, it was by no means clear that this would translate into a formal treaty. The Berlin crisis seemed to demonstrate that in the absence of a clear American commitment to defend Western European and the capability of doing so, these countries would always be prone to abandon the West German state and perhaps other vital positions as well.

Of course the Europeans were not only worried about the Red Army. As several historians have rightfully emphasized, they also feared the Germans.[82] As had been evident during the London Conference, Britain, France, and the Benelux nations believed that in promoting a West German government, the Americans were imprudently forfeiting the security controls stipulated at Potsdam and Yalta. During the blockade, that apprehension became more salient as the Americans tried to enlarge the prerogatives granted to the West Germans.

In a host of fields—reparations, prohibited industries, control of the Ruhr, and demilitarization provisions—the U.S. position seemed unduly lax.[83] For this reason the promise of a North Atlantic defensive treaty, which gave security against German as well as Soviet aggression, seemed essential. Indeed, the creation of NATO was so closely intertwined with the birth of the West German government that in April 1949, the State Department used the signing ceremonies for the treaty as the occasion to conclude the negotiations on the West German basic law and on an occupation statute that delineated the reduced power of the occupiers.[84] Highlighting the connection to Truman, the new secretary of state Dean Acheson emphasized that:

the success of these negotiations on German affairs has been greatly facilitated by the conclusion of the North Atlantic Treaty. Without it, I
doubt that we would have come to a successful conclusion of these
agreements.[85]

If the formation of NATO and the creation of a West German state
were reciprocal processes, it is also true that the Soviet interference
with the Berlin access routes had facilitated both. Once it was clear that
the airlift was succeeding, canny U.S. officials perceived that the ongoing crisis was actually strengthening their hand in both negotiations
and they would do well to prolong it.

At the time, most Americans simply assumed that Washington was
anxious to relieve the pressure on Berlin with a quick capitulation by
Moscow. Indeed, the conventional histories of the Cold War describe a
dramatic moment in February 1949, when Stalin made a public statement intimating that he might be willing to lift the blockade without
any Western concessions on currency. According to this account, an
alert Chip Bohlen instructed Philip Jessup to inquire of Jacob Malik,
the Soviet ambassador at the UN, whether Stalin's remarks had any
"special significance." The official reply did not come until mid-
March, when the Russians agreed that the currency question could be
deferred until after a new Council on Foreign Ministers meeting. That
concession led to a fresh round of negotiations, which culminated six
weeks later in a Soviet decision to end their obstruction of the access
routes.

Such a description contains grains of truth. U.S. policy-makers
certainly wanted to know whether the Soviets would lift the travel
restrictions even if there were no Western concessions on Berlin's
currency. From that vantage point Stalin's remarks aroused their
curiosity. However, apart from the unwitting president, those policy-
makers most involved in the German question feared that if a settlement came too soon—before the basic law and the NATO treaty were
finished—long-standing fissures on the Western side would open up.

Reflecting such apprehension, Bohlen reminded Jessup that it was
"of utmost importance that we keep under constant review the timing
of the discussions . . . on the Berlin situation."[86] The Malik talks had
clarified "the present Soviet attitude," and now that this was known
there was no need for haste. Bohlen considered that the "real advantage

to U.S. policy" could be the "lifting of the blockade without the payment on the part of the three powers of any political price." Hence the United States would peg the negotiations to the events in Bonn, where the West German Parliamentary Assembly was still deliberating. Given the complexity of the East-West issues, Jessup should be able "to quicken or slacken the tempo without arousing Soviet suspicions."

For American officials, the real achievement that spring was the completion of the West German basic law and the signing of the NATO treaty. President Truman thought these agreements "the best thing that had been done in our administration," for it had "carried forward our efforts for peace in the world and prosperity." [87] Not until these tasks were complete would the United States provide the Soviets with a face-saving way to end their ill-starred "blockade."

4.

On May 12, 1949—one minute past midnight—the lights went on in the western sectors of Berlin as cars, trucks, and trains resumed their travel into and out of the city. As one feature of their deal with the Russians, the Americans had conceded an item they had resisted for ten months—the convening of a four-power Council of Foreign Ministers to discuss the future of Germany. This appeared to be a safe option once the West German basic law was complete and the NATO treaty settled.

Yet now that the partition of Germany was a virtual certainty, George Kennan, the head of the State Department's policy planning staff, registered his dissent. Since the inception of the Berlin confrontation, the author of "containment" had become increasingly leery of his own handiwork. For months his staff had been working on the details for plan A ("A Program for Germany"), which provided for free elections in a united Germany. The resulting government would become sovereign except for certain "reserved areas," where a new Allied Control Council could override decisions by majority vote. The key to Kennan's proposal was the elimination of the occupation zones, a drastic reduction in the number of foreign troops, and the redeployment of those forces to the border areas.

At least in a military sense, plan A would create a kind of neutral zone in the heart of Europe, which might later be enlarged as great-power tensions abated. Yet Kennan's superiors were hostile to the idea. They would rather leave an estimated 180,000 Soviet troops near the Rhine than do anything to jeopardize partition. To Kennan this predilection was tragic since it meant freezing the division of Europe for years to come and ensuring that the competition between the two sides would become preeminently military.

The confrontation in Berlin was not simply an episode in the early Cold War, it was the occasion when the conflict assumed its definitive shape. It is therefore hardly surprising that it has been shrouded in myth. For most Americans then and now the compelling story has always been the intrepid pilots. The "remembrance" speech of President Clinton on the tarmac of Tempelhof airport was simply the echo of the commentary fifty years before. As described in a characteristic lead feature of *Time* magazine:

> The incessant roar of the planes—that typical and terrible Twentieth Century sound, a voice of cold mechanized anger—filled every ear in the city. It reverberated in the bizarre stone ears of the hollow, broken houses; it throbbed in the weary ears of Berlin's people who were bitter, afraid, but far from broken; it echoed in the intently listening ear of history. The sound meant one thing: the West was standing its ground and fighting back.[88]

In Berlin and countless places thereafter, the mission of the United States would be to hold fast against the aggressive hordes.

A more accurate account of the Berlin encounter suggests certain large themes, which have long been debated by Cold War historians, but which have never been incorporated into a serious national discussion.

One is the heretical notion that the isolation of East Germany and Eastern Europe under total Soviet control was perhaps avoidable. In the immediate aftermath of World War II, Stalin was clearly bent on using the presence of the Red Army to reshape the societies under its authority. But despite more than a decade of "new documents" flowing out of the Eastern archives, there is still no evidence that he intended to transform all these places into mini-Soviet states or that he expected to dominate them for very long.

Moreover, as historians Norman Naimark, Vladimir Zubok, and Constantine Pleshakov have amply demonstrated, there are many reasons to suppose that Stalin was looking for a deal in Germany and that he was prepared to make significant concessions to bring one about. Perhaps when it was time to hammer out the final details and to actually loosen the bonds on the eastern zone, the Soviet leadership would have faltered. Yet this is something we will never know, because by the spring of 1947 the United States and Britain had closed the door to that contingency.

A second theme is the distinctive way in which American leaders were learning to define "national security." After 1948, what they meant by this was military superiority and a "credible" nuclear striking force. In subsequent years, this would appear to the American people as something inevitable—not really a choice, but merely an outcome forced on the United States by Soviet aggression.

Yet as George Kennan well understood, the military competition was a direct result of the decision to divide Germany and to leave Berlin as a permanent locus of contention in the heart of Europe. Kennan also recognized that, in an era of nuclear weapons, even military superiority might not protect the United States from catastrophic events.

Kennan's colleagues saw matters differently. With less imagination they could not so easily envision the day when the USSR would be a nuclear rival, and by the time this happened, the crucial decisions were already in place. Yet in adopting a high-risk approach to national security these colleagues were also reflecting priorities that Kennan shared. For they were not simply thinking about America's physical safety but about protecting its political and economic system. From that standpoint, the danger of reunifying Germany and possibly reknitting the European continent was that the Marshall Plan would be undermined and plans for reintegrating the capitalist economies of Western Europe disrupted.

This leads to a third and arguably most important theme: namely, the enhanced power of the bureaucracies and the lack of public accountability. In opting for schism, U.S. policy-makers did not take the American people into their confidence nor did they significantly involve elected officials. Despite his famous saying that the "buck stops here," with regard to Europe Harry Truman was a detached president, who had very little comprehension of the issues. Though fearful that war would break out in Berlin, he never familiarized himself with the Soviet position, nor did he grasp the connection between the writing of the West German basic law and Russian interference with the city's access routes.

If Truman was out of the loop, so too was the Congress. There was never a point, either before or during the Berlin crisis, where Congress debated the division of Germany. Members were paying close attention to the Marshall Plan and there was wide support for the inclusion of the West German zones. What legislators did not realize was that the partition of the country had become an administration preference. Thus as late as June 1949, when Secretary of State Dean Acheson testified before the Senate Foreign Relations Committee, the powerful Senator Vandenberg was startled to learn that Acheson did not want an agreement with the Soviets. Didn't this mean, Vandenberg queried, that there would be "a permanent Cold War"?[89] Not necessarily "permanent," responded Acheson, but the task would be "to see who develops more strength."

It is astonishing to consider that during the entire Berlin crisis—with its obvious potential for armed conflict—U.S. policy was set without significant involvement by any elected officials. This abdication framed the public's ignorance of the issues. Absent accountable leaders able and willing to outline the existing options, there was little opportunity for democratic discussion. Lacking pertinent information, citizens were relegated to the sidelines, where their only role was to cheer for the airlift.

Forty years later the Cold War ended and with it the division of Europe. That outcome has spawned a "triumphalist" history, which obscures the nature and costs of American decision making in this arena.

By depriving the Soviet Union of the fruits of its World War II victory over Germany, the Truman administration created an imbalance of power in Europe, which consigned the nations of the East to decades of exclusive Soviet control. Moreover, the ensuing military competition had wide-ranging international effects. For it triggered a tragically expensive arms race and endowed even remote places on the globe with a strategic significance they might not otherwise have held. Eventually millions would die in proxy wars—in Korea, Vietnam, and elsewhere—and the self-determination of many countries would be subordinated to the U.S.-Soviet rivalry.

From the perspective of the present, perhaps the most durable and harmful consequence was the creation of a permanent American "national security state," organized around military solutions. Faced with fresh challenges in the Middle East, Condoleezza Rice and the team of Cheney, Rumsfeld, and Bush exhibit the same preference for coercion over diplomacy as their Cold War forebears. And not surprisingly, they see in the shifting "tectonic plates" an "opportunity" to repeat, in this oil-rich region, the presumed successes of the European project.

7

The United States, the United Nations, and the Other Post–Cold War World Order: Internationalism and Unilateralism in the American Century

Jessica Wang

I am not here as a public official, but as a citizen of a troubled world who finds hope in a growing consensus that the generally accepted goals of society are peace, freedom, human rights, environmental quality, the alleviation of suffering, and the rule of law.

> Jimmy Carter, Nobel Peace Prize
> acceptance speech, December 2002 [1]

To Americans, immigration is our problem. Soccer is our problem. This is American unilateralism.

> Jorge Montano, former Mexican
> ambassador to the United States, on
> the eve of the U.S.-Mexico game,
> World Cup 2002 [2]

The September 11 attacks and their aftermath opened a new and wrenching chapter in the history of the post–Cold War world, and the need for fresh thinking about the nature of the international system and the place of the United States within it has become ever more urgent. Since the end of the U.S.-Soviet conflict, it has been common to speak of a unipolar post–Cold War order, in which the United States plays the dominant role in structuring the international system. Proponents of American globalism tout the need for American strength as the crucial guarantor of order and stability within the Hobbesian anarchy that reigns among nation-states, while detractors condemn the American pursuit of power as a hegemonic, imperialist enterprise. Few, however, would question the primacy of the United States as the determinative component of contemporary international relations. This point of consensus among both boosters and critics of American foreign policy reflects a long-held tendency to understand international configurations of power and their history in terms of individual nation-states or blocs of states, from the system of balance-of-power politics that dominated Europe from the mid–seventeenth century until the dawn of World War II, to the bipolar world of Cold War superpower confrontation, to the unipolar framework of the present.[3]

There is another post–Cold War order afoot, however. Over the past century, a competing version of the international system, one premised upon the submission of nation-states to international institutions, the rule of law, and the will of the global community, has doggedly persisted throughout the worst periods of chaos and violence. This legal-institutional internationalism, which envisioned the possibility of fundamentally reworking the structures of the international system, surpassing the political limitations of the nation-state, and putting an end to military conflict, possessed extensive political influence both within the United States and around the world throughout the first half of the twentieth century. The Cold War set the United States upon a different path, however, as the nation's newfound predominance combined with anticommunist ideology to produce a more narrow, pragmatic discourse about international relations that viewed the idea of transcending the imperatives of power as but a fantasy. But international institutions and legal norms continued to evolve, and the current patchwork of nongovernmental organizations, the United Nations, and an expanding international legal regime now plays a significant role in efforts to keep the peace, promote national self-determination, protect human rights, and address other global problems.

The United States, meanwhile, has increasingly set itself apart from this other post–Cold War order in recent years. Although the

United States was once one of the major supporters of a strengthened international legal order, the Cold War prompted profound shifts in the American political imagination toward a more unilateral, U.S.-centered worldview. The national recollection of internationalism as a central part of the American past has been virtually obliterated, and instead, the prism of memory has transformed historical contingencies into a different set of inevitabilities about the necessity for American power and freedom of action. Consequently, most Americans, even among those who pay close attention to global affairs, know relatively little about the history of the United Nations or the internationalist aspirations that were once a powerful political force in the United States. In response to this void in understanding, this essay charts out a parallel history of the Cold War and post–Cold War periods, one in which internationalist ideals and institutions began to rival nation-states as arbiters of world affairs. The history of internationalism and U.S.-UN relations transcends mere academic interest: understanding this aspect of past experience offers potential means for rekindling a more creative, open-ended sense of possibilities for American foreign policy in the twenty-first century.

PRELUDE: AMERICAN INTERNATIONALISM AND THE POLITICS OF PEACE, 1899–1945

The founding of the United Nations marked the culmination of a half-century of efforts around the world to create a community of nations that could transcend the harsh and frequently violent order that seemed the norm of international relations by the end of the nineteenth century. Although the United States had its own imperial designs, the projection of American power abroad generated strong political pressures against the prevailing assumptions of international relations. Congress developed a powerful anti-imperialist bloc, and a domestic peace movement gained considerable reach and influence. No presuppositions about the nature of nation-states and the workings of the world system remained unchallenged, as internationalists of varied stripes contemplated the expansion of international law and the creation of new international institutions as means of replacing military confrontation and warfare with arbitration and the rule of law. Within the worldview of early twentieth-century progressivism, which believed strongly that the exertion of human will could fundamentally transform existing social realities, the grand aspiration of recasting relations between nations into something beyond a Darwinian struggle of power against power seemed within reach.

As a result of the Cold War, Americans have largely forgotten the deeply ingrained nature of legal internationalism in American political culture prior to World War II. In the decades following the First Hague Conference in 1899, a diverse and spirited cacophony of voices clamored for alternatives to power politics and warfare, as a rough consensus across the political spectrum embraced the possibility of remaking the international order and rendering war obsolete. Peace organizations prospered during the 1900s and 1910s, and their membership spanned the ranks of prominent businessmen, political leaders, clergymen, professionals, intellectuals, progressive reformers, and socialist activists. Among the conservative business advocates, Andrew Carnegie was among the most active, and his corporate wealth helped to establish the mainstream character of discussions about international arbitration, the establishment of a permanent world court, the need to restrain national sovereignty, the possibility of world federalism, and other internationalist endeavors.[4]

All three progressive presidents—Theodore Roosevelt, William Howard Taft, and Woodrow Wilson—also supported the creation of an international legal infrastructure that could contain conflict between nations and promote the ideal of global community. Roosevelt backed the early work of the Hague Court, publicly endorsed the goals of the 1907 National Arbitration and Peace Conference, lent the prestige of the presidency to the organization of the Second Hague Conference, also held in 1907, and embraced the idea of a League of Peace.[5] Although remembered more often for "dollar diplomacy," Taft was also an ardent legal internationalist, and the creation of a new international judicial system motivated him above all else. As president, he pursued arbitration treaties with France and Britain as first steps toward the supranational judicial power he hoped would govern international relations in the future, and he frequently spoke before peace groups, worked actively on behalf of the American Society of International Law, and enjoyed the political support of the Chicago Peace Society and other major peace organizations.[6]

Wilson, of course, is the best-known internationalist of all American presidents, and his dedication to the League of Nations paved the way for the creation of the United Nations a quarter-century later.[7] Historians usually emphasize the League's failures, but even as the League demonstrated the limits of post–World War I internationalism, it also helped to legitimate the status of international law, encourage the formation of additional international organizations, and establish other significant precedents as the central institutional embodiment of internationalist principles.[8] Although the League ultimately could not keep the peace, it still served as an important indicator that the international order could become an arena in which individual nation-states did not constitute the sole determinants of world affairs.

At the same time, the U.S. refusal to join the League poses an obvious challenge to any depiction of the pre–World War II period as the heyday of American internationalism. The rejection of the League and the more general history of congressional intransigence toward treaty ratification is often invoked to explain American resistance to legal internationalism and suggest its inevitability given the structure of American politics. Isolationism, however, did not necessarily imply American unilateralism during the early twentieth century. The isolationists feared international institutions and their power, but as anti-imperialists, they sought alternative paths to creating a better, more just world. During the 1920s, as the devastation of the war reenergized the search for world peace, Senator William E. Borah (R-Idaho), a powerhouse in the progressive, isolationist wing of the Senate, became a leading figure behind the outlawry of war movement, which sought to use moral suasion, the removal of legal legitimacy from armed conflict, and reductions in armaments to promote a change in ethical and legal norms that would ultimately prevent nations from violence against each other. In 1928, Borah's efforts resulted in the signing of the Kellogg-Briand Pact, which required its signatories to "condemn recourse to war for the solution of international controversies and renounce it as an instrument of national policy in their relations with one another." Ultimately, some fifty nations, including the United States, major European powers, the Soviet Union, and Japan, agreed to be parties to the treaty, and for a brief, hopeful moment, much of the world formally abjured the use of war.[9]

The liveliness of early twentieth-century debates about world peace is difficult to recapture, and it is easy to be cynical. The long record of American intervention throughout the Caribbean and elsewhere during the Roosevelt and Wilson presidencies does little to build confidence in the progressive presidents' internationalist pretensions. Nor does the racialized language of civilization that dominated internationalist thought a century ago sit well with contemporary attitudes. The Americans who promoted legal internationalism rarely envisioned its benefits extending beyond the white, European world. Carnegie's idea for a League of Peace, for example, included only the United States, Great Britain, France, Russia, and Germany, and it represented less a formula for a new international order than great-power politics by another name.[10] The League of Nations promised to be more inclusive, but Wilson still did not look beyond white, European countries when he called for national self-determination. A young Nguyen Ai Quoc's (later Ho Chi Minh) appeal to Wilson at Versailles on behalf of Vietnamese independence went unanswered.[11]

Nor could efforts to create a new international order boast much success by the 1930s. Taft's arbitration treaties went down to defeat in the Senate, as did American membership in the League of Nations. The Kellogg-Briand Pact's invocation of moral suasion as an alternative to institutional solutions also quickly collapsed with the Japanese occupation of Manchuria, followed by fascist Italy's invasion of Ethiopia, and the start of World War II in Europe. Neither the Treaty of Versailles, the League of Nations, the Harding administration's complex Washington treaty system, nor the Kellogg-Briand Pact prevented the deadliest war of the twentieth century.[12] The atomic bombings of Hiroshima and Nagasaki provided a grim capstone to a conflict that killed at least sixty million people around the world.

It would thus be an exaggeration to see the United States as a paragon of legal internationalism and its virtues in the pre–World War II years, but the shortcomings and failures of early twentieth-century internationalism should not obscure the contrasts between past and current political realities. In the first half of the twentieth century, American political culture did offer an openness to the possibility of peace as a permanent state of affairs, a liveliness of debate over ways to transcend the anarchic tendencies of an international system of self-interested nation-states, and even a willingness to conceive of limitations on American sovereignty and greater modesty in American ambitions for the sake of international stability. It is difficult to imagine a similarly rich discussion taking place in the mainstream of American politics today. Instead, the transition from the immediate postwar enthusiasm for the United Nations to the bipolar world order of the Cold War, and the marginalization of the UN within America's Cold War foreign policy, displaced cooperative, communitarian visions of world order and consigned them to the outer reaches of American politics.

INTERNATIONALIST PLATEAU:
THE UNITED STATES AND THE CREATION
OF THE UNITED NATIONS

World War II produced a complex mixture of despair and hope that transformed the American debate over international organization. On the one hand, the war's sheer brutality, combined with the utter barbarity of the Holocaust, seemed to demonstrate the futility of human nature ever overcoming its dark, violent side. At the same time, however, the destructiveness of the war and the portent of the nuclear age reinforced the sense that humankind had to develop alternatives to armed conflict at all costs. These contradictory sentiments received full expression in American deliberations over the United Nations, as the internationalist hopes of the prewar period melded with the angst and desperation of the war's end to produce the new international body.

In the years since the UN's founding, scholars have emphasized the hyperbole and intensity of hope surrounding its creation, as American politicians and the press sold the UN with lofty statements about the prospects for world peace, and the American public rallied behind the new organization.[13] Critics, meanwhile, cite the structural limitations of the UN that marred it from the very beginning, especially the veto power possessed by the five permanent members of the Security Council, and lambast the privileges of power that undermine the institution's universalist claims to equality of representation.[14] From the vantage point of the last months of World War II and the early postwar years, however, American discussions about the UN looked rather different. Admittedly, there was plenty of hype, as well as genuine hope. Senator Charles W. Tobey (R-New Hampshire) was typical in declaring the

United Nations "the greatest step yet taken by mankind towards world peace."[15] Proposals for world federalism also experienced a postwar resurgence, as many intellectuals believed that only the formation of a truly international community could forestall the next global calamity. In the March 1946 issue of the *Atlantic Monthly,* for example, Thomas K. Finletter, who would later emphasize the maintenance of American nuclear superiority as secretary of the Air Force in the early 1950s, forcefully proclaimed the need for world government, even though it would be a "bitter pill" for a United States accustomed to its sense of sovereignty and independent nationhood.[16] The organized world-government movement also experienced a postwar boost. In February 1947, Norman Cousins triumphantly announced the "organic merger of all the important world government organizations" into the United World Federalists, and he exuberantly reported that the different organizations had reached a general consensus about the need to use the United Nations as the basis for a future world government.[17] Even the physicist Edward Teller, better known for his staunch anticommunism and unwavering devotion to nuclear weapons development (as well as his role as one of the models for Stanley Kubrick's Dr. Strangelove), held faith in the potential of international organization during the early postwar years. As late as the summer of 1948, Teller declared world government "our only hope for survival" and insisted upon it as a necessary long-term goal.[18]

At the April 1945 San Francisco conference and in the months following, however, an undercurrent of caution, and even pessimism, also dominated discussions of the UN. Even as they uttered the requisite paeans to peace, politicians and commentators also emphasized the UN's structural limitations, and they articulated an evolutionary view that recognized international organization and the world order as a work in progress, in which the UN was a preliminary step rather than a finished product. The necessity for the UN lay not in the brilliant new world it promised to create, but in the catastrophic destruction and human misery that it provided a chance to avoid. Senator Arthur H. Vandenberg (R-Michigan), the ranking Republican on the Senate Foreign Relations Committee and a key U.S. delegate at San Francisco, typified this outlook. Formerly a strict isolationist, Vandenberg, then a Michigan newspaper owner and editorialist, had opposed American entry into the League of Nations, and throughout the 1920s and 1930s he frequently articulated the standard opposition to entangling alliances that would curtail American freedom of action. World War II and the increasingly destructive capabilities of modern technology, however, convinced Vandenberg and other isolationists that the United States had to construct and participate in a cooperative postwar international order, and the UN offered the prospect of such cooperation while at the same time preserving American prerogatives through the veto.[19] As he introduced the UN Charter to the Senate at the end of June 1945, however, Vandenberg highlighted the document's shortcomings even as he praised its potential. He declared that he had "no illusions regarding its imperfections" and "no pretensions that it guarantees its own benign aims." Nonetheless, the United Nations constituted "an experiment which must be bravely undertaken in behalf of peace." Although the UN might fail, there was an obligation to try. "I prefer the chance," Vandenberg observed, "rather than no chance at all." The possibility of World War III, which would "open new laboratories of death too horrible to contemplate," required a new effort at international organization.[20]

Such criticisms served the political purpose of warding off charges that international organization represented naive idealism, but they also reflected a keen awareness of the actual international climate surrounding the UN's creation. Vandenberg conceded that the veto power of the permanent members risked reducing the United Nations to a military alliance dominated by the United States, Great Britain, and the Soviet Union, but he argued that one had to deal with the world as it was, not as one would like it to be. "The truth of the matter," Vandenberg contended, "is that we confront a condition, not a theory. . . . The 'condition' is that Britain, Russia, and America control the dominating force-factors of the earth, and are calculated to thus continue for the foreseeable years ahead. To ignore this realism in our peace plans would be to wander in a wishful dream."[21] The UN, its backers insisted, in a tacit allusion to the failures of the League of Nations, embodied a combination of pragmatism and idealism that necessarily incorporated the hard facts of geopolitical life circa 1945. The knowledge that the UN constituted a beginning and not an end, however, softened the blow of international realities and the boundaries they circumscribed.

This concept of international organization as an entity still coming into being suffused early discussions of the UN Charter. President Truman's speech at the final session of the San Francisco conference, for example, stressed that the charter was not the final word. "This charter, like our own Constitution," he observed, "will be expanded and improved as time goes on. No one claims that it is now a final or a perfect instrument. It has not been poured into a fixed mold. Changing world conditions will require readjustments—but they will be the readjustments of peace and not of war."[22] Harold E. Stassen, one of the American delegates at San Francisco, similarly told a Washington, D.C., audience in June 1945 that the "greatness" of the UN Charter lay in its potential to evolve, "in the fact that it has within it the room for growth and adjustment and change under future world transitions and experiences. It is drafted, not for a world standing still but for a world that is dynamic and living."[23] In July, as the Senate took up debate over ratification of the charter, Senator Tom Connally (D-Texas) stressed that the UN was no panacea, but merely a step away from the brink of destruction. He stated, "We advance it [the Charter] not as a magical instrument which will guarantee that there shall be no more wars." The Charter did offer "an advance over the ground where we now stand." But the UN's success, he warned, depended upon constant effort: "Those who want to join a league that is magic, that requires no care, that requires no fuel, that requires no sacrifice on our part, that requires the sending of no troops by us if it comes to that point, are doomed to disappointment. There is no such league; there never has been such a league. There has got to be constant cooperation of the nations of the earth in support of the spirit as well as the letter of the Charter and the high purposes which it envisions."[24] Senator J. William Fulbright (D-Arkansas) similarly emphasized that the maintenance of peace was a process, not a finished product. "Peace is not a negative, static concept," he explained. "It is not a tranquil state of felicity and blessedness. It is a positive method of adjusting the endless conflicts inherent in the nature of restless and energetic men."[25] Thus the UN came into being at a time when the political imagination conceived of both the new organization and the international order as objects in flux that would change and grow with the times. The Cold War, however, imposed a new temporal sense that fixed U.S.-Soviet conflict into permanent reality and consigned internationalism to the backwater of American foreign policy.

THE UNITED STATES, THE UNITED NATIONS, AND THE COLD WAR ORDER

The limited optimism that surrounded the founding of the UN soon gave way to a rapidly growing pessimism, even before the outlines of the Cold War became clear. In December 1945, *The New Republic* grimly observed that the atomic bomb, "which outdated UNO [the United Nations Organization] before it ever got beyond the blueprint stage," combined with the lack of a fully worked-out peace agreement among the wartime allies, meant that the UN had "two strikes already against it."[26] In the following year, as the depths of U.S.-Soviet confrontation became increasingly apparent, internationalists attacked the resurgence of nationalism and lamented the concomitant weakening of the UN's prospects. On the heels of the controversy over Soviet withdrawal from Iran in March 1946, just the latest crisis in the uncertainty that reigned over international relations during the months since the end of the war, *The New Republic* deplored the "slanderous distortions of the aims of the United Nations" and pronounced it "hard to believe that the peoples of Britain, of America, of the USSR, of Iran and China, are peaceful, law-abiding citizens who want to live as part of one, united world."[27] Senator Claude Pepper (D-Florida) also sensed the changed international atmosphere, and he decried the "blind alley of nationalism, isolationalism, or unilateralism" and the breakdown of unity between the United States, Great Britain, and Russia upon which the UN depended.[28] By the fall of 1946, a sense of gloom had firmly set in. As Marcel Hoden, formerly private secretary to the Secretary-General of the League of Nations in the 1930s, observed in *The Nation,* "Never since 1938 has there been more talk of war."[29]

With the rise of the Cold War, the United States turned away from the commitment to international law and international institutions that had been a central part of American political culture throughout the first half of the twentieth century. Within the Truman administration, early enthusiasm for the UN as a prelude to a new kind of politics gave way to the projection of American power in the face of the Soviet threat. American policy toward Greece, which the Truman administration set within the larger context of the Cold War and the need to counter Soviet influence, demonstrated the shift in the UN's status. In the weeks leading up to Truman's congressional address on aid to

Greece and Turkey, in which the president outlined the Truman Doctrine and declared America's broader commitment to the containment of communism, State Department officials characterized Greece as an important test for the UN, and they emphasized the consistency between U.S. aid and the principles of the UN Charter.[30] Soon after the Truman Doctrine speech, however, the administration took steps to distance itself from the internationalist political machinery of the UN. Faced with public criticism for pursuing policy independent of the world organization, the administration considered addressing a letter to the Secretary-General. On March 18, Dean Rusk, then a lower-level State Department official, advised Undersecretary of State Dean Acheson that such a communication, although it offered certain advantages, risked establishing an undesirable precedent that could unduly expand UN jurisdiction and restrain American foreign policy in the future. The next day, at a meeting between Acheson, Secretary of War Patterson, and Secretary of the Navy Forrestal, Acheson stated the letter would not be sent. According to the meeting minutes, Acheson observed that "we might as well face the fact that UN will not settle problems of this type and that it is impossible for the UN to intervene in cases involving subversive movements."[31]

From then on, although American officials maintained a facade of public support for the UN, American policy toward Greece treated the world organization as more a public relations problem than a serious framework for the pursuit of international relations. As John Allphin Moore Jr. and Jerry Pubantz have observed, the Truman Doctrine marked the administration's transition to "cold war mode; gone was the universalist preoccupation with the United Nations as the chief vehicle of U.S. foreign policy."[32] Although the legislation authorizing U.S. aid to Greece and Turkey contained an amendment that required the cancellation of aid in the event of a Security Council or General Assembly resolution condemning such aid, Acheson later characterized the rider as mere "window dressing" meant to placate critics.[33] Over the following months, administration officials seemed more concerned with maintaining an appearance of consistency with UN principles for the sake of world opinion than actually upholding those principles.[34] From the perspective of U.S. policy, the United Nations had become part instrument and part obstacle for the waging of the Cold War.[35]

Until 1970, the United Nations generally provided a friendly forum for America's Cold War aims. In particular, the Korean war demonstrated the utility of the world body for legitimating American foreign policy. The Soviet Union temporarily walked out of the UN early in 1950 in protest over the refusal to seat the People's Republic of China, and the Soviet withdrawal allowed the United States to wage the war with the UN's imprimatur. The U.S. also held sway in the General Assembly. Until the mid-1950s, it could generally count on a two-thirds majority for votes favorable to American goals, and it held a simple majority throughout the 1960s. During these years, American dominance was so powerful that the U.S. never invoked its Security Council veto.[36] Given the weight of numbers, the United States rarely appeared in open defiance of the United Nations during the early decades of the Cold War.[37]

Despite this overwhelming influence, however, the United States nonetheless consistently dismissed the United Nations and its mechanisms for promoting international peace and stability, turning instead toward American-centered means in order to wage the Cold War. George F. Kennan's reflections on the nature of foreign relations captured the American turnabout against UN-centered internationalism. Kennan had earlier gone so far as to denounce the use of the UN in the Korean war as "fuzzy-minded idealism," and in his well-known 1951 primer on U.S. foreign relations, *American Diplomacy, 1900–1950,* he continued his attack. "The most serious fault of our past policy formulation," he argued, lay in "the legal-moralistic approach to international problems" that "runs like a red skein through our foreign policy of the last fifty years." Although Kennan could not define this approach to policy precisely, he identified it with the basic framework of international law and organization that had developed over the past fifty years: "It has in it something of the old emphasis on arbitration treaties, something of the Hague Conferences and schemes for universal disarmament, something of the more ambitious American concepts of the role of international law, something of the League of Nations and the United Nations, something of the Kellogg Pact, something of the idea of a universal 'Article 51' pact, something of the belief in World Law and World Government."[38] For Kennan, the reality of the world order lay in the conflict between nation-states, and not in the community of nations that had been evolving since the turn of the century.

In lieu of an internationalism that emphasized American responsibility to the community of nations, the Cold War prompted an aggressively U.S.-centered foreign policy dedicated to the narrow pursuit of national security through the containment of communism. By the early 1950s, the U.S. had organized alternative arrangements for collective security, through regional alliances such as the OAS, NATO, ANZUS, and SEATO, that offered less cumbersome means for implementing U.S. objectives around the world. The United States also did not hesitate to act unilaterally and ride roughshod over the United Nations. In the early 1950s, CIA-backed coups in Iran and Guatemala clearly contravened the principles of the UN Charter. Following the American-inspired military coup against the democratically elected Arbenz government in Guatemala, President Jacobo Arbenz Guzman appealed to the Security Council to condemn American aggression. The United States adroitly maneuvered to keep Guatemala off the Security Council's agenda by strong-arming its European allies, Britain and France, as well as sharply reprimanding UN Secretary-General, Dag Hammarskjöld, when their support seemed to waver.[39] The two coups sent a clear message: as far as the United States was concerned, American power, not international authority, would determine the path of the Cold War.

Vietnam soon became another hotbed of American unilateralism. In the mid-1950s, the U.S. had already defied international will by subverting the Geneva Accords and rendering impossible the work of the International Control Commission created to monitor and oversee the peace process. The Johnson administration's debate over escalation in 1964–65 illustrates even more starkly the disregard and cynicism with which American policy–makers had come to view the UN.

A few political figures opposed American involvement early on, and they continued to articulate alternatives in terms that resonated with the earlier U.S. commitment to internationalist principles. Senators Wayne Morse (D-Oregon) and Mike Mansfield (D-Montana) pressed the administration to seek peace through the United Nations, and Morse in particular stressed the obligations of the United States under the UN Charter.[40] Undersecretary of State George Ball, perhaps the sole dissenter within the administration over its Vietnam policy, also urged his superiors not to lose "the moral approbation of most UN members."[41] Such voices within the corridors of power were few, however, and no match for the vision of American power that held sway by the 1960s.

The primary architects of America's Vietnam policy viewed the United Nations as an object for manipulation, to be consulted only insofar as necessary to project an image of American compliance with international opinion. In May 1964, for example, as National Security Advisor McGeorge Bundy pushed for a gradual buildup of American military force in Vietnam, he recommended an approach to the Security Council as a mere "exercise," a prelude to "a formal announcement by us and our friends that the requirements of the UN resolution (whether or not it was vetoed) are not being met." The announcement would serve "to clarify again that we have tried the UN and that it is not our fault that there has been an inadequate response."[42] Early the following year, when Mansfield warned that military intervention in Vietnam was doomed to fail and urged Johnson to seek a solution through the UN, Bundy replied that such an effort would be pointless: "From the Secretary-General on down, we are unable to find any expert on the UN who sees any prospect that it can act effectively in the present situation in Vietnam."[43] Bundy's assertion was false— U Thant wanted desperately to establish peace in Vietnam and had already been trying to persuade the United States to enter negotiations with North Vietnam, but he faced an uncooperative Johnson administration and, in particular, the contempt of Secretary of State Dean Rusk.[44]

U.S. relations with the United Nations worsened further over the following decades as American perceptions failed to catch up with profound changes in the geopolitical landscape. The history of international relations since World War II has long been written through the prism of Cold War, bipolar conflict, but in the long run, decolonization and its aftermath may prove to have a more enduring and significant legacy. The emergence of nations through decolonization nearly doubled the UN's membership by 1960, and most of the UN's new members viewed the world's problems as lined up along the North-South axis. American foreign policy, which preferred to view all conflicts through the lens of the East-West struggle, was ill-equipped to deal with the aspirations of long-repressed peoples. Most of the new nations suspected the intent of both the USSR and the United States and sought a course outside the confines of the Cold War framework; from the American perspective, this insistence upon autonomy suggested vulnerability to communist subversion.[45] The tensions between the United States and the newly independent nations of Asia and Africa, as well as the rest of what at the time was called the Third World, soon produced an open rupture between the U.S. and the UN.

As of 1970, the U.S. was already at odds with world opinion, including its closest European allies, because of the Vietnam War. The rise of the Third World within the United Nations further exacerbated the breach. In 1968, seventy-seven UN members organized the Group of 77 (which soon expanded to include over a hundred nations) to provide a counterweight to American power and promote the interests of small, impoverished nations faced with Northern economic dominance. As Gary B. Ostrower has described it, "The Group of 77 was the incarnation of the cultural change that Charles Malik had described: sympathetic to social and economic radicalism, deeply hostile of what it defined (correctly or not) as imperialism, dogmatic about race and intolerant of western legalism."[46] During the early 1970s, the Group of 77 articulated an agenda sharply at odds with American foreign policy: it extended an invitation to Yasir Arafat to address the General Assembly, rejected liberal economic policy in favor of a New International Economic Order, and sponsored the November 1975 General Assembly resolution that condemned Zionism as a form of racism. The American ambassador to the UN, Daniel Patrick Moynihan, viewed the Group of 77 as a threat to all the UN stood for; during his stormy tenure, he denounced the New International Economic Order as "tyranny by the majority" and generally followed a policy of confrontation. Moynihan's frequent attacks, career UN diplomat Brian Urquhart later recalled, "struck a xenophobic chord across large sections of the American public" and served as both cause and harbinger of things to come.[47]

Relations between the United States and the United Nations warmed briefly during the Carter years, but improved outward appearances did not signify a fundamental change in the relatively low status of the United Nations within U.S. foreign policy. The enthusiasm over Andrew Young's tenure as UN ambassador also failed to mask persistent tensions between the United States and the "Third World UN," as symbolized by the temporary American withdrawal from the International Labor Organization in 1977 in protest of the ILO's positions on Israel.[48] Disputes between the United States and the United Nations worsened a few years later as the Reagan administration's assertiveness in the global arena clashed with the UN's efforts to exert its independence. The Reagan years prompted what the political scientist Robert W. Gregg later characterized as "an orgy of UN-bashing."[49] During the early 1980s, the U.S. suspended its involvement in the International Atomic Energy Agency for six months, and it pulled out of UNESCO for the next nineteen years. At one point, Reagan indicated that if the United Nations itself wanted to leave the United States and station its headquarters elsewhere, Americans would be perfectly happy to see the world organization pull up its stakes.[50] The *New York Times* identified "a national mood of disenchantment with the United Nations."[51] Congress, seeing little gain in continued investment in an institution that so often contradicted American aims, sought to pull the fiscal plugs. In 1983, the Kassenbaum amendment cut U.S. contributions to the UN by $500 million over four years, and in 1985, the Gramm-Rudman Act exercised further cuts. Within three years, U.S. payments totaled less than half of what the United States was assessed, and the United Nations, forbidden under the charter to borrow money, faced severe financial straits.[52] The United States began to resist the international legal order as well. In May 1984, the World Court issued a provisional ruling (formalized two years later) against the United States over its violations of international law in connection with American support for the Nicaraguan contras. The United States, in a move that perhaps foreshadowed the current American attitude toward the International Criminal Court, promptly withdrew recognition of compulsory jurisdiction on the part of the World Court.[53]

By the mid-1980s, the Cold War had reduced American internationalism to a shadow of its former self. Brian Urquhart later recalled the grim mood among the advocates of global community. He observed:

> In Reagan's Washington, there seemed to be an open season on a variety of multilateral or international arrangements which were the fruit of years of painstaking work and negotiation. Some neoconservative ideologues even advocated the virtues of "global unilateralism" for the United States. . . . They [the administration and neoconservatives]

seemed to view the United Nations as a troublesome sideshow. . . . The conservative right apparently believed that if the UN was not effectively dominated by the United States, did not respond unquestioningly to United States values or priorities, and failed to function as a bastion against the Soviet Union, it was not the international organization the United States ought to belong to.[54]

For Urquhart, Secretary of State George P. Shultz's critique, delivered at the fortieth-anniversary celebration of the UN charter, captured the derision and contempt the United Nations faced from the United States by the mid-1980s. Shultz, Urquhart wrote, "spoke of the world organization as if it was a delinquent schoolboy who had flunked his exams. . . . It was a depressing performance."[55]

Other observers also worried about the "twilight of internationalism" and condemned what they viewed as an increasingly worrisome trend toward American unilateralism in world affairs. Disrespect for the rule of law appeared rampant, and the United States's once-strong support for an internationalism based on the primacy of international norms, restraint in the use of force, and commitment to international organization seemed to have faded.[56] Driven by a mentality that failed to recognize the majority of nations that sought a neutral existence outside the parameters of U.S.-Soviet conflict, the United States had abandoned its early enthusiasm for the United Nations in favor of an American-centered, Cold War order. From the American perspective, by the 1980s the UN had become little more than a noisy, intransigent, and ultimately irrelevant force in the struggle for power that defined world affairs.

THE UNITED NATIONS, INTERNATIONALISM, AND THE REMAKING OF THE WORLD ORDER

In 1945, the founders of the United Nations had emphasized that the world organization's success depended on continued cooperation between the major wartime allies. The Cold War soon diminished the UN's role and sharply limited its ability to effect major changes in the nature of international relations. As one scholar observed in the late 1960s, "Throughout the history of the United Nations the impact of the systemic environment on the Organization has far surpassed the impact of the Organization on the [international] system."[57] Nonetheless, throughout the postwar decades, the United Nations continued to evolve, just as so many American officials had once predicted it would. Even in a climate of American unilateralism and the Cold War's domination of the international agenda, the UN quietly succeeded in promoting new norms about the conduct of human affairs, and for nations around the world, it provided an important alternative to the balance-of-power politics that defined the U.S.-Soviet conflict.

From the perspective of smaller nations, the United Nations remained a source of hope that the international arena could transcend the anarchical relations of individual nation-states. For example, internationalist ideals defined the agenda of the 1955 Bandung conference, in which representatives and leaders from some thirty African and Asian nations established the organized nonaligned movement in order to chart a path independent of the U.S.-Soviet conflict. As the Bandung conferees called for tolerance and peaceful coexistence between nations, as well as an end to racism and colonialism, they appealed repeatedly to the principles of the UN Charter and the need to strengthen the United Nations. Most of those in attendance were from newly independent nations, and Bandung represented a postcolonial effort to move the world beyond the domination of the many by the few.

Anticommunist ideology had submerged the language of internationalism and world peace within American political culture by the 1950s, but that language remained compelling elsewhere in the world.[58] Few Americans have ever examined what transpired at Bandung; reading the official speeches fifty years later, one is struck by the optimism and passion behind the sentiments expressed there, and the refreshing counterpoint they offer to an era mired in the stridency of the Cold War. At Bandung, Indonesian president Sukarno gave impassioned voice to internationalist principles as he called upon governments to follow "the highest code of morality and ethics" and warned that the world could not afford to "indulge in power politics."[59] Indonesian Prime Minister Sastroamidjojo also emphasized the dangers posed by the "present precarious balance of power" and called for a true peace based not on relations of domination, but on tolerance, cooperation, and recognition of national self-determination.[60]

The Bandung delegates counted on the United Nations to play the pivotal role in creating an internationalist world order, but they were not uncritical of the world organization. In particular, the representatives of Arab states articulated their anger and distress over Palestine and charged the UN with failing to live up to its own regime of human rights and respect for nationalities. As they articulated their grievances, however, they also made clear their staunch belief that solutions to world problems lay in a strengthened United Nations and the active promotion of the UN Charter. Egyptian and Arab nationalist leader Gamal Abdel Nasser, who would soon be known also as one of the stalwarts of the nonaligned movement, stressed Egypt's "unshaken faith in the new international order which was inaugurated in the Charter of the United Nations" and insisted that the path toward world peace lay in sustaining the ideals of the charter and the Universal Declaration of Human Rights. "The game of power politics," he added, "must be stopped if the existing international tensions [are] to come to an end."[61] Although he faulted the UN for failing to uphold human rights in Palestine, he made clear his devotion to a UN-centered world order. Other delegates, including representatives from Ceylon, Libya, Iraq, Pakistan, and Lebanon, also pronounced their dedication to the UN Charter. Even as some of them found fault with the United Nations, they also believed the organization needed to play a more active role in world affairs.[62] Carlos P. Romulo, head of the Philippine delegation and one of the key contributors to the formulation of the Universal Declaration of Human Rights, captured the consensus at Bandung that there existed an international order that superseded the interests of individual nation-states. "Issues of freedom, equality, and growth," Romulo observed, "are no longer merely national problems but *world* problems." Although the United Nations was "more a mirror of the world than an effective instrument for changing it," the organization remained a place of promise, "a place where man, not quite yet a reasonable animal, is trying very hard to become one."[63]

Such sentiments did not exist merely as lofty, but forlorn, hopes in the midst of the U.S.-Soviet conflict. Through a long-term process mired in obstacles and disappointments—partly the result of the Cold War political climate and partly the product of the UN's own institutional structure—the United Nations nonetheless succeeded in pushing international relations in the direction of internationalist principles. As one scholar observed back in 1970, "The postwar era, for all the inadequacies of contemporary international organization, produced truly revolutionary developments."[64] In the years since, the UN's prominence in world affairs has only increased, particularly since the end of the Cold War. On the whole, for over fifty years now, the United Nations has fostered progress in a wide range of significant and worthwhile areas. The growing acceptance of the universality of human rights, the invention of peacekeeping as a means of managing international disputes, the rise of humanitarian intervention within nation-states, the promotion of an international legal regime able to prosecute war crimes and crimes against humanity, and the expansion of a rich international order structured by formal institutions and the diverse activities of thousands of nongovernmental organizations all derive much of their legitimacy and influence from the UN's efforts.

Until the 1940s, human rights remained but a nascent concept in international relations, but it gained normative status in the aftermath of World War II. As Mary Ann Glendon has observed, the United Nations' 1948 Universal Declaration of Human Rights, combined with the Nuremberg Principles and the 1948 Genocide Convention, "became a pillar of a new international system under which a nation's treatment of its own citizens was no longer immune from outside scrutiny."[65] Although the Universal Declaration lacked enforcement mechanisms and the imprimatur of international law, as a statement of principle it established new standards for conduct that nations violated at their peril. Nations did not cease to persecute their own citizens, but the idea of human rights prompted political countercurrents that could not be ignored. In the early 1960s, Malcolm X defined the cause of African Americans in terms of human, rather than civil, rights, and sought UN condemnation of American racism precisely because he understood the power of ideas and world opinion. The Universal Declaration also provided legitimacy and influence to human rights organizations founded in the 1960s and 1970s, including Amnesty International and Human Rights Watch, and over the last thirty years, such NGOs have played a major role in calling attention to the worst abuses of nations around the world. In more recent years, at the 1993 UN World Conference on Human Rights and the 1995 UN World Conference on Women, the United Nations also provided an important platform for the recognition of women's rights as human rights, and the growing international concern with the conditions of women around the world owes much to the United Nations and the exertions of NGOs that placed women's issues on the world's agenda. Nascent enforcement mechanisms have also evolved over the last several decades, and with the establishment of new institutions such as the International Criminal Court, global tolerance for human rights violations may continue to shrink in the future.[66]

The development of peacekeeping also demonstrated the UN's capacity for creative political evolution even in the midst of the Cold War. Although the United Nations was founded to maintain international peace and security, the UN charter did not anticipate the mechanism of peacekeeping, that is, the use of neutral forces brought in with the consent of warring parties to help preserve tenuous peace agreements. When the United Nations Emergency Force was deployed at the end of the 1956 Suez crisis, peacekeeping constituted, as Peter R. Baehr and Leon Gordenker have observed, "an unprecedented device."[67] In his memoir, Brian Urquhart also emphasized the novelty of peacekeeping: "The modus operandi of peacekeeping operations, now commonplace, was then a first experiment, a complete innovation. We were asking soldiers, against all tradition and training, to take part in nonviolent operations in a critical situation—operations, moreover, which were not under the control of their own governments. The new peacekeeping operations touched on the most delicate issues of military psychology, national sovereignty, international politics, and national and international law."[68] Peacekeeping prompted a new understanding about the use of force, in which the maintenance of peace required a visible military presence without the actual firing of weapons. As Urquhart explained, "The real strength of a peacekeeping operation lies not in its capacity to use force, but precisely in its *not* using force and thereby remaining above the conflict and preserving its unique position and prestige. The moment a peacekeeping force starts killing people, it becomes a part of the conflict it is supposed to be controlling, and therefore a part of the problem."[69]

Given the difficulty of sustaining cease-fires in unstable situations, peacekeeping has understandably had an uneven record. In the 1950s and 1960s, for example, partial success in the Middle East stood alongside failure in the Congo.[70] The constraints of Cold War politics also limited the scope of UN peacekeeping operations. Nonetheless, peacekeeping became a regular function of the United Nations, and it has come to play a highly visible and significant role in the promotion of peace and stability around the world. The awarding of the 1988 Nobel Peace Prize to the United Nations Peacekeeping Forces, one of five Nobel Peace Prizes associated with the United Nations, signified the importance of UN peacekeepers' contributions to world affairs. The prize recognized the peacekeepers as the embodiment of "the manifest will of the community of nations to achieve peace through negotiations" and lauded their creative transformation of military force into an instrument of nonviolence.[71]

The synergistic relationship between the United Nations and nongovernmental organizations has also contributed to the reshaping of the international political landscape over the last several decades. In the 1920s, the Covenant of the League of Nations pioneered the extension of international authority to private organizations by recognizing and supporting the humanitarian efforts of the International Red Cross. The UN Charter built upon this precedent by mandating consultation with nongovernmental organizations in the UN's Economic and Social Council. In practice, this limited consultative status has provided NGOs informal access to the entire UN bureaucracy, including the General Assembly and the Security Council, and as a result, NGOs have built considerable influence through the UN system. With the UN's support, NGOs have added the voice of what some observers call "international civil society" to international relations, an arena traditionally dominated by the official governments of nation-states. The situation is not entirely new—as Akira Iriye has recently emphasized, the history of nongovernmental organizations as a component of international relations dates back to the late nineteenth century, and had the UN never existed, NGOs undoubtedly would have still persisted with their work. The UN has aided their efforts, however, by providing NGOs with official status and a friendly forum to pursue agendas in diverse areas, including human rights, humanitarian intervention, environmental protection, arms control, health, and international development.

Consequently, nongovernmental organizations have been able to play a major role in setting the terms of policy debates at the international level. For example, in the areas of women's rights, the environment, and humanitarian relief, nongovernmental organizations have become increasingly visible, especially since the end of the Cold War. The aforementioned promotion of women's rights around the world owes much to the cooperative efforts of NGOs and the UN. Similarly, environmental groups, numbering literally in the hundreds, helped define the international environmental agenda at the 1992 UN Conference on Environment and Development in Rio de Janeiro; five years later, environmental organizations also participated in policy formulation at the 1997 UN Conference on Climate Change in Kyoto. NGOs, often but not always in partnership with the UN, have also been near the front lines of the worst post–Cold War conflicts, dispensing humanitarian relief in Bosnia, Chechnya, Rwanda, Kosovo, and elsewhere, as well as training an insistent spotlight on the most criminal abuses of power wherever they take place around the world.[72]

THE UNITED STATES, THE UNITED NATIONS, AND THE POST–COLD WAR WORLD ORDER

As this brief survey indicates, during the Cold War, much of the world continued to look to the UN as an alternative to power politics, and the organization itself established and experimented with new means of promoting peace, stability, and human dignity that stretched the boundaries of a world order based on sovereign nation-states. During the first stage of the post–Cold War era, from the fall of the Berlin Wall in 1989 to the destruction of the World Trade Center in 2001, the UN-centered internationalist order made considerable headway in demonstrating its viability and importance as a force in world affairs. The Gulf War constituted a key turning point. For the first time, the UN, released from the constraints of the Cold War, was able to promote collective security along the lines envisioned in the UN Charter. Although critics of the Gulf War have emphasized oil interests and American dominance of the international scene, the UN resolutions authorizing use of force to repel the invasion of one member state by another cannot be easily reduced to the unfettered pursuit of American interest and the reduction of the UN to a mere instrumentality.[73] The United States naturally worked to shape the international will toward the American agenda, but it also had to follow world opinion. By seeking the imprimatur of the UN and a broad international coalition, rather than following a wholly unilateral course as some, such as

British Prime Minister Margaret Thatcher, recommended, the United States accepted certain limits placed by the international community. A decade later, American conservatives denounced the earlier decision not to overthrow Saddam Hussein's regime, as if the failure to do so constituted a grievous error of the moment. They seemed conveniently to forget that the tenuous and difficult partnerships of 1990–91, particularly with the major Arab states, specifically forbade taking the war to Baghdad, and that a decision by the first Bush administration to exceed its international mandate would have provoked world enmity. By contrast, the current Bush administration has had few qualms about inciting international rancor. As a career diplomat observed in his resignation letter, tendered during the buildup to the 2003 war on Iraq, *"oderint dum metuant"* appears to have become official U.S. policy, at the risk of potentially devastating consequences.[74]

As Robert W. Gregg has observed, one may criticize the United States's UN diplomacy leading up to the 1991 Gulf War on a variety of grounds—that it was cynical and coercive, and that it paid mere lip service to the American obligation, under the charter, to seek peaceful solutions before resorting to warfare. To that extent, the U.S.-UN relationship differed little from what it had been since the 1950s. But at the same time, the post–Cold War context of the Gulf crisis also led the United States to deal seriously with the UN for the first time in years, as well as make major concessions in light of international opinion, and the United Nations emerged from the war with renewed vigor and autonomy.[75] As a result, during the years between the first Gulf War and the second in 2003, the UN's stature grew dramatically. In addition to the initiatives on human rights and the environment, UN peacekeeping expanded at a rapid pace in the 1990s. Between 1988 and 1998, the UN launched well over twice as many peacekeeping operations as it had in its entire previous history, including efforts in Angola, El Salvador, Cambodia, Haiti, the Balkans, and other hot spots struggling to establish political stability. UN peacekeeping also expanded beyond the maintenance of cease-fires to include new functions, such as presiding over troop withdrawals and monitoring elections.[76] There were salutary developments on the legal front as well. Not only did the International Court of Justice rebound from its Cold War doldrums, but more recently, after a century of gradual codification of humanitarian law, the international legal structure for prosecuting war crimes and crimes against humanity has also begun to come of age. In 1993, the Hague convened the first war crimes tribunal since the Nuremburg trials in order to prosecute crimes committed in Bosnia. With the recent ratification of the Rome Statute and the establishment of the International Criminal Court, the world now has, for the first time, a standing court for the prosecution of war crimes and crimes against humanity.[77]

As yet, this UN-centered international order functions far from perfectly. The institutions and treaty arrangements for upholding the principles of the UN Charter are still relatively young, and they frequently collide with the aspirations of individual nation-states. The international community's consistent failure to respond adequately to genocide over the last half century signifies one of the most wrenching shortcomings of the UN system. Humanitarian intervention in the face of the worst forms of human brutality poses inherent challenges because the UN Charter recognizes the primacy of both national sovereignty and individual dignity. The international community is still improvising its responses in cases when the two prove irreconcilable, and the complexities of international relations militate toward inaction. In 1999, the UN harshly evaluated its failure to respond effectively to the Rwandan genocide of 1994, but at the same time, Russia's friendly relationship with Serbia prevented the Security Council from mobilizing a quick response to events in Kosovo. Perhaps more extensive diplomacy might have yielded a UN response, but President Bill Clinton, himself haunted by the American failure to act in Rwanda, opted for an end run around the UN and organized the NATO bombing campaign that put an end to ethnic cleansing in Kosovo.[78]

Such failures in the UN's mission to keep the peace and protect human rights, however, should be understood as the product of the global community's nascent character, and not inherent flaws of the internationalist vision. The world order envisioned by the UN Charter is still in a constant process of coming into being, and its capacities pale compared to the magnitude of global problems. Nonetheless, the United Nations has made considerable inroads in establishing its own legitimacy as a political presence on the world stage, as well as promoting creative political, legal, and military responses to crises and adverse conditions around the world. The greater threat to the UN's success comes not from the allegedly impractical, pie-in-the-sky character of internationalist hopes, but from the resurgence of American power since the end of the Cold War.

Unlike most of the world, the United States has not greeted the UN's post–Cold War rise to prominence with enthusiasm. One might have postulated a revival of pre–World War II internationalism after the disintegration of the Soviet Union, but old patterns of thought die hard. Indeed, in many quarters, post–Cold War triumphalism vindicated the strategies of the previous decades. According to various lines of thought, the peaceful collapse of the Soviet Union demonstrated the virtue of American vigilance and tough-mindedness in the face of the Communist threat, and it justified a range of policy choices, from the doctrine of mutual assured destruction to the defense buildup of the 1980s. Decisions that then reflected ideological commitments or improvised responses to exigencies of the time have even been rewritten in hindsight as bold, carefully constructed strategies to ensure final victory in the Cold War.[79]

As a result, the collapse of the Soviet Union reinforced American tendencies toward unilateralism, and long before the crisis that resulted in a new American war on Iraq, the United States had become one of the major obstacles to internationalist aspirations. Although Presidents Bill Clinton and George W. Bush proclaimed their commitment to multilateralism, the actions of the United States spoke otherwise. In recent years, the United States has received heavy criticism around the world for its opposition to a ban on land mines, its failure to ratify the Kyoto Protocol on climate change, its resort to the NATO-led bombing campaign in Kosovo rather than relying upon action under UN auspices, its decision to discard single-handedly the 1973 ABM Treaty in order to pursue strategic missile defense, and its stalwart opposition to the International Criminal Court. Until 1999, the American refusal to keep up with its dues payments to the UN (by then, U.S. arrears topped $1.6 billion) also cast the United States as a less than committed citizen of the world.[80]

As a result of persistent American defiance of international will, world opinion has grown increasingly critical of American unilateralism. In May 2001, in response to continued American attacks on the UN and the refusal of the U.S. to meet its financial obligations, the UN Economic and Social Council voted the U.S. off the United Nations Human Rights Commission. Later that month, Amnesty International issued a scathing report that cited American opposition to the land-mine ban and the International Criminal Court, as well as other developments, as evidence that the United States was "as frequently an impediment to human rights as it is an advocate." When President Bush visited Sweden in the summer of 2001, some 10,000 protesters turned out to demonstrate against American policies on strategic missile defense, the environment, and the death penalty. The following year, the United States further inflamed the debate over the International Criminal Court by demanding immunity for American peacekeeping forces and threatening to pull the plug on UN peacekeeping operations in Bosnia-Herzegovina and elsewhere if such immunity were not forthcoming. Leaders in Europe, Canada, Mexico, and elsewhere responded bitterly to the American attack on the ICC. In this tense international atmosphere, even World Cup soccer could become an occasion for a former Mexican diplomat to decry American unilateralism.[81]

Even before the diplomatic crisis over Iraq, the divide between international opinion and the direction of U.S. foreign policy had thus grown painfully obvious. In recent years, government officials, media organs, and interested observers around the globe have decried American tendencies toward unilateralism on an almost daily basis and pled for greater sensitivity to the repercussions of American actions beyond U.S. borders. Although the United States briefly enjoyed a wave of sympathy and support in the aftermath of the September 11 attacks on the World Trade Center and the Pentagon, since then the Bush administration's war against terror, especially its insistence on making Iraq the latest battlefield, only heightened anxieties about the projection of American power in the international arena. During the six months leading up to the U.S.-led invasion of Iraq in March 2003, the Bush administration encountered little other than confirmed opposition as it tried to earn support for American military intervention. Instead, most of the world preferred to look elsewhere, to the moral authority of the United Nations, for leadership.[82]

World opinion and international organization ultimately failed to prevent military conflict, and the war on Iraq has led some observers to predict, or even pronounce, the death of the UN system.[83] That conclusion seems premature, however, for a variety of reasons. First, the United States still cannot declare Iraq a job well done, the Bush administration's protestations to the contrary notwithstanding. Although military victory came relatively easily, during the weeks following the end of the war, the persistence of civil chaos, the collapse of basic infrastructure within the country, and the inability of ordinary Iraqis to go about their daily business with a minimal expectation of personal safety pointed to the utter inadequacy of postwar planning on the part of the United States. The hasty replacement of General Jay Garner as civilian administrator of Iraq a scant three weeks after his arrival, apparently in response to continued looting and street violence, shortages in food, water, and other basic necessities of life, and frequent reports of women unable to leave their homes in broad daylight for fear of kidnapping and rape, underscored the incoherence of American occupation policy.[84] It would be premature to gauge the long-term effects of the war, but it certainly seems clear that the Bush administration failed to anticipate and adequately meet Iraq's principal needs in the conflict's immediate aftermath. The administration's early determination to prevent the UN, with its extensive experience in providing police power and humanitarian aid in unstable political situations, from playing a significant role in the postwar reconstruction of Iraq also needlessly exacerbated postwar difficulties. Moreover, as of this writing (October 2003), organized resistance to the American occupation has grown steadily. Regular acts of sabotage against oil pipelines and power facilities, multiple daily attacks on American soldiers, and increasingly bold acts of terror, such as the bombings of the Jordanian embassy and the UN's headquarters in Baghdad that killed over thirty people, a car bombing of a mosque in Najaf that left about a hundred dead, including a prominent Shiite cleric, an attack on the hotel where Deputy Secretary of Defense Paul D. Wolfowitz was staying during his visit to Baghdad, and a dramatic series of suicide car bombings in Baghdad that left dozens dead and hundreds wounded, indicate a highly unstable situation that does not augur well for the Bush administration's state-building aspirations.[85]

It also seems difficult to argue that the war has significantly enhanced American security. Although the White House cited the threat from weapons of mass destruction as its main rationale for preemptive warfare, the United States has thus far failed to uncover significant caches of biological and chemical weapons, or dramatic proof of a thriving Iraqi nuclear weapons program. One cannot dismiss completely the possibility that banned weapons might yet be discovered, but the complete absence of such weapons deployed and ready for use has led to growing concerns and criticisms within the Central Intelligence Agency, the military, and Congress about the quality of the information that provided the main rationale for the war. The apparent inadequacy of intelligence information concerning weapons of mass destruction was further compounded by the failure of the U.S. military to secure suspected weapons sites, which were instead looted as the military continued its headlong rush to Baghdad. The administration hailed early findings, such as the uncovering of two trailers initially believed to have been biological weapons facilities, but none of these discoveries has withstood close scrutiny, and at this point, the American intelligence community has all but conceded its credulousness in accepting reports of Iraqi weapons programs by Iraqi defectors and expatriates at face value.[86] Nor has convincing evidence surfaced of the close linkages between Saddam Hussein and Al Qaeda alleged by the Bush administration. Meanwhile, in Afghanistan, Hamid Karzai's government maintains only a tenuous hold on power, and at this point it is hard to believe any Iraqi connection to international terrorism posed a greater threat to American security than the apparent regrouping of Al Qaeda operatives in uncontrolled areas along the Afghanistan-Pakistan border, as well as in east Africa and other parts of the world.[87] The May 2003 suicide bombings of compounds in Saudi Arabia that housed large numbers of Americans and other foreigners also raises the question of whether or not the Bush administration has identified the right battlegrounds in its war against terrorism.[88]

For its part, the UN system remains intact despite the damage wrought by American actions, and developments during the run up to the war on Iraq demonstrated the significance of the UN's authority even as the United States worked actively to undermine that authority. First, although the Bush administration apparently decided in advance to pursue military action against Iraq regardless of the outcome of prewar diplomacy, its assessment of American interest deemed it preferable to gain UN approval, if possible. Hence the United States went through the motions of renewed UN weapons inspections in Iraq under Security Council Resolution 1441, and in March 2003 it launched a strenuous diplomatic effort to obtain a second Security Council resolution authorizing the use of force. Although the UN ultimately could not prevent the war, the attractions of possible Security Council approval were sufficient to delay the war's start for a period of months. The Bush administration's official line that the United States was part of a "coalition of the willing" arrayed against Saddam Hussein also highlighted the symbolic importance of international support, even as the war remained, overwhelmingly, an American operation. (By contrast, the United States did not deploy the language of coalition during the Vietnam War, and few Americans today remember that Australian and South Korean troops, as well as Thai mercenary soldiers, fought in Vietnam at the request of the United States.) Second, the failure of the United States even to obtain a simple majority vote in the Security Council in favor of a second resolution and force a French veto, despite intense efforts to round up the necessary votes, particularly from the small African nations of Cameroon, Guinea, and Angola, speaks to the greater autonomy of the post–Cold War United Nations, as compared to the ability of American carrots and sticks to sway important Security Council votes in earlier decades.[89] Third, the willingness of so many leaders around the world to insist publicly that only the UN could legitimately authorize military action to enforce UN resolutions regarding Iraq indicates the esteem in which the world organization is held, as both a symbol and a potential counterweight to American power. Americans also hold the United Nations in high regard—up until the eve of the war, opinion polls consistently suggested the American public's preference for continued UN weapons inspections in Iraq and UN sanction prior to the beginning of military action.[90] Meanwhile, the American doctrine of preemptive warfare has not earned significant support—to that extent, the rest of the world has not accepted the American attempt to rewrite the international rules of conduct. Finally, with the deteriorating security situation in Iraq and the rising monetary costs of the American occupation, the United States has found itself unable to do away entirely with its own need for the United Nations. The Bush administration's desire for both American control and international assistance has produced constant vacillation over the UN's role in Iraq's reconstruction, and negotiations over the purpose and extent of the world organization's participation continue, but growing dismay within the United States over the economic burden of the occupation (about $1 billion per week) appears to have rendered long-term unilateralism financially untenable.[91] All of these developments indicate that the UN Charter has not yet, as Michael J. Glennon recently contended, "gone the way of the Kellogg-Briand Pact."[92]Although frequently honored in the breach, the principles of the charter remain the stated norms of international behavior, and most nations seem to believe that a stronger UN would serve their national interests.

Of course, one must acknowledge that the war provided yet another stark reminder of the UN's limitations. Periodic failure is written into its institutional structure, in the lack of adequate mechanisms to enforce the international community's will, and particularly in the veto power, which preserves the perquisites of the great powers that emerged victorious in World War II. But it is equally important to recognize the achievements of internationalism within the sharp constraints of a hybridized international system that has grafted international organization onto a world of independent nation-states. Despite enormous obstacles, over the last six decades the United Nations has managed to become not just a powerful moral symbol, but a real political force in world affairs.

CONCLUSION: THE UN-CENTERED WORLD (GET USED TO IT)

A January 2003 cover page of the *New York Times Magazine* blared, "The American Empire (Get Used to It)."[93] The United States might do better, however, to adapt to a more interdependent world, with the United Nations at its core. The critical question of the twenty-first century is whether the United States will choose to be a cooperative partner in "the other post–Cold War order," or if it will continue to pursue the politics of predominance that emerged during the Cold War. As Americans ponder the answer to this question, they ought to remember that internationalism is neither a foreign import nor a province of the political margins. It was a real and valid proposition to most Americans throughout the first half of the twentieth century, and it remains a real and valid proposition to much of the world today.

Cynics will argue that internationalism faded in the United States for good reason, and the rest of the world ought to follow suit. The proliferation of ethnic conflict and violence around the world in recent years, not to mention the dangers posed by international terrorism, seems to speak to the futility of expecting peoples and nations to be their better selves. Advocates of world peace and international cooperation have always been vulnerable to charges of impracticality, precisely because experience so often seems to suggest that their goals are unobtainable. Not all pasts are usable, and while the creation of a true community of nations or the appeal to moral suasion may sound like admirable sentiments, the world as an array of power against power appears too often to correspond to actual reality.[94]

Geopolitical considerations also militate against a voluntary renunciation of empire on the part of the United States. American dedication to peace politics reached its height at a time when the center of world power still lay in Europe. The schizophrenic character of American foreign relations—its combination of imperial ambition and sympathy toward the rights of small nations—perhaps owes much to the United States's liminal turn-of-the-century position as a country inferior to the major European powers but itself a growing force in world affairs. Alternative conceptions of world order offered a means for the United States to play a larger role in international relations than its actual status implied; to that extent, it is no coincidence that the United States abandoned those alternatives once it realized a preponderance of power.[95] Traditional geopolitics rewards the powerful, and current political trends do not indicate much willingness on the part of policymakers to rethink the virtues of American hegemony.

Nonetheless, the international system has shown signs of fundamental change. The relatively peaceful collapse of communism in Eastern Europe in 1989, contrary to all expectations, demonstrated that creative political possibilities are not confined to the distant past or the realm of fancy. In recent years, the renewed vigor of humanitarian intervention and the widespread efforts to address world problems through international agreements ranging from the Ottawa Treaty banning land mines to the Rome Statute of the International Criminal Court to the Kyoto Protocol on climate change suggests that to some extent, despite American opposition, institutionalized internationalism has never been stronger. The hard-won UN-brokered agreements with Indonesia that secured independence for East Timor in 1999, after decades of violent repression during which the most powerful members of the international community turned a blind eye, provide testimony to the continued political viability and value of the UN's work.[96] At the same time, however, the new Pax Americana has placed institutionalized internationalism at its greatest risk since the 1930s, and world problems continue to multiply. To echo former president Jimmy Carter's sentiments in his 2002 Nobel address, internationalism offers a realm of possibility, and there are concrete developments that provide a basis for hope, but not without remembering that we remain within the confines of a deeply troubled world.

Part IV

The Present

8

The Three Cold Wars

Chalmers Johnson

Reflecting their traditional preoccupations with Europe, most American political elites accept as obvious that "the Cold War is over." What they really mean is that in Europe, the Cold War seemed to end with the breaching of the Berlin Wall in 1989 and the collapse of the Soviet Union in 1991. They tend to ignore or be ignorant of the simultaneous Cold Wars in East Asia and Latin America, which had different ideological and material foundations and which continued unabated after the demise of the communist camp.

In East Asia, the confrontation with China has long preoccupied American strategists above all others, but they have been forced to guard what they say and take an indirect approach because of China's growing economic power and because any conflict with China would seriously overstretch American military and financial capabilities. Ironically enough, China has been proceeding in ways the United States once hoped it would, effectively dismantling Leninism without the political instability of the former Soviet Union and becoming one of the most capitalist (and fastest growing) economies on earth. By so doing, however, it is rapidly approaching superpower status and possibly threatening American dominance over East Asia.

On the Korean peninsula, the artificial division imposed in 1945 by the United States and the Soviet Union persists, although relations between the two Korean entities themselves have improved. In June 2000, the leaders of North and South Korea met in Pyongyang, the North Korean capital, and started a process looking toward the reunification of the country without interference from any outside power. The meeting allowed President Kim Dae Jung of South Korea to proclaim, "The North will no longer attempt unification by force and, at the same time, we will not do any harm to the North. The most important outcome of the summit is that there is no longer going to be any war."[1] Unfortunately, this statement may no longer be true. President Kim won the 2000 Nobel Peace Prize for this breakthrough, but he did not fully calculate how threatening his initiative was to the interests of American militarism and the military-industrial complex. President George W. Bush's "axis of evil" speech of January 29, 2002—singling out Iran, Iraq, and North Korea as the next targets for American pre-emptive attack—did much to undermine the emerging hopes for peace on the Korean peninsula. By mid-2003, relations between North Korea and the United States, with South Korea as an increasingly alarmed and anti-American bystander, had become perhaps the most threatening on earth, including the possible use of nuclear weapons.

Similarly, the Cold War in Latin America is not only not over but, in July 2000, entered a new, more virulent stage in Colombia and other Andean nations with the escalation of United States military intervention under cover of fighting the drug war. Following directly on the U.S.'s Vietnam-like operations in Central America throughout the 1980s, this new phase in South America includes clandestine operations by U.S. Army Special Forces, support for right-wing death squads in Colombia and Bolivia, mammoth arms sales, and an indifference to the effects of powerful herbicides on the environment and water supply. Throughout the 1990s, the United States was extremely active in training Latin American and Caribbean military officers in the techniques of "foreign internal defense" (indistinguishable from state terrorism) and in attempting to quarantine Cuba as a threat to stability in the region.

The Soviet Union disintegrated because of ideological rigidity in its economic institutions, imperial overstretch, and an inability to reform. Its collapse produced a crisis of credibility for the United States. For the first forty years after World War II, the Soviet menace was the U.S.'s prime justification for its worldwide and multifaceted operations against communism. When this rationale for empire disappeared, it was revealed that the United States had also pursued many other, not-publicly-acknowledged objectives beyond balancing and containing the Soviet Union. The United States had grown accustomed to its hegemony over the parts of the world not dominated by the Soviet Union, and it intended to maintain and enlarge them.

When the Cold War seemed to end, the U.S. did not demobilize but instead reinforced its system of alliances and bases around the world and launched extensive strategic and intellectual efforts to find new threats and situations that demanded its policing. These included a self-declared "humanitarian war" against Serbia, renewed intervention in the Chinese civil war on behalf of Taiwan, an extremely provocative stance toward North Korea, and, after the terrorist attacks of September 11, 2001, on New York's World Trade Center and the Pentagon, a unilateral assertion of American hegemony over the entire world under the guise of fighting a presidentially declared war on terrorism. This led to two American wars—against Afghanistan in 2001–2002 and against Iraq in 2003—with the addition of many new military bases in both the targeted and the adjacent countries. The cockpit of American imperialism shifted to the Middle East and focused on U.S. struggles to dominate Persian Gulf oil, advance the putative interests of Israel, and ensure that the Islamic nations were unable to develop or cooperate with each other in confronting Anglo-American imperialism. Nonetheless, the traditional Cold War battlefronts in Europe, Asia, and Latin America did not disappear. The United States was preoccupied with its operations in Central and Southwest Asia, but it continued to defend and try to enlarge the enclaves it had long controlled in other parts of the world. My purpose in this essay is to try to identify the commonalities and differences among the original three Cold Wars and to point out what did not end when the Cold War itself was said to have ended.

COLD WAR I: EUROPE

Until his death in 1983, Raymond Aron was an independent French intellectual who passionately defended U.S. foreign policy in postwar Europe against the views of most other French and Western European observers. His views express clearly the conventional wisdom on the Cold War in Europe: "It was evident to anyone viewing inter-state relations in accordance with the traditional, if not eternal, categories that the aim [of the United States] in 1946 and 1947 was to prevent the Soviet Union from filling the vacuum created by the disappearance of the Third Reich and the exhaustion of the theoretically victorious older nations. . . . If a United States military 'protectorate' still exists in Europe twenty years later, it is because the Europeans themselves expressed an urgent wish for it. . . . Success in Europe required neither limited war, counterrevolution, nor the CIA."[2] It should be noted that at the time Aron wrote, he was fully informed about and participated in numerous CIA operations in Europe that were in some cases similar to the totalitarian practices of the Soviet Union that he criticized. Nonetheless, his views, as far as they go, are accurate enough.[3] The United States succeeded in Europe by default—as the French say, *faute de mieux,* for want of something better. The truth of the matter is that the U.S. did not so much win the European Cold War as the Soviet Union unquestionably lost it.

Stalin created the USSR's postwar empire of East European satellites by force, just as the United States created its empire of military bases in East Asia. Neither empire could or would have come into being in any other way. By the "Soviet Union's empire," I mean the seven people's democracies in Eastern Europe that formed the heart of the communist camp until its collapse in 1989—namely, East Germany, Poland, Czechoslovakia, Hungary, Romania, Albania, and Bulgaria. Its American equivalent was the system of satellites the United States created in East Asia, including at one time puppet regimes in Thailand, South Vietnam, the Philippines, and Taiwan but with only Japan and South Korea still retaining their Cold War status. Both superpowers also resorted to force against popular movements to hold their respective empires together—the Soviet Union in 1956 in Budapest and in 1968 in Prague; the United States from 1950 to 1953 in Korea and from 1954 to 1975 in Vietnam.[4]

On November 9, 1989, the people of East Berlin tore down the wall that had divided their city since 1961; and on October 3, 1990, Germany was formally reunited. At the Soviet-American summit meeting in Malta in December 1989, President George H.W. Bush declared that the Cold War was over. The Americans succeeded in Europe because they were, with some qualifications, on the side of democracy. The Soviets lost the Cold War in Europe and subsequently disintegrated in part because of their overreliance on totalitarianism. Nonetheless, the alliance based on a common commitment to democracy by the United States and the leading nations of Europe became seriously frayed during the first post–Cold War decade. Because of its attempt to advance its own unacknowledged imperial project, the

United States squandered the goodwill it had accumulated since the Marshall Plan. European nations became alarmed by the United States's behavior and increasingly voted with coalitions of nations intended to balance American power. Finally, in the spring of 2003, France and Germany refused to join America's illegal invasion of Iraq. Overwhelming majorities in every democratic nation on earth, including significant numbers in the United States itself, opposed unsanctioned aggression against Iraq.

Well before this climactic event, European nations were openly questioning American leadership. In November 1999, the UN, by a vote of fifty-four to four with seventy-three abstentions, adopted a resolution sponsored by Russia, China, and Belarus calling on the parties to the Antiballistic Missile Treaty of 1972 "to refrain from the deployment of antiballistic missile systems for a defense of the territory of its country and not to provide a base for such a defense." Only the U.S., Israel, Latvia, and Micronesia voted against the resolution. Thirteen of the fifteen members of the European Union abstained, while the other two, France and Ireland, voted for the resolution. Before the resolution was adopted, France proposed an amendment calling for efforts to stop the spread of weapons of mass destruction and their means of delivery. It was approved by twenty-two votes to one, with ninety-five abstentions. The United States cast the only negative vote.[5] The United States was unfazed by its isolation. On December 13, 2002, the U.S. ambassador to Moscow delivered a formal notice of President Bush's unilateral decision to withdraw from the ABM Treaty, which became effective six months from that date.

Similarly, only two countries, the U.S. and Somalia, refused to sign the UN Convention on the Rights of the Child, which calls on nations not to recruit into their militaries individuals under the age of eighteen (the U.S. military occasionally takes a seventeen-year-old).[6] The U.S. has also steadfastly opposed creating an International Criminal Court to try leaders charged with genocide and has refused to sign the international treaty against the use of land mines, even though both sides in Korea, where the U.S. claims they are indispensable, have started to remove the mines in order to reopen rail service between the two halves of the country.

American unilateralism is destroying the democratic coalition the U.S. forged during the European Cold War. There are many examples, perhaps the most important being the United States's program to build a comprehensive antiballistic missile defense. If actually deployed, such a system threatens to undermine all treaties that have existed for over thirty years for the prevention of nuclear war and to launch a new nuclear arms race. When combined with the October 1999 failure of the U.S. Congress to ratify the Comprehensive Test-Ban Treaty and the Pentagon's continued maintenance of a stockpile of nuclear warheads at Cold War levels, the American national missile defense (NMD) appears to Europeans as a determination to go it alone regardless of the views of the rest of the world. It should also be noted that without European cooperation, no missile defense of any sort can ever be effective since at least some of the radars on which it depends would have to be based in Greenland, which is Danish territory and is at present unavailable for American use.[7]

In March 2002, the press exposed the Bush administration's still secret Nuclear Posture Review, actually delivered to Congress on January 8, 2002, in which it reversed a twenty-year-old policy of maintaining nuclear weapons only for deterrence and as a last resort. The new statement listed seven countries as potential future nuclear targets: Russia, Iraq, Iran, North Korea, China, Libya, and Syria. The review specifically cited a military confrontation with China over the status of Taiwan as an instance in which the United States might resort to nuclear weapons.[8] In May 2002, the United States actually signed a treaty with Russia in which both countries pledged to reduce their strategic nuclear arsenals to between 1,700 and 2,200 warheads over a ten-year period. However, this development was vitiated by the United States's insistence that rather than destroy its warheads it would merely put them in storage.[9] There was also no parallel agreement addressing Russia's concerns about the U.S.'s development of a missile defense system.

These are not mere differences in capabilities or perspectives between the U.S. and its European allies. Paul H. Nitze, perhaps the most experienced of all American Cold War strategists, has concluded, "I can think of no circumstances under which it would be wise for the United States to use nuclear weapons, even in retaliation for their prior use against us. . . . It is the presence of nuclear weapons that threatens our existence. . . . It would be safe now to dispose, unilaterally, of our nuclear arsenal."[10] Nitze argues that the development of precision-guided conventional munitions has rendered nuclear weapons obsolete. An equally qualified strategist, General George Lee Butler, a thirty-three-year veteran of the U.S. Air Force and in 1991 commander of the Strategic Air Command, asks, "How [can one] fathom a historical view that can witness the collapse of communism but fail to imagine a world rid of nuclear weapons?" General Butler advocates abolishing the command he used to head. "Surely," he writes, "we still comprehend that to threaten the deaths of tens or hundreds of millions of people presages an atrocity beyond anything in the record of mankind." [11] That such comprehension does not and may never exist is suggested by the hysteria in the United States during 1999 and 2000 over whether China had stolen American nuclear secrets and the search for a Chinese spy within the American nuclear weapons laboratories.

During the Cold War the United States regarded Western Europe as the ultimate domino, the area of the world that could not under any circumstances be lost to the Soviet Union. The U.S. therefore built there its strongest alliances and even went along with the futile efforts of Britain, France, and the Netherlands to reestablish their colonial empires in East Asia. But America's imperial pretensions are now unraveling these transatlantic ties, as are many issues other than nuclear weaponry. So far from admiring America's values, many Europeans see the frequent use of the death penalty in the United States as openly racist. Similarly, the early release from a six-months' prison sentence of Marine Captain Richard Ashby, who piloted the jet that in February 1998 cut a skiers' gondola cable in northern Italy and plunged twenty vacationers to their deaths, seems to reflect America's imperial arrogance. Equally irritating to Europeans is America's illicit reading of every fax, telex, e-mail, phone call, and computer data message transmitted by satellite around the world and, since 1971, its attaching tapping pods to most underwater cables—the so-called Echelon program—particularly since Echelon's "collection requirements" include the private economic activities of America's leading allies. [12]

Even NATO's one and only war, the bombing of Serbia and Kosovo during the spring of 1999, seriously divided the members of NATO. What looked like a belated intervention by the democracies against Serbia's ethnic cleansing turned out to be a demonstration of America's military technology and led to charges of war crimes. China claimed that the war in Kosovo was merely a test of America's advanced weaponry, and this is why NATO intervened without UN or other legal sanction and why more Chinese died in the war (as a result of the American bombing of China's embassy in Belgrade) than Americans, who suffered no casualties at all.[13] Amnesty International concluded that the bombing of Radio Television Serbia on April 23, 1999, "was a deliberate attack on a civilian object and as such constitutes a war crime," and Human Rights Watch found that of the approximately 500 Yugoslav civilians killed, "half died because of NATO violations of laws and practices on protecting civilians."[14]

The Cold War in Europe is over, but that development has not ushered in a period of stable peace—largely because the United States government had and still has other objectives. In retrospect it appears that both the Soviet Union and the United States lost the Cold War in Europe. Even more ironic, America's military adventurism in Iraq produced a working cooperation among France, Germany, and Russia—something that American foreign policy long sought to forestall—and did more to compel the uniting of Europe, including its acquisition of a military capability, than any other international event. Nowhere did America's Cold War triumphalism result in greater and less easily reversed net losses.

COLD WAR II: EAST ASIA

The greatest single disaster in post–World War II American foreign policy was the failure of the U.S. to understand and adjust to the Chinese revolution. This failure started during World War II and persists to the present day. Ever since it became clear, shortly after Japan's surrender in the summer of 1945, that China would be convulsed by civil war and that the likely victor would be the Chinese Communist Party, the United States has been obsessed by China's growing power and by the potential challenge a renascent China might offer to American hegemony in East Asia and ultimately to its covert Cold War project to create a global capitalist order led by the United States. Except for the two decades after Nixon's 1971 opening of a dialogue with China and his aligning the U.S. with China against the Soviet Union, American Cold War policy in East Asia has been hostile to China. Today, with China's own redirection of its efforts to catch up economically with the rest of East Asia, American policy still vacillates—on the one hand it seeks to profit from and tries to influence China's economic development while on the other it maintains massive military forces directed against China and contends that the only thing maintaining stability in East Asia is the presence of these American military forces.

All the major elements of postwar American imperialism in East Asia follow from this obsession with China. They include the decision to end the immediate postwar efforts to democratize Japan and instead to make it into the primary American base for military operations in East Asia. A corollary of this policy was to isolate Japan economically from its traditional markets in China. As a consequence, in order for Japan to regain any form of economic viability, the U.S. had to open its own market to Japan on uniquely favorable terms. As the American embassy in Tokyo reported to the Department of State in 1960, "Our economic policy accorded Japan a fair and reasonable share of our market as premise and precondition for U.S.-Japan relationships in political and security fields and has led to substantial expansion of Japanese exports, making possible Japan's present economic prosperity." [15] This policy is still in effect today—in return for basing 100,000 American troops in Japan and South Korea, Japan still takes as its due privileged access to the American economy and protectionist barriers against American sales and investment in the Japanese market. The result is huge excess capacity in Japan, the severe hollowing out of American manufacturing industries, and the largest trade imbalances (in favor of Japan) ever recorded between two economies.

At the time of the proclamation of the Chinese People's Republic in October 1949, the United States could not decide what to do. Should it follow normal international practice and recognize the new regime or succumb to the gathering forces of reaction and McCarthyism within the United States and pretend that Chiang Kai-shek's regime in exile in Taiwan still represented China? As James L. Peck has shown, the outbreak of war in Korea on June 25, 1950, provided a way out of this dilemma.[16] Even though the U.S. entered the Korean War with UN sanction, its simultaneous action to prevent the Chinese Communists from taking over Taiwan was purely unilateral and created what is today still one of the most volatile issues in international relations in the Pacific. For the first two decades after 1949, the United States recognized the regime in Taiwan as the legitimate government of China, supported Taiwan as the occupant of China's permanent seat in the UN, maintained a total economic embargo against the mainland, and, despite massive evidence to the contrary, tried to characterize the Chinese revolution as a manifestation of Soviet imperialism. Chiang Kai-shek became the model for a long list of military dictators whom the United States installed, sponsored, or protected in Taiwan, South Korea, South Vietnam, the Philippines, Thailand, and Indonesia because they were anticommunist. Like Chiang and many of his counterparts in the Soviet satellites in Eastern Europe, most of these dictators were corrupt, brutal, and incompetent. Nowhere in East Asia did the United States promote democracy; its belated appearance in the Philippines, South Korea, and Taiwan came about as a result of domestic protest movements against what had become increasingly unpopular American-supported regimes.

The United States fought savage wars with China—literally in Korea and figuratively in Vietnam, where it sought to discredit Mao's theory of people's war. The latter provoked serious divisions within the American electorate and contributed to the United States's growing reputation as an imperialist bully. More than anything else, however, these wars gave the conduct of American foreign relations outside of Europe its special characteristics—a reliance on abstract formulae and slogans (such as a *global communist conspiracy, counterinsurgency,* the *free world, captive nations*) rather than undertaking serious empirical investigations of local political and economic conditions; excessive use of the American military and employment of undue violence; and clandestine operations to unseat inconvenient governments or to prop up unpopular but pro-American ones (in Iran, Guatemala, Japan, the Bay of Pigs, the Congo, South Korea, South Vietnam, the Dominican Republic, the Philippines, Indonesia, Chile, Angola, Nicaragua, Somalia, and Haiti to name only the best-known cases). By the time the Soviet Union had disappeared, dependence on these methods had almost totally replaced America's traditional use of diplomacy, foreign aid, and efforts to project the United States as a model for other nations.

The fundamental basis of the Cold War in Europe was a struggle between totalitarianism and democracy; the USSR was on the wrong side of this confrontation. The fundamental basis of the Cold War in East Asia was a struggle for liberation from prewar European, American, and Japanese colonialism; the United States was on the wrong side of this struggle. Despite knowing that most of the revolts in East Asia were driven by popular domestic nationalism, the U.S. persisted in characterizing these movements as led by Communists taking orders from Moscow. Such myopia also propelled the United States into the fatal blunder of supporting attempts by the European powers to reclaim their East Asian colonies after they had been driven from them by Japanese armies during World War II. Even in South Korea, in setting up its puppet regime, the United States propped up numerous Koreans who had collaborated with the Japanese colonialists. In no place did these American policies succeed; in Vietnam, American ideological rigidity came close to producing a revolution within its own society—the ultimate form of blowback from ill-conceived foreign operations. Today, when anticolonial nationalism has proven victorious everywhere in East Asia (except for the still-divided Korea), there is a legacy of distrust of American motives because the U.S. for so long failed to appreciate the force of these nationalisms.

When the Soviet Union collapsed, the United States initially seemed to accept that some relaxation of its imperial controls over East Asia was appropriate. In 1992, it allowed the Philippines to expel the U.S. Navy from its largest overseas base, at Subic Bay, and it undertook some minor cuts in its deployed military forces. It also shifted its foreign policy toward Japan to emphasize the inequitable economic relations between the two countries rather than the strengthening of American military bases. In 1993, the American-created single-party regime in Japan collapsed owing to the irrelevance of its sole qualification for holding power—anticommunism—and the U.S. did nothing to save it. Nonetheless, almost instantly after the disappearance of the Soviet Union, American strategists, aided by China's repression of protesters at Tiananmen in 1989, began to vilify China and to make a domestic case that China was the successor to the USSR and the justification for America's global hegemony.

By 1995, the United States had fully recovered its imperialist acumen. The Pentagon's Nye Report of 1995 authorized the permanent basing of 100,000 U.S. troops in Japan and South Korea, and a new visiting-forces agreement was signed with the Philippines by which

U.S. troops were reintroduced there.[17] Meanwhile, the Liberal Democratic Party returned to power in Japan and resumed its unprecedented trade surpluses with the U.S. despite (or because of) its own faltering economy. The 1997 Asian economic meltdown that began in Thailand, South Korea, and Indonesia revealed the dangers of their having followed American economic advice and pressure. It also had the effect of discrediting the Association of Southeast Asian Nations and its Asian Regional Forum as nascent multilateral organizations capable of dealing with East Asian problems without outside interference. The United States was back, fully committed to maintaining its empire in the Asia-Pacific region even though it was still engaged in an internal argument over whether it should engage China or try to contain it.

One key element of post–Cold War American imperialism in the area has been a persistent exaggeration of alleged threats posed by two of the remaining, formally communist countries of the area—China and North Korea. In May 1999, for example, the U.S. Congress issued its so-called Cox Report, named after Christopher Cox, a Republican representative from Newport Beach, California. Cox claimed that China had pilfered secret data on seven of the U.S.'s most advanced thermonuclear weapons. He also said that the stolen information included computer codes, allegedly essential to the design of nuclear warheads, which most likely came from secret computers at America's nuclear weapons laboratories. Led by the *New York Times,* the mass media sensationalized this report and set off a hunt for a spy at the Los Alamos National Laboratory in New Mexico. A *New York Times* editorial contended, "The Cox Committee has performed an invaluable service with its unsparing investigation."[18]

Needless to say, the spy was soon found in the person of an American scientist of Chinese ancestry (from Taiwan, not China), Wen-ho Lee. Federal authorities threatened Lee with death (like the Rosenbergs), tried to extract a confession from him, and then confined him in a jail in New Mexico under conditions similar to those the French imposed on Captain Alfred Dreyfus when they sentenced him to Devil's Island. The whole case ultimately fell apart for lack of evidence, and it also seemed likely that the Department of Energy and the Federal Bureau of Investigation had singled out Lee (as the French did Dreyfus) because of his race. Anti-Semitism and anti-Chinese racism were at the heart of both famous spy manias. When an FBI agent admitted to a federal judge that he had lied in his testimony against Lee, the government sought a plea bargain arrangement that freed Lee.

Early in the case, journalist Robert Scheer of the *Los Angeles Times*—the Émile Zola of this affair—wrote, "The China threat exists only in the minds of politicians who are playing fast with national security concerns and the *New York Times,* which was awarded a Pulitzer Prize for publicizing their most stark warnings."[19] Over a year later, even the *New York Times* sought to excuse its behavior. It said it had been misled by "government officials who previously insisted that the downloaded data contained the 'crown jewels' of America's nuclear arsenal that could change the global balance of power if transferred to a hostile power."[20] China, it seems, still inspires McCarthyism in the United States.[21]

The other great focus of America's exaggeration of supposed military threats from East Asia has been North Korea. The Pentagon has based much of its case for a national missile defense on North Korea's alleged development of nuclear weapons and long-range missiles. But the evidence for these capabilities has repeatedly failed to stand up. For example, during 1998 and 1999, Lt. Gen. Patrick Hughes, then head of the Defense Intelligence Agency, circulated to members of Congress raw intelligence that he said showed North Korea was secretly building an underground nuclear reactor. When the Americans exerted pressure on North Korea to inspect the place Hughes had identified as the site of the hidden plant, it was found not only to contain no machinery of any kind but to be too small to have contained a reactor. When the Americans returned in May 2000 for a further inspection, it was still empty.[22]

Even more embarrassing, in November 1999, the Space Imaging Company of Thornton, Colorado, used its own private spy satellite, the Ikonos, to photograph the alleged North Korean missile-launch site. The Ikonos has a resolving power down to one meter, which is comparable to military surveillance satellites. Looking at the Ikonos pictures, the Federation of American Scientists declared, "It is quite evident that this facility was not intended to support, and in many respects is incapable of supporting, the extensive test program that would be needed to fully develop a reliable missile system." It called the North Korean base, completed in 1988, "barely worthy of note, consisting of the most minimal imaginable test infrastructure." The

Ikonos pictures also called into doubt the steady stream of intelligence on North Korea then coming from South Korean sources: one of Seoul's alleged North Korean defectors had said that all agricultural villages had been removed from the vicinity of the test site but there they still were in the new pictures.[23]

Despite many such cases, members of the U.S. Congress refused to accept that the Cold War in East Asia could be ending. On July 27, 2000, well after the Koreans had already launched their own peace initiatives, the House of Representatives Policy Committee, whose chairman is the hyperbolic Christopher Cox, released a report on the situation there. Its opening lines are: "North Korea is not merely a dictatorship: it is a uniquely monstrous tyranny that has tormented the Korean people for half a century, creating the most completely totalitarian and militarized state in human history. Today, even while North Korea is faltering on the edge of economic collapse, it poses one of the greatest threats to American and allied interests anywhere around the globe."[24]

More ominous in its long-term implications than such propaganda, the Pentagon has on numerous occasions asserted that even if the two halves of Korea were reunited, it intends to keep a military force based there.[25] Since South Korea vastly exceeds North Korea in expenditures on weapons and is twice as populous and at least twenty-five times richer than its northern counterpart, the American military is clearly not needed for its defense.[26] The American presence there is, in fact, a warning to China that the United States intends to preserve its imperial enclaves in the East Asian area.

Under the George W. Bush administration, America's relations with North Korea steadily worsened. In September 2002, the White House asserted in its National Security Strategy a right to wage preventive war. This rhetoric gained an almost immediate reality for North Korean leader Kim Jong Il and his associates when the Americans began to mobilize a powerful invasion force on the borders of Iraq, also included in Bush's list of nations targeted for regime change. Watching Iraq being destroyed by the world's richest and most heavily armed country, North Korea prepared to defend itself in the only way it thought the Americans could understand. It withdrew from the Nuclear Nonproliferation Treaty, expelled international inspectors, and restarted an old power reactor that it had mothballed in accordance with the North Korean-U.S. agreement of 1994.

On April 6, 2003, Pyongyang announced that only by arming itself with a "tremendous military deterrent" could it guarantee its own security. "The Iraqi war shows that to allow disarming through inspection does not help avert a war but rather sparks it. . . . This suggests that even the signing of a nonaggression treaty with the U.S. would not help avert a war." Much like a comment attributed to Winston Churchill during the Battle of Britain, North Korea was now telling its citizens, "If you've got to go, take one with you." The places it threatens to take with it are Seoul and its population of eleven million, the thirty-eight American bases on Okinawa, and as many Japanese cities as it can hit (though in actual fact it may not have the capability of reaching as far as either Okinawa or the Japanese mainland with nuclear-tipped missiles). At the very least, however, were it to arm itself with nuclear weapons, it would certainly spark a nuclear arms race in East Asia.

During 2002 and 2003, South Korean public opinion shifted radically on the issue of North Korea. The prosperous and well-informed people of the South know that their fellow Koreans, hungry, desperate, oppressed but exceedingly well-armed, are trapped by the ironies of the end of the Cold War and by the harshness of the Kim Jong Il regime, but are also being pushed into an exceedingly dangerous corner by the pride and arrogance of the Americans in their newly proclaimed role as the reigning global military colossus. The South no longer much fears the North—so long as it is not being pushed to extreme acts by Washington. They fear instead the enthusiasm for war emanating from Washington and the constant problems generated by American troops based in South Korea over the past fifty years.

North Korea has been attempting, albeit fitfully and with great trepidation, to come in from the cold in somewhat the same way China did so successfully over the past twenty years. As Kim Dae Jung understood, the U.S. and South Korea should be magnanimous winners instead of megalomaniacal warmongers. No surrounding nation—not the Republic of Korea, nor Japan, nor China, nor Russia—wants or sees the need for a renewed civil war on the Korean peninsula. Now that the generation that fought the Korean War in the South, the

North, and the United States is passing from the scene, the time is ripe for younger people with more flexible approaches to resolve this last remaining Cold War legacy—a hostile peninsula divided at the DMZ. It is only in the U.S. that the departure of this generation seems to have created such a case of historical amnesia that a new generation is prepared to start a war there all over again.

Equally irresponsibly, the United States has started to upgrade its extensive military relationship with Taiwan. Since the mainland-Taiwan military confrontation of 1996 (which occurred on the eve of Taiwanese elections and was intended to prevent a unilateral Taiwanese declaration of independence), the Clinton administration authorized the Pentagon, in the words of the veteran China correspondent Jim Mann, "to conduct the kind of strategic dialogue with Taiwan's armed forces that had not been permitted by any administration since 1979."[27]

Taiwan is one of the United States's wealthiest customers for weapons, and it already possesses a retaliatory capacity against mainland China that effectively neutralizes the threat of genuine combat in the Taiwan Strait. The real danger is that war could result because of political miscalculations. China has repeatedly indicated that it does not want to incorporate Taiwan through the use of military force. At the same time, it cannot tolerate a unilateral secession of what by every principle and precedent of international law is its territory. Given the blunders of the United States fifty years ago, there is no solution to the Taiwan problem. Only the maintenance of the status quo and a further passage of time can offer any resolution. Unfortunately, United States imperialist pretensions stand in the way of such prudence.

COLD WAR III: LATIN AMERICA

It is said that dead men tell no tales, but in Latin America they are speaking with exceptional clarity—revealing the sordid details of U.S. Cold War foreign policy toward the area. In 1992, in Asunción, Paraguay, a survivor of the regime of former dictator General Alfredo Stroessner stumbled on five tons of reports and photographs left over from Operation Condor. This operation, begun in 1975, was a cooperative effort among military and police officials of Brazil, Argentina, Chile, Paraguay, Uruguay, and Bolivia to identify, torture, and kill as many representatives of workers and advocates of democracy as they could find. Such records also exist in other Latin American countries, but in the words of Juan Garcés, the Spanish lawyer who brought the 1998 suit against General Augusto Pinochet of Chile on charges of genocide, "in Paraguay they didn't manage to hide it all."[28] Baltazar Garzón, the Spanish judge who sought the extradition of Pinochet from England after his arrest there on October 16, 1998 (and, more recently of Argentine generals and admirals), collected more than 1,500 pages of evidence from the archives before American officials moved in to sanitize them.

Elsewhere in Latin America, incriminating archives of terror are also coming to light. In June 2000, an Argentine judge asked Brazil for information about three Argentine citizens who disappeared in Brazil when both countries were under military rule. To the surprise of virtually all observers, Brazil's highest court ordered that all documents relating to Operation Condor be turned over to Argentine authorities.[29]

At El Aguacate, eighty miles east of Tegucigalpa, Honduras, at the abandoned military base the U.S. built in 1983 to wage what the Associated Press calls its "Cold War fight against communism," jail cells and the bodies of torture victims have been uncovered. El Aguacate is just one of several sites in Honduras being investigated on the basis of witnesses' testimony and records. During the 1980s, Honduras was the CIA's largest station on earth; it was used to train some 14,000 Nicaraguan counterrevolutionaries (Contras) for operations across the border.[30]

On August 24, 2000, acting on a warrant for extradition signed by Judge Garzón, Mexican authorities arrested Ricardo Miguel Cavallo at Cancún while he was trying to flee the country back to Argentina. Many victims of the Argentine junta, 1976–1983, have identified Cavallo as "Serpico," the head torturer at the Escuela Mecánica located inside naval headquarters at Buenos Aires. The arrest was unprecedented since Mexico usually resists all efforts to extradite fugitives within its borders. As the *New York Times* put it, "[Mexico] became a kind of haven for Latin American military officers suspected of cold-war crimes, just as Argentina once was a refuge for Nazis."[31] During the reign of the Argentine junta, military officers killed at least 30,000 people, and another 5,000 disappeared. Their relatives invented a new term for them, *los desaparacedos*. Between 1991 and 1998, a small unit in the Argentine Ministry of Health treated some 31,102 torture victims. To this day no torturer has been investigated or tried, and no compensation has been paid.[32]

The breakthrough in producing these and other revelations about the Cold War in Latin America was the arrest of Pinochet in England. Until that time the United States remained absolutely tight-lipped about the CIA's knowledge of and participation in the Chilean military's overthrow of Salvador Allende in 1973 and about the roles of graduates of the U.S. Army's School of the Americas in Operation Condor. But Spain's request for Pinochet's extradition caused many of his victims in Latin America and Europe to speak out and this forced the United States at least to pretend to cooperate in an international effort to reveal the truth about crimes against humanity in which it had been implicated.

There are also two high-profile cases involving the United States directly that had never been resolved—the 1973 murders in Santiago by Pinochet's secret police unit, DINA (Dirección de Inteligencia Nacional), of two U.S. citizens, Charles Horman, age thirty-one a filmmaker and writer, and his colleague Frank Teruggi, age twenty-four; and DINA's assassination on September 26, 1976, in Washington of the former Chilean ambassador to the United States, Orlando Letelier, and his twenty-five-year-old American companion, Ronni Karpen Moffitt.

In January 2000, the British Home Secretary Jack Hall tried to spare the United States embarrassment by denying Spain's warrant for extradition and allowing Pinochet to return to Chile. However, the preferential treatment of Pinochet kept the issue of his crimes alive, and President Clinton ordered the CIA to make public its files on the Pinochet regime. It has yet to do so completely and, in August 2000, CIA director George Tenet defied the president and refused to declassify records that he said "would reveal too much about CIA sources and methods."[33] But it was too late. Enough has already been released under Clinton's order to make clear the role played by the United States in Latin America under cover of the Cold War.

The "methods" that the CIA declines to reveal to the American public include its routine practice of turning over the names of people it wants executed to military and police authorities that it has trained and helped put in power. It can then pretend that it had nothing to do

with their subsequent deaths, even expressing shock and disappointment at the excesses of its former pupils. This was the pattern of
American operations in Indonesia from General Suharto's rise to
power in 1965 to the American refusal in the autumn of 1999 to get involved in rescuing the victims of Indonesian army terror in East
Timor.[34] The CIA employed these same methods in bringing Pinochet
to power and in its relations with Operation Condor.

In 1982, the French film director Constantin Costa-Gavras released
Missing, his motion picture about the deaths of Horman and Teruggi.
Twenty years after it was first shown, virtually all of the details in the
film have now been confirmed, including the execution of the two
young men on September 19, 1973, in the Santiago sports arena because they knew too much about American involvement in the military coup that had just taken place on September 11. The film's scenes
of Horman's wife's repeatedly asking State Department officers "Can
they order an American to disappear without consulting the Americans first?" and the American military and naval attachés prodding
the wife to give them the names of all of her husband's Chilean friends
have been substantiated by newly released documents. When the
American ambassador is portrayed as saying to Horman's father that
his son was probably kidnapped by leftists in order to embarrass the
new government, we now know this was typical of the U.S. embassy's
activities at the time of Allende's overthrow.

The documents the State Department released in February 2000
had been divulged in 1980 but now previously blacked-out sections
were restored. These new sections make clear that the State Department knew from virtually the day of their disappearance that the two
Americans had been killed by Pinochet. Embassy officials further
speculated that "the Chileans would not have done so without a green
light from U.S. intelligence."[35] The *New York Times* has also noted that
"American intelligence and military officials may have encouraged
General Augusto Pinochet's security forces to round them up even
though it was clear that the two men, like thousands of Chileans arrested during the same period, were likely to be mistreated, if not
killed."[36]

The assassination of Letelier is even more damning. After having
served as foreign minister in the Allende government, he came to
Washington in 1975 as an associate fellow of the Institute of Policy

Studies and professor of international relations at American University. He was killed in a car-bomb explosion on the orders of General Manuel Contreras, the director of DINA. All of this has long been known. What is new is that on September 18, 2000, the CIA released a document revealing for the first time that in 1975 General Contreras was "a paid CIA asset" and that contacts with him continued long after he had dispatched his agents to Washington to kill Letelier.[37]

This revelation about Contreras is just one important instance within a general pattern. The Asunción archives showed that "United States officials backed Condor nations not only with military aid but also with information" and that U.S. Army Colonel Robert Thierry helped General Stroessner set up his police-state apparatus and train his police officers. They also showed that FBI operatives had supplied the Pinochet regime with the names of Chileans in their files. "The F.B.I. [has] defended the sharing of information with Chile as standard practice among law enforcement agencies of governments friendly to Washington."[38] In the July 2000 release of documents on Chile that President Clinton ordered, the FBI disclosed for the first time that it had collected information on the activities in Chile of Frank R. Teruggi, whose bullet-ridden body was found in the Santiago morgue ten days after he disappeared.[39] The Brazil files disclosed that "The first known mention of Operation Condor came in a 1976 cable from the American Embassy in Buenos Aires, and American agents worked closely with security officials in the region, many of whom had studied at the United States–run School of the Americas."[40]

The Cold War in Latin America is different from those in Europe or East Asia. Long before the issue of communism appeared in the Americas, the United States had been intervening economically and militarily to support American corporations and to prevent the development of governments backed by strong populist movements. As early as 1953, well before the arrival of Fidel Castro on the scene and looking forward to the CIA's overthrow the following year of Guatemala's democratic government, the National Security Council wrote in a highly classified statement of American policy toward the area: "There is a trend in Latin America toward nationalistic regimes maintained in large part by appeals to the masses of the population. . . . It is essential to arrest the drift in the area toward radical and nationalistic regimes."[41]

The 1959 Cuban revolution turned out to be an ideological godsend for the United States. The U.S. had long sought some way to redirect popular resentment in Latin America away from the exploitative activities of American multinational corporations—including the United Fruit Company in Central America and the copper-mining companies in Chile. Positing a communist threat to the area was the best strategy the United States had ever found. Fidel and Ché lent great credibility to the United States's old fears about outside forces threatening the independence of its Latin American neighbors. Recognizing that there was no way it could rely on democratic forces in Latin America, since they knew all too well which foreign country was actually threatening their independence, the United States therefore turned to the armies of Latin America for its allies and preferred political leaders.

One of the most important institutions of American foreign policy is the U.S. Army's School of the Americas, founded in Panama in 1946 and moved to Fort Benning, Georgia, in 1984 after Panamanian President Jorge Illueca called it "the biggest base for destabilization in Latin America" and evicted it. Its curriculum includes counterinsurgency, military intelligence, interrogation techniques, sniper fire, infantry and commando tactics, psychological warfare, and jungle operations.[42] Although some members of Congress have long tried to shut it down, the Pentagon and the White House have always found ways to keep it in the budget. In May 2000, the Clinton administration sought to provide new camouflage for the school by changing its name to the Defense Institute for Hemispheric Security Cooperation and transferring authority over it from the Department of the Army to the Department of Defense. Congressman Joseph Moakley (D-Massachusetts) referred to this reform as "putting perfume on a toxic dump" and continued, "The School of the Americas has trained some of the most brutal assassins, some of the cruelest dictators, and some of the worst abusers of human rights the Western Hemisphere has ever seen. If we don't stand for human rights down in Georgia, how can we possibly expect to promote them anywhere else in the world?"[43]

The School of the Americas (SOA, also known in Latin America as the School of Assassins) has trained over 60,000 military and police officers from Latin American and Caribbean countries. Among SOA's most illustrious graduates are the dictators Manuel Noriega (who is serving a forty-year sentence in an American jail for drug trafficking) and Omar Torrijos of Panama; Guillermo Rodrigues of Ecuador; Juan Velasco Alvarado of Peru; Leopoldo Galtieri, former head of Argentina's junta; and Hugo Banzer Suarez of Bolivia. Other alumni include the former military officer and leader of the Salvadoran death squads, Roberto D'Aubuisson, who according to the United Nations Truth Commission for El Salvador, orchestrated the assassination on March 24, 1980, of the archbishop of El Salvador, Oscar Romero, and helped plan the assault by the U.S.–trained Atlacatl Battalion against El Mozote village on December 11, 1981, that killed some 767 unarmed men, women, and children. The UN Commission recovered as many shell casings as it could find at El Mozote. All were stamped as having been manufactured for the U.S. government at Lake City, Missouri.

An equally prominent participant in Operation Condor and a graduate of the SOA is Colonel Pablo Belmar of the Chilean DINA. He was one of thirty officers named in the 1998 Spanish human rights case against General Pinochet. Colonel Belmar was charged with being a participant in the torture and murder in 1976 in Santiago of Carmelo Soria, a UN official and Spanish citizen. Soria's car and body were dumped in a Santiago canal in order to make his death appear accidental. Colonel Belmar graduated from SOA's basic arms orientation course in 1968 and was invited back to Fort Benning in 1987 as a guest instructor of human rights.

According to the human rights organization School of the Americas Watch, one out of every seven commanders of DINA was a graduate of SOA. A typical graduate, 1st Lt. Armando Fernandez Larios, class of 1970, was one of two DINA agents who in 1974 killed General Carlos Prats González, Allende's defense minister, and his wife in Buenos Aires. He was also indicted by a U.S. grand jury in 1979 for his involvement in the assassination of Letelier in Washington, D.C. Both General Prats and Letelier were murdered with car bombs.[44] Augusto Pinochet himself did not study at the SOA, but he gave the school a ceremonial sword that in 1991 was on prominent display in the office of the commandant.

The end of Operation Condor did not bring an end to the tortures, murders, and disappearances of advocates of democracy in Latin America. The name of Vladimiro Montesinos, SOA class of 1965, was prominently in the news in 2000 when as head of Peruvian military intelligence and President Alberto Fujimori's closest adviser, he was caught bribing an opposition politician. The United States helped him escape into exile in Panama.[45] The Americas Watch Report on human rights in Peru claims that Montesinos was responsible for the disappearances of nine university students and a professor on July 18, 1992. Four officers have testified that Montesinos took an active part in torturing them.[46] Not incidentally, Montesinos has also been implicated in deals to sell 10,000 AK-47 assault rifles to the FARC (Fuerzas Armadas Revolucionarias de Colombia), Colombia's largest guerrilla group.[47]

Colombia has sent over 10,000 soldiers to train at the SOA, more than any other country. Both Human Rights Watch and the Department of State in their annual reports on Colombia link SOA graduates to the Colombian military and paramilitary death squads and to murders, kidnappings, and thefts that occurred in 1999. The presence of so many SOA graduates in Colombia is probably one element behind the United States's decision during July 2000 to open full military operations there. According to U.S. estimates, 40 percent of Colombian territory is held by either two Colombian rebel groups or by right-wing paramilitaries allied with the Colombian Army. Although Colombia was already the third largest recipient of U.S. foreign aid in the world, the amount it will receive rose spectacularly after the installation of George W. Bush as president. The American Seventh Special Forces Group from Fort Bragg, North Carolina, has been sent to train Colombian troops at a secret base near the confluence of the Caquetá and Orteguaza Rivers. The American embassy in Bogotá has declared the area off-limits to all foreign and domestic journalists.[48]

Even though the Colombian civil war is at least thirty-six years old, the United States has become alarmed about the growing production of cocaine in rebel-held territory. It has therefore formulated a $7.5 billion strategy, called Plan Colombia, to train three anti-narcotic battalions, composed of 3,000 Colombian soldiers, who will be flown into combat aboard sixty Huey-2 and Black Hawk helicopters that the U.S. has supplied. FARC's coca laboratories are actually located in the Peruvian jungles, and cocaine is transported down the Amazon River to the United States and Europe, just as the river is used to import munitions. FARC has also threatened to invade Ecuador if the U.S. uses it as a base for aerial operations. The probability is therefore high that all the countries that border on Colombia will become embroiled in a general insurgency. The United States also plans a campaign of aerial defoliation against Colombian fields using a new, not fully-tested biological fungicide. Brazil fears that runoff from these operations will poison the region's waters and that direct military operations will push thousands of Colombian refugees into the Brazilian state of Amazonas. According to the late journalist Tad Szulc, Plan Colombia, like U.S. operations in Vietnam, was "developed by men and women who know little of Colombia's history, culture, and politics."[49] Plan Colombia is only the latest manifestation of the third and oldest Cold War, that in Latin America.

Three years after its inception, the American counterinsurgency in Colombia was a dreadful failure. During 2002, FARC killed nine local mayors and forced hundreds to resign, while, as reported by Peter Clark, the paramilitaries were responsible for most of the 184 assassinations of trade unionists—by far the highest rate in the world.[50] Cocaine continued to be widely available in the United States, and the amount of land in the Andean countries devoted to coca cultivation, about 540,000 acres, remained stable for the past fifteen years. America's money spent on Colombia has been almost entirely wasted. The struggle there offers yet another illustration that the musclebound American military is ineffective as an instrument of sociopolitical policy.

The attitudes and policies that underlie American post–Cold War triumphalism are not easily changed. They have their roots in the tense postwar situation in Europe, the United States's obsession with China following the communist victory there, and the discovery that anticommunism could advance traditional American interests in Latin America. The imperialism that was bolstered by these ideological positions was always there but came into the open only with the end of the European Cold War and the United States's trumpeting of its status as the "last remaining superpower."

These tendencies were greatly exacerbated by the terrorist attacks of September 11, 2001. The president claimed that the United States was declaring war on terrorism although he failed to follow up legally, in terms of the constitutional stipulations requiring that Congress declare war. The undeclared war on terrorism allowed the government to whip up patriotic fervor and to suppress discussion of the attackers' motives. Any attempt to explain why the terrorists felt justified in attacking the World Trade Center and the Pentagon was denounced as "siding with the terrorists," as Attorney General John Ashcroft did in Congressional testimony. One result was that politicians worldwide instantly hijacked the concept and redesignated their own enemies as terrorists, claiming to be following the example of the United States in attacking them militarily. In the Middle East, the Israeli government abandoned all efforts to achieve peace with the Palestinians and instead attacked them with tanks and helicopter gunships; and in South Asia, the United States found itself drawn into the fifty-five-year-old Kashmir dispute between India and Pakistan. This latter long-standing conflict threatens nuclear war between the two countries, which both claim Kashmir. The United States's declaration of war on terrorism has greatly accelerated the imperial overstretch that the United States was already experiencing before the end of the Cold War in Europe. The danger is that the United States may insensibly be following in the footsteps of the Soviet Union, its erstwhile super-power competitor. The delusions of Cold War triumphalism contributed mightily to this development.

9

Still Stuck in the Big Muddy

Marilyn B. Young

I recall all too well the nightmare of Vietnam. . . . I am determined to do everything in my power to prevent this country from becoming involved in another Vietnam nightmare.

Senator Robert Byrd, June 29, 2002

. . . it is possible that the destruction of September 11 uncovered the suppressed remains of Vietnam.

Wolfgang Schivelbusch,
The Culture of Defeat

We're going to get better over time. We've always thought of post-hostilities as a phase distinct from combat. . . . The future of war is that these things are going to be much more of a continuum. . . . This is the future for the world we're in at the moment. We'll get better as we do it more often.

Lawrence Di Rita, special assistant
to Secretary of Defense Rumsfeld,
July 18, 2003

There seem to be only two kinds of war the U.S. can fight: World War II or Vietnam. The conviction on the part of some Americans and many politicians that the United States could (or should or would) have won the war in Vietnam is a convenient mechanism for getting around a remembered reality of defeat. An alternate strategy is to concentrate the national mind on World War II, skipping not only Vietnam but also Korea. In recent movie and television serials World War II is depicted as a long, valiant struggle that the U.S. fought pretty much on its own, winning an exceptionally clean victory that continues to redeem all Americans under arms anywhere at any point in history.[1] In virtually every military action since 1975, the administration in charge has tried to appropriate the images and language of World War II. Thus, *seriatim,* Noriega, Aidid, Milosevic, and Saddam Hussein (twice) were roundly denounced as the Adolf Hitler du jour; September 11, 2001, of course, is the twenty-first-century Pearl Harbor. Nevertheless, in each of these wars or war-like events, some journalist or politician was bound to ask the fearful question: is this another Vietnam?

What is it that people fear in a repetition of Vietnam? Military and political defeat, of course, but beyond that the daily experience of an apparently endless war, one that registered on the home front not in calls for sacrifice and heroism but rather domestic division, resistance to the draft, high desertion rates, urban riots, popular suspicion of the government, a steadily rising number of U.S. dead and wounded, the shame-inducing images of napalmed Vietnamese children, the reluctant knowledge of American atrocities like My Lai. In his speech in June 2002, Senator Byrd listed his own nightmare images: "the anti-war protests and demonstrations, the campus riots, and the tragic deaths at Kent State, as well as the resignation of a president. And I remember all too well the gruesome daily body counts. . . ."[2]

Because the Vietnam War cannot be assimilated to a triumphal American narrative, presidents must regularly pick their way around it. They have done so mainly by taking its public-relations failings to heart rather than by contemplating its history or meaning. Despite calling Vietnam a noble crusade, Ronald Reagan was in no mood to risk repeating other aspects of the conflict. Money and arms substituted for U.S. combat troops in both Nicaragua and El Salvador, and when a suicide bomber killed over 200 U.S. Marines in Lebanon, Reagan quickly withdrew the rest. At the same time, to demonstrate that the world's mightiest military power was not afraid to use its power directly (and to justify a military budget that never responded to the end of any war, including the Cold War), small, predictably winnable mini-wars were waged against small, largely defenseless countries. Operation Urgent Fury made it clear to all Grenadians, and most particularly its left-leaning government, that neither the U.S. nor those students it sent abroad to get medical degrees, could be pushed around. Six years later, the first Bush administration taught

General Noriega and the people of Panama a similar lesson in Operation Just Cause.

The victories in Operations Urgent Fury and Just Cause were useful and their titles ambitious enough. Yet they were painted on too small a canvas to take the sting out of defeat in Vietnam. For that, more troops would have to travel longer distances, use greater firepower, and engage a real army. When Saddam Hussein seized more of Kuwait than the administration of the first President Bush thought necessary, the stage was set for a military extravaganza that might indeed, as the president so fervently hoped, "kick the Vietnam syndrome once and for all." Vietnam, by negative example, had taught the civil and military branches of the government how to market a war as well as how to fight one. It was all in the timing: enough time to engage the easily distractable imagination of the public but not so much time that boredom set in, or worse, anxiety. Operation Desert Shield, the period from August 1990 to mid-January 1991, served to create a steadily intensifying crisis atmosphere. Network TV and its cable rival, CNN, used the time to settle on appropriate logos and their musical accompaniment. Operation Desert Storm, first as thirty-nine days of sustained and furious bombing and then in the form of a massive ground invasion, was the longed-for release. The desert theme, modest, descriptive, worked so well that some years later, Clinton, without regard for its World War II invocation of the German enemy, named one of his attacks on Iraq Desert Fox.

Media cooperation was essential if Deserts Storm and Shield were successfully to overcome memories of Vietnam. Early in the war, General Norman Schwarzkopf pointed out that inflated "body count" figures had led many Americans to distrust military press briefings. Alternately, when believed, they had upset people. Therefore, there would be no body count in the Gulf War. Thus, through over a month of bombing and a week of ground fighting, no estimates of Iraqi losses were ever offered, nor did the press demand them. The result was a televised war relatively innocent of dead bodies; a war that, except for the bombing of a Baghdad air raid shelter and the repeated shots of desperate oil-soaked cormorants, would not spoil one's dinner. Indeed, the wildlife allegedly destroyed by Saddam Hussein's "ecological terrorism" substituted for images of humans wounded by American

bombs. After the war, CBS revealed that one particularly sad cor-
morant, whose struggle for life was shown over and over again on TV,
had actually been the victim of an oil spill caused not by Iraqi sabotage
but by Allied bombing. By the end of the war, it had become possible to
take the enemy as not people, but machines; the tanks, busses, cars,
which jammed the highway out of Kuwait City seemed to have fled on
their own, so that their charred hulks contained no human remains.
There was thus a visual purity to the U.S. victory that successfully
masked its savagery.

The sense of purity was conveyed by a cooperative press, but the administration took no chances: the press was tightly controlled as well.
In Vietnam, reporters learned to treat military press briefings with the
respect they deserved: five o'clock follies they were called and widely
mocked. Reporters understood it was the task of the military to report
victory; it was the reporters' task to find out what was going on. This is
not to romanticize the role of the press in Vietnam. The overwhelming
majority of reporters supported the war, and their criticisms were
rarely based on principle but rather on tactics. Even so, the reporters
made clear the cavernous abyss between what the U.S. military and
State Department wished the public to believe and what seemed to the
press to be the case. The abyss was called the "credibility gap," and it
meant that people began to treat government handouts with an unprecedented degree of skepticism. Since Vietnam the military has been
careful not to allow this process to repeat itself. "Three Pentagon press
officers," James LeMoyne reported during the first Gulf War, "said
that they spent significant time analyzing reporters' stories in order to
make recommendations on how to sway coverage in the Pentagon's
favor." Reporters who asked "hard questions" were warned that their
"antimilitary" attitude would count against them. On-camera TV interviews were halted in the middle if the press officer didn't like what
was being said; reporters who filed stories on troop doubts about the
war found their access to senior military men curtailed and the soldiers
themselves were subjected to close questioning by their officers.[3] The
troops were also carefully briefed on how to talk to the press. "Say you
are highly trained," Anthony Swofford was told. "Say you're excited to
be here and you believe in the mission and that we'll annihilate the
Iraqis." When a marine in the company argues that it's un-American

to censor speech, the staff sergeant responds: "You are marines. There is no such thing as speech that is free. You must pay for everything you say. Especially the unauthorized crap."[4]

Throughout Gulf War I, generals and retired generals, admirals and retired admirals were given hours of TV time to speculate, point with pointers, describe in sensuous detail the operation of this or that weapon. The Middle East experts of choice, like the military men, supported the president's policy. The peace side received airtime, but in proportions that effectively marginalized it. Peace demonstrations in Europe went uncovered and demonstrations and marches in the U.S. did not fare much better. Told by Vietnam revisionists that the media had created the peace movement by showing it on TV, the networks exercised due caution.

In the war against terrorism via the war in Afghanistan, there was a similar unanimity of expert opinion, but far fewer visuals. No generals instructed the public in the fine points of the map of Afghanistan, no reporters accompanied the troops. When a reporter for the *Washington Post* tried to reach the site of a missile attack on an alleged Al Qaeda target, he was stopped at gunpoint.[5] But a press too tightly controlled becomes restive and the Pentagon has been alert to invent other means of containing the media. During Gulf War I, the entire population had the experience of being in the nose cone of a missile as it descended towards its target; the camera did not show the view from the ground looking up. It was difficult to imagine what greater service the news media could offer a warring state. But that was before *Survivor* offered a new model. According to the *New York Times,* the Pentagon planned to "promote its war effort through television's genre of the moment, the reality series." Over the protests of its news division the ABC entertainment division would produce a thirteen-part series offering, according to the press release, "compelling personal stories" of America's fighting men and women. "There's a lot of other ways to convey information to the American people than through news organizations," Rear Adm. Craig R. Quigley pointed out. "That's the principal means," the admiral went on, "but if there is an opportunity to tell about the courage and professionalism of our men and women in uniform on prime-time television for thirteen straight weeks, we're going to do it. That's an opportunity not to be missed."[6]

By the second Gulf War, the military had arrived at a more perfect

form: the embedded press corps that has, by and large, fulfilled its pun-
ning name. At one point in the war, the TV talk show host Charlie
Rose conducted a telephone interview with Frederik Balfour, a *Business Week* correspondent who was embedded in the 3rd Infantry. Balfour had opposed the war before it began, but now riding along with
the troops, dependent upon them for his protection, he found it was
impossible not to feel part of their "cause." Rose next asked Colin
Soloway, *Newsweek* correspondent with the 101st Airborne Division,
if he'd been able to go along on any Apache helicopter missions. No,
Soloway explained regretfully, Apache helicopters only have seats for
the two pilots. Still, he was able to view the videotape when the helicopters returned to base and the pilots were glad to "walk him
through" whatever engagement they had conducted. The TV audience did not get to see the tapes—any more than they had during Gulf
War I.

Looking back on the first Gulf War, it would seem the first President Bush had done everything right. In addition to avoiding that
which must not be done—conscription, an uncontrolled press, body
counts, gradual escalation—Bush had done that which should be
done: send a massive force immediately; accuse the enemy of atrocities
before such an accusation could be made against the U.S.; keep American casualties to an absolute minimum; give the victorious troops a
victory parade. Yet the Vietnam syndrome lingered. If the first test of
the political success of a war is the reelection of those who made it, then
despite all these preparations the administration had failed. If the second test is how the war is represented in popular culture, the failure
proved even greater. The only notable movie to come out of the war,
Three Kings, depicted the conflict as Vietnam on speed: a war of multiple betrayals and massacres; a war without honor or sense. For all the
efforts of the administration to re-create World War II, Gulf War I
never achieved the necessary majesty. It remained a punitive war
against an oil ally who had gotten out of hand and had to be punished.
The first President Bush chose to retain a presumably chastened Saddam Hussein in power. American troops did not march triumphantly
through the streets of Baghdad as they had in Berlin and Tokyo. The
Gulf War planners, many of whom, like Colin Powell, had fought in
Vietnam, put great thought and energy into avoiding that war's dangers and they succeeded. Still, they could not make war good again.

Clinton's military expeditions, undertaken with a clear memory of what the Vietnam War had been about and why he had opposed it, fared no better. In Somalia, the Clinton administration worked towards the World War II formula by naming one of that country's many warlords as its Hitler and proceeding to hunt him and his lieutenants down. In the course of those unsuccessful efforts, a famine-stricken population, which had initially welcomed U.S. intervention, turned famously ugly. Eighteen dead Americans and 1,000 dead Somalis later, Clinton withdrew U.S. forces. For most of the public, the lesson drawn was that if you couldn't have World War II and didn't want Vietnam, it was best to stay home, or to participate from 30,000 feet up. Thus, in Kosovo, safe in the skies, the U.S. Air Force played its part, prevailing over a "pint-sized nation whose entire gross national product amounted to one-sixteenth of the Pentagon's budget. . . ."[7] It was a model intervention: no Americans were hurt and the stock market soared.

Clinton's use of military force was one response to the ghost of Vietnam; George H.W. Bush's more robust resort to arms, another. But neither could meet the contradictory need of the country to see itself as both supremely powerful *and* forever an underdog; both the only redeemer and the preeminent victim. In Vietnam its power had not prevailed, it was not the underdog, it had redeemed no one and nothing and, however frequently Vietnam veterans were called upon for surrogate victim duty, it was difficult to avoid the sense that Vietnam itself remained the main victim. And then came September 11.

For a time, it seemed that terrible event would succeed in burying the ghost of Vietnam. It gave the U.S. a moral authority it had not had since Franklin Delano Roosevelt. In addition, once Bush had declared war on terrorism (a recurring declaration starting with the presidency of Ronald Reagan) the rhetoric not only of World War II but of the Cold War as well returned. In the manner of the Cold War, the war against terrorism was perforce endless; in the manner of World War II, it was a struggle against enemies of consummate wickedness, an Axis of Evil. Best of all, this particular endless war against evil would require little home-front effort beyond continuing to consume at normal or preferably exorbitant levels. The first battle in the new war, overthrowing the Taliban, proved to be only a minor challenge to the military. What happened in Afghanistan thereafter—warlord rule, a possible revivification of the Taliban, the devastated countryside—detained neither the Bush administration nor the general public. The relentless march to war against Iraq, long urged by the second President Bush's close advisers, could now begin.

Yet at a narrative level, the combination of Cold War and World War II stumbled. The most important institutional legacy of World War II, the United Nations, for a time almost brought the march to a complete halt. The grand coalition of Gulf War I would not reenlist and the administration was reduced to recruiting international support through highly publicized bribery and threats, only to achieve a Coalition of the Willing made up, among others, of Eritreans and Solomon Islanders. Administration insistence that Saddam Hussein had weapons of mass destruction, up to and including nuclear weapons, joined a collective memory of how World War II ended with the dominant fears of the Cold War era but convincing proof of the existence of the weapons could not be assembled. Not only was the World War II template elusive, but the Vietnam War returned in the form of a mass antiwar movement, global in scope, broadly inclusive, spontaneously organized, clearly and repeatedly saying no to war.

Nothing could have deflected the administration from having its war. Yet the sharp outlines of a victorious war story quickly blurred. Instead of the orderly march into the defeated capital past the cheering thousands: looting, arson, anarchy, peaceful demonstrators shot and killed, shouts of "down with America." Instead of a ceremonial turning over of power to the new rulers, historically the moment that legitimized the new order, senior American officers sat alone on the plush sofas of an empty palace. An historian, Wolfgang Schivelbusch, observed that the "absence of the vanquished from their place at the table of surrender resonated as a sinister silence, like a tragedy ending without a dying hero's last words." The scene of the generals in the palace was a "scene of ersatz surrender, for the simple reason that the defeated regime had vanished without a trace."[8]

The most famous surrender scene in twentieth-century U.S. history took place on the deck of the battleship USS *Missouri* on September 2, 1945. It was a ceremony, John Dower has written, "laden with symbolism." The ship bore the name of President Truman's home state, it flew the flag that had flown from the White House on Pearl Harbor day as well as the one Commodore Perry had flown as he sailed into Tokyo Bay in 1853. Japan's "utter subjugation was reinforced by the dramatic setting of the surrender ceremony itself."[9] At the end of Gulf War II, George W. Bush, appropriately costumed, copiloted a Navy jet onto the deck of the aircraft carrier *Abraham Lincoln,* which had had to put out to sea a bit in order to make the landing feasible. There were no Iraqis there, of course, only cheering American sailors and a largely admiring press corps. But if the surrender was ersatz, so was the victory speech, for openly to declare victory would require the release of Iraqi prisoners of war and no one wanted to do that. Nor, for that matter, did the president wish to announce the return of peace, as General MacArthur had on board the *Missouri.* Instead, in a great mix of historical references, Bush called upon the spirits of war presidents past (Roosevelt, Truman, Kennedy, and Reagan)[10] in the course of announcing a victory in "one battle" in the ongoing war against terrorism, a victory comparable to the Allied landings in Normandy and the battle of Iwo Jima.[11] But what neither Bush nor the press had foreseen was the ongoing resistance to U.S. occupation on the part of various Iraqi groups, a resistance that takes a daily toll in American and Iraqi dead.

Initially the Vietnam syndrome referred to the reluctance of the public to engage in war. Now, it seems clear, it is the government of the country that is caught in its grip, convinced that the only cure for that long-ago defeat is yet more war. But redeeming Vietnam is only one function of the wars the U.S. has fought since September 11, 2001. The other, perhaps more significant purpose, is to extend, selectively, the benefits the Cold War had brought to the U.S. over its forty-five-year life span, regrettably lost owing to the Soviet Union's withdrawal from the field and its subsequent disappearance.

The majority of Americans in the summer of 1950 (some 57 percent according to a Gallup poll) believed that with the "police action" in Korea, World War III had begun.[12] Writing shortly after the fall of the Taliban government in Afghanistan, Eliot Cohen, director of Strategic Studies at Johns Hopkins University School of Advanced International Studies, made the same calculation in an important op-ed piece for the *Wall Street Journal* shortly after the war in Afghanistan had begun.[13] It was crucial, Cohen argued, to call things by their right name. The "less palatable but more accurate name" for the war on terrorism is "World War IV." "The Cold War was World War III," Cohen wrote, and World War IV resembles it in many ways: it is global; it will require "a mixture of violent and nonviolent efforts"; it will last a very long time; and "it has ideological roots." The enemy now is "militant Islam," and in this war, Afghanistan was "just one front in World War IV, and the battles there just one campaign." Cohen envisioned at least two others: in Iraq and in Iran.

Norman Podhoretz pursued this theme in a long essay several months later entitled "How to Win World War IV," and former CIA director James Woolsey embraced the same idea, predicting that World War IV was likely to last longer than World Wars I and II but "hopefully not the full four-plus decades of the Cold War."[14] Notable among all three commentators was their evident zest for war. Podhoretz was explicit: "I fully realize," he wrote, "that we are judged both by others and by ourselves, as lacking the stomach and the skills to play even so limited an imperial role as we did in occupying Germany and Japan after World War II." He sometimes doubted the country's capabilities in this regard, and worried about the long history of national inattention and passivity. "Yet," he concluded, "given the transfiguring impact of major wars on the victors no less than on the vanquished, who can tell what we may wind up doing and becoming as we fight our way through World War IV?" The prospect of what the U.S. (or any other warring state) might become as it fought its way through the twenty-first century did not give Podhoretz pause. He was confident everybody in the world would be better off and that victory in World War IV would mean, as President Bush proclaimed, "an age of liberty here and across the world."

In terms of public rhetoric, domestic security policies, militarization of foreign policy and culture, curtailment of civil liberties, a pervasive sense of fear and threat, the war on terrorism is the Cold War redux. It takes little historical imagination to see in the permanent war against terrorism a continuation of what was initially imagined as a permanent war against communism. The use the Bush administration has made of September 11 echoes the use the Truman administration made of the North Korean attack against South Korea, and the war against Iraq extends the analogy (for Syngman Rhee think Chalabi). Out of the ashes of the Korean War and ground zero came analogous convictions about the efficacy of force, the fear that compromise or concession signaled weakness, and the irrelevance of the local causes of conflict. The Korean War enabled the U.S. to fund the remilitarization of Europe and Japan, create an expanded alliance system, build a chain of military bases that spanned the globe (Japan, South Korea, Taiwan, the Philippines, Thailand, Australia, Diego Garcia, Saudi Arabia, Ethiopia, Turkey, Greece, Italy, Spain, Portugal, Germany, England, Iceland), and establish an ever-expanding nuclear arsenal. Out of September 11 and the war against Iraq, the U.S. has dismantled an alliance system it declared overly constricting and expanded its chain of military bases into new areas of the world: Iraq, Afghanistan, Uzbekistan, Djibouti, Pakistan, Georgia, Kazakhstan, Bulgaria, Yugoslavia (former), in addition to existing base facilities in Kuwait, Saudi Arabia, and Turkey. The combination effectively embraces the richest areas in the world for oil exploration and development.[15]

Ominously, the administration has pressed for and received funding to renew nuclear weapons research and testing, in disregard of the Comprehensive Test Ban and the Nuclear Nonproliferation Treaties. The Pentagon's nuclear posture review argues for a "new triad" approach to nuclear planning: "New capabilities must be developed to defeat emerging threats such as hard and deeply buried targets, to find and attack mobile and relocatable targets, to defeat chemical or biological agents and to improve accuracy and limit collateral damage." The need for these new weapons is based on "classified intelligence" indicating that more than seventy countries have underground facilities of which "at least 1,100" are thought to be "strategic command centers or weapons bases." The administration is committed to useable nuclear weapons as a means of deterring "smaller countries" from developing nuclear weapons systems. "Under this theory," the *New York Times* reports, "those countries may now believe that the stigma of using a large nuclear weapon against them is so great that the United States would never do so." A "less devastating weapon" would thus be a more credible threat.[16]

Inherent in the Cold War from its outset was the possibility it could end through the evolution of the Soviet Union into one of Us. Although the Soviet Union never formally surrendered and several Communist states remain at large, much of the American public was persuaded that the U.S. had "won" the Cold War, even that peace, with its expected dividends, had arrived. But terrorism is a tactic, not an ideology, one the weak will always have available for use against the strong. In the war on terrorism, the administration of the second President Bush may have discovered the model for permanent war in a unipolar world.

10

Remembrance of Empires Past: 9/11 and the End of the Cold War

Corey Robin

Busy giddy minds with foreign quarrels.
> —*Henry IV,* Part 2

In 2000, I spent the better part of a late summer interviewing William F. Buckley and Irving Kristol. I was writing an article for *Lingua Franca* on the defections to the left of several younger right-wing intellectuals, and wanted to hear what the movement's founding fathers thought of their wayward sons. Over the course of our conversations, however, it became clear that Buckley and Kristol were less interested in these ex-conservatives than they were in the sorry state of the conservative movement and the uncertain fate of the United States as a global empire. The end of communism and the triumph of the free market, they told me, were mixed blessings. Conservative victories, these developments had nevertheless rendered the United States ill-equipped for the post–Cold War era. Americans now possessed the most powerful empire in history. At the same time, they were possessed by one of the most antipolitical ideologies in history: the free market. According to its more aggressive idealists, the free market is a harmonious order, promising an international civil society of voluntary exchange, requiring little more from the state than the occasional enforcement of laws and contracts. For Buckley and Kristol, this was too bloodless a notion upon which to found a national order, much less a global empire. It did not provide the passion and élan, the gravitas and authority, that the exercise of American power truly required, at home and abroad. It encouraged triviality and small-minded politics, self-interest over the national interest—not the most promising base from which to launch an empire. What's more, the right-wingers in charge of the Republican Party didn't seem to realize this.

"The trouble with the emphasis in conservatism on the market," Buckley told me, "is that it becomes rather boring. You hear it once, you master the idea. The notion of devoting your life to it is horrifying if only because it's so repetitious. It's like sex." Conservatism, Kristol added, "is so influenced by business culture and by business modes of thinking that it lacks any political imagination, which has always been, I have to say, a property of the left." Kristol confessed to a deep yearning for an American empire: "What's the point of being the greatest, most powerful nation in the world and not having an imperial role? It's unheard of in human history. The most powerful nation always had an imperial role." But, he continued, previous empires were not "capitalist democracies with a strong emphasis on economic growth and economic prosperity." Because of its commitment to the free market, the United States lacked the fortitude and vision to wield imperial power. "It's too bad," Kristol lamented. "I think it would be natural for the United States . . . to play a far more dominant role in world affairs. Not what we're doing now but to command and to give orders as to what is be done. People need that. There are many parts of the world, Africa in particular, where an authority willing to use troops can make a very good difference, a healthy difference." But with public discussion moderated by accountants—"There's the Republican Party tying itself into knots. Over what? Prescriptions for elderly people? Who gives a damn? I think it's disgusting that . . . presidential politics of the most important country in the world should resolve around prescriptions for elderly people. Future historians will find this very hard to believe. It's not Athens. It's not Rome. It's not anything"—Kristol thought it unlikely that the United States would take its rightful place as the successor to empires past.[1]

Since 9/11, I've had many occasions to recall these conversations. September 11, we have been told, shocked the United States out of the complacent peace and prosperity that set in after the Cold War. It has forced Americans to look beyond their borders, to understand at last the dangers that confront a world power. It has reminded us of the goods of civic life and of the value of the state, putting an end to that fantasy of creating a public world out of private acts of self-interested exchange. It has restored to our woozy civic culture a sense of depth and seriousness, of things "larger than ourselves." Most critical of all, it has given the United States a coherent national purpose and focus for imperial rule. A country that seemed for a time unwilling to face up to its international responsibilities is now prepared, once again, to bear any burden, pay any price, for freedom. This changed attitude, the argument goes, is good for the world. It presses the United States to create a stable and just international order. It is also good, spiritually, for the United States. It forces us to think about something more than peace and prosperity, to remind us that freedom is a fighting faith rather than a cushy perch.

Like any historical moment, 9/11—not the terrorist attacks or the day itself but the imperial political culture it has spawned—has multiple dimensions. Some part of this new dispensation is the product of a surprise attack on civilians, and the efforts of U.S. leaders to provide some measure of security to an apprehensive citizenry. Some part of it flows from the subterranean political economy of oil, from the desire of U.S. elites to secure access to energy reserves in the Middle East and Central Asia, and to wield oil as an instrument of geopolitics. But while these factors play a considerable role in determining U.S. policy, they do not explain entirely the politics and ideology of the imperial moment itself. To understand that dimension, we must look to the impact on American conservatives of the end of the Cold War, of the loss of communism and the ascendancy of the free market as the organizing principle of the domestic and international order. For it is conservative dissatisfaction with that order that now drives, in part, their effort to create a new one.

For neoconservatives who thrilled to Ronald Reagan's crusade against communism, all that was left after the Cold War was Reagan's other passion—his sunny entrepreneurialism and market joie de vivre—which found a welcome home in Bill Clinton's America. While neocons are certainly not opposed to capitalism, they do not believe it is the highest achievement of civilization. Their vision is more exalted. They aspire to the epic grandeur of Rome, the ethos of the pagan warrior—or moral crusader—rather than that of the comfortable bourgeois. Since the end of the Cold War, that vision has received short shrift, eclipsed by the embrace of free markets and free trade. Undone by their own success, neoconservatives are not happy with the world they created. And so they have taken up the call of empire, providing the basso profundo to a swelling chorus, which now includes many progressive voices as well. Though they have complete faith in American power, the neocons are uncomfortable with using it for the mere extension of capitalism. They seek to create an international order that will be a monument for the ages, a world that is about something more than money and markets.

But, as I will suggest, this envisioned imperium may not provide such an easy resolution to the challenges confronting the United States. Already, the American empire is coming up against daunting obstacles in the Middle East and Central Asia, suggesting how elusive the reigning idea of the new imperialists—that the United States can govern events, that it can make history—truly is. Domestically, the cultural and political renewal that many imagine 9/11 has produced is proving a difficult achievement, the victim of a free-market ideology that shows no sign of abating. While it is still too soon to make any definitive assessment, there are already enough signs to suggest that 9/11 will not—and perhaps cannot—fulfill the role ascribed to it by the neocons of empire.

9/11: THE DREAM

Immediately following the attacks on the World Trade Center and the Pentagon, intellectuals, politicians, and pundits—not on the radical left, but mainstream conservatives and liberals—breathed an audible sigh of relief, almost as if they welcomed the strikes as a deliverance from the miasma Buckley and Kristol had been criticizing. The World Trade Center was still on fire and the bodies entombed there scarcely recovered when Frank Rich announced that "this week's nightmare, it's now clear, has awakened us from a frivolous if not decadent decade-long dream." What was that dream? The dream of prosperity, of surmounting life's obstacles with money. During the 1990s, Maureen Dowd wrote, we hoped "to overcome flab with diet and exercise, wrinkles with collagen and Botox, sagging skin with surgery, impotence with Viagra, mood swings with anti-depressants, myopia with laser surgery, decay with human growth hormone, disease with stem cell research and bioengineering." We "renovated our kitchens," observed David Brooks, "refurbished our home entertainment systems, invested in patio furniture, Jacuzzis and gas grills"—as if affluence might free us of tragedy and difficulty.[2] This ethos had terrible domestic consequences. For Francis Fukuyama, it encouraged "self-indulgent behaviour" and a "preoccupation with one's own petty affairs." It also had international repercussions. According to Bush administration official Lewis Libby, the cult of peace and prosperity found its purest expression in Bill Clinton's weak and distracted foreign policy, which made "it easier for someone like Osama bin Laden to rise up and say credibly, 'The Americans don't have the stomach to defend themselves. They won't take casualties to defend their interests. They are morally weak.' " According to Brooks, even the most casual observer of the pre-9/11 domestic scene, including Al Qaeda, "could have concluded that America was not an entirely serious country."[3]

But after that day in September, more than a few commentators claimed, the domestic scene was transformed. America was now "more mobilized, more conscious and therefore more alive," wrote Andrew Sullivan. George Packer remarked upon "the alertness, grief, resolve, even love" awakened by 9/11. "What I dread now," Packer confessed, "is a return to the normality we're all supposed to seek." For Brooks, "the fear that is so prevalent in the country" after 9/11 was "a cleanser, washing away a lot of the self-indulgence of the past decade." Revivifying fear, Brooks argued, eliminated the anxiety of prosperity, replacing a disabling emotion with a bracing passion. "We have traded the anxieties of affluence for the real fears of war."[4]

> Now upscalers who once spent hours agonizing over which Moen faucet head would go with their copper farmhouse-kitchen sink are suddenly worried about whether the water coming out of pipes has been poisoned. People who longed for Prada bags at Bloomingdale's are suddenly spooked by unattended bags at the airport. America, the sweet land of liberty, is getting a crash course in fear.[5]

Today, Brooks concluded, "commercial life seems less important than public life. . . . When life or death fighting is going on, it's hard to think of Bill Gates or Jack Welch as particularly heroic."[6]

Writers repeatedly welcomed the galvanizing moral electricity

now coursing through the body politic. A pulsing energy of public resolve and civic commitment, which would restore trust in government—perhaps, according to some liberals, even authorize a
revamped welfare state—a culture of patriotism and connection, a
new bipartisan consensus, the end of irony and the culture wars,
a more mature, more elevated presidency.[7] According to a reporter at
USA Today, President Bush was especially keen on the promise of 9/11,
offering himself and his generation as exhibit A in the project of domestic renewal. "Bush has told advisors that he believes confronting
the enemy is a chance for him and his fellow baby boomers to refocus
their lives and prove they have the same kind of valor and commitment their fathers showed in WWII."[8] And while the specific source
of Christopher Hitchens's elation may have been peculiarly his own,
his self-declared schadenfreude assuredly was not: "I should perhaps
confess that on September 11 last, once I had experienced all the usual
mammalian gamut of emotions, from rage to nausea, I also discovered
that another sensation was contending for mastery. On examination,
and to my own surprise and pleasure, it turned out to be exhilaration.
Here was the most frightful enemy—theocratic barbarism—in plain
view. . . . I realized that if the battle went on until the last day of my
life, I would never get bored in prosecuting it to the utmost."[9] With its
shocking spectacle of death and galvanizing fear, 9/11 offered a dead
or dying culture the chance to live again.

Internationally, 9/11 forced the United States to reengage the
world, to assume the burden of empires without embarrassment or
confusion. Where the first George Bush and Bill Clinton had fumbled
in the dark, searching for a doctrine to guide the exercise of U.S. power
after the collapse of the Soviet Union, the mission of the United States
was now clear: to defend civilization against barbarism, freedom
against terror. As Condoleezza Rice told *The New Yorker,* "I think the
difficulty has passed in defining a role. I think September 11th was one
of those great earthquakes that clarify and sharpen. Events are in
much sharper relief." An America thought to be lost in the quicksand
of free markets, individualism, and isolation was now recalled to a
consciousness of a world beyond its borders, and to a willingness to
sustain casualties on behalf of a U.S.-led global order. As Clinton's former undersecretary of defense concluded, "Americans are unlikely to
slip back into the complacency that marked the first decade after the

Cold War." They now understood, in the words of Brooks, that "evil exists" and that "to preserve order, good people must exercise power over destructive people."[10]

Future historians, I suspect, will look back upon these and other similar reactions to September 11 with some bewilderment. Not just because so many writers and politicians opened their arms to the political fallout from mass death. More significant is that September 11 has given them an opportunity to air their long-brewing contempt for the very peace and prosperity that preceded it. On September 12, one might have expected expressions of sorrow over the bursting of bubbles—economic, cultural, and political. But instead, many saw 9/11 as a thunderous judgment upon—and necessary corrective to—the frivolity and emptiness of the 1990s. We would have to reach back almost a century—to the opening days of World War I, when the "marsh gas of boredom and vacuity"[11] enveloping another free-trading, globalizing fin de siècle exploded—to find a parallel to our present moment.

To understand this spirit of relief and rejoice, we must return to the waning days of the Cold War, those years between the late 1980s and early 1990s when American elites first realized that the United States could no longer define its mission in terms of the Soviet menace. While the end of the Cold War unleashed a wave of triumphalism in the United States and Western Europe, it also provoked among elites an anxious uncertainty about U.S. foreign policy. With the defeat of communism, many asked, how should the United States define its role in the world? Where and when should it intervene in foreign conflicts? How big a military should it field? Underlying these arguments was a deep unease about the size and purpose of American power. The United States seemed to be suffering from a surfeit of power, which made it difficult for elites to formulate any coherent principles to govern its use. As Richard Cheney, the first President Bush's secretary of defense, acknowledged in February 1992, "We've gained so much strategic depth that the threats to our security, now relatively distant, are harder to define." Almost a decade later, the United States would still seem, to its leaders, a floundering giant. As Condoleezza Rice noted during the 2000 presidential campaign, "The United States has found it exceedingly difficult to define its 'national interest' in the absence of Soviet power." So uncertain about the national interest did political elites become that a top Clinton defense aide—and subsequent dean of Harvard's Kennedy School—would eventually throw up his hands in defeat, declaring the national interest to be whatever "citizens, after proper deliberation, say it is"—an abdication simply unthinkable during the Cold War reign of the Wise Men.[12]

When Clinton assumed office, he and his advisers took stock of this unparalleled situation—where the United States possessed so much power that it faced, in the words of Clinton National Security Advisor Anthony Lake, no "credible near-term threat to [its] existence"—and concluded that the primary concerns of American foreign policy were no longer military but economic. After summarily rehearsing the various possible military dangers to the United States, President Clinton declared in a 1993 address, "We still face, *overarching everything else,* this amorphous but profound challenge in the way humankind conducts its commerce." The great imperative of the post–Cold War era was to organize a global economy where citizens of the world could trade across borders. For that to happen, the United States had to get its own economic house in order—"renewal starts at home," said Lake—by reducing the deficit (in part through reductions in military spending), lowering interest rates, supporting high-tech industry, and promoting free trade agreements. Because other nations would also have to conduct a painful economic overhaul, Lake concluded that the primary goal of the United States was the "enlargement of the world's free community of market democracies."[13]

Clinton's assessment of the challenges facing the United States was partially inspired by political calculation. He had just won an election against a sitting president who had not only led the United States through victory in the Cold War but had also engineered a stunning rout over the Iraqi military. A southern governor with no foreign policy experience—and a draft-dodger to boot—Clinton concluded that his victory over Bush meant that questions of war and peace no longer resonated with American voters the way they might have in an earlier age.[14] But Clinton's vision also reflected a conviction, common to the 1990s, that the globalization of the free market had undermined the efficacy of military power and the viability of traditional empires. Force was no longer the sole, or most effective, instrument of national will. Power now hinged upon economic performance, the dynamism of a nation's prosperity, and the attractiveness of its culture. As Joseph Nye, Clinton's assistant secretary of defense, would come to argue, "soft power"—the cultural capital that made the United States so admired around the globe—was as important to national preeminence as military power. In perhaps a first for a U.S. official, Nye invoked Gramsci to argue that the United States would only maintain its position of hegemony if it persuaded—rather than forced—others to follow its example. "If I can get you to *want* to do what I want," wrote Nye, "then I do not have to force you to do what you do *not* want to do."[15] To maintain its standing in the world, the United States would have to outcompete other national economies, all the while ensuring the spread of its free-market model and pluralist culture. The greatest dangers confronting the United States were that it would not reform its economy, or that it would abuse its military superiority and provoke international hatred. The problem confronting the United States was not that it did not have enough power, but that it had too much. To render the world safe for globalization, the United States would have to be defanged, or, at a minimum, significantly curtailed in its imperial aspirations.

For many American intellectuals and politicians, particularly those conservatives who yearned for and then celebrated socialism's demise, Clinton's promotion of easygoing prosperity was a horror. Affluence produced a society without difficulty and adversity. Material satisfaction induced a loss of social depth and political meaning, a lessening of resolve and heroic verve. "In that age of peace and prosperity," David Brooks would write, "the top sitcom was *Seinfeld,* a show about nothing." Robert Kaplan emitted barb after barb about the "healthy, well fed" denizens of "bourgeois society," too consumed with their own comfort and pleasure to lend a hand—or shoulder a gun—to make the world a safer place. "Material possessions," he concluded, "encourage docility."[16] Throughout the 1990s, the lead item of intellectual complaint, across the political spectrum, was that the United States was insufficiently civic-minded or martial, its leaders and citizens too distracted by prosperity and affluence to take care of its inherited institutions, common concerns, and worldwide defense. Respect for the state was supposed to be dwindling, as was political participation and local volunteerism.[17] Indeed, one of the most telling signs of the waning imperative of the Cold War was the fact that the 1990s began and ended with two incidents—the Clarence Thomas–Anita Hill hearings, and the Supreme Court decision during the 2000 presidential election controversy—casting scandalous suspicion on the nation's most venerated political institution.

For influential neocons of the *Weekly Standard* persuasion, Clinton's foreign policy was even more of an anathema. Not because the neocons were unilateralists arguing against Clinton's multilateralism, or isolationists or realists critical of his internationalism and humanitarianism.[18] Clinton's foreign policy, they argued, was too driven by the imperatives of free-market globalization. It was proof of the oozing decadence taking over the United States after the defeat of the Soviet Union, a sign of weakened moral fiber and lost martial spirit. In an influential manifesto published in 2000, Donald and Frederick Kagan could barely contain their contempt for "the happy international situation that emerged in 1991," which was "characterized by the spread of democracy, free trade, and peace," and which was "so congenial to America" with its love of "domestic comfort." According to Kaplan, "The problem with bourgeois societies" like our own "is a lack of imagination. A person raised in a middle- or upper-middle-class suburban environment"—the soccer moms, for instance, so insistently championed by Republicans and Democrats alike—does not care about the world outside her narrow confines. "Peace," he complained, "is pleasurable, and pleasure is about momentary satisfaction." It was "obtainable only through a form of tyranny, however subtle and mild." It erased the memory of bracing conflict, robust disagreement, the luxury of defining ourselves "by virtue of whom we were up against."[19]

Though conservatives are often reputed to favor wealth and prosperity, law and order, stability and routine—all the comforts of bourgeois life—most of Clinton's conservative critics hated him for his pursuit of these very virtues. Clinton's free-market obsessions betrayed an unwillingness to embrace the murky world of power and violent conflict, of tragedy and rupture. His foreign policy was not just unrealistic; it was insufficiently dark and brooding. "The striking thing about the 1990s zeitgeist," complained Brooks, "was the presumption of harmony. The era was shaped by the idea that there were no fundamental conflicts anymore." Conservatives thrive on a world filled with mysterious evil and unfathomable hatreds, where good is always on the defensive and time is a precious commodity in the cosmic race against corruption and decline. Coping with such a world requires pagan courage and an almost barbaric *virtù,* qualities conservatives embrace over the more prosaic goods of peace and prosperity. It is no accident that Paul Wolfowitz, the darkest of these dark princes of pessimism, was a student of Allan Bloom (in fact, Wolfowitz makes a cameo appearance in *Ravelstein*, Saul Bellow's novel about Bloom), for Bloom—like many other influential neoconservatives—was a follower of the political theorist Leo Strauss, whose quiet odes to classical virtue and ordered harmony veiled his Nietzschean vision of torturous conflict and violent struggle.[20]

But there was another reason for the neocons' dissatisfaction with Clinton's foreign policy. Many of them found it insufficiently visionary and consistent. Clinton, they claimed, was reactive and ad hoc rather than proactive and forceful. He and his advisors were unwilling to imagine a world where the United States shaped rather than responded to events. Breaking again with the usual stereotype of conservatives as nonideological muddlers, figures like Wolfowitz, Libby, Kaplan, Richard Perle, Frank Gaffney, Kenneth Adelman, and the father-son teams of Kagan and Kristol, called for a more ideologically coherent projection of U.S. power, where the "benign hegemony" of American might would spread "the zone of democracy" rather than just extend the free market. They wanted a foreign policy that was, in words of praise that Robert Kagan would later use to describe Senator Joseph Lieberman, "idealistic but not naïve, ready and willing to use force and committed to a strong military, but also committed to using American power to spread democracy and do some good in the world." As early as the first Bush administration, the neocons were insisting that the United States ought, in Cheney's words, "to shape the future, to determine the outcome of history," or, as the Kagans would later put it, "to intervene decisively in every critical region" of the world, "whether or not a visible threat exists there." They criticized those Republicans, in Robert Kagan's words, who "during the dumb decade of the 1990s" suffered from a "hostility to 'nation-building,' the aversion to 'international social work' and the narrow belief that 'superpowers don't do windows.' "[21] What these conservatives longed for was an America that was genuinely imperial—not just because they believed it would make the United States safer or richer, and not just because they thought it would make the world better, but because they literally wanted to see the United States *make* the world. They sought, in other words, to create history—to commit the very sins that they had long accused Marxists and other ideologues of committing: hubris, worship of state power, and utopian aspiration.

At the most obvious level, 9/11 has confirmed what the conservatives have been saying for years: The world is a dangerous place, filled with hostile forces who will stop at nothing to see the United States felled. More important, 9/11 has given conservatives an opportunity—and audience—to articulate, without embarrassment, the vision of imperial American power they have been quietly nourishing for years. "People are now coming out of the closet on the word empire," Charles Krauthammer accurately observes. Unlike empires past, conservatives claim, this one will be guided by a benign, even beneficial vision of worldwide improvement. Because of America's sense of fair play and benevolent purpose—unlike Britain or Rome, the United States has no intention of occupying or seizing territory of its own—this new empire will not generate the backlash that all previous empires have generated. As a *Wall Street Journal* writer says, "We are an attractive empire, the one everyone wants to join." In the words of Rice, "Theoretically, the realists would predict that when you have a great power like the United States it would not be long before you had other great powers rising to challenge it. And I think what you're seeing is that there's at least a predilection this time to move to productive and cooperative relations with the United States, rather than to try to balance the United States."[22] By creating an empire, the United States will no longer have to respond to immediate threats, to "wait upon events while dangers gather," as President Bush put it in his 2002 state of the union address. It will now "shape the environment," anticipate threats, thinking not in months or years, but in decades, perhaps centuries. The goal here is what Cheney, acting on the advice of Wolfowitz, first outlined in the early 1990s: to ensure that no other power ever arises to challenge the United States, to ensure that no regional powers ever attain preeminence in their local theaters. The emphasis, then, is on the preemptive and predictive, to think in the Hegelian terms of becoming rather than in the more staid Anglo terms of being. As Richard Perle put it, vis-à-vis Iraq, "What is essential here is not to look at the opposition to Saddam as it is today, without any external support, without any realistic hope of removing that awful regime, but to look at what could be created."[23]

For conservatives, this is a heady time, a moment when their simultaneous commitment and hostility to the free market may finally be satisfied. No longer hamstrung by the numbing politics of affluence and prosperity, they believe they can count on the public to respond to the call of sacrifice and destiny, confrontation and evil. With danger and security the watchwords of the day, the American state will be newly sanctified—without opening the floodgates to economic redistribution. 9/11 and the American empire, they hope, may at last resolve those cultural contradictions of capitalism that Daniel Bell noticed long ago but which have only truly come to the fore since the defeat of communism.

9/11: THE REALITY

It is of course too soon to make any definitive assessment of the domestic and international situation of the United States, post-9/11, but mounting evidence suggests that the American empire envisioned by conservatives is encountering more than a few obstacles, at home and abroad. In order to field the neocon empire, U.S. leaders will have to overcome, or at least provide a more realistic strategy for coping with, the problem of blowback. But instead of confronting this issue, the Bush administration dismisses it out of hand. In addition, since 9/11, whenever the U.S. military has faltered, popular support for aggressive militarism has dissipated, suggesting that the domestic base for such an empire is thin. Even the imperial warriors in the Bush administration have proven themselves, first in Afghanistan and now in Iraq, profoundly, almost congenitally, uninterested in the concrete tasks of empire-building. Finally, as almost every sober analyst of the current situation has pointed out, the United States finds itself today the object of such intense worldwide hatred in part because of the imperial power and economic hegemony that it wields. The only long-term solution to the problem of terrorism, they claim, is to pursue a combination of criminal indictments and prosecutions and political and economic reforms of the sort that would distribute power more equitably, both within and between states. Far from pursuing a prudent path to security, they argue, the United States is embarking upon a reckless path toward danger and instability, which will ultimately redound to the detriment of America itself.[24]

One of the most disturbing aspects of the new imperial vision is its total disregard for the problem of blowback, which Chalmers Johnson described to such devastating effect in his prescient book, published before 9/11. In *Blowback,* Johnson cites a 1997 Pentagon report, which states, "Historical data show a strong correlation between U.S. involvement in international situations and an increase in terrorist attacks against the United States. In addition, the military asymmetry that denies nation states the ability to engage in overt attack against the United States drives the use of transnational actors [i.e., terrorists]."[25] If this report is correct, it means that a major element of the neocon strategy—increased military involvement throughout the world—will only increase the likelihood that states and non-state actors will rely upon terrorist attacks against the United States in the future. Practically every commentator has pointed out that 9/11 taught Americans they are not invulnerable, that in an interdependent, global world, it is simply impossible to guarantee total immunity from terrorist attack. This permanent vulnerability to terrorist attack—not just on American soil but in countries and territories around the world where the United States has overseas military bases[26]—plus the realities of blowback, suggest a future that can only be more dangerous for Americans, at home or abroad.

Indeed, in the very same month that the neocons and their media allies were going public with their vast new vision of American imperial power, the United States military announced plans for a radical reduction in U.S. troops in Saudi Arabia. The U.S. presence there, claimed one senior military officer, is "destabilizing to the government," and American troops, added a base commander, are "sitting ducks." In that same month, a Japanese district court found a United States serviceman stationed in Okinawa guilty of raping a young woman, merely the latest in a string of criminal convictions against the 26,000 American troops in Okinawa (between 1972 and 1995, U.S. troops in Okinawa have been connected to 4,716 crimes), which have fanned widespread anti-American opposition within Okinawa and Japan.[27] Despite the claims of the Bush administration that the invasion of Iraq was a necessary step in the war on terrorism, even its most utopian defenders have been forced to acknowledge that the invasion and now occupation of that country have been a lightning rod for terrorist activity. With Al Qaeda and other anti-American groups rallying to beleaguered Iraq as the frontline in their war against the United

States, the predictions of opponents of the war have proven all too correct.

Despite the history of blowback, the administration, its intellectual gurus, and its media defenders dismiss it as a threat to imperial power. Blowback simply does not jibe with how they understand the nature and origin of terrorism. With terrorism classified as a symptom of unfathomable evil or antimodernist hostility to Western values, it does not—and cannot—register as a reaction to imperial power. After the invasion and occupation of Afghanistan, the administration came to believe, according to a former high-level intelligence official, that it did not need to worry about the problem of blowback. "They went against the established experts on the Middle East who said it [the bombing of Afghanistan] would lead to fundamental insurrections in Saudi Arabia and elsewhere. Not so, and anyone who now preaches any approach of solving problems with diplomacy is scoffed at. They're on a roll." Even though it took Osama bin Laden some ten years after the stationing of U.S. troops in Saudi Arabia to exact his revenge against the United States, even though the administration prides itself on thinking in terms of decades, the failure of blowback to materialize within three months of the Afghanistan war was taken as proof positive that blowback was no longer a threat—a point reinforced by a December 2001 presentation at the White House by Middle East historian Bernard Lewis. According to one White House staffer, Lewis said, "In that part of the world, nothing matters more than resolute will and force," which, according to an eye-opening *New Yorker* report, means that "the United States needn't proceed gingerly for fear of inflaming the 'Arab street,' as long as it is prepared to be strong."[28]

In and of itself, blowback might not prove such a formidable problem, at least not in the short term; after all, other empires have weathered it for a period of time. What makes blowback such a destabilizing factor over the long haul is that despite all the talk of the United States being prepared to take casualties in the war on terrorism, at moments when that war has seemed to blunder or miscarry, naysayers in the media and the Democratic Party—not to mention in Western Europe—have emerged to criticize the Bush administration and put it on the defensive. In late October and early November 2001, after a mere few weeks of bombing had failed to dislodge the Taliban, critics started murmuring their fears that the war in Afghanistan would be a reprise of the Vietnam quagmire.[29] As the war in Iraq came to be a reality, Europeans voiced their growing discomfort with the Bush administration's pursuit of the Axis of Evil, culminating in the unprecedented display of international opposition to the war on February 15, 2003. Democrats have begun, however tentatively, to probe the edges of acceptable criticism of the war, trying to identify Bush's weak spots in order to offer some form of loyal opposition. As the 2004 presidential campaign moves into its final season, voicing that criticism has become a litmus test of electability among the candidates.[30]

True, none of these critics has yet to challenge the full-throttle military premise of Bush's policies, but their periodic appearance, particularly in times of trouble or defeat, suggests that the administration's vision is politically viable only so long as it is successful. And, of course, this is as it must be: Because the centerpiece of the neoconservative promise is that the United States can govern events—that it can determine the outcome of history—their entire vision stands or falls on success or failure. Any suggestion that events lie beyond their control, their vision collapses. Indeed, it only took a week in late March 2002 of horrific bloodshed in Israel and the Occupied Territories—and the resulting accusations that "Bush fiddles in the White House or Texas, playing Nero as the Mideast burns"—for the planned empire to start, if not unraveling, then at least to be seriously called into question. No sooner had violence in the Middle East begun to escalate, when even the administration's defenders began jumping ship, suggesting that any invasion of Iraq would have to be postponed indefinitely. As one of Reagan's high-level national security aides put it, "The supreme irony is that the greatest power the world has ever known has proven incapable of managing a regional crisis." The fact, this aide added, that the administration had been so maniacally "focused on either Afghanistan or Iraq"—the two key outposts of imperial confrontation—while the Middle East was going up in flames "reflects either appalling arrogance or ignorance."[31] Likewise, during the summer of 2003, when it became apparent that the war on Iraq, though officially declared won and over, was settling into a prolonged, difficult, violent, and nasty guerilla campaign against an occupying power.

Ironically, insofar as the Bush administration avoids those conflicts, such as that between the Israelis and Palestinians, where it might fail, it is forced to forgo the very logic of imperialism that it seeks to avow. In other words, the neoconservative ideology of empire, premised as it is on the ability of the United States to control events, cannot accommodate failure, but by avoiding failure, the imperialists are forced to acknowledge that they cannot control events. As former Secretary of State Lawrence Eagleburger has observed of the crisis in the Middle East, Bush realizes "that simply to insert himself into this mess without any possibility of achieving any success is, in and of itself, dangerous, because it would demonstrate that in fact we don't have any ability right now to control or affect events"[32]—precisely the admission that the neocons cannot afford to make. This catch-22 is no mere problem of logic or consistency: It betrays the essential fragility of the imperial position itself.

That fragility also reflects the hollowness of the neocons' imperial vision. Though the neocons see imperialism as the cultural and political counterpart to free markets, they have not yet come to terms with how the conservative opposition to government spending, rooted in free-market ideology, renders the United States unlikely to make the necessary investments in nation-building that imperialism requires. It has been less than two years, as of this writing, since the United States promised the people of Afghanistan that it would never abandon them, and already it's clear that the Bush administration has done just that. Outside of Kabul, warlords rule the country, women's rights are nonexistent, heroin production is up, infrastructure and roads have not been built, and the Taliban has publicly launched a war of attrition to force an increasingly cash-strapped United States from the field. Former Clinton administration official Richard Holbrooke has gone so far as to claim that Afghanistan "is in extreme danger of falling back into the hands of warlords and drug lords and terrorists. And if this happens, Afghanistan will once again become a sanctuary for attacks against the United States." Ahmed Wali Karzai, brother of Afghan President Hamid Karzai, says much the same: "It is like I am seeing the same movie twice and no one is trying to fix the problem. What was promised to the Afghans with the collapse of the Taliban was a new life of hope and change. But what was delivered? Nothing. Everyone is back in business."[33] Postwar reports about the American occupation of Iraq reveal an administration not only unprepared for a guerilla campaign against the occupying powers, but also blithely indifferent to the task of nation-building. Presuming that a combination of private contractors and Iraqi oil flows would secure independence and democracy in Iraq, the administration had demonstrated that its imperial feathers are little more than the dissembling plumage of its free-market eagle.

On the domestic front, there is little evidence to suggest that the 9/11 political and cultural renewal imagined by most commentators—the revival of the state, the return of shared sacrifice and community, the deepening of moral awareness—has taken place, or will take place. September 11 may have temporarily increased popular trust in government and interest in public affairs,[34] but it has done little to displace among elites the free-market ideology that makes government action—outside the realm of national security—an instant source of suspicion. So long as the nation's dominant political language and practices glorify the market, no amount of civic cheerleading or wartime fervor can create a genuine *civitas*. We may live in a postmodern age, but no one is *that* postmodern. There is still a lived reality for all to see, and if that reality contradicts the claims of national leaders, the calls for shared sacrifice and common purpose will be heard for what they are—cheap rhetoric rather than genuine public philosophy.

Prior to September 11, President Bush pushed through Congress the most extensive tax cut since the early days of the Reagan administration. After September 11, congressional Republicans pushed through, twice, even more tax cuts for the wealthy. Though the tax cuts have imposed serious constraints on the ability of the U.S. to fight the war on terrorism, Bush and the Republicans show no sign of backing off from them. When politicians, moreover, have proposed government intervention in national-security-related sectors of the economy, free-marketeers in the Republican Party have been surprisingly effective at stymieing them. In March 2002, for example, sixty-two senators, including nineteen Democrats, rejected higher fuel-efficiency standards in the automobile industry, which would have reduced dependence upon Persian Gulf oil. Missouri Republican Christopher Bond felt so unencumbered by the need to pay homage to state institutions in time of war that he claimed on the Senate floor, "I don't want to tell a mom in my home state that she should not get an S.U.V. because Congress decided that would be a bad choice." Even more telling was just how vulnerable proponents of higher standards were to these antistatist, market arguments. John McCain, for example, was instantly put on the defensive by the notion that the government would be interfering with people's private market choices. He was left to argue that "no American will be forced to drive any different automobile," as if that would have been a dreadful imposition in this new era of wartime sacrifice and solidarity.[35]

Or consider the December 2001 announcement of Ken Feinberg, head of the September 11 Victims' Compensation Fund created by Congress, that families of victims would receive compensation for their loss based in part on the salary each victim was earning at the time of his or her death. After the attacks on the World Trade Center and the Pentagon, Congress had taken the unprecedented step of assuming national responsibility for restitution. Though the inspiration for this decision was to forestall expensive lawsuits against the airlines industry, many observers took it as a signal of the new dispensation: in the face of national tragedy, political leaders were finally breaking with the jungle survivalism of the Reagan-Clinton years. But even in death, the market—and the inequalities it generates—was the only language America's leaders knew how to speak. Abandoning the notion of shared sacrifice, Feinberg opted for the actuarial tables to figure out appropriate compensation packages. The family of a single sixty-five-year-old grandmother earning $10,000 a year—perhaps a minimum-wage kitchen worker—would draw $300,000 from the fund, while the family of a thirty-year-old Wall Street trader would get $3,870,064. The men and women killed on September 11 were not equal citizens of a democracy; they were private earners, and rewards would be distributed accordingly. Even more telling, virtually no one—not even the commentators and politicians who denounced the Feinberg calculus for other reasons—criticized this aspect of his decision.[36]

Even within and around the military, the ethos of patriotism and shared destiny remains secondary to that of the market. The government's desire not to spend too much money and thereby raise taxes has forced American soldiers in Afghanistan and Iraq to actually spend their own money on much-needed personal items of war: night-vision goggles, desert camouflage boots, baby wipes, better radios and communications equipment, and bigger rucksacks.[37] In a little-noticed article in the *New York Times,* military recruiters have confessed that they still entice potential enlistees not with the call of patriotism or duty but with the promise of economic opportunity. As one recruiter put it, "It's just business as usual. We don't push the 'Help our country' routine." When the occasional patriot bursts into a recruiting office and says, "I want to fight," a recruiter explains, "I've got to calm them down. We're not all about fighting and bombing. We're about jobs. We're about education."[38] Recruiters admit that they continue to target immigrants and people of color—on the assumption that it is these constituencies' lack of opportunity that drives them to the military. The Pentagon's publicly acknowledged goal, in fact, is to increase the number of Latinos in the military from the current 10 percent to 22 percent. Recruiters have even slipped into Mexico, with promises of instant citizenship to poor noncitizens willing to take up arms on behalf of the United States. According to one San Diego recruiter, "It's more or less common practice that some recruiters go to Tijuana to distribute pamphlets, or in some cases they look for someone to help distribute information on the Mexican side."[39] In December 2002, as the United States prepared to invade Iraq, New York Democratic congressman Charlie Rangel decided to confront this issue head-on by proposing a reinstatement of the draft. Noting that immigrants, people of color, and the poor were shouldering a greater percentage of the military burden than their numbers in the population warranted, Rangel argued that the United States should distribute the domestic costs of empire more equitably. If middle-class white kids were forced to shoulder arms, he claimed, the administration and its supporters might think twice before going to war. His proposed legislation went nowhere.

The fact that the war has not yet imposed the sort of sacrifices on the population that normally accompany national crusades has provoked no small measure of concern among political and cultural elites. "The danger, over the long term," writes the *Times*'s R. W. Apple, "is loss of interest. With much of the war to be conducted out of plain sight by commandos, diplomats and intelligence agents, will a nation that has spent decades in easy self-indulgence stay focused?" Not long after he declared the age of glitz and glitter over, Frank Rich found himself publicly agonizing that "you'd never guess this is a nation at war." Prior to 9/11, "the administration said we could have it all"; since 9/11, the administration has been saying much the same thing. A former aide to LBJ told the *New York Times,* "People are going to have get involved in this. So far it's a government effort, as it should be, but people aren't engaged."[40] Without consecrating the cause in blood, observers fear, Americans will not have their commitment tested, their resolve deepened. As Doris Kearns Goodwin complained on *The NewsHour:*

> Well, I think the problem is we understand that it's going to be a long war but it's hard for us to participate in that war in a thousand and one ways the way we could in World War II. You could have hundreds of thousands joining the armed forces. They could go to the factories to make sure to get those ships, tanks, and weapons built. They could have victory gardens. They could feel not simply as we're being told: Go back to your ordinary lives. It's harder now. We don't have a draft in the same way we did although there's some indication I'd like to believe that that younger generation will want to participate. My own youngest son who just graduated from Harvard this June has joined the military. He wants that three-year commitment. He wants to be part of what this is all about instead of just going to work for a year and going to law school, he wants to be a part of this. And I suspect there will be a lot of others like that as well. But somehow you just keep wishing that the government would challenge us. Maybe we need a Manhattan Project for this antibiotics vaccine production. We were able to get cargo ships down from 365 days in World War II to one day by the middle with that kind of collective enterprise. And I think we need to be mobilized, our spirit, our productivity, much more than we were.[41]

In what may be the strangest spectacle of the entire war, the nation's leaders are now scrambling to find things for people to do—not because there's much to be done, but because without something to do, leaders worry, the ardor of ordinary Americans will grow cold. Since these tasks are unnecessary—and mandating them would violate the norms of market ideology—the best the president and his colleagues have come up with is to announce Web sites and toll-free numbers where enterprising men and women can find information about helping out the war effort. As Bush declared in North Carolina the day after his 2002 state of the union address, "If you listened to the speech last night, you know, people were saying, 'Well, gosh, that's nice, he called me to action, where do I look?' Well, here's where: at usafreedomcorps.gov. Or you can call this number—it sounds like I'm making a pitch, and I am. This is the right thing to do for America. 1-877-USA-CORPS." What are the duties these volunteers are to perform? If they are doctors or health care workers, they can enlist to help out during emergencies. And everyone else? They can serve in neighborhood watch programs to guard against terrorist attacks—in North Carolina. Or they can report suspicious activities to the authorities.[42]

Thus far, political elites have failed to turn 9/11 into the galvanizing instrument of an American renaissance. What's more, they probably can't. For without a wrenching transformation of the economy and a reconsideration of the aggressively free-market ideals that have guided American policy for the last two decades—neither of which seems likely—there is no incentive for elites or citizens to invent themselves anew.

MACHIAVELLIAN MOMENTS

We thus face an extremely dangerous situation. On the one hand, we have a group of political and cultural elites whose vision of American power is recklessly utopian, who seem increasingly disconnected from any coherent conception of the national interest. On the other hand, we have a domestic population that shows little interest in sustaining such a far-flung empire. Rather than resolving the contradictions laid bare by the collapse of the Soviet Union—the tension between the free market and imperial aspiration—the current moment seems to be, if not exactly exacerbating them, then at least doing little to assuage them. The political order projected by Bush and his advisers—and their supporters in the media and academia—is just that: a projection, a jerry-built structure that can only last so long as the United States is able to put down, with minimum casualties, any challenge to its power. If this assessment is correct, we may well be entering one of those famed Machiavellian moments discussed by J.G.A. Pocock a quarter-century ago—those moments when a republic opts for the grandeur and frisson of empire, and is forced to confront the fragility and finitude of all political forms, including its own.

We may also be seeing, and I suggest this in only the most tentative of ways, the slow decomposition of the American ruling class.[43] Ever since the end of the Cold War—some might even say the Vietnam War—there has been a growing disconnect between the culture and ideology of U.S. business elites and that of political warriors like Wolfowitz and the other neocons. Where the Cold War saw the creation of a semi-coherent class of Wise Men who brought together, however jaggedly, the worlds of business and politics—men like Dean Acheson and the Dulles brothers—the Reagan years and beyond have witnessed something altogether different. On the one hand, we have a younger generation of corporate magnates who, though ruthless in their efforts to secure benefits from the state, have none of the respect or passion for the state that their older counterparts had. While certainly willing to take from the public till, they are contemptuous of politics and government. These new CEOs respond to their counterparts in Tokyo, London, and other global cities, and so long as the state provides them with what they need and does not interfere unduly with their operations, they leave it to the apparatchiks.[44] As one Silicon Valley executive said to Thomas Friedman, when asked by Friedman how often he talks about Iraq, Russia, or foreign wars, "Not more than once a year. We don't even care about Washington. Money is extracted by Silicon Valley and then wasted by Washington. I want to talk about people who create wealth and jobs. I don't want to talk about unhealthy and unproductive people. If I don't care about the wealth destroyers in my own country, why should I care about the wealth destroyers in another country?"[45]

On the other hand, with neocons like Wolfowitz and Brooks, the Kagans and the Kristols, we have a new class of political elites who have little contact with the business community, whose primary experiences outside of government have been in either academia, journalism, think tanks, or some other part of the culture industry. As corporate elites set their sites upon an increasingly global economy, these ideologues have been given, it seems, the run of the farm. They traffic in ideas, and see the world as a vast landscape of intellectual projection. Unconstrained by even the most interested of interests, they are free to advance their cause, in the Middle East and elsewhere. Indeed, according to press reports, most corporate elites, both in the United States and internationally, and even in the oil industry, have been either uninterested in or firmly opposed to the Bush administration's far-flung expedition in Iraq.[46] Like their corporate counterparts, the neocons view the world as their stage, but unlike their corporate counterparts, they are preparing for an altogether more theatrical, otherworldly drama. Their endgame, if they have one, is an apocalyptic confrontation between good and evil, civilization and barbarism—categories of pagan conflict diametrically opposed to the world-without-borders vision of America's free-trading, globalizing elite.

NOTES

Introduction: Cold War Triumphalism and the Real Cold War
by Ellen Schrecker

1. For a useful survey of the reasons for the fall of the Soviet Union, see Stephen Kotkin, *Armageddon Averted: The Soviet Collapse, 1970–2000* (New York: Oxford University Press, 2001).
2. Richard Perle, "Military Power and the Passing of the Cold War," in Charles W. Kegley Jr. and Kenneth L. Schwab, eds., *After the Cold War: Questioning the Morality of Nuclear Deterrence* (Boulder: Westview Press, 1991), 33.
3. Joshua Muravchik, "Losing the Peace," *Commentary* 94, no. 1 (July 1992), 39.
4. *Ibid.,* 41.
5. Margaret Thatcher, "Ronald Reagan: The Greatness of His Achievements," *Vital Speeches of the Day* 64, no. 8 (February 1, 1998), 226.
6. Francis Fukuyama claimed that the SDI transformed the Soviet Union because it "threatened to make obsolete an entire generation of Soviet nuclear weapons, and shifted the superpower competition into areas like microelectronics and other innovative technologies where the Soviet Union had serious disadvantages." Francis Fukuyama, *The End of History and the Last Man* (New York: Free Press, 1992), 75; Jay Winik, *On the Brink: The Dramatic, Behind-the-Scenes Saga of the Reagan Era and the Men and Women Who Won the Cold War* (New York: Simon & Schuster, 1996), 295.
7. Ann Coulter, *Treason: Liberal Treachery from the Cold War to the War on Terrorism* (New York: Crown Forum, 2003), 160–61.
8. Bob Dole, "The Best Days Are Yet to Come," August 15, 1996, *Vital Speeches of the Day* 62, no. 22 (September 1, 1996), 679.
9. Jack Kemp, speech to Republican national convention, August 15, 1996, *ibid.,* 679.
10. Lynne V. Cheney, *Telling the Truth: Why Our Culture and Our Country Have Stopped Making Sense—and What We Can Do About It* (New York: Simon & Schuster, 1995), 29.
11. http://www.whitehouse.gov/news/releases/2003/01/20030128-19.html (accessed Sept. 14, 2003).
12. Coulter, *Treason,* 166.
13. Fukuyama, *The End of History,* 93.
14. Nelson Lichtenstein, "Market Triumphalism and the Wishful Liberals," 103.
15. John Fousek, *To Lead the Free World: American Nationalism and the Cultural Roots of the Cold War* (Chapel Hill: University of North Carolina Press, 2000), 128.
16. For a thorough (and thoroughly entertaining) exposition of the tenets of market fundamentalism see Thomas Frank, *One Market Under God: Extreme Capitalism, Market Populism, and the End of Economic Democracy* (New York: Doubleday, 2000).
17. George Soros, *Open Society (Reforming Global Capitalism)* (New York: Public Affairs, 2000), xxiv.

18. Irving Kristol, quoted in Michael S. Sherry, *In the Shadow of War: The United States Since the 1930s* (New Haven: Yale University Press, 1995), 496.

19. Chalmers Johnson, "The Three Cold Wars," 244.

20. Ronald R. Fogelman, "Strategic Vision and Core Competencies: Global Reach—Global Power," *Vital Speeches of the Day* 63, no. 4 (December 1, 1996), 998.

21. George H.W. Bush, quoted in Gilbert Achar, *The Clash of Barbarisms: Sept. 11 and the Making of the New World Disorder* (New York: Monthly Review Press, 2002), 9.

22. Mary Kaldor, *The Imaginary War: Understanding the East-West Conflict* (Oxford: Basil Blackwell, 1990), 244–45.

23. William Appleman Williams, quoted in Leo Ribuffo, "Moral Judgments and the Cold War: Reflections on Reinhold Niebuhr, William Appleman Williams, and John Lewis Gaddis," 41.

24. Sherry, *In the Shadow of War,* 88, 124–25; Fousek, *To Lead the Free World,* 41–43; Andrew D. Grossman, *Neither Dead Nor Red: Civil Defense and American Political Development During the Early Cold War* (New York: Routledge, 2001); Ann Markusen, Peter Hall, Scott Campbell, and Sabina Deitrick, *The Rise of the Gunbelt: The Military Remapping of Industrial America* (New York: Oxford University Press, 1991), 235.

25. Bruce Cumings, *The Origins of the Korean War: The Roaring of the Cataract, 1947–1950* (Princeton, NJ: Princeton University Press, 1990), 17; Ellen Schrecker, *Many Are the Crimes: McCarthyism in America* (Boston and New York: Little, Brown, 1998).

26. Richard E. Neustadt and Ernest R. May, *Thinking in Time: The Uses of History for Decision Makers* (New York: Free Press, 1986), 75. For a discussion of the uses of nostalgia, albeit in a somewhat different context, see Arjun Appadurai, *Modernity at Large: Cultural Dimensions of Globalization* (Minneapolis: University of Minnesota Press, 1996), 74–77.

27. For an insightful discussion of the uses of World War II imagery, see Sherry, *In the Shadow of War,* 351–52, 399.

28. Winik, *On the Brink,* 257–58; Kim Holmes, "Geo-conservatism," *Policy Review,* no. 71 (Winter 1995), 38. For a recent unflattering portrayal of President Truman, see Arnold Offner, *Another Such Victory: President Truman and the Cold War, 1945–1953* (Stanford: Stanford University Press, 2002).

29. Thomas E. Mann, "What Bush Can Learn from Truman," *New York Times,* October 6, 2002, Week in Review, 13.

30. Nicholas Lemann, "The Next World Order," *The New Yorker,* April 1, 2002, 44.

31. Charles J. Hanley, Sang-Hun Choe, and Martha Mendoza, *The Bridge at No Gun Ri: A Hidden Nightmare from the Korean War* (New York: Henry Holt, 2001).

32. Sherry, *In the Shadow of War,* 336; Marilyn Young, "Still Stuck in the Big Muddy."

33. Corey Robin, "Remembrance of Empires Past: 9/11 and the End of the Cold War."

34. Leo Ribuffo, "Moral Judgments and the Cold War: Reflections on Reinhold Niebuhr, William Appleman Williams, and John Lewis Gaddis."

35. On the demonization of the enemy during World War II, see John W. Dower, *War Without Mercy: Race and Power in the Pacific War* (New York: Pantheon Books, 1986).

36. Bruce Cumings, "Time of Illusion: Post–Cold War Visions of the World," 99; Melvyn P. Leffler, *A Preponderance Of Power: National Security, the Truman Administration, and the Cold War* (Stanford: Stanford University Press, 1992); Michael S. Sherry, *Preparing for the Next War: American Plans for Postwar Defense* (New Haven: Yale University Press, 1977).

37. Kaldor, *The Imaginary War,* 5 and *passim.*

38. John Lewis Gaddis, *The Long Peace: Inquiries into the History of the Cold War* (New York: Oxford University Press, 1987).

39. John J. Mearsheimer, "Back to the Future: Instability in Europe after the Cold War," *International Security* 15, no. 1 (Summer 1990), 51.

40. Soros, *Open Society,* 305.

41. Mary Kaldor, *New and Old Wars: Organized Violence in a Global Era* (Cambridge: Polity Press, 1999), 81.

42. Mary L. Dudziak, *Cold War Civil Rights: Race and the Image of American Democracy* (Princeton: Princeton University Press, 2000); Fousek, *To Lead the Free World,* 132–39.

43. Sherry, *In the Shadow of War,* 228; R.C. Lewontin, "The Cold War and the Transformation of the Academy," in Noam Chomsky et al., *The Cold War and the University: Toward an Intellectual History of the Postwar Years* (New York: The New Press, 1997), 1–34.

44. Fousek, *To Lead the Free World,* 161; Penny von Eschen, *Race Against Empire: Black Americans and Anticolonialism, 1937–1957* (Ithaca: Cornell University Press, 1996); Gerald Horne, *Black and Red: W.E.B. DuBois and the Afro-American Response to the Cold War, 1944–1963* (Albany: State University of New York Press, 1986); Robert Korstad and Nelson Lichtenstein, "Opportunities Found and Lost: Labor, Radicals, and the Early Civil Rights Movement," *Journal of American History* 75 (1988): 786–811; Stuart W. Leslie, *The Cold War and American Science* (New York: Columbia University Press, 1993); Rebecca Lowen, *Creating the Cold War University: The Transformation of Stanford* (Berkeley and Los Angeles: University of California Press, 1997).

45. For a sophisticated assessment of the price of Cold War militarization, see Catherine Lutz, *Homefront: A Military City and the American 20th Century* (Boston: Beacon Press, 2001). See also Hogan, *Cross of Iron,* 482.

46. Hogan, *Cross of Iron,* 277–84.

47. Eisenhower, speech, April 1953, quoted in Sherry, *In the Shadow of War,* 195.

48. Bruce J. Schulman, "Slouching Toward the Supply Side: Jimmy Carter and the New American Political Economy," in Gary M. Fink and Hugh Davis Graham, *The Carter Presidency: Policy Choices in the Post–New Deal Era* (Lawrence: University Press of Kansas, 1998), 63–64.

49. Kotkin, *Armageddon Averted,* 40. Tsaba Bekes, remarks delivered at Conference on Cold War Triumphalism, International Center for Advanced Studies, New York University, April 2002.

50. Markusen et al., *The Rise of the Gunbelt.*

51. Sherry, *In the Shadow of War,* 71.

52. Markusen et al., *The Rise of the Gunbelt,* 253.

53. The most developed argument here is that of Mary Kaldor, *The Baroque Arsenal* (New York: Hill and Wang, 1981). See also Markusen, *The Rise of the Gunbelt,* 33–35.

54. For a more extensive discussion of the decline of the steel industry, see Judith Stein, *Running Steel, Running America: Race, Economic Policy, and the Decline of Liberalism* (Chapel Hill: University of North Carolina Press, 1998).

55. *The Defense Monitor* 29, no. 3 (2000) 1; Ben Friedman, "When Is a Nuke Not a Nuke?" *The Defense Monitor* 31, no. 3 (March 2002) 5; Michael Klare, *Rogue States and Nuclear Outlaws: America's Search for a New Foreign Policy* (New York: Hill and Wang, 1995), 120.

56. *The Defense Monitor* 28, no. 4 (1999), 5.

57. William Stueck, "Placing Jimmy Carter's Foreign Policy," in Fink and Graham, *The Carter Presidency,* 259–60; *The Defense Monitor* 21, no. 6 (1992), 10.

58. Klare, *Rogue States and Nuclear Outlaws,* 50.

59. *The Defense Monitor* 25, no. 8 (October 1996), 1; Friedman, "When Is a Nuke Not a Nuke?"

60. Charles W. Kegley Jr. and Kenneth L. Schwab, "At Issue: Deterrence in the Post–Cold War Era," in Kegley and Schwab, eds., *After the Cold War: Questioning the Morality of Nuclear Deterrence* (Boulder: Westview, 1991), 3; Tamar Gabelnick, "Under Attack! U.S. Arms Export Controls Targeted on All Fronts," *The Defense Monitor* 31, no. 7 (August 2002).

61. Robert Alvarez, "The Legacy of Hanford," *The Nation,* August 18–25, 2003; Korey Capozza, "Northern Exposure," *ibid.; The Defense Monitor* 23, no. 2 (1994) 7; *ibid.,* 24,

no. 8 (1995), 6. For a comprehensive account of the local impact of the American military, see Lutz, *Homefront.*
62. Markusen et al., *Rise of the Gunbelt,* 248–53. See Lisa McGirr, *Suburban Warriors: The Origins of the New American Right* (Princeton: Princeton University Press, 2001) for a detailed portrayal of the political culture of one of the most important of those areas.
63. Carolyn Eisenberg, "The Myth of the Berlin Blockade and the Early Cold War."
64. Grossman, *Neither Dead Nor Red.*
65. Sherry, *In the Shadow of War,* 179.
66. Daniel Patrick Moynihan, *Secrecy: The American Experience* (New Haven and London: Yale University Press, 1998), 59, 78–79.
67. Moynihan, *Secrecy,* 154.
68. Chalmers Johnson, "The Three Cold Wars."
69. *The Defense Monitor* 22, no. 8 (1993), 2.
70. Bruce G. Blair, "Nuclear Time Warp," *The Defense Monitor* 31, no. 5 (May 2002), 1.
71. For a perceptive discussion of the current form of demonization, see Bruce B. Lawrence, "Conjuring with Islam, II," *Journal of American History* 89, no. 2 (September 2002), 488–90.
72. Kaldor, *Baroque Arsenal,* 149–55.
73. *The Defense Monitor* 21, no. 6 (1992), 2–10.
74. Jessica Wang, "Whatever Happened to World Peace? Internationalism and the American Political Imagination, 1898–2002," paper delivered at Conference on Cold War Triumphalism, International Center for Advanced Studies, New York University, April 2002.
75. Eisenberg, "The Myth of the Berlin Blockade."
76. Jessica Wang, "The United States, the United Nations, and the Other Post–Cold War World Order: Internationalism and Unilateralism in the American Century."
77. Kaldor, *New and Old Wars;* Michael T. Klare, *Resource Wars: The New Landscape of Global Conflict* (New York: Henry Holt, 2001), 223–24.

1. Moral Judgments and the Cold War: Reflections on Reinhold Niebuhr, William Appleman Williams, and John Lewis Gaddis by Leo P. Ribuffo

Part of this article was adapted from Leo P. Ribuffo, "What Is Still Living in the Ideas and Example of William Appleman Williams?" *Diplomatic History* 25 (Spring 2001), 309–316.

1. Walter LaFeber, *America, Russia, and the Cold War, 1945–1966* (New York: Wiley, 1967), 40.
2. Reinhold Niebuhr, *Moral Man and Immoral Society* (New York: Scribner's, 1932). For useful accounts of Niebuhr's intellectual evolution from writers of various political and theological perspectives, see Richard Wightman Fox, *Reinhold Niebuhr: A Biography* (New York: Pantheon, 1985); Donald B. Meyer, *The Protestant Search for Political Realism, 1919–1941* (Berkeley: University of California Press, 1960); Arthur M. Schlesinger Jr., "Reinhold Niebuhr's Role in American Political Thought and Life," in *The Politics of Hope* (Boston: Houghton Mifflin, 1962); June Bingham, *Courage to Change: An Introduction to the Life and Thought of Reinhold Niebuhr* (New York: Scribner's, 1961); Gordon Harland, *The Thought of Reinhold Niebuhr* (New York: Oxford University Press, 1960); Paul Merkley, *Reinhold Niebuhr: A Political Account* (Montreal: McGill University Press, 1975); Ronald H. Stone, *Reinhold Niebuhr: Prophet to Politicians* (Nashville: Abingdon, 1972); Henry B. Clark, *Serenity, Courage, Wisdom: The Enduring Legacy of Reinhold Niebuhr* (Cleveland: Pilgrim Press, 1994); Robin W. Lovin, *Reinhold Niebuhr*

and Christian Realism (Cambridge: Cambridge University Press, 1995); and Colm Mc-Keogh, *The Political Realism of Reinhold Niebuhr: A Pragmatic Approach to Just War* (New York: St. Martin's, 1997).

3. Reinhold Niebuhr, *The Children of Light and the Children of Darkness: A Vindication of Democracy and a Critique of Its Traditional Defense* (New York: Scribner's, 1944), 32–33.

4. Reinhold Niebuhr, *The Irony of American History* (New York: Scribner's, 1962). In his *Spiritual Politics: Religion and America Since World War II* (New York: Simon & Schuster, 1989), Mark Silk coined the term *celebrity theologian* and cited Niebuhr as the premier case in point. Merkley, *Niebuhr: Political Account,* 174. Merkley provides the best account of Niebuhr as a Cold War ideologist.

5. Niebuhr, *Irony,* 7–8, 155–58, 167.

6. *Ibid.,* 28, 3, 36, 38. Reinhold Niebuhr and Alan Heimert, *A Nation So Conceived: Reflections on the History of America from Its Early Visions to Its Present Power* (London: Faber and Faber, 1963), 36.

7. Niebuhr, *Irony,* 35, 74, 38.

8. Niebuhr and Heimert, *Nation So Conceived,* 134–35, 141–42; Niebuhr, *Irony,* 109.

9. Niebuhr, *Irony,* viii, 3, 19; Niebuhr and Heimert, *Nation So Conceived,* 149.

10. Niebuhr, *Irony,* 109, 105, 55; Niebuhr and Heimert, *Nation So Conceived,* 144.

11. Niebuhr, *Irony,* 146–47.

12. Niebuhr, *The Structure of Nations and Empires: A Study of the Recurring Patterns and Problems of the Political Order in Relation to the Unique Problems of the Nuclear Age* (New York: Scribner's, 1959), 259, 282; Niebuhr, *Faith and Politics: A Commentary on Religious, Social and Political Thought in a Technological Age* (New York: Braziller, 1968), 216. This collection contains essays published between the mid-1950s and 1968.

13. Niebuhr and Paul Sigmund, *The Democratic Experience: Past and Present* (New York: Praeger, 1969), 5, 11; Niebuhr, *Structure of Nations,* 21; Niebuhr, *The Self and the Dramas of History* (New York: Scribner's, 1955); Niebuhr, *Faith and Politics,* 127, 214–17.

14. Niebuhr, *Structure of Nations,* 235, 245; Niebuhr, *Faith and Politics,* 202–4, 206–7, 209, 236.

15. Niebuhr, *Structure of Nations,* 209, 215, 235; Niebuhr, *Faith and Politics,* 211, 216–17, 226, 236–37.

16. Niebuhr, *Structure of Nations,* 168, 248, 235, 237, 252, 282.

17. Niebuhr and Sigmund, *Democratic Experience,* 13; Niebuhr, *Faith and Politics,* 208, 236; Niebuhr, *Structure of Nations,* 282, 295; Niebuhr and Sigmund, *Democratic Experience,* 14.

18. Niebuhr, *Structure of Nations,* 267, 269, 274; Niebuhr and Sigmund, *Democratic Experience,* 5.

19. Fox, *Reinhold Niebuhr,* 274–79; Merkley, *Niebuhr: Political Account,* 196–98; Niebuhr, *Faith and Politics,* 252.

20. Harland, *Thought of Reinhold Niebuhr,* 196; McKeogh, *Political Realism,* 172–73; Fox, *Reinhold Niebuhr,* 264; Niebuhr, *Faith and Politics,* 241, 250–51; Niebuhr, *Structure of Nations,* 176.

21. Niebuhr, *Faith and Politics,* 257, 261; Fox, *Reinhold Niebuhr,* 285; Mitchell K. Hall, *Because of Their Faith: CALCAV and Religious Opposition to the Vietnam War* (New York: Columbia University Press, 1980), 8–9, 20, 30.

22. Niebuhr, *Faith and Politics,* 261, 267.

23. *Ibid.,* 257–58, 261, 268.

24. *Ibid.,* 234–35.

25. Niebuhr, *Irony,* 3.

26. William Appleman Williams, *The Contours of American History* (Chicago: Quadrangle, 1966), 472.

27. "William Appleman Williams," in Henry Abelove et al., ed., *Visions of History* (New York: Pantheon, 1984), 129; Henry W. Berger, ed., *A William Appleman Williams Reader:*

Selections from His Major Historical Writings (Chicago: Ivan R. Dee, 1992), 340; William Appelman Williams, History as a Way of Learning (New York: New Viewpoints, 1973), 193; Williams, The Roots of the Modern American Empire: A Study of the Growth and Shaping of Social Consciousness in a Marketplace Society (New York: Random House, 1969), 449; Williams, Some Presidents: From Wilson to Nixon (New York: Vintage, 1972), 84. For Williams's biography and intellectual evolution, see Paul H. Buhle and Edward Rice-Maximin, William Appleman Williams: The Tragedy of Empire (New York: Routledge: 1995), 1–144; James Livingston, "Social Theory and Historical Method in the Work of William Appleman Williams," Diplomatic History 25 (Spring 2001), 275–82; William G. Robbins, "William Appleman Williams: 'Doing History Is Best of All. No Regrets,' " in Lloyd C. Gardner, ed., Redefining the Past: Essays in Diplomatic History in Honor of William Appleman Williams (Corvallis: Oregon State University Press, 1986), 3–19; Berger, "Introduction," in Berger, Williams Reader, 11–33; and Kevin Mattson, Intellectuals in Action: The Origins of the New Left and Radical Liberalism, 1945–1970 (University Park: Pennsylvania State University Press, 2002), 145–85.

28. "Williams," in Abelove, Visions, 128; Berger, Williams Reader, 340–41.
29. Williams, Some Presidents, 21; and The Tragedy of American Diplomacy (New York: Delta, 1959, 2d rev. ed., 1972), 10; "Williams," in Abelove, Visions, 132.
30. Williams, Tragedy, 20.
31. Williams, "Conclusion: The Critics of the American Empire Open a Door to Create an American Community," in Williams, ed., From Colony to Empire: Essays in the History of American Foreign Relations (New York: Wiley, 1972), 476; Williams, Contours, 183.
32. Williams, Contours, 222; Williams, Empire as a Way of Life: An Essay on the Causes and Character of America's Present Predicament Along with a Few Thoughts About an Alternative (New York: Oxford University Press, 1980).
33. Williams, Tragedy, 9; Williams, Roots, 258.
34. Williams, America Confronts a Revolutionary World: 1776–1976 (New York: William Morrow, 1976), 133.
35. Williams, Tragedy, 18–57; Williams, The Great Evasion: An Essay on the Contemporary Relevance of Karl Marx and the Wisdom of Admitting the Heretic into the Dialogue About America's Future (Chicago: Quadrangle Books, 1964), 44; "Williams," in Abelove, Visions, 108.
36. Williams, Great Evasion, 35.
37. Williams, "Conclusion," 480–81.
38. Williams, Tragedy, 58–161; Williams, "Colony," 482.
39. Williams, Tragedy, 162–201; Berger, Williams Reader, 114. For the best discussion of Williams and the so-called isolationists (a term he rejected), see Justus D. Doenecke, "William Appleman Williams and the Anti-Interventionist Tradition," Diplomatic History 25 (Spring 2001), 283–91.
40. Williams, Contours, 462–63; Williams, Some Presidents, 56, 59.
41. Williams, Tragedy, 297. Italics in the original.
42. Ibid., 206, 210–11; "Williams," in Abelove, Visions, 135.
43. Williams, Way of Learning, 371.
44. Williams, Tragedy, 292; Williams, Williams Reader, 339.
45. Williams, Tragedy, 309, 288.
46. Ibid., 286–87; Williams, Great Evasion, 19.
47. Williams, Great Evasion, 69–70.
48. Ibid., 52, 54.
49. Williams, Some Presidents, 31; Williams, Contours, 485; Williams, "Colony," 481; "Williams," in Abelove, Visions, 134–35, 140; Buhle and Rice-Maximin, William Appleman Williams, 158.
50. Williams, Tragedy, 309, 288.
51. Williams, Some Presidents, 85, 87, 95; Williams, "Critics of Empire," 485–86.

52. Williams, *America Confronts a Revolutionary World*, 112, 182–83, 194, 199.
53. Williams, *Way of Learning*, 383; "Williams," in Abelove, *Visions*, 131, 135–37, 139; Williams, *Williams Reader*, 387–88.
54. "Williams," in Abelove, *Visions*, 131, 136–37, 139.
55. Buhle and Rice-Maximin, *William Appleman Williams*, 235.
56. *Ibid.*, 234–35; Berger, *Williams Reader*, 391.
57. Berger, *Williams Reader*, 377–78.
58. John Lewis Gaddis, "The Tragedy of Cold War History," *Diplomatic History* 17 (Winter 1993), 15.
59. *Ibid.*, 16.
60. Gaddis, "On Moral Equivalency and Cold War History," *Ethics and International Affairs* (1996), 131–32. While some heirs to the Popular Front tradition may believe that Soviet foreign policy was morally equivalent to—or better than—that of the United States, I cannot think of a serious American historian who argues this position or even makes the point in passing. The closest seems to be Gabriel Kolko, who criticized both the United States and the Soviet Union for respectively crushing the European left and letting it be crushed. For example, see Kolko, *The Politics of War: The World and United States Foreign Policy, 1941–1945* (New York: Vintage, 1968).
61. Gaddis, *The United States and the Origins of the Cold War, 1941–1947* (New York: Columbia University Press, 1972), 358–60. For Gaddis's background, see "Gaddis, John Lewis," in Jeff Chapman and John D. Jorgenson, eds., *Contemporary Authors: A Bio-Bibliographical Guide to Current Writers in Fiction, General Nonfiction, Poetry, Journalism, Drama, Motion Pictures, Television, and Other Fields*, vol. 56 (Detroit: Gale, 1997), 142–43.
62. Gaddis, *The Landscape of History: How Historians Map the Past* (New York: Oxford University Press, 2002), 7, 10, 43, 55, 102, 105, 122, 140.
63. *Ibid.*, 33, 49, 61, 82, 117, 129.
64. *Ibid.*, 127; Gaddis, "Moral Equivalency," 138, and *The United States and the End of the Cold War: Implications, Reconsiderations, Provocations* (New York: Oxford University Press, 1992), 186.
65. Gaddis, *Russia, the Soviet Union, and the United States: An Interpretive History* (New York: Wiley, 1978).
66. Gaddis, *Strategies of Containment: A Critical Appraisal of Postwar American National Security Policy* (New York: Oxford University Press, 1982), vii; Gaddis, *End of the Cold War*, 6, 7, 9, 12.
67. Gaddis, *The Long Peace: Inquiries into the History of the Cold War* (New York: Oxford University Press, 1987), 226; Gaddis, *Strategies*, 356–57, italics in the original.
68. Gaddis, *Long Peace*, 7, 9, 235; Gaddis, *Strategies*, 334; Gaddis, *End of the Cold War*, 13; Gaddis, *We Now Know: Rethinking Cold War History* (New York: Oxford University Press, 1997), 55.
69. Gaddis, *End of the Cold War*, 13; Gaddis, *Strategies*, 140–41; Gaddis, *Russia, the Soviet Union, and the United States*, 213.
70. Gaddis, *Long Peace*, 216, 230, 232, 234; Gaddis, *End of the Cold War*, 177; Gaddis, *Russia, the Soviet Union, and the United States*, 246.
71. Gaddis, *Long Peace*, 216.
72. Gaddis, "Moral Equivalency," 136, 137.
73. Gaddis, "Tragedy of Cold War History," 5, 10–12; Gaddis, *Landscapes of History*, 117–18.
74. Gaddis, "Tragedy of Cold War History," 11–12; Gaddis, "Moral Equivalency," 142, 145; Gaddis, *We Now Know*, 291, 293.
75. Gaddis, *We Now Know*, 282, 283, 290; Gaddis, "Moral Equivalency," 138.
76. Gaddis, *End of the Cold War*, 49, 53.
77. *Ibid.*, 57.
78. Gaddis, *Strategies*, 127–97; Gaddis, *We Now Know*, 129–31, 210–11, 289.
79. Gaddis, *End of the Cold War*, 58–59.

80. *Ibid.,* 59. For a more generous interpretation of Carter's understanding of Niebuhr, see Leo P. Ribuffo, "God and Jimmy Carter," in Ribuffo, *Right Center Left: Essays in American History* (New Brunswick, NJ: Rutgers University Press, 1992), 214–48.

81. Gaddis, "Tragedy," 13–14; Gaddis, *End of the Cold War,* 60; Gaddis, *We Now Know,* 292.

82. Gaddis, *Landscape,* 127; Gaddis, "Tragedy," 11; Gaddis, "Moral Equivalency," 148.

83. Gaddis, *Strategies of Containment,* 337–39; Gaddis, *We Now Know,* 166, 178, 187–88, 293.

84. Gaddis, *We Now Know,* 284–85, 291.

85. For the argument that some members of the Truman administration toyed with a spheres-of-influence settlement in 1945–46, see Marc Trachtenberg, *A Constructed Peace: The Making of the European Settlement, 1945–1963* (Princeton: Princeton University Press, 1999).

86. John Keegan, *The First World War* (New York: Vintage, 1998), 3. I am indebted to a discussion with Gaddis himself for this point. When I heard him present a version of his argument to a small group slightly more than a decade ago, he suggested that anyone making my critique might point to the World War I dead. On the Belgians in the Congo, see Adam Hochschild, *King Leopold's Ghost: A Story of Greed, Terror, and Heroism in Colonial Africa* (New York: Mariner, 1999).

87. Williams, *Tragedy,* 2.

88. For my views on the Afghanistan war, see Ribuffo, "One Cheers for This Military Intervention, Two Cheers for Cosmopolitan Isolationism," *Journal of the Historical Society* 2 (Spring 2002), 203–14.

89. *The National Security Strategy of the United States* is available at www.whitehouse.gov/nsc/nss.

90. John Lewis Gaddis, "A Grand Strategy of Transformation," *Foreign Policy,* November–December 2002.

91. Williams, *Roots,* 452. For useful discussions on the left about these issues, especially the problem of humanitarian intervention, see "Humanitarian Intervention: A Forum," *The Nation,* July 14, 2003, 11–20; and "Comments and Opinions," *Dissent,* Summer 2003, 5–13.

2. Time of Illusion: Post–Cold War Visions of the World
by Bruce Cumings

1. Russell Jacoby, *The Last Intellectuals: American Culture in the Age of Academe* (New York: Basic Books, 1987).

2. See the critique of postmodernism on the left in Norman Geras, *Discourses of Extremity* (New York: Verso, 1990), 61–168.

3. Mary Kaldor, "After the Cold War," *New Left Review* 180 (March–April 1990), 33. Prof. Kaldor has been one of the most clear-sighted analysts of the Cold War system.

4. Roberto Mangabiera Unger, *Knowledge and Politics* (New York: Free Press, 1975). The first part of this book offers a stunning critique of liberal politics.

5. Alasdaire MacIntyre, *After Virtue: A Study in Moral Theory* (Notre Dame: University of Notre Dame Press, 1981), 33. See also MacIntyre, *Whose Justice? Which Rationality?* (Notre Dame: University of Notre Dame Press, 1988).

6. Barrington Moore, Jr., *Social Origins of Dictatorship and Democracy: Lord and Peasant in the Modern World* (New York: Beacon Press, 1966), 505–8.

7. United States Institute of Peace, "Prospects for Conflict or Peace in Central and Eastern Europe" (May 1990), 1.

8. Louis Hartz, *The Liberal Tradition in America* (New York: Houghton Mifflin, 1955).

9. Louis Hartz, *The Founding of New Societies* (New York: Harcourt, Brace & World, 1964), 3–22.

10. *Ibid.,* 9.

11. Alan Cowell, "Ashcroft Soaks Up a World of Complaints," *New York Times,* January 25, 2003, A8.
12. In the 1960s Mao Zedong was asked to comment on the real meaning of the French Revolution. He responded that not enough time had yet passed to know.
13. Hitchens, "How Neoconservatives Perish: Good-bye to 'Totalitarianism' and All That," *Harper's,* July 1990, 65–70. In 2003 Hitchens became a neoconservative himself, supporting Bush's invasion of Iraq among other things. Political acrobats ought to know better than to leave such a conspicuous paper trail.
14. John Mearsheimer, "Back to the Future," *International Security* 15, no. 1 (Summer 1990) (also the shorter version in *The Atlantic Monthly*); Francis Fukuyama, *The End of History and the Last Man* (New York: Free Press, 1992) (hereinafter abbreviated *End of History*); Samuel P. Huntington, *The Clash of Civilizations and the Remaking of World Order* (New York: Simon & Schuster, 1996).
15. *The National Interest* 16 (Summer 1989).
16. *New York Times Magazine,* October 22, 1989.
17. Nicholas Wade, "A Dim View of a 'Posthuman Future,' " *New York Times,* April 2, 2002, D1, D4.
18. Fukuyama, *End of History,* 304.
19. *Ibid.,* 162.
20. *Ibid.,* 311.
21. *Ibid.,* 312, 330–35.
22. Kaufmann quoted in Keith Ansell-Pearson, *An Introduction to Nietzsche as Political Thinker: The Perfect Nihilist* (Cambridge: Cambridge University Press, 1994), 89, 105–7.
23. Friedrich Nietzsche, *Beyond Good and Evil,* trans. Walter Kaufmann (New York: Vintage, 1966) 211.
24. Didier Eribon, *Michel Foucault,* trans. Betsy Wing (Cambridge, MA: Harvard University Press, 1991), 189.
25. *Ibid.,* 19–20.
26. Karl Polanyi, *The Great Transformation* (Boston: Beacon Press, 1944), 119–21.
27. Friedrich Nietzsche, *The Will to Power,* trans. Walter Kaufmann and R.J. Hollingdale (New York: Vintage, 1968), 267.
28. Sir L. Stephen, quoted in Polanyi, *The Great Transformation,* 121.
29. Michel Foucault, *Power/Knowledge,* ed. Colin Gordon (New York: Pantheon Books, 1980), 96.
30. Fukuyama, *End of History,* 296–97.
31. Friedrich Nietzsche, *Untimely Meditations,* trans. R.J. Hollingdale (Cambridge and New York: Cambridge University Press, 1983), 116.
32. *Ibid.,* 62–66.
33. *Ibid.,* 104, 107–8.
34. Spencer R. Weart, *Never at War: Why Democracies Will Not Fight One Another* (New Haven and London: Yale University Press, 1998). For a typical political-science account see Bruce Russett, *Grasping the Democratic Peace: Principles for a Post–Cold War World* (Princeton: Princeton University Press, 1993). Both his book and Weart's provide extensive bibliographical guidance to the democratic peace literature.
35. John J. Mearsheimer, *The Tragedy of Great Power Politics* (New York and London: W. W. Norton & Company, 2001), xi.
36. *Ibid.,* 2–3.
37. *Ibid.,* 31.
38. *Ibid.,* 181, 400.
39. Quoted in Mearsheimer, *Tragedy of Great Power Politics,* 26.
40. Huntington, *The Clash of Civilizations,* 158–61.
41. *Ibid.,* 46.

42. *Ibid.*, 312–16.
43. *Novus ordo seclorum* is on the American national seal and the dollar bill, although in the latter case it resides under a cyclops eye hovering above a pyramid, a Masonic or Illuminati symbol that has drawn the blank stares of American conspiracy theorists from the origin of the nation right down to the local-yokel "militias" that came to the media's attentions in the aftermath of the 1995 bombing of the federal building in Oklahoma City.
44. Huntington, *The Clash of Civilizations* 68–69, 311.
45. *Ibid.*, 305–8.
46. Robert Latham, *The Liberal Moment: Modernity, Security, and the Making of the Postwar International Order* (New York: Columbia University Press, 1997).
47. Eric Schmitt and James Dao, "U.S. Is Building Up Its Military Bases in Afghan Region," *New York Times*, January 9, 2002, A1.

3. Market Triumphalism and the Wishful Liberals
by Nelson Lichtenstein

1. As quoted in Tom Frank, *One Market Under God: Extreme Capitalism, Market Populism, and the End of Economic Democracy* (New York: Anchor Books, 2000), 5.
2. *Ibid.*, 23–40; James Arnt Aune, *Selling the Free Market: the Rhetoric of Economic Correctness* (New York: Guilford Press, 2001), 8.
3. Gilder quoted in Frank, *One Market Under God*, 3; Francis Fukuyama, "The End of History," *The National Interest* (Spring 1989), 14–15. Fukuyama's essay and his subsequent books have already generated a considerable historiography. See, for example, Philip Abbott, " 'Big' Theories and Policy Counsel: James Burnham, Francis Fukuyama, and the Cold War," *Journal of Policy History* 14 (Fall 2002), 417–30.
4. *The National Security Strategy of the United States of America*, September 17, 2002, at http://www.whitehouse.gov/nsc/nssall.html.
5. As quoted in William Greider, *One World Ready or Not: The Manic Logic of Global Capitalism* (New York: Touchstone Books, 1998), 212.
6. Frank, *One Market Under God*, 211.
7. Anders Lewis, e-mail, H-Labor, May 27, 2003, seth@suscom-maine.net.
8. Michael Lewis, "Why You?" *New York Times Magazine*, September 23, 2001, 70–71.
9. Michael Cox, "American Power Before and After 11 September: Dizzy with Success?" *International Affairs* 78, no. 2 (2002), 289–91.
10. Bennett Harrison and Barry Bluestone, *The Great U-Turn: Corporate Restructuring and the Polarizing of America* (New York: Basic Books, 1988), 3–52; Godfrey Hodgson, *The World Turned Right Side Up: A History of the Conservative Ascendancy in America* (Boston: Houghton Mifflin, 1996), 186–215; Robert Kuttner, *Everything for Sale: the Virtues and Limits of Markets* (New York: Alfred Knopf, 1997), 68–109; Thomas and Mary Edsall, *Chain Reaction: the Impact of Race, Rights, and Taxes on American Politics* (New York: W.W. Norton, 1991), 154–97.
11. David Pilling, "Japanese Companies: How Could a Corporate Sector That Dominated the World a Decade Ago Have Become So Unproductive?" *Financial Times*, April 21, 2003, 9; Paul Krugman, *The Return of Depression Economics* (New York: W. W. Norton, 1999). The once-vaunted "four tigers"—South Korea, Hong Kong, Taiwan, and Singapore—also had their troubles, but south China, whose labor relations and regulatory regime resembles that of nineteenth-century Pittsburgh, has roared ahead. It is fast becoming the twenty-first-century workshop of the world.
12. Hodgson, *The World Turned Right Side Up*. And see especially Chapter 8, "The Strange Death of John Maynard Keynes," 186–215.
13. Howard Brick, "Talcott Parsons's 'Shift Away from Economics,' 1937–1946," *Journal of American History* 87, no. 2 (September 2000), 511.

14. See most recently, and from the right, Aaron Friedberg, *In the Shadow of the Garrison State: America's Anti-statism and Its Cold War Grand Strategy* (Princeton: Princeton University Press, 2000).

15. The *Times Literary Supplement* names the book as one of the 100 most influential books to appear since the end of World War II. A new edition has just appeared, in which Bell asserts "the resumption of history" along with the continuing "end of ideology" at the dawn of the twenty-first century. Daniel Bell, *The End of Ideology: On the Exhaustion of Political Ideas in the Fifties* (Cambridge, MA: Harvard University Press, 1960, 2000), xi–xxviii.

16. Brick, "Talcott Parsons's 'Shift Away from Economics,'" 507, 511; Brick, *Age of Contradiction: American Thought and Culture in the 1960s* (New York: Twayne Publishers, 1998), xiv–xv, 54–57.

17. Jordan Schwarz, *Liberal: Adolf A. Berle and the Vision of an American Era* (New York: The Free Press, 1987), 60.

18. Richard Pells, *Radical Visions and American Dreams: Culture and Social Thought in the Depression Years* (New York: Harper & Row, 1973), 69–70; Schwarz, *Liberal: Adolf A. Berle,* 59. See also Thomas K. McCraw, "In Retrospect: Berle and Means," *Reviews in American History* 18 (1990), 578–96.

19. Schwarz, *Liberal: Adolf A. Berle,* 353. The Twentieth Century Fund mission statement is from 1948, when Berle was a board member. He would serve as chair from 1950 to 1970.

20. Adolf Berle, "Property, Production, and Revolution, a Preface to the Revised Edition," *The Modern Corporation and Private Property* (New York: Harcourt, Brace, and World, 1968), xxvi. Tellingly, Berle relied on the old socialist slogan (in italics) to define the direction of contemporary social change. I thank Howard Brick for this reference.

21. John Medearis, "Schumpeter, the New Deal, and Democracy," *American Political Science Review* 91, no. 4 (December 1997), 819–33.

22. Joseph Schumpeter, *Capitalism, Socialism and Democracy* (New York: Harper & Row, 1942, 1975), 134, 143; and see also Arnold Heertje, ed., *Schumpeter's Vision: Capitalism, Socialism and Democracy After 40 Years* (New York: Praeger, 1981), especially Tom Bottomore, "The Decline of Capitalism Sociologically Considered," 22–44; and Arthur Smithies, "Schumpeter's Predictions," 130–49.

23. Volker Berghahn, *America and the Intellectual Cold Wars in Europe* (Princeton: Princeton University Press, 2001), 96–113 *passim;* Hugh Wilford, *The CIA, the British Left and the Cold War: Calling the Tune* (London: Frank Cass, 2003).

24. Peter Drucker, *The Concept of the Corporation* (New York: John Day Company, 1946, 1972), 8.

25. *Ibid.,* 12; and nearly fifty years later Drucker still held much the same evolutionary view. See Peter Drucker, *Post-Capitalist Society* (New York: HarperBusiness, 1993), 4–9.

26. Drucker, *Concept of the Corporation.* This viewpoint was given a powerful, comparative elaboration by another influential, émigré theorist of industrial society. See "The Bureaucratization of Economic Enterprises," in Reinhard Bendix, *Work and Authority in Industry* (Berkeley: University of California Press, 1956, 1974), 198–253 *passim.*

27. For much more along this theme, see Howard Brick, "The Postcapitalist Vision in Twentieth-Century American Social Thought," paper prepared for the conference "Capitalism and Its Culture: Rethinking Twentieth-Century American Social Thought," University of California, Santa Barbara, February 28–March 1, 2003.

28. Arthur Schlesinger Jr., *The Vital Center* (Boston: Houghton Mifflin, 1949), 173. The book is still in print, still in the news, and in his recent autobiography endorsed once again half a century after it first appeared. Arthur Schlesinger Jr., *A Life in the 20th Century: Innocent Beginnings, 1917–1950* (Boston: Houghton Mifflin, 2000), 522.

29. Schlesinger, *The Vital Center,* 154, 174.

30. James Cochrane, *Industrialism and Industrial Man in Retrospect: A Critical Review of the Ford Foundation's Support for the Inter-University Study of Labor* (New York: The Ford Foundation, 1979), 61–80.

31. Richard M. Bissell Jr., *Reflections of a Cold Warrior: From Yalta to the Bay of Pigs* (New Haven: Yale University Press, 1996), 30–79 *passim;* Evan Thomas, *The Very Best Men: Four Who Dared: the Early Years of the CIA* (New York: Simon & Schuster, 1995), 87–97; and see in particular two excellent essays: Nils Gilman, "Modernization Theory, the Highest State of American Intellectual History," and David Engerman, "West Meets East: The Center for International Studies and Indian Economic Development," both in Engerman, Gilman, Mark H. Haefele, and Michael E. Latham, *Staging Growth: Modernization, Development, and the Global Cold War* (Amherst: University of Massachusetts Press, 2003), 47–80, 199–224.

32. Cochrane, *Industrialism and Industrial Man in Retrospect,* 92–95.

33. Kerr, Dunlop, et al., "Industrialism and Industrial Man Reconsidered: Some Perspectives on a Study Over Two Decades of the Problems of Labor and Management in Economic Growth," typescript 1974, in Clark Kerr papers, unprocessed, Institute of Industrial Relations, UC Berkeley. It is difficult to calculate total expenditures over the two decades, especially when home institution funds are added it. The Ford Foundation's first full grant came to more than $400,000, close to $4 million in 2000 dollars.

34. *Ibid.,* 80–95, 118–19; Clark Kerr, John T. Dunlop, Frederick Harbison, and Charles A. Myers, *Industrialism and Industrial Man* (Cambridge, MA: Harvard University Press, 1960), 12, and see in particular Chapter 3, "The Industrializing Elites and Their Strategies," and Chapter 9, "The Rule Makers and the Rules," 47–76, 234–63. John Dunlop is generally recognized as the author of the concept of a "web of rules." See his highly influential *Industrial Relations Systems* (Cambridge, MA: Harvard University Press, 1958). Some twelve books and twenty articles were published during the 1950s alone under the auspices of the Kerr-Dunlop Inter-University Study. Bruce Kaufman, *The Origins and Evolution of the Field of Industrial Relations in the United States* (Ithaca, NY: ILR Press, 1993), 94–95.

35. Paddy Riley, "Clark Kerr: From the Industrial to the Knowledge Economy," paper delivered at the conference, "Capitalism and Its Culture: Re-thinking Twentieth Century Social Thought," UC Santa Barbara, March 1, 2003.

36. C. Wright Mills, *The New Men of Power: America's Labor Leaders* (Urbana: University of Illinois Press, 1948, 2001), 233, 237; on Franz Neumann, whose work greatly influenced Mills, see H. Stuart Hughes, "Franz Neumann Between Marxism and Liberal Democracy," in *The Intellectual Migration: Europe and America, 1930–1960,* ed. Donald Fleming and Bernard Bailyn (Cambridge, MA: Harvard University Press, 1969), 446–62.

37. Scholarship on C. Wright Mills is once again flourishing. For one of the best short studies, see Kevin Mattson, *Intellectuals in Action: The Origins of the New Left and Radical Liberalism, 1945–1970* (University Park: Pennsylvania State University Press, 2002), 43–96.

38. This perspective, which denies the hegemony of a postwar labor-management accord or a consensus liberalism, is advanced in Rick Perlstein, *Before the Storm: Barry Goldwater and the Unmaking of the American Consensus* (New York: Hill and Wang, 2001); Meg Jacobs, *Pocketbook Politics: Economic Citizenship in Twentieth-Century America* (forthcoming, Princeton University Press); and Lichtenstein, *State of the Union: A Century of American Labor* (Princeton: Princeton University Press, 2002), 98–140.

39. This idea was first brought to my attention in Maurice Isserman and Michael Kazin, "The Failure and Success of the New Radicalism," in Steve Fraser and Gary Gerstle, *The Rise and Fall of the New Deal Order, 1930–1980* (Princeton: Princeton University Press, 1989), 225–26.

40. Adolf Berle Jr., *Power Without Property: A New Development in American Political Economy* (New York: Harcourt, Brace and Company, 1959), 11–26; Robert Booth Fowler, *Believing Skeptics: American Political Intellectuals, 1945–1964* (Westport, CT: Greenwood Press, 1978), 176–86.

41. James Miller, *"Democracy Is in the Streets": From Port Huron to the Siege of Chicago* (New York: Simon & Schuster, 1987), 232–33.

42. John Kenneth Galbraith, *The New Industrial State* (Boston: Houghton Mifflin, 1967), 263–64, 274, 280–81.

43. Virginia Postrel, "Looking Forward," *Forbes,* September 18, 2000, 108.

44. As quoted in Mark Gerson, *The Neoconservative Vision: From the Cold War to the Culture Wars* (Lanham, MD: Madison Books, 1996), 221.

45. Daniel Bell, *The Coming of Post-Industrial Society: A Venture in Social Forecasting* (New York: Basic Books, 1973, 1976, 1999), 298.

46. Francis Fukuyama, "Getting It Right," *National Interest* (Winter 1999), 130.

47. The Tofflers had been Communists, or close to the party, during the late 1940s. They were members of that youthful cohort who worked for Henry Wallace and then industrialized. By the time they came out of a Cleveland factory in the 1950s, they had repudiated Marxism, but not its sense that history moves by grand socio-technical stages. Gingrich had been a fan since the early 1970s. See the excellent essay by John Judis, "Newt's Not-So-Weird Gurus: In Defense of the Tofflers," *The New Republic* 213 (October 9, 1995), 16–24.

48. Jeffery Halprin, "Getting Back to Work: The Revaluation of Work in American Literature and Social Theory, 1950–1985," (Ph.D. diss., Boston University, 1987), 42–89, 114–67 *passim,* Dublin quoted at 57; Clark Kerr, "The Prospect for Wages and Hours in 1975" (1958), in Kerr, *Labor and Management in Industrial Society* (Garden City, NY: Doubleday, 1964), 203–31.

49. Brick, *The Age of Contradiction,* 54.

50. Charles Sabel and Jonathan Zeitlin, "Alternatives to Mass Production," *Past and Present,* revised and updated in Zeitlin and Sabel, *Worlds of Possibilities: Flexibility and Mass Production* (New York: Cambridge University Press, 1994); Michael Piore and Charles Sabel, *The Second Industrial Divide: Possibilities for Prosperity* (New York: Basic Books, 1984), 19–48.

51. Piore and Sabel, *Second Industrial Divide,* 133–64.

52. Robert Reich, *The Next American Frontier* (New York: Penguin Books, 1983), 246.

53. Piore and Sabel, *Second Industrial Divide,* 261, 305–6. And see also Shoshana Zuboff, *In the Age of the Smart Machine: The Future of Work and Power* (New York: Basic Books, 1984). Piore, Sabel, and Zuboff stood on the left but their faith in a technocratic progressivism fed rather easily into the Reaganite optimism of such technomarket futurists as George Gilder and Ben Wattenberg.

54. As quoted in Kim Moody, *Workers in a Lean World: Unions in the International Economy* (New York: Verso, 1997), 43–44.

4. Cold War Triumphalism and the Deformation of the American Economy by Michael A. Bernstein

1. For comments on previous drafts of this essay, I am most grateful to Marc Favreau, Allen Hunter, Ellen Schrecker, Christopher Simpson, and the participants at the "Conference on Cold War Triumphalism" held at the International Center for Advanced Studies at New York University in April 2002.

2. The data discussed here are best summarized and presented in Edward N. Wolff, *Top Heavy: The Increasing Inequality of Wealth in America and What Can Be Done About It* (New York: The New Press, 2002), 67–68 and 38–39.

3. That the income tax reductions of the Program for Economic Recovery put before the Congress by President Reagan were, in fact, a political contrivance to benefit the most privileged in the electorate is vividly demonstrated in the memoirs of the president's director of the Office of Management and Budget, David Stockman. Stockman in particular referred to the budget strategy as a "Trojan horse" deployed on behalf of the rich. See his *The Triumph of Politics: How the Reagan Revolution Failed* (New York: Harper &

Row, 1986). In this regard it is interesting to note that a 1995 study by the Organization for Economic Cooperation and Development, which assessed sixteen industrialized nations, concluded the United States had the greatest spread between the top 10 percent and bottom 10 percent of the income distribution. From 1979 until 1995, earnings for those in the top decile relative to those in the last decile rose a bit over 21 percent The Federal Reserve Board has similarly reported that the richest 10 percent of the American population hold a bit over two-thirds of the total national wealth; over the period 1983 to 1995, this segment garnered 70 percent of the total rise in the national wealth. See Edmund S. Phelps, *Rewarding Work: How to Restore Participation and Self-Support to Free Enterprise* (Cambridge, MA: Harvard University Press, 1997).

4. See Michael A. Bernstein, "Understanding American Economic Decline: The Contours of the Late-Twentieth-Century Experience," in *Understanding American Economic Decline,* eds. Michael A. Bernstein and David Adler (New York: Cambridge University Press, 1994), 22–24. Another example of the sheer magnitude of the military-spending strategies embraced by the Reagan administration is afforded by comparative data on proportionate commitments to defense. By the end of the 1980s, the United States distributed 6.1 percent of national product to defense. France, by comparison, allocated 3.5 percent; the Federal Republic of Germany, 3.1 percent; and Japan, a bit less than one percent. A good example of the illegitimate claim by proponents of supply-side economics that the Reagan tax cuts had stimulated recovery is Lawrence Lindsey, *The Growth Experiment: How the New Tax Policy Is Transforming the U.S. Economy* (New York: Basic Books, 1990). It beggars the imagination to suggest that, in the absence of the "military Keynesianism" practiced by Ronald Reagan, the American economy would have grown as it did throughout the 1980s.

5. By the early 1990s, the antitax sentiments of the public had been manipulated and inflamed to such an extent that calls for the reform of the Internal Revenue Service (IRS) became increasingly popular. They ranged from suggestions that the Service transform itself from an enforcement mission to a customer service posture. Some radicals even suggested that the Service be eliminated entirely. Interestingly enough, while those political leaders in favor of reform offered little substantiation for the alleged abuses of the agency, save for the parading of a select group of tearful taxpayers before special investigative committees (whose stories of ill-treatment in audits and of overly aggressive garnishment of taxes were devoid of explanations as to why the Service targeted them in the first place), they more often than not helped to create the very problems they wanted resolved. Systematic budget cuts over the years had affected IRS like any other federal bureau—the frustration of citizens who sought Service advice on taxes, only to be rewarded with unhelpful taped phone messages and form letters, was primarily grounded in the staff cuts at the IRS that budget hawks had implemented. Small wonder then that many IRS critics did not also convene investigations of the agency's increasingly weakened ability to police tax fraud and avoidance.

6. In his remarkable study of *The Business Response to Keynes: 1929–1964* (New York: Columbia University Press, 1981), Robert Collins vividly demonstrates how the American business community had once been entirely persuaded by Keynes's view of the interactions between enterprise, households, and individual decision-making in the marketplace.

7. George Bush's travails as the nation's forty-first president provided a unique example of the new classical economic "chickens" coming home to roost. Within the first year of his term, it became obvious that federal tax cuts had so unbalanced the federal ledger that the nation's capital markets were at risk given the enormous amounts of borrowing undertaken by the Treasury. Forced ultimately to ask for a tax increase, the president found himself hounded by the right wing of his own party as the 1992 campaign approached. Most analysts believe these intra-party struggles played a significant part in weakening Bush's bid for reelection. Bill Clinton's subsequent triumph, as the first

Democrat to reach the White House in twelve years, was a striking representation, in the political realm, of the inherent contradictions to be found in a national fiscal policy recast by Reaganism. See, in this regard, Peter Passell, "The Tax-Rise Issue: Bush Rationale vs. Economists," *New York Times,* May 10, 1990, A14. No less an authority than Richard Darman, Director of the Office of Management and Budget under President George H.W. Bush, ultimately claimed that the combination of Reagan tax cuts and increased military spending constituted the largest and most undisciplined addition to federal debt in the nation's history. See his *Who's in Control?: Polar Politics and the Sensible Center* (New York: Simon & Schuster, 1996).

8. In his memoir, *Who's in Control?,* Richard Darman argues that the massive rise in the national debt during the 1980s was far more the result of increased military spending than it was due to the cost of social spending (especially antipoverty) programs. It is well worth noting that, at the same time, a rhetorical sleight-of-hand took place so subtle as to provoke little if any comment. Increasingly, politicians, economists, and voters alike spoke of what were once called "transfer-payments" (such as Medicare, Medicaid, Aid to Families with Dependent Children, food stamps, and Social Security) as "entitlements." The former label, of course, was freighted with operational and technical meaning drawn from the national income accounts. By contrast, the latter evoked notions of engrossment at public expense by those possibly unworthy. Just as one could be "entitled" to something, one could just as arguably be "disentitled." Thus it became easier to speak of program elimination, zero-base budgeting, means-testing, and an array of efforts at retrenchment unthinkable a decade or more earlier. In such simple yet profound changes in word choice, conservatives found yet another weapon in their determination to disestablish the mixed economy of the Cold War era. See Gareth Davies, *From Opportunity to Entitlement: The Transformation and Decline of Great Society Liberalism* (Lawrence: University Press of Kansas, 1996).

9. See John B. Taylor, "Changes in American Economic Policy in the 1980s: Watershed or Pendulum Swing?," *Journal of Economic Literature* 33 (1995), 777–84, as well as Richard M. Alston, J.R. Kearl, Michael B. Vaughan, "Is There a Consensus Among Economists in the 1990s?," *American Economic Review* 82 (1992), 203–20. American Economic Association President Gerard Debreu offered interesting speculations about the tendencies of modern economists to indulge an introverted formalism in his presidential address in 1991: "The Mathematization of Economic Theory," *American Economic Review* 81 (1991), 1–7. For a thorough narrative concerning twentieth-century changes in the thinking and practice of American economists, see my *A Perilous Progress: Economists and Public Purpose in Twentieth Century America,* (Princeton: Princeton University Press, 2001), especially Chapters 5–6.

10. The authorship "shares" reported in a 1983 study for the period 1973–1978 were, respectively, 54 percent in the *American Economic Review,* 58 percent in the *Journal of Political Economy,* and 74 percent in the *Quarterly Journal of Economics.* See E. Ray Canterbery and Robert Burkhardt, "What Do We Mean by Asking If Economics Is a Science?," in Alfred Eichner, ed., *Why Economics Is Not Yet a Science* (Armonk, NY: M.E. Sharpe, 1983), 15–40. On the articulation of alternative scientific "paradigms," the classic reference is Thomas S. Kuhn, *The Structure of Scientific Revolutions* (Chicago: University of Chicago Press, 1962). Nearly two decades ago, Hyman P. Minsky argued that the scholarly debates among Keynesians and monetarists during the 1970s were really nothing of the sort. Given that "the competing camps used the same economic theory," the substance of their dispute was minor and the potential outcomes of its resolution hardly innovative. See his *Stabilizing an Unstable Economy* (New Haven: Yale University Press, 1986), 102, 138. Independent of the formulation of opinion within the economics profession, there is the broader issue of how public attitudes on economic matters were (and are) framed. The entire question of the role of the financial press and of nonprofit organizations in both setting the terms of public debate on policy issues and influencing

public understanding of them is a significant matter for further historical inquiry. In this regard, see, for example, Wayne Parsons, *The Power of the Financial Press: Journalism and Economic Opinion in Britain and America* (New Brunswick, NJ: Rutgers University Press, 1990), and Jean Stefancic and Richard Delgado, *No Mercy: How Conservative Think Tanks and Foundations Changed America's Social Agenda* (Philadelphia: Temple University Press, 1996). Also see Robert Parry, "Who Buys the Right?," *The Nation,* November 18, 1996, 5–6. Above and beyond the power of policy pundits and the media, there is also the puzzle of how individuals gain access to the necessary information and skills to formulate appropriate and sophisticated positions on economic questions—an issue made all the more complex by the fact that such questions often require quantitative skills sorely lacking in large proportions of the electorate. See my "Numerable Knowledge and Its Discontents," *Reviews in American History* 18 (1990), 151–64.

11. See "Let's Not Take Feel-Good Economics Too Far," *Business Week,* October 20, 1997.

12. It is interesting to consider that at the very time such changes in the outlook of the profession took place, opportunities for the employment of economists in the private sector increased dramatically. No doubt a parallel development, in this regard, was the transition in the aspirations of new generations of students who sought out careers in the corporate world rather than, as their predecessors had done a few decades before, positions in the government service. Equally intriguing is the fact that the anti-statism of this new cadre of young economists had close formal (if not substantive) similarities with that of an earlier generation who, in the 1960s most especially, as a New Left had excoriated government professionals as servants of a malicious power elite. On the notion of *laissez-nous-faire,* see William Appleman Williams. *The Contours of American History* (Chicago: Quadrangle Books, 1961, 1966).

13. A particularly vivid, if strident, representation of these arguments is Susan Lee, *Hands Off: Why the Government Is a Menace to Economic Health* (New York: Simon & Schuster, 1996). An historical perspective on American attitudes regarding regulation is provided by Rudolph J.R. Peritz, *Competition Policy in America, 1888–1992: History, Rhetoric, Law* (New York: Oxford University Press, 1996).

14. See, for example, James Risen and Douglas Jehl, "Bush to Call for Freeze on New Regulations," *Los Angeles Times,* January 31, 1992, A1, A14; Edwin Chen, "White House Pushes Deregulation," *Los Angeles Times,* January 31, 1992, D4; and James Risen, "Clinton Kills Controversial Quayle Panel," *Los Angeles Times,* January 23, 1993, A14. Thomas Petzinger Jr. provides a thorough survey of the impacts of deregulation in the American aviation industry in his *Hard Landing: The Epic Contest for Power and Profits That Plunged the Airlines into Chaos* (New York: Random House, 1996).

5. "Papers of a Dangerous Tendency": From Major Andre's Boot to the VENONA Files by Maurice Isserman and Ellen Schrecker

1. George Will, "Cold Water on the Left's Myths," *Washington Post,* April 21, 1995, 21.

2. David Brion Davis, ed., *The Fear of Conspiracy: Images of Un-American Subversion from the Revolution to the Present* (Ithaca, NY: Cornell University Press, 1971), xiii.

3. Michael Rogin, *Ronald Reagan, the Movie and Other Episodes in Political Demonology* (Berkeley and Los Angeles: University of California Press, 1987), 68.

4. The colonists were, of course, well aware of English precedent for their own penchant for document-writing; as Pauline Maier notes in tracing the origins of the Declaration of Independence that "The milestones of English history are marked not so much by stone documents as by parchment documents. . . . ," Maier, *American Scripture: Making the Declaration of Independence* (New York: Knopf, 1997), 50. Americans, however, had a much stronger sense of starting anew than their English forebears, whose unwritten constitution was believed, somewhat fancifully, to draw on traditions of governance

stretching back to the pre–Norman Conquest and mostly undocumented era of Anglo-Saxon self-rule.

5. The classic depiction of this process is found in Perry Miller's *Errand into the Wilderness* (Cambridge: Harvard University Press, 1956).

6. Quoted in Carl N. Degler, *Out of Our Past: The Forces That Shaped Modern America,* 2d edition (New York: Harper & Row, 1970), 82–83. Among those Americans trying their hands at declaration-writing in the heady early days of the American Revolution was one Benedict Arnold of New Haven, a captain in the Connecticut Foot Guards. Clare Brandt, *The Man in the Mirror: A Life of Benedict Arnold* (New York: Random House, 1994), 20.

7. *Ibid.,* 220.

8. Richard Hofstadter, *The Paranoid Style in American Politics and Other Essays* (New York: Knopf, 1966), 29. Emphasis in the original.

9. Brandt, *The Man in the Mirror,* 233.

10. Jedidiah Morse, "The Present Dangers and Consequent Duties of the Citizens," in Davis, ed., *The Fear of Conspiracy,* 47.

11. Hofstadter, *Paranoid Style,* 35–36.

12. Many of the original VENONA documents are available on the Internet at www.nsa.gov/docs/venona.

13. Harvey Klehr, John Earl Haynes, and Fridrikh Igorevich Firsov, *The Secret World of American Communism* (New Haven: Yale University Press, 1995); Klehr, Haynes, and Kyrill M. Anderson, *The Soviet World of American Communism* (New Haven: Yale University Press, 1998); Allen Weinstein and Alexander Vassiliev, *The Haunted Wood: Soviet Espionage in America—The Stalin Era* (New York: Random House, 1999); Haynes and Klehr, *Venona: Decoding Soviet Espionage in America* (New Haven: Yale University Press, 1999); and Eric Breindel and Herbert Romerstein, *The Venona Secrets* (Washington, DC: Regnery, 2000). Additional works utilizing these documents include Nigel West and Oleg Tsarev, *The Crown Jewels: The British Secrets at the Heart of the KGB Archives* (London: HarperCollins, 1998); and Robert Louis Benson and Michael Warner, eds., *Venona: Soviet Espionage and the American Response, 1939–1957* (Washington, DC: National Security Agency, Central Intelligence Agency, 1996). Additional evidence, of decidedly mixed reliability, comes from the growing memoir literature by former KGB agents and their collaborators. See for example, Pavel Sudoplatov and Anatolii Sudoplatov with Jerrold L. Schecter and Leona P. Schecter, *Special Tasks: The Memoirs of an Unwanted Witness—A Soviet Spymaster* (Boston: Little, Brown, 1994); Alexander Feklisov with Sergei Kostin, *The Man Behind the Rosenbergs* (New York: Enigma, 2001); Christopher Andrew and Vasili Mitrokhin, *The Sword and the Shield: The Mitrokhin Archive and the Secret History of the KGB* (New York: Basic Books, 1999).

14. We made this point repeatedly in our own writings. See, for example, Maurice Isserman, "Notes from Underground," *The Nation,* June 12, 1995; Isserman, "Guess What—They Really Were Spies," *Forward,* January 29, 1999; Isserman, "They Led Two Lives," *New York Times Book Review,* May 9, 1999; Ellen Schrecker, review of Harvey Klehr, John Earl Haynes, and Kyrill M. Anderson, *The Soviet World of American Communism, Journal of American History,* March 1999; Schrecker, "The Spies Who Loved Us?," *The Nation,* May 24, 1999; Isserman and Schrecker, "The Right's Cold War Revisionism," *The Nation,* July 24–31, 2000.

15. Thomas Powers, "The Plot Thickens," *New York Review of Books,* May 11, 2000, 59.

16. Hofstadter, *Paranoid Style,* 29.

17. See the excellent biography by Kathryn S. Olmsted, *Red Spy Queen: A Biography of Elizabeth Bentley* (Chapel Hill: University of North Carolina Press, 2002.)

18. Feklisov, *The Man Behind the Rosenbergs,* 120.

19. New York to Moscow, December 5, 1944, no. 1715, Benson and Warner, *Venona,* 385.

20. Weinstein and Vassiliev, *The Haunted Wood,* 162.

21. *Ibid.*, 178; Feklisov, *The Man Behind the Rosenbergs,* 125–28.
22. Weinstein and Vassiliev, *The Haunted Wood,* 160.
23. Klehr and Haynes, *The American Communist Movement: Storming Heaven Itself* (New York: Twayne, 1992), 179; Theodore Draper, *The Roots of American Communism* (New York: Viking, 1957); Draper, *American Communism and Soviet Russia: The Formative Period* (New York: Viking, 1960); Klehr, *The Heyday of American Communism: The Depression Decade* (New York: Basic Books, 1984).
24. Mark Naison, *Communists in Harlem During the Depression* (Urbana: University of Illinois Press, 1983); Robin D.G. Kelley, *Hammer and Hoe: Alabama Communists During the Great Depression* (Chapel Hill: University of North Carolina Press, 1990); Maurice Isserman, *Which Side Were You On? The American Communist Party During the Second World War* (Middletown, CT: Wesleyan University Press, 1982).
25. Theodore Draper, "American Communism Revisited," *New York Review of Books,* May 9, 1985.
26. Klehr and Haynes, *The American Communist Movement,* 108; Irving Howe and Lewis Coser, *The American Communist Party: A Critical History* (New York: Praeger, 1957, 1962), 434.
27. Haynes and Klehr, *Venona,* 7.
28. John Haynes, "The Cold War Debate Continues: A Traditionalist View of Historical Writing on Domestic Communism and Anti-Communism," *Journal of Cold War Studies* 2, no. 1 (2000), 114.
29. Haynes and Klehr, *Venona,* 7.
30. Breindel and Romerstein, *The Venona Secrets.*
31. Jerrold and Leona Schecter, *Sacred Secrets: How Soviet Intelligence Operations Changed American History* (Washington, DC: Brassey's, Inc., 2002).
32. For the most judicious discussion of the impact of espionage on the development of the Soviet bomb, see David Holloway, *Stalin and the Bomb: The Soviet Union and Atomic Energy, 1939–1956* (New Haven: Yale University Press, 1994). See also Vladislav Zubok and Constantine Pleshakov, *Inside the Kremlin's Cold War from Stalin to Khrushchev* (Cambridge, MA: Harvard University Press, 1996), 62, 150.
33. Harvey Klehr, "Spies Like Us," *Weekly Standard,* July 1–8, 2002, 37.
34. The conditions for admission to the Communist International were reprinted in Helmut Gruber, ed., *International Communism in the Era of Lenin* (Greenwich, CT: Fawcett, 1967), 287–92.
35. Cited in Klehr, Haynes, and Firsov, *Secret World of American Communism,* 73.
36. Steve Nelson, James R. Barrett, Rob Ruck, *Steve Nelson, American Radical* (Pittsburgh: University of Pittsburgh Press, 1981), 101. As Harvey Klehr noted, "To be publicly identified as a Communist," in many places in the U.S. in the 1930s, "was to risk grave penalties." Klehr, *Heyday of American Communism,* 158.
37. Nelson et al., *Steve Nelson,* 137–52.
38. Haynes, Klehr, and Firsov, *Secret World of American Communism,* 240.
39. Alfred Kazin, *Starting Out in the Thirties* (Boston: Little Brown, 1965), 83.
40. E.P. Thompson, "Socialist Humanism, An Epistle to the Philistines," *New Reasoner* I (Summer 1957).
41. Weinstein and Vassiliev, *The Haunted Wood,* 75.
42. *Ibid.,* 15.
43. See Ronald Radosh and Joyce Milton, *The Rosenberg File,* 2d ed. (New Haven: Yale University Press, 1997), 29.
44. Theodore Hall, in *Secrets, Lies & Atomic Spies,* 2002. 60 min. Boston: WGBH/Nova and Somerville, Mass., Powderhouse Productions. Tug Yourgrau, producer and director.
45. Teletype, New York to Director, November 30, 1945, Elizabeth Bentley, NY FBI File, #432.

46. Gary May, *Un-American Activities: The Trials of William Remington* (New York: Oxford University Press, 1994), 129.
47. Haynes, "Cold War Debate," 114.
48. John Lewis Gaddis, *We Now Know: Rethinking Cold War History* (Oxford: Clarendon Press, 1997), 294.
49. Nicholas von Hoffman, "Was McCarthy Right About the Left?" *Washington Post,* April 14, 1996.
50. As Thomas Powers noted in a review of *Venona* and related books, McCarthy "never found even a single genuine Communist in the government; none of those he named recklessly during his hour on the stage was ever proved to have been a spy; and none of them appear in the VENONA traffic or the documents published by [Allen] Weinstein and others." Thomas Powers, "The Plot Thickens," *New York Review of Books,* May 11, 2000, 54.
51. Weinstein and Vassiliev, *The Haunted Wood,* 300.
52. Benson and Warner, *Venona,* xxx.
53. Arthur Herman, *Joseph McCarthy: Reexamining the Life and Legacy of America's Most Hated Senator* (New York: The Free Press, 2000); Kevin Smant, "Joseph McCarthy and the Historians," *Continuity,* no. 26 (Spring 2003), 154. For a critical response to Herman's book, see Alonzo L. Hamby, "Reds Under the Bed," *New York Times Book Review,* December 12, 1999, 32.
54. Ann Coulter, *Treason: Liberal Treachery from the Cold War to the War on Terrorism* (New York: Crown Forum, 2003), 39.
55. Haynes, "Cold War Debate," 92.
56. Arnold Beichman, "Communism's Last Stronghold," *Washington Times,* June 3, 1996.
57. David Horowitz, "Ordeal by Slander," *Salon.com,* December 6, 1999.
58. Roger Kimball, "One Book on Communism That Should Shake the World," *Wall Street Journal,* April 11, 1995.
59. Jerry L. Martin and Anne D. Neal, "Defending Civilization: How Our Universities Are Failing America and What Can Be Done About It," American Council of Trustees and Alumni, November 2001.

6. The Myth of the Berlin Blockade and the Early Cold War
by Carolyn Eisenberg

1. Remarks by National Security Advisor Condoleezza Rice on terrorism and foreign policy, Paul H. Nitze School of International Affairs, Johns Hopkins University, April 29, 2001.
2. David McCullough, *Truman* (New York: Simon & Schuster, 1992).
3. George F. Kennan (Mr. X), "The Sources of Soviet Conduct," *Foreign Affairs* (July 1947).
4. William Clinton, Address at the Tempelhof Airlift Ceremony, May 14, 1998, White House Press Office.
5. William Stivers, "Soviet Supply of West Berlin, 1948-49," *Diplomatic History* (Fall 1997).
6. For a more extended discussion of this theme, see Carolyn Eisenberg, *Drawing the Line: The American Decision to Divide Germany, 1944-49* (New York: Cambridge University Press, 1996).
7. Shortly after the London CFM adjourned, American intelligence agencies began predicting a Soviet move against Berlin. Robert Murphy to Secretary of State, December 24, 1947, *Foreign Relations of the United States* (*FRUS*), 1947, II: 905; Walter Bedell Smith to Secretary of State, December 23, 1947, *ibid.,* 908; R.H. Hillenkoetter to the president, December 22, 1948, RG 226 Records of the Office of Strategic Services, Leahy File #123,

"Memos to and from the President," Modern Military Branch, National Archives (MMNA).

8. Protocol Between the United States, the United Kingdom and the Soviet Union Regarding the Zones of Occupation in Germany and the Administration of Greater Berlin, *FRUS, the Conferences at Malta and Yalta:* 118–21; Agreement on Control Machinery in Germany, *ibid.:* 124–27; Allied Statement on Control Machinery in Germany, June 5, 1945; Senate Committee on Foreign Relations, *Documents on Germany, 1944–59,* 18–20; Amending Agreement on Zones of Occupation and Administration of the 'Greater Berlin' Area," July 26, 1945, *ibid.:* 21–24.

9. Reporting to Whitehall, General Robertson noted that Clay "is determined that the discussions shall fail, and is instructing his men that they must look for a good opportunity and a good cause." Robertson to Strang, March 12, 1948, Foreign Office, 371/79587/Public Record Office (PRO); Clay to Department of the Army, February 5, 1948, Jean Edward Smith, *The Papers of General Lucius D. Clay,* vol. 2 (Bloomington: Indiana University Press, 1974), 553–54; Clay/Draper Teleconference, February 10, 1948, *ibid.,* 559; Wisner to Lovett, March 10, 1948, *FRUS,* 1948, II: 879–82.

10. Murphy to Secretary of State, January 8, 7, 9, 1948, *FRUS* 1948: 10–16, 19–20; Robertson to FONOFF, January 13, 1948, FO 371/70572/PRO; Robertson to Pat Dean, January 27, 1948, FO 371/70579/PRO.

11. Communique Issued at the Recess of the London Conference on Germany, March 6, 1948, *FRUS,* 1948, II: 141–43.

12. Berlin to FONOFF, April 5, 1948, FO 371/70585/PRO; Robertson to FONOFF, June 9, 1948, FO 371/70593/PRO; Clay to Draper, June 10, 1948, Jean Smith, ed., *Clay Papers* II: 673–74.

13. See Samuel J. Walker, "No More Cold War: American Foreign Policy and the 1948 Peace Offensive," *Diplomatic History* (Winter 1981), 75–91.

14. Memorandum of Conversation by Secretary of State, May 11, 1948, 1948 *FRUS,* 1948, IV: 860–61; Caffrey to Secretary of State, May 12, 1948, *ibid.:* 863; Durbrow to the Secretary of State, May 12, 1948, *ibid.:* 865; Durbrow to the Secretary of State, May 18, 1948, *ibid.:* 970–71.

15. For documentation of the London discussions, see *FRUS,* 1948, II: 191–312. The results are outlined in Communique of the London Conference on Germany, June 7, 1948, *ibid.:* 313–16.

16. Lewis Douglas to the Secretary of State, June 1, 6, 7, 1948, FRUS, 1948, II: 363, 365–67; Harvey to FONOFF, June 8, 1948, FO 371/70584/PRO.

17. Robertson to FONOFF, June 8, 1948, FO 371/70564/PRO; Robertson to FONOFF, June 10, 1948, FO 371/70584/PRO; Konrad Adenauer, *Memoirs, 1945–53* (Chicago: Regnery, 1965).

18. Clay to Sokolovsky, June 18, 1948, RG 84 US POLAD, Murphy Correspondence, Federal Records Center, Suitland Maryland (FRC); Sokolovsky to Clay, June 20, 1948, *ibid.*

19. See discussion in Manuel Gottlieb, *The German Peace Settlement and the Berlin Crisis* (New York: Paine-Whitman, 1960), 190–97.

20. The clearest statement of the Soviet position is contained in Soviet Reply, July 14, 1948, in Margaret Carlyle, ed., *Documents on International Affairs* (New York: Oxford University Press, 1952), 589–92.

21. These tactical issues constitute the focus of much of the literature in the field. See especially John R. Oneal, *Foreign Policy Making in Times of Crisis* (Columbus: Ohio University Press, 1982); Avi Shlaim, *The United States and the Berlin Blockade: A Study in Crisis Decision-Making* (Berkeley: University of California Press, 1983); Daniel F. Harrington, "The Berlin Blockade Revisited," *International History Review* (February 1984), 88–112.

22. Soviet Reply, July 14, 1948.

23. Extensive documentation on the Moscow talks is contained in *FRUS,* 1948, II, and *Clay*

Papers, II. Yet for a behind-the-scenes understanding of the dynamics of the talks, I found the unpublished records of the British Foreign Office to be indispensable.

24. Smith to Secretary of State, August 31, 1948, *FRUS,* 1948, II: 1092–97.

25. Bohlen to Secretary of State, Lovett, Hickerson, and Kennan, August 4, 1948, RG 59 Bohlen MSS, Department of State, National Archives (DSNA); Clay for Bradley and Royall, August 4, 1948, *Clay Papers* II: 752–53.

26. Harrison to FONOFF, August 25, 1948, FO 371/70510/PRO.

27. For Military Governor's talks, see *Clay Papers* II: 798–856.

28. Marshall to Smith, August 25, 1948, *FRUS,* 1948, II: 1085; Smith to Secretary of State, 1948, *ibid.:* 999–1006; Smith to Secretary of State, August 25, 1948, *ibid.:* 1078–79.

29. Clay-Draper Teleconference, September 19, 1948, *Clay Papers* II: 855–68.

30. Acting Secretary of State to American Diplomatic and Consular Officers, September 26, 1948, *FRUS,* 1948, II: 1186–87.

31. For discussion of Truman's peace initiative see Robert J. Donovan, *Conflict and Crisis: The Presidency of Harry S. Truman, 1945–48* (New York: W. W. Norton, 1977), 422–25; Clark Clifford and Richard Holbrooke, *Counsel to the President* (New York: Random House, 1991), 231–34; David McCullough, *Truman,* 685–87; Forrest G. Pogue, *George C. Marshall, 1945–49* (New York: Viking, 1987), 407–8.

32. Dean Rusk to Lewis Douglas, September 15, 1948, RG 335 Berlin Book III, MMNA.

33. Draper to Clay, October 5, 1948, RG 335 SAOUS 000.1 Germany, MMNA; Bohlen to Marshall, October 8, 1948, *FRUS,* 1948, II: 1214–16.

34. Draft Resolution Urging Implementation of the Four-Power Directive on Berlin and a Meeting of the Council of Foreign Ministers on Germany. Submitted to the UN Security Council, October 22, 1948, in U.S. Senate Committee on Foreign Relations, *Documents on Germany,* 137–38; Harvey to FONOFF, October 14 and 19, 1948, FO 371/10519/PRO.

35. The Americans especially wanted to escape from the provisions of the August 30 Moscow Directive. Bohlen to Jessup, October 19, 1948, RG Bohlen MSS, DSNA.

36. Conclusions of the Cabinet, November 15, 1948, FO 371/70522/PRO; JF Dulles to Thomas Dewey, October 21, 1948, FO 371/70520/PRO.

37. Bohlen to Jessup, October 26, 1948, RG 59 Bohlen MSS, DSNA.

38. See Trygve Lie, *In the Cause of Peace* (New York: The Macmillan Company, 1954), 205–12; U.K. Delegation to FONOFF, November 11, 1948, FO 371/70522/PRO; U.S. Del (Paris) to Secretary of State, November 12, 1948, RG 335 SAOUS 123.7, MMNA.

39. U.S. Delegation (Paris) to Secretary of State, November 12, 1948, RG 335 SAOUS 123.7, MMNA.

40. Bohlen to Jessup, November 5, 1948, RG 59 Bohlen MSS, DSNA; Jessup to Lovett, October 29, 1948, *FRUS,* 1948, II: 1228–30; G.A. Lincoln, Memo Summarizing Conversation Between Mr. Hickerson, Mr. Beam, and Col. Lincoln, October 30, 1948, RG 335 SAOUS 123.5 Germany, MMNA; Paris to FONOFF, November 12, 1948, FO 371/70523/PRO.

41. Shlaim, *The United States and the Berlin Blockade, 1948–49,* 368–69. In his article, Jessup observes, "It is striking how often one person after another stressed the point that we must convince others that we really wanted a settlement. The suspicion of our motives did not seem to slacken." Yet Jessup's dispatches from the period indicate some of the reasons for the doubts. Philip Jessup, "The Berlin Blockade and the Use of the United Nations," *Foreign Affairs* 50 (October 1971), 171.

42. Clay to Murphy, November 24, 1948, *Clay Papers* II: 937; Jessup to Marshall, November 24, 1948, FRUS, 1948, II: 1262–63; Murphy to Bohlen, November 24, 1948, *ibid.:* 1260–62.

43. A focal point was the forthcoming municipal elections. The Soviet Kommandant had objected to the electoral ordinance, which had been drafted by the City Assembly. Spurred by the Americans, the City Assembly decided to defy the Soviets and proceed

with the balloting on December 5. Murphy to Secretary of State, November 26, 1948, RG 84 US POLAD, Frankfort TS: Berlin Cables, FRC; Bohlen to Jessup. November 22 and 26, 1948, RG 59 Bohlen MSS, DSNA.

44. Murphy to Secretary of State, November 26, 1948, RG 84 Frankfurt TS, Folder: Berlin cables, Box 84, FRC.

45. Bohlen to Jessup, December 1948, RG 59 Bohlen MSS, DSNA.

46. U.K. Delegation to FONOFF, December 11, 1948, FO 371/70526/PRO; FONOFF to Paris, December 14, 1948, *ibid.;* Lovett to the Embassy in Paris, December 16, 1948, *FRUS,* 1948, II: 1279–81; Jessup to State Department, December 16, 1948, RG 336 SAOUS 000.1 Germany, MMNA.

47. Committee of Experts on the Berlin Currency, Record of Meeting Held in Secretary of State's Room on December 29, 1948, FO 371/76537/PRO.

48. Bevin to Franks, January 11, 1949, FO 371/76539/PRO. In the final phases the British and French failed to support the Bramuglia proposal, but neither would they support the American plan that seemed to them palpably fraudulent. GHP Gifford, Minute, February 14, 1949, FO 371/76544/PRO.

49. M. Gordon, Technical Committee on Berlin Currency and Trade: meetings at Geneva, 25 January–7 April, Impressions. FO 3717/6544/PRO.

50. D.M Gordon, Technical Committee on Berlin Currency: U.K. Delegation to FONOFF, February 5, 1949, FO 371/76544/PRO.

51. So concerned were the British about the compromising contents of this report that they directly urged Trygve Lie not to publish it. FONOFF to U.K. delegation, February 16, 1949, FO 371/76544/PRO.

52. Smith, *My Three Years in Moscow* (Philadelphia: Lippincott, 1950), 253.

53. Murphy to Secretary of State, June 26, 1948, *FRUS,* 1948, II: 918–19.

54. Forrestal Diary, June 27–28, 1948, in Millis, ed., *The Forrestal Diaries; The Inner History of the Cold War,* ed. Walter Millis with E. S. Duffield (New York: Viking, 1951), 452–54.

55. See, for example, David McCullough, *Truman,* 630.

56. Oneal, *Foreign Policy Making in Time of Crisis,* fn 51, 284.

57. Millis, *Forrestal Diaries,* 455. See important discussion of this issue in Herken, *Winning Weapon,* 258–59.

58. Kenneth W. Condit, *The History of the Joint Chiefs of Staff and National Policy,* vol. 2 (Wilmington, DE: Glazier, 1979), 139; Major Harry Borowski, "A Narrow Victory: The 1948 Berlin Blockade and the American Military Response" (Unpublished Paper), Washington, DC: AHA Convention, 1979.

59. Clay to Bradley, July 15, 1948, *Clay Papers* II, 739–40; Robertson to FONOFF, July 16, 1948, FO 371/70502/PRO; FONOFF Conversation with Lovett, July 15, 1948, FO 371/70504/PRO.

60. James Forrestal, Dinner with General Clay, July 21, 1948, Millis, *The Forrestal Diaries,* 439–40.

61. Secretary Royall to the Secretary of Defense, July 10, 1948, RG 335 SAOUS 0001.4, MMNA.

62. Royall to the Secretary of Defense, July 10, 1948; Draper, Memorandum of Conversation with Averell Harriman, RG 335 SAOUS 000.1 Germany, MMNA.

63. See discussion in Steven Rearden, *History of the Office of the Secretary of Defense, the Formative Years* (Washington, DC: Office of the Secretary of Defense, 1984), 425–32.

64. Forrestal, July 15, 1945, in Millis, *Forrestal Diaries,* 458–59.

65. The fullest description of this meeting comes from David Lilienthal, *The Journals of David Lilienthal, II: The Atomic Energy Years, 1945–50* (New York: Harper & Row, 1964), 388–92; Millis, *Forrestal Diaries,* 460–61.

66. Cited in Lilienthal, *Journals,* 391.

67. Truman was also responding to factors that he did not raise in this meeting, including

the jurisdictional battling between the Navy and the Air Force. Rearden, *Secretary of Defense,* 430.

68. *Ibid.,* 434.

69. Millis, *Forrestal Diaries,* 462–63.

70. Royall to Secretary of Defense, July 10, 1948, RG 335 Draper/Voorhees, MMNA. Clay to Draper, July 19, 1948, *Clay Papers,* II: 743–46; Secretary of Defense, A Report to the National Security Council on U.S. Military Courses of Action with Respect to the Situation in Berlin, July 28, 1948, President's Secretary File (PSF), Box 204, Harry S. Truman Library (HST).

71. Robert Ferrell, ed., *Off the Record: The Private Papers of Harry S. Truman* (New York: Harper & Row, 1980), 148–49.

72. Lilienthal, *Journals* II: 406–8.

73. Forrestal Diaries, September 7, 1948, 2474–75, Forrestal MSS, Princeton University (PU); Rearden, *Secretary of Defense,* 297.

74. NSC 30, "United States Policy on Atomic Weapons," September 10, 1948, *FRUS, 1948,* I: 624–28.

75. *Ibid.;* Rearden, *Secretary of Defense,* 436; Millis, *Forrestal Diaries,* 486–87.

76. David Rosenberg, "The Origins of Overkill: Nuclear Weapons and Atomic Strategy," in Norman A. Graebner, ed., *The National Security: Its Theory and Practice, 1945–1960* (New York: Oxford University Press, 1986), 131.

77. David Alan Rosenberg, "American Atomic Strategy and the Hydrogen Bomb Decision," *Journal of American History* (June 1979), 69–71. While Rosenberg emphasizes the technological factors that made the improvement of the atomic arsenal feasible, my own view is that the experience of a serious crisis in Berlin spurred those developments forward.

78. Franks to FONOFF, October 6, 1948, FO 371/70518/PRO; Robertson to Kirkpatrick, October 6, 1948, *ibid.*

79. Extract from Record of Meeting at the Quai d'Orsay, October 4, 1948, FO 371/70519/PRO; Memorandum of Conversation, Berlin Situation, October 6, 1948, RG 59 Bohlen MSS, DSNA.

80. CIA, Review of the World Situation, October 20, 1948, PSF Box 204 (HST).

81. In March 1948, Senator Vandenberg had introduced a carefully worded resolution permitting American support for the Western Union. Timothy P. Ireland, *Creating the Entangling Alliance: The Origins of the North American Treaty Organization* (Westport, CT: Greenwood, 1981), 93–112.

82. Melvyn P. Leffler, *A Preponderance of Power: National Security, the Truman Administration, and the Cold War* (Stanford, CA: Stanford University Press, 1992), 279–86.

83. Eisenberg, *Drawing the Line,* 469–74.

84. Murphy, Tentative Outline of Approach in the Discussions with the British and French Foreign Ministers on Germany, March 30, 1948, *FRUS,* III: 140–42; Memorandum of Conversation by the Secretary of State, April 5, 1949, fn 5, *ibid.:* 163; Agreed Memorandum regarding the Principles Governing the Exercise of Powers and Responsibilities of German Federal Republic, April 8, 1949, and Occupation Statute Defining the Powers to Be Retained by the Occupation Authorities, April 8, 1949, *ibid.:* 178–83.

85. Acheson to Truman, Negotiations on Germany, April 8, 1949, PSF Box 163, HST; Ireland, *Entangling Alliance,* 138–41.

86. Bohlen to Jessup. Murphy et al., April 15, 1949, RG 59 Bohlen MSS, Box 2, DSNA.

87. Memorandum of Conversation by the Chief of Protocol, April 7, 1949, *FRUS, 1949,* III: 173–75.

88. "The Siege," *Time,* July 12, 1948.

89. U.S. Senate, Committee on Foreign Relations, Hearing Held in Executive Session, Results of the Foreign Ministers Conference, June 22, 1949, 23–29.

7. The United States, the United Nations, and the Other Post–Cold War World Order: Internationalism and Unilateralism in the American Century by Jessica Wang

1. The full text of Carter's Nobel lecture can be found on the Nobel Foundation Web site: www.nobel.se/peace/laureates/2002/carter-lecture.html (January 2003).

2. Richard Boudreaux, "Crucial Game Against the U.S. Means the World to Mexicans," *Los Angeles Times,* June 16, 2002, A1, A14.

3. Akira Iriye, *Global Community: The Role of International Organizations in the Making of the Contemporary World* (Berkeley and Los Angeles: University of California Press, 2002) both acknowledges this trend and provides an important exception.

4. On Carnegie's efforts on behalf of peace, see David Patterson, *Toward a Warless World: The Travail of the American Peace Movement, 1887–1914* (Bloomington and London: Indiana University Press, 1976), 139–42 and 147–48. See also Carnegie's own writings and speeches, including: "A League of Peace," October 17, 1905, and "Honor and International Arbitration," 1910, reprinted in Burton J. Hendrick, ed., *The Miscellaneous Writings of Andrew Carnegie,* vol. 2 (New York: Doubleday, Doran and Company, 1933), 221–71 and 272–88 respectively; "Peace Versus War: The President's Solution," *Century Illustrated Monthly Magazine* 80 (May/October 1910), 307; and "Arbitration," *Contemporary Review* 100 (August 1911), 176. I am grateful to my research assistant, Marissa de Siena, for helping me to understand Carnegie's conception of world peace, as well as other aspects of peace politics during the first decades of the twentieth century.

5. Patterson, *Toward a Warless World,* 109–10, 116, and 129; and Frank Ninkovich, *Modernity and Power: A History of the Domino Theory in the Twentieth Century* (Chicago and London: University of Chicago Press, 1994), 14. Roosevelt's internationalism ended, however, where national sovereignty and imperial aspirations began. Unsympathetic to the anti-imperialist wing of the peace movement, he pursued military intervention in Colombia and Santo Domingo without qualms, and he refused to countenance international agreements that threatened to restrict American sovereignty. In 1912, William I. Hull, a Quaker pacifist and history professor at Swarthmore College, aptly described Roosevelt as "the Dr. Jekyll and Mr. Hyde of the Peace Movement." Quoted in Patterson, *Toward a Warless War,* 182.

6. Ninkovich, *Modernity and Power,* 20–36; and Patterson *Toward a Warless World,* Chap. 9. Ninkovich observes, "Taft's true love was an international court backed by world opinion that would dispense impartial justice on the basis of legal principles without regard for national sensibilities." Ninkovich, 34.

7. On Wilson's internationalism, and the domestic coalition of progressives and socialists that informed his political vision, see Thomas J. Knock, *To End All Wars: Woodrow Wilson and the Quest for a New World Order* (Princeton: Princeton University Press, 1992).

8. On the League's significance, see David Armstrong, Lorna Lloyd, and John Redmond, *From Versailles to Maastricht: International Organisation in the Twentieth Century* (Houndmills and London: Macmillan Press Ltd., 1996), Chaps. 1 and 2.

9. Outlawry of war was the brainchild of Chicago lawyer Salmon O. Levinson. For his original proposal, see Salmon O. Levinson, "Outlawry of War," Chicago, American Committee for the Outlawry of War, December 25, 1921. On Borah and the outlawry of war movement, see John Chalmers Vinson, *William E. Borah and the Outlawry of War* (Athens: University of Georgia Press, 1957). The text of the Kellogg-Briand Pact can be found at the Web site of the Yale Law School's Avalon Project: www.yale.edu/lawweb/avalon/kbpact/kbpact.htm (April 2002).

10. The quotation is from Carnegie, "Arbitration," 169. On the importance of the idea of civilization to early twentieth-century foreign policy, see Frank Ninkovich, "Theodore Roosevelt: Civilization as Ideology," *Diplomatic History* 10 (Summer 1986), 221–45.

11. One should be cautious about dismissing universalism because of the racism within its origins. As Akira Iriye has observed, and as Ho's appeal to Wilson indicates, although cultural prejudices failed to match the universalist pretensions of internationalist rhetoric, pluralist discourse had a power of it own that cannot be reduced to the biases of its adherents. Throughout the pre–World War I years, intellectuals from around the world pressured Western nations to live up to their inclusive language of internationalism, and their demands raised prospects for the realization of universalist ideals on a grand scale. Akira Iriye, *Cultural Internationalism and World Order* (Baltimore and London: Johns Hopkins University Press, 1997), 41–49.

12. The Washington treaty system consisted of the Five-Power, Four-Power, and Nine-Power treaties, established in 1921–22 to restrict naval rearmament and stabilize Asia. Walter LaFeber, *The American Age: United States Foreign Policy at Home and Abroad Since 1750* (New York: W. W. Norton & Company, 1989), 319–23.

13. On the unrestrained American optimism surrounding the UN in 1945, see, for example, John Allphin Moore Jr. and Jerry Pubantz, *To Create a New World? American Presidents and the United Nations* (New York: Peter Lang Publishing, Inc., 1999), Chap. 2; Armstrong, Lloyd, and Redmond, *From Versailles to Maastricht*, 65; and Gary B. Ostrower, *The United Nations and the United States* (New York: Twayne Publishers, 1998), 44.

14. See, for example, Phyllis Bennis, *Calling the Shots: How Washington Dominates Today's UN* (New York: Olive Branch Press, 1995), Chap. 1.

15. Americans United for World Government, Inc., "Talk Delivered by Senator Charles W. Tobey," August 6, 1946, Box 44, Folder 5, Harold C. Urey Papers, Mandeville Department of Special Collections, University of California San Diego, San Diego, CA.

16. Thomas K. Finletter, "Timetable for World Government," *Atlantic Monthly* 177 (March 1946), 53–60. The quotation is from page 56.

17. Norman Cousins to Harold C. Urey, February 28, 1947, Box 44, Folder 5, Urey papers.

18. Edward Teller, "Comments on the 'Draft of a World Constitution,' " *Bulletin of the Atomic Scientists* 4 (July 1948), 204.

19. On Vandenberg and the founding of the UN, see James A. Gazell, "Arthur H. Vandenberg, Internationalism, and the United Nations," *Political Science Quarterly* 88 (September 1973), 375–94.

20. Senate, 79th Cong., 1st sess., *Congressional Record* (June 29, 1945), vol. 91, pt. 5: 6981 and 6982.

21. *Ibid.,* 6984.

22. "Address in San Francisco at the Closing Session of the United Nations Conference," June 26, 1945, *Public Papers of the Presidents of the United States: Harry S. Truman, 1945* (Washington, DC: U.S. Government Printing Office, 1961), 139.

23. Address by Harold E. Stassen, July 5, 1945, entered into the record by Senator Tom Connally (D.-Texas), Senate, 79th Cong., 1st sess., *Congressional Record* (July 6, 1945), vol. 91, pt. 6, 7276.

24. Senate, 79th Cong., 1st sess., *Congressional Record* (July 23, 1945), vol. 91, pt. 6, 7953.

25. *Ibid.,* 7962. For other contemporary expressions of this evolutionary conception of the UN, see, in addition to the Senate debate in the *Congressional Record,* Sumner Welles, "The Vision of a World at Peace," *Virginia Quarterly Review* 21 (Autumn 1945), 481–96, esp. 481–82; Edward R. Stettinius, "Founder of the United Nations," *The New Republic* 114 (April 15, 1946), 555–58; and Frank Gervasi, "The Brave Beginning," *Collier's* 118 (July 6, 1946), 12–13.

26. "Two Strikes on UNO," *The New Republic* 113 (December 24, 1945), 852.

27. "For an End to Slander," *The New Republic* 114 (April 1, 1946), 427.

28. Claude Pepper, "A Program for Peace," *The New Republic* 114 (April 8, 1946), 470–73. The quotation is from page 470.

29. Marcel Hoden, "The Roots of Discord," *The Nation* (November 9, 1946), 518.

30. See United States Representative on the Commission of Investigation (Ethridge) to the

Secretary of State, February 21, 1947, *Foreign Relations of the United States: 1947,* vol. 5, *The Near East and Africa* (Washington, DC: U.S. Government Printing Office, 1971), 37–39; and Report by the Subcommittee on Foreign Policy Information of the State-War-Navy Coordinating Committee, undated, but approved by the SWNCC on March 3, 1947, *Foreign Relations of the United States: 1947,* vol. 5, 76–79. In the February 21 telegram, Ethridge argued that both American security and the "future of UN are bound up in situation here" and stressed that the "UN is our best hope at moment." The report by the Subcommittee on Foreign Policy Information observed that economic aid to Greece was "consistent with the wholehearted support which the United States is giving to the United Nations" and observed that "the national security of the United States depends to a large degree on the maintenance of the principles of the United Nations."

31. Memorandum by the Director of the Office of Special Political Affairs (Rusk) to the Under Secretary of State (Acheson), March 18, 1947, *Foreign Relations of the United States: 1947,* vol. 5, 124–26. The minutes of the March 19 meeting between Acheson, Patterson, and Forrestal are discussed and quoted in the "Editorial Notes" on pp. 126–27.

32. Moore and Pubantz, *To Create a New World,* 64.

33. Dean Acheson, *Present at the Creation: My Years in the State Department* (New York: W. W. Norton & Company, 1969), 224.

34. See, for example, Memorandum of Conversation, by the Deputy Director of the Office of Near Eastern and African Affairs (Villard), July 9, 1947, 216; Secretary of State to Governor Dwight P. Griswold, at Washington, July 11, 1947, 222; and Secretary of State to the American Mission for Aid to Greece, November 4, 1947, 398, all in *Foreign Relations of the United States: 1947,* vol. 5.

35. On this point, consult Ostrower, *The United Nations and the United States,* Chap. 3. See also Leland M. Goodrich, "San Francisco in Retrospect," *International Journal* 25 (Spring 1970), 247–48.

36. Armstrong et al., *From Versailles to Maastricht,* 88; Ostrower, *The United Nations and the United States,* 125. The UN Charter requires a two-thirds majority vote on "important questions" brought before the General Assembly, and a simple majority on all other issues. For a copy of the UN Charter, consult the UN Web site: www.un.org.

37. By contrast, the Soviet Union exercised its veto frequently during the UN's early years. In some cases, the U.S. engineered votes on issues in expectation of a Soviet veto, as a way to bolster an image of Soviet intransigence within the UN. Armstrong et al., *From Versailles to Maastricht,* 68.

38. George F. Kennan, *American Diplomacy, 1900–1950* (Chicago and London: University of Chicago Press, 1951), 95. Kennan's reference to "fuzzy-minded idealism" is quoted in Moore and Pubantz, *To Create a New World,* 69, n. 81.

39. Ostrower, *The United Nations and the United States,* 76–77; and Caroline Pruden, *Conditional Partners: Eisenhower, the United Nations, and the Search for a Permanent Peace* (Baton Rouge: Louisiana State University Press, 1998), 108–19. As a measure of the distance from immediate postwar internationalism, and the self-proclaimed internationalism of both Eisenhower and Secretary of State Dulles, to the unilateralism of Cold War policy, Pruden notes that "the administration never seriously considered pursuing its objectives in Guatemala through either universal or regional multilateral organizations." Pruden, 110.

40. For Morse's attitude, see "Summary Record of the 526th Meeting of the National Security Council, Washington, April 3, 1964, 2 P.M.," *Foreign Relations of the United States: 1964–1968,* vol. 1, *Vietnam 1964* (Washington, DC: U.S. Government Printing Office, 1992), 223–24. Morse elaborated upon U.S. obligations under the UN Charter in a June 1965 memorandum that McGeorge Bundy (president's special assistant for national security affairs) termed "the tightest case I have seen for taking Vietnam to the UN." "Memorandum from the President's Special Assistant for National Security Affairs (Bundy) to President Johnson," June 24, 1965, *Foreign Relations of the United States:*

1964–1968, vol. 3, *Vietnam, June–December 1965* (Washington, DC: U.S. Government Printing Office, 1996), 44; Morse's memorandum is reproduced on pp. 28–33. For Mansfield's viewpoint, see "Memorandum from Senator Mike Mansfield to President Johnson," February 8, 1965, *Foreign Relations of the United States: 1964–1968,* vol. 2, *Vietnam, January–June 1965,* 205.

41. "Letter from the Under Secretary of State (Ball) to the Secretary of State," Enclosure, May 31, 1964, *Foreign Relations of the United States: 1964–1968,* vol. 1, 404.

42. "Draft Memorandum from the President's Special Assistant for National Security Affairs (Bundy) to the President," May 25, 1964, *Foreign Relations of the United States: 1964–1968,* vol. 1, 376. Similarly, in February of the following year, after a U.S. attack on a military base in North Vietnam, the administration sent a letter to the UN secretary-general in order "to preempt any effort of a UN member to call a UN Security Council Meeting to discuss the situation in Vietnam." "Summary Notes of the 547th Meeting of the National Security Council," February 8, 1965, *Foreign Relations of the United States: 1964–1968,* vol. 2, *Vietnam, January–June 1965* (Washington, DC: U.S. Government Printing Office, 1996), 188. In South Vietnam, Ambassador Maxwell Taylor similarly explained to the South Vietnamese government that the communication merely constituted "preemptive action" to take "the initiative from those countries who might wish to call us before the UN bar as the guilty party." "Telegram from the Embassy in Vietnam to the Department of State," February 15, 1965, *Foreign Relations of the United States: 1964–1968,* vol. 2, 271.

43. "Letter from the President's Special Assistant for National Security Affairs (Bundy) to Senator Mike Mansfield," February 9, 1965, *Foreign Relations of the United States: 1964–1968,* vol. 2, 211.

44. On U Thant's efforts to negotiate a settlement in Vietnam, and the tensions between him and the Johnson administration, see Brian Urquhart, *A Life in Peace and War* (New York: Harper & Row, 1987), 190; and Thomas M. Franck, *Nation Against Nation: What Happened to the U.N. Dream and What the U.S. Can Do About It* (New York and Oxford: Oxford University Press, 1985), 154–58. See also the editorial note in *Foreign Relations of the United States: 1964–1968,* vol. 2, 337 on U Thant's efforts to arrange peace talks. "Memorandum from Acting Secretary of State Ball to President Johnson," February 13, 1965, *Foreign Relations of the United States: 1964–1968,* vol. 2 observes that "U Thant, the French, and India have already called for some form of negotiation," and "Ambassador Stevenson has reported that there is substantial sentiment in the United Nations favoring negotiation." On February 15, as the administration deliberated further military action in the context of international pressure for a peace settlement, William P. Bundy advised Dean Rusk, "The complexity and difficulty of these issues argue strongly for *not* seeking to litigate them in the UN." "Memorandum from the Assistant Secretary of State for Far Eastern Affairs (Bundy) to Secretary of State Dean Rusk," February 15, 1965, *Foreign Relations of the United States: 1964–1968,* vol. 2, 280.

45. See, for example, Dwight D. Eisenhower, *Waging Peace, 1956–1961* (Garden City, NY: Doubleday & Company, Inc., 1965), 230, where Eisenhower observed, "The danger of Communist military aggression . . . was being somewhat discounted, while more subtle infiltration and subversion under the cloak of promises of Communist aid to uncommitted countries were becoming more noticeable." In 1956, Secretary of State John Foster Dulles famously condemned neutralism as an "immoral and short-sighted conception." "Dulles Talk Aims to Assure Allies," *New York Times,* June 10, 1956, 24. Some scholars have pointed out that the Eisenhower administration's actual attitude toward neutralism was far more nuanced than much of its public rhetoric. See, for example, Michael A. Guhin, *John Foster Dulles: A Statesman and His Times* (New York and London: Columbia University Press, 1972), 252–64; and H.W. Brands, *The Specter of Neutralism: The United States and the Emergence of the Third World, 1947–1960* (New York and London: Columbia University Press, 1989); see also Eisenhower's own comments in "Remarks at

the Pageant of Peace Ceremonies," December 17, 1954, *Public Papers of the Presidents of the United States: Dwight D. Eisenhower, 1954* (Washington, DC: U.S. Government Printing Office, 1960), 356; and "The President's News Conference of June 6, 1956," *Public Papers of the Presidents of the United States: Dwight D. Eisenhower, 1956* (Washington, DC: U.S. Government Printing Office, 1958), 554–55, and 556–57, n. 1. At the same time, however, there is no question that the administration distrusted the nonaligned movement and believed in the necessity of winning the Third World over to the American point of view. In addition, leaders of nonaligned nations encountered more direct pressure than public rhetoric necessarily indicated. Norodom Sihanouk, for example, later recalled the attitude of the U.S. ambassador to Cambodia as follows: "No nations could conceivably remain neutral in the struggle against world communism. . . . Not to be with the U.S. in this crusade was to be against her [ellipsis in original]." Norodom Sihanouk, as related to Wilfred Burchett, *My War with the CIA: Cambodia's Fight for Survival* (Middlesex, England and London: Penguin Books, 1973), 76. Here I must thank Geoffrey Robinson for assistance on the relationship between the Eisenhower administration and the nonaligned movement (and for other citations, particularly in notes 62, 77, and 96), as well as for our many conversations over the past several years about internationalism, world affairs, international organization, human rights, and humanitarian intervention.

46. Ostrower, *The United Nations and the United States,* 134.

47. Moore and Pubantz, *To Create a New World,* 223; Ostrower, *The United Nations and the United States,* 134–36, 155. The quotation is from Urquhart, *A Life in Peace and War,* 264.

48. The phrase "Third World UN" comes from Armstrong, et al., *From Versailles to Maastricht,* Chapter 4. For details regarding the reasons for U.S. withdrawal from the ILO, see Armstrong, et al., 101–2.

49. Robert W. Gregg, *About Face? The United States and the United Nations* (Boulder, CO and London: Lynne Rienner Publishers, 1993), 3.

50. *Ibid.,* 68–69.

51. Bernard D. Nossiter, "Questioning the Value of the United Nations," *New York Times Magazine,* April 11, 1982, 17.

52. Ostrower, *The United Nations and the United States,* Chap. 9; Gregg, *About Face?,* Chap. 4. In the early 1960s, the United States had sharply criticized the Soviet Union and France for withholding payments for UN peacekeeping operations in the Congo. In theory, a nation could lose its vote in the General Assembly for failure to pay dues, but in the interests of universalism, no such penalty resulted at the time, thereby creating a precedent for U.S. arrears two decades later.

53. Ostrower, *The United Nations and the United States,* 188.

54. Urquhart, *A Life in Peace and War,* 326–27. For an example of the conservative opinion that "a world without the UN would be a better world," see Burton Yale Pines, ed., *A World Without the UN: What Would Happen If the UN Shut Down* (Washington, DC: The Heritage Foundation, 1984). The quotation is from page xix. See also the conservative commentator Charles Krauthammer's "Let It Sink," *The New Republic* 197 (August 24, 1987), 18–23.

55. Urquhart, *A Life in Peace and War,* 371.

56. See, for example, Thomas L. Hughes, "The Twilight of Internationalism," *Foreign Policy* 61 (Winter 1985–86), 25–48; and Robert C. Johansen, "The Reagan Administration and the U.N.: The Costs of Unilateralism," *World Policy Journal* 3 (Fall 1986), 601–41. One scholar later described the Reagan administration as "at its outset . . . the most unilateralist, nationalistic, and ideological of any presidential team since at least 1945." David P. Forsythe, *The Politics of International Law: U.S. Foreign Policy Reconsidered* (Boulder, CO and London: Lynne Rienner Publishers, 1990), 122.

57. Oran R. Young, "The United States and the International System," *International Organization* 22 (Autumn 1968), 902.

58. On anticommunism's effects on the politics of peace in the United States, see Robbie Lieberman, " 'Does that Make Peace a Bad Word?' American Responses to the Communist Peace Offensive, 1949–1950," *Peace and Change* 17 (April 1992), 198–228. The Cold War produced rifts within the organized peace movement as well. For example, on the split over NATO within world government groups, see Atlantic Union Committee, press release, March 15, 1949, Box 10, Folder 10, Urey papers; and United World Federalists, "North Atlantic Pact and Related Military Considerations," March 27, 1949, Box 95, Folder 7, Urey papers.

59. Sukarno, April 18, 1955, *Vital Speeches of the Day* 21 (June 1, 1955), 1251.

60. Sastroamidjojo, April 18, 1955, *Vital Speeches of the Day* 21 (June 1, 1955), 1253.

61. Gamal Abdel Nasser, April 18, 1955, *Vital Speeches of the Day* 21 (June 1, 1955), 1257 and 1258.

62. From *Vital Speeches* 21 (June 1, 1955) see, in particular, John Kotelawala, prime minister of Ceylon, April 18, 1955, 1254–56; Mahmud Bey Muntasser, ambassador of Libya, April 18, 1955, 1258–59; Mohammad Fadhil Jamali, Iraqi delegation, 1259–61; Mohammed Ali, prime minister of Pakistan, April 19, 1955, 1261–63; and Sami Solh, prime minister of Lebanon, April 19, 1955, 1267–68. For a full-fledged account of the conference by a rare American observer, see Richard Wright, *The Color Curtain: A Report on the Bandung Conference* (London: Dobson Books Ltd., 1956).

63. Carlos P. Romulo, April 18, 1955, *Vital Speeches* 21 (June 1, 1955), 1271.

64. Wolfgang Friedman, "The United Nations and the Development of International Law," *International Journal* 25 (Spring 1970), 282.

65. Mary Ann Glendon, *A World Made New: Eleanor Roosevelt and the Universal Declaration of Human Rights* (New York: Random House, 2001), xvi.

66. On the general history of human rights and its normative power since the Universal Declaration, see Glendon, *A World Made New*, Chaps. 11 and 12, and epilogue; and Peter R. Baehr and Leon Gordenker, *The United Nations in the 1990s* (New York: St. Martin's Press, 1992), Chap. 5. For Malcolm X's appeals, see, for example, George Breitman, ed., *Malcolm X Speaks: Selected Speeches and Statements* (New York: Pathfinder Press, 1965), especially "The Ballot or the Bullet," "The Black Revolution," and "Appeal to African Heads of State." Malcolm X was hardly alone among African Americans in pursuing an internationalist strategy for civil rights—during the Cold War, many prominent African Americans viewed the international arena as an important source of support. See, for example, Brenda Gayle Plummer, *Rising Wind: Black Americans and U.S. Foreign Affairs, 1935–1960* (Chapel Hill and London: University of North Carolina Press, 1996), especially Chaps. 5–6; and Penny M. von Eschen, *Race Against Empire: Black Americans and Anticolonialism, 1937–1957* (Ithaca, NY and London: Cornell University Press, 1997). On women's rights as human rights, consult Radhika Coomaraswamy, "Reinventing International Law: Women's Rights as Human Rights in the International Community," *Bulletin of Concerned Asian Scholars* 28 (April–June 1996), 16–26.

67. Baehr and Gordenker, *The United Nations in the 1990s*, 83. See also Armstrong, et al., *From Versailles to Maastricht*, 76–77.

68. Urquhart, *A Life in Peace and War*, 137.

69. *Ibid.*, 179. See also Urquhart, "On U.N. Peacekeeping," *New York Times*, December 19, 1983, A19.

70. Armstrong, et al., *From Versailles to Maastricht*, 76–81 and 105–7.

71. The quotation is from the citation of the Norwegian Nobel Committee, "The Nobel Peace Prize for 1988," found on the Nobel Foundation Web site: www.nobel.se/peace/laureates/1988/press.html (October 2002). The observation about military force and nonviolence is found in the presentation speech by Egil Aarvik, chairman, Norwegian Nobel Committee, "The Nobel Peace Prize 1988," www.nobel.se/peace/laureates/1988/presentation-speech.html (October 2002).

72. On the general history of NGOs, consult Iriye, *Global Community*. On the relationship

between the United Nations and NGOs, and their activities in various policy areas, see Peter Willetts, ed., *"The Conscience of the World": The Influence of Non-Governmental Organisations in the UN System* (Washington, DC: The Brookings Institution, 1996); and Thomas G. Weiss and Leon Gordenker, eds., *NGOs, the UN, and Global Governance* (Boulder, CO and London: Lynne Rienner Publishers, Inc., 1996).

73. Many scholars of the UN agree on this point: see, for example, Gregg, *About Face?*, Chap. 5; Armstrong, et al., *From Versailles to Maastricht,* 124–25; Moore and Pubantz, *To Create a New World,* 289–303, especially 300–3. As Robert W. Gregg notes, "A bumper sticker seen on U.S. highways asserted that there would have been no hue and cry, much less an Operation Desert Storm, had Kuwait's principal export been broccoli. . . . There is almost certainly some truth in its message, as evidenced by subsequent reluctance to confront Serbia over its assault on Bosnia. . . . .But the alacrity with which the Security Council challenged Saddam Hussein and ratcheted up its challenge to his annexation of Kuwait still suggests a strong commitment to fundamental Charter principles and a willingness to go well beyond rhetorical creed protection." Gregg, 112. Gary B. Ostrower's account is rather more pessimistic, however, and emphasizes the extent to which the U.S. could mold the UN to its own purposes during the Gulf War. Ostrower, *The United Nations and the United States,* 196–202.

74. "Let them hate, so long as they fear." John Brady Kiesling, interviewed by Melissa Block, "All Things Considered," National Public Radio, March 7, 2003. A full copy of Kiesling's eloquent resignation letter can be found in House, 108th Cong., 1st sess., *Congressional Record* (March 4, 2003), vol. 149, no. 34: E363–64.

75. Gregg, *About Face?,* Chap. 5, especially 115–16. On page 128, Gregg observes, "But although opinion may have been divided regarding U.S. policy during the Gulf crisis, there can be no denying that the UN figured more prominently and more positively in that policy than it had in many years. There had clearly been an about-face from the UN bashing that had been the hallmark of U.S. policy toward the global organization in the 1980s."

76. For a complete list of peacekeeping operations through 1998, see the appendix in Ostrower, *The United Nations and the United States,* 253–55. Gregg, *About Face?,* 96, discusses the expansion of UN peacekeeping functions.

77. On the post–Cold War recovery of the International Court of Justice, see Armstrong, et al., *From Versailles to Maastricht,* 121. Gary Jonathan Bass, *Stay the Hand of Vengeance: The Politics of War Crimes Tribunals* (Princeton: Princeton University Press, 2000); Yves Beigbeder, *Judging War Criminals: The Politics of International Justice,* (New York: St. Martin's Press, 1999); and Howard Ball, *Prosecuting War Crimes and Genocide: The Twentieth Century Experience* (Lawrence: University Press of Kansas, 1999) address war crimes tribunals and their history. Information on the Rome Statute and the International Criminal Court can be found on the UN Web site: www.un.org/law/icc (October 2002).

78. On genocide in the twentieth century, consult Samantha Power's magisterial history: *"A Problem from Hell": America and the Age of Genocide* (New York: Basic Books, 2002).

79. For an example of this conservative revisionism, see Jay Winik, *On the Brink: The Dramatic, Behind-the Scenes Saga of the Reagan Era and the Men and Women Who Won the Cold War* (New York: Simon & Schuster, 1996), which argues that the Reagan administration intentionally shifted from an assumption of perpetual U.S.-Soviet confrontation to a strategy of winning the Cold War once and for all.

80. In 1999, the United States agreed formally to meet its obligations, in exchange for reforms within the UN bureaucracy. The terrorist attacks of September 11, 2001, provided added impetus for the United States to settle its debts: shortly afterwards, the House approved a payment of $582 million, and the following September, the House authorized the final payment on past dues. Juliet Eilperin, "House Approves U.N. Payment," *Washington Post,* September 25, 2001, A1; and "Final UN Dues Payment," *San Diego Union-*

Tribune, September 26, 2002, A15; both accessed through www.lexis-nexis.com/universe.

81. Christopher Marquis, "Washington Angry Over Losing Rights Seat," *New York Times,* May 4, 2001, A13; Norman Kempster, "U.S. 'Impediment' to Human Rights, Report Declares," *Los Angeles Times,* May 30, 2001, A18; Robin Wright, "Swedes Bare Scorn in Street Theater Mockery of Bush," *Los Angeles Times,* June 15, 2001, A5, A6; Robin Wright, "New Europe Speaks with Louder Voice," *Los Angeles Times,* June 18, 2001, A1, A4; William Orme, "U.S. Demands Immunity for Its Peacekeepers," *Los Angeles Times,* June 20, 2002, A3; William Orme, "Dispute May End U.N. Role in Bosnia," *Los Angeles Times,* July 1, 2002, A1, A4; William Orme, "Peace Missions Are Put in Doubt," *Los Angeles Times,* July 3, 2002, A1, A9; William Orme, "Canada, Mexico Oppose U.S. Stance on Court," *Los Angeles Times,* July 11, 2002, A3; Richard Bourdreax, "Crucial Game Against the U.S. Means the World to Mexicans," *Los Angeles Times,* June 16, 2002, A14. For general observations regarding the post–Cold War tendency toward American unilateralism, see Charles William Maynes, "America's Fading Commitment to the World," *Global Focus: U.S. Foreign Policy at the Turn of the Millennium,* ed. Martha Honey and Tom Barry (New York: St. Martin's Press, 2000), 85–106; and Michael Byers, "The World According to Cheney, Rice and Rumsfeld," *London Review of Books,* February 21, 2002, 14–15.

82. See, for example, the statements of Nelson Mandela, quoted in Mike Cohen, "Mandela Criticizes U.S. on Iraq," *Washington Post* (electronic edition: www.washingtonpost.com, September 2002), September 2, 2002.

83. See, for example, Michael J. Glennon, "Why the Security Council Failed," *Foreign Affairs* 82 (May/June 2003), 16–35.

84. On the immediate instability in postwar Iraq, see, for example, Richard Leiby, "For Crime Victims in Iraq, No Place to Turn," *Washington Post,* May 12, 2003, C1; Peter Slevin, "Baghdad Anarchy Spurs Call for Help," *Washington Post,* May 13, 2003, A1; Carol Morello, "Iraqi Women Out of the Picture: Prominence in Public Life Disappears in Postwar Fear," *Washington Post,* May 17, 2003, A1; Edmund L. Andrews and Susan Sachs, "Iraq's Slide into Lawlessness Squanders Good Will for U.S.," *New York Times,* May 19, 2003, sec. 1, 1; and Edmund L. Andrews, "Iraq's Looters Tearing Up Archaeological Sites," *New York Times,* May 23, 2003, A1. On Garner's arrival and quick replacement, see David Rhode, with Michael Moss, "American Overseer in Iraq Returns to a Kurdish Zone," *New York Times,* April 23, 2003, A12; Steven R. Weisman, "U.S. Set to Name Civilian to Oversee Iraq," *New York Times,* May 2, 2003, A18; and Patrick E. Tyler, "New Overseer Arrives in Iraq in U.S. Shuffle," *New York Times,* May 13, 2003, A1. More recent information indicates that the State Department anticipated the United States's post-combat difficulties, but the Bush administration downplayed the risks. Eric Schmitt and Joel Brinkley, "State Department Foresaw Trouble Now Plaguing Iraq," *New York Times* (electronic edition: www.nyt.com, October 2003), October 19, 2003. Some of these articles were accessed online at www.lexis-nexis.com/universe (May 2003).

85. Patrick E. Tyler, "Troops Attacked in Baghdad in Fresh Signs of Resistance," *New York Times,* June 2, 2003, A1 and A10; John Tierney, "Postwar GI Deaths Now Exceed Toll from War," *New York Times,* August 27, 2003, A10; Dexter Filkins and Robert F. Worth, "11 Die in Baghdad as Car Bomb Hits Jordan's Embassy," *New York Times,* August 8, 2003, A1; "Huge Suicide Blast Demolishes U.N. Headquarters in Baghdad," *New York Times,* August 20, 2003, A1, A8, and A9; Neil MacFarquhar, "Commentators in Arab World Call Attack a Catastrophe," *New York Times,* August 23, 2003, A13; Patrick J. McDonnell and Tracy Wilkinson, "Blast Kills Scores at Iraq Mosque," *Los Angeles Times,* August 30, 2003, A1: Thom Shanker, "Wolfowitz's Hotel Is Attacked in Baghdad," *New York Times* (electronic edition: www.nyt.com, October 2003), October 19, 2003; Dexter Filkins and Alex Berenson, "34 Killed in 5 Suicide Bombings in Baghdad: 200 Are In-

jured in 45 Minutes of Mayhem," *New York Times,* October 28, 2003, A1, A8. Some of these articles were accessed online at www.lexis-nexis.com/universe (September 2003).

In addition, a furloughed American soldier's account of ordinary Iraqis' intense enmity toward U.S. troops is disturbingly reminiscent of the American experience during the Vietnam War. In October 2003, Specialist Juan Castillo, who was stationed west of Baghdad, described the situation in Iraq as "madness" and the war as "a waste." He continued, "And the people there hate us. If we were rolling through a town and they were cheering, hell yeah, it would make us feel better. But when they're not co-operating and throwing rocks and giving us evil looks, we don't want to be there. We're conquerors to them. It wasn't supposed to be like that." Jeffrey Gettleman, "On Fur-lough, Soldier Savors Every Moment," *New York Times,* October 15, 2003, A16; on American soldiers in Vietnam, see Christian G. Appy, *Working Class War: American Combat Soldier and Vietnam* (Chapel Hill and London: University of North Carolina Press, 1993), Chap. 7.

86. Barton Gellman, "Frustrated, U.S. Arms Team to Leave Iraq," *Washington Post,* May 11, 2003, A1; Ian Traynor, "Nuclear Watchdog Fears Terrorist Dirty Bomb After Looting at Al-Tuwaitha, *The Guardian* (London), May 14, 2003, 16; James Risen, "CIA Studying Prewar Ratings of Iraqi Threat," *New York Times,* May 22, 2003, A1 and A16; Greg Miller, "Analysis of Iraqi Weapons 'Wrong,' " *Los Angeles Times,* May 31, 2003, A1 and A12; Douglas Jehl, "Iraqi Trailers Said to Make Hydrogen, Not Biological Arms," *New York Times,* August 9, 2003, A1 and A6; Bob Drogin, "U.S. Suspects It Received False Iraq Arms Tips, *Los Angeles Times,* August 28, 2003, A1 and A4. In October, the Iraq Survey Group's preliminary report found evidence of the Hussein regime's interest in acquiring or developing unconventional weapons, but, to the ire of both Republicans and Democrats within Congress, no signs of existing weapons themselves. James Risen and Judith Miller, "No Illicit Arms Found in Iraq, U.S. Inspector Tells Congress," *New York Times,* October 3, 2003, A1, A12. Some of these articles were accessed online at www.lexis-nexis.com/universe (May 2003).

87. On the continued threat of Al Qaeda in various parts of the world, as well as the persis-tence of the Taliban in Afghanistan, see David Johnston, with Don van Natta, Jr., "U.S. Officials See Signs of a Revived Al Qaeda," *New York Times,* May 17, 2003, A1; Carlotta Gall, "Five Are Arrested in Reported Plan to Set Off Bomb in Kandahar," *New York Times,* May 26, 2003, A9; Jacki Lyden, "U.S. Readies Policy Shift in Afghanistan," *All Things Considered,* National Public Radio, August 2, 2003, audio link available at www.npr.org (September 2003); Paul Watson, "Taliban Finds New Strength in Paki-stan," *Los Angeles Times,* August 31, 2003, A1 and A4; David Rhode, "Taliban Raids Widen in Parts of Afghanistan," September 1, 2003, A1 and A4. Meanwhile, the failure of the U.S. to produce convincing evidence of Iraq's ties to international terrorism has led the Central Intelligence Agency to undertake a review of the government's prewar intelligence. Consult James Risen, "Prewar Views of Iraq Threat Are Under Review by CIA," *New York Times,* May 22, 2003, A1; and "Reviewing the Intelligence on Iraq," *New York Times,* May 26, 2003, A14. Some of these articles were accessed online at www.lexis-nexis.com/universe (May 2003).

88. Glenn Kessler and Alan Sipress, "Western Targets Bombed in Riyadh," *Washington Post,* May 13, 2003, A1.

89. On American manipulation of the United Nations, see Bennis, *Calling the Shots.*

90. In December 2002, one poll suggested that 63 percent of Americans felt war would be justified only if there was serious evidence of weapons violations by Iraq. Maura Reynolds, "Most Unconvinced on Iraq War," *Los Angeles Times,* December 17, 2002, 1. In February 2003, another poll indicated that 59 percent of Americans believed UN weapons inspectors should be given more time before any resort to war. Patrick E. Tyler and Janet Elder, "Poll Finds Most in U.S. Support Delaying a War," *New York Times,* February 14, 2003, A1. As late as March 10, polls indicated that 52 percent of Americans

preferred to give UN weapons inspectors more time, although a majority (55 percent) also indicated they would back U.S. military action without the approval of the Security Council. Adam Nagourney and Janet Elder, "Growing Number in U.S. Back War, New Survey Finds," *New York Times,* March 11, 2003, A1. On the general tendency of the American public to hold more favorable views of the UN than those of the American political leadership, see Edward C. Luck, *Mixed Messages: American Politics and International Organization, 1919–1999* (Washington, DC: Brookings Institution Press, 1999).

91. On the Bush administration's back-and-forth stance over the UN's role in Iraq, see Christopher Marquis, "U.S. May Be Forced to Go Back to U.N. for Iraq Mandate," *New York Times,* July 19, 2003, A1 and A7; Steven R. Weisman with Felicity Barringer, "U.S. Abandons Idea of Bigger U.N. Role in Iraq Occupation," *New York Times,* August 14, 2003, A1 and A10; Douglas Jehl, "U.S. Now Signals It Might Consider U.N. Force in Iraq," *New York Times,* August 28, 2003, A1 and A10. On October 16, 2003, U.S. diplomacy managed to produce a unanimous vote in favor of UN Security Council Resolution 1511, which supported efforts by the so-called Coalition Provisional Authority to reconstitute civil government in Iraq. Felicity Barringer, "Unanimous Vote by U.N.'s Council Adopts Iraq Plan," *New York Times,* October 17, 2003, A1, A12. Major American allies remained unenthused, however. France and Germany were particularly disturbed by the lack of a clear and quick timetable for the establishment of Iraqi governmental authority, and the resolution did not produce immediate promises of massive financial aid from the international community, as the Bush administration had hoped.

92. Glennon, "Why the Security Council Failed," 23.

93. *New York Times Magazine,* January 5, 2003, 1.

94. For such a critique of internationalism and the UN system, see Glennon, "Why the Security Council Failed." Following a classic realist analysis, one reminiscent of Kennan in the 1950s, Glennon argued that the nation-state's self-interested pursuit of power remains the central, incontrovertible fact of international relations, and nothing will ever change that reality. As a result, he contended, "architects of a new world order must therefore move beyond castles in the air—beyond imaginary truths that transcend politics." Glennon, 32. But rather than naturalize the nation-state, as Glennon does, one should recall that nations are historical constructs that have evolved over time. The nation-state is not a fact of nature, and it is a fallacy to think of it as a completely immutable form of social organization.

95. In the early 1970s, Walter LaFeber observed, "During the twentieth century the internationalist concepts initiated by Root had been unsuccessfully adjusted by Stimson, dazzlingly transformed by Acheson, and then narrowed and carried to one logical conclusion of unilateralism by John Foster Dulles and Henry Kissinger. Although several of these men, particularly Root and Dulles, believed at one time in the possibilities of international legal machinery, they either modified or dropped this faith when they perceived that such machinery might severely restrict American self-interest or, as between 1945 and the mid-1960s, the United States could go it alone without needing the machinery." "Internationalism as a Current in the Peace Movement: A Symposium," in *Peace Movements in America,* ed. Charles Chatfield (New York: Schocken Books, 1973), 184.

96. For a concise and moving account of East Timor's struggle for independence and the critical role the UN played in 1999, see Geoffrey Robinson, " 'If You Leave Us, We Will Die,' " *Dissent* 49 (Winter 2002), 87–99.

8. The Three Cold Wars by Chalmers Johnson

1. Kim Dae Jung, "Only a Unified Korea Can Survive in the Coming Information Age," *Los Angeles Times,* June 18, 2000.

2. Raymond Aron, *The Imperial Republic* (Englewood Cliffs, NJ: Prentice-Hall, 1974), 38, 39, 150.

3. See Frances Stonor Saunders, *The Cultural Cold War: The CIA and the World of Arts and Letters* (New York: The New Press, 1999), 90, 391–92, 394.

4. For further development of this argument, see Chalmers Johnson, *Blowback: The Costs and Consequences of American Empire* (New York: Metropolitan Books, 2000).

5. Anthony Goodman, "U.N. Adopts Draft Against U.S. Anti-Missile Defense," Reuters, November 5, 1999.

6. Barbara Crosette, "Tying Down Gulliver with Those Pesky Treaties," *New York Times,* August 8, 1999.

7. James Brooke, "Greenlanders Wary of a New Role in U.S. Defenses," *New York Times,* September 18, 2000.

8. William M. Arkin, "Secret Plan Outlines the Unthinkable," *Los Angeles Times,* March 10, 2002; and David G. Savage, "Nuclear Plan Meant to Deter," *Los Angeles Times,* March 11, 2002.

9. "U.S. and Russia Agree Big Arms Cut," *Financial Times,* May 14, 2002.

10. Paul H. Nitze, "A Threat Mostly to Ourselves," *New York Times,* October 28, 1999.

11. George Lee Butler, "The General's Bombshell," *Washington Post,* January 20, 1997.

12. William Pfaff, "Germany's Special Relationship with U.S. Is Ending Badly," *International Herald Tribune,* March 28, 2000; "Careful, They Might Hear You," *The Age* (Melbourne), May 23, 1999; and Jeffrey Richelson, "Desperately Seeking Signals," *Bulletin of the Atomic Scientists,* March/April 2000, 47–51.

13. *New York Times,* July 18, 1999.

14. Steven Erlanger, "Rights Group Says NATO Bombing in Yugoslavia Violated Law," *New York Times,* June 8, 2000.

15. Telegram from Embassy in Japan to the Department of State, June 24, 1960, *Foreign Relations of the United States, 1958–1960,* vol. 18, 378.

16. James L. Peck, "Ideal Illusions: China, Globalism, and the National Security World, 1947–1968," Ph.D. dissertation, New York University, 1996 (Ann Arbor, MI: UMI Dissertations, 1997), 210 *et passim.*

17. See Chalmers Johnson and E.B. Keehn, "East Asian Security: The Pentagon's Ossified Strategy," *Foreign Affairs* 74 no. 4 (July–August 1995), 103–14; and Walden Bello and Ehito Kimura, "Why the Protectorate Survives," Northeast Asia Peace and Security Network, Special Report, June 23, 1999, http://www.nautilus.org/.

18. Editorial, *New York Times,* May 26, 1999.

19. *Los Angeles Times,* May 11, 1999.

20. Editorial, *New York Times,* September 12, 2000.

21. See Chalmers Johnson, "In Search of a New Cold War," *Bulletin of the Atomic Scientists,* September/October 1999, 44–51.

22. James Risen, "Ferreting Out North Korea's Nuclear Secrets: U.S. Intelligence Experts at Odds," *New York Times,* August 5, 2000.

23. Federation of American Scientists, "Space Imaging Ikonos," November 1, 1999, January 11, 2000, www.fas.org; and William J. Broad, "Spy Photos of Korea Missile Site Bring Dispute," *New York Times,* January 11, 2000.

24. House Policy Committee, Christopher Cox, Chairman, "Clinton-Gore Aid to North Korea Supports Kim Jong-il's Million-Man Army," July 27, 2000, http://policy.house. gov/documents/perspectives/2000/nk.htm. Also see Steven Lee Myers, "Pentagon Says North Korea Is Still a Dangerous Military Threat," *New York Times,* September 22, 2000. An example of exaggerated military reporting on these issues is Jim Lea, "NK Missile at Launch Site," *Pacific Stars & Stripes,* July 21, 1999.

25. See Doug Bandow, "Korean Détente: A Threat to Washington's Anachronistic Military Presence?" *Foreign Policy Briefing* (Cato Institute), no. 59, August 17, 2000; Jane Perlez,

"South Korean Says North Agrees U.S. Troops Should Stay," *New York Times,* September 11, 2000; and "U.S. Secretary of Defense: Need to Maintain 100,000 U.S. Troops in Asia," *Yomiuri Shimbun* (Tokyo), September 23, 2000.

26. Kim Ji-ho, "N.K. Lags Far Behind S. Korea in Military Power," *Korea Herald,* January 12, 2000.

27. *Los Angeles Times,* July 24, 1999.

28. Diana Jean Schemo, "Files in Paraguay Detail Atrocities of U.S. Allies," *New York Times,* August 11, 1999.

29. Larry Rohter, "Brazil Opens Files on Region's Abuses in Age of Dictators," *New York Times,* June 9, 2000.

30. Freddy Cuevas, Associated Press, "Military Base or Murder Scene?" *San Diego Union-Tribune,* August 18, 1999.

31. Tim Weiner and Ginger Thompson, "Wide Net in Argentine Torture Case," *New York Times,* September 11, 2000.

32. Clifford Klauss, "Pinochet Case Reviving Voices of the Tortured," *New York Times,* January 3, 2000.

33. See Vernon Loeb, "Top C.I.A. Officials Won't Declassify Some Chile Files," *Washington Post,* August 11, 2000; and Christopher Marquis, "White House to Revisit Chile Files That C.I.A. Wants to Block," *New York Times,* September 14, 2000.

34. Allan Nairn, "U.S. Complicity on Timor," *The Nation,* September 27, 1999, 5–6.

35. Diana Jean Schemo, *New York Times* service, "CIA Linked to Killing of 2 Americans in Chile," *San Diego Union-Tribune,* February 13, 2000.

36. "The Truth About Chile," *New York Times,* editorial February 15, 2000.

37. See Peter Kornbluh, Director, Chile Documentation Project, National Security Archive, "CIA Acknowledges Ties to Pinochet's Repression," September 19, 2000, http://www.gwu.edu/~nsarchiv/news/20000919/index.html; and Kornbluh, "CIA Outrages in Chile," *The Nation,* October 16, 2000, 4–5.

38. *New York Times,* August 11, 1999.

39. Diana Jean Schemo, "F.B.I. Watched an American Who Was Killed in Chile Coup," *New York Times,* July 1, 2000.

40. *New York Times,* June 9, 2000.

41. NSC 144, March 4, 1953; quoted in Peck, "Ideal Illusions," 73.

42. W.E. Gutman, "Politics of Assassination: The Bloody Legacy of the U.S. Army School of the Americas," http://www.pangaea.org/street_children/latin/soa.htm.

43. Steven Lee Myers, "Protesting War School for Foreigners," *New York Times,* November 22, 1999; and "School of the Americas," http://www.house.gov/moakley/iss_scham.htm. Also see "Watching What the Army Teaches," *New York Times* editorial, November 21, 1999; and Steven Lee Myers, "Army Training School to Rise Again, Recast but Unmoved," *New York Times,* May 20, 2000.

44. See http://www.soaw.org, s. v. School of the Americas Graduates.

45. Sebastian Rotella, "Fujimori Insists He Retains Firm Grip on Peru's Helm," *Los Angeles Times,* September 20, 2000; Sebastian Rotella, "Peru: Fujimori and His Secretive Spy Chief Did Business in the Shadows," *Los Angeles Times,* September 25, 2000; and Christopher Marquis, "U.S. Says Asylum in Panama Helped Avert a Coup in Peru," *New York Times,* September 26, 2000.

46. http://www.soaw.org, School of the Americas Graduates, s. v., Peru, Vladimiro Lenin Montesinos Torres.

47. http://www.soaw.org, "Peruvian Intelligence Chief Named in Scandals Is SOA Grad," September 18, 2000.

48. Larry Rohter, "In U.S.-Trained Force, Colombia Unites War on Rebels and Drugs," *New York Times,* July 29, 1999.

49. Tad Szulc, "The Ghost of Vietnam Haunts 'Plan Colombia,' " *Los Angeles Times,* Au-

gust 20, 2000; and "The Price of War, Beyond Colombia," Stratfor.com's Global Intelligence Update, September 27, 2000, http://stratfor.com/.

50. Peter Clark, "Failed 'Plan' in Colombia," *The Nation,* posted online July 31, 2003.

9. Still Stuck in the Big Muddy by Marilyn B. Young

1. More daringly, Hollywood returned to Vietnam itself in the 2002 movie *We Were Soldiers,* in which a battlefield victory early in the war obscured the ultimate defeat. For more on this see Marilyn B. Young, "In the Combat Zone," *RHR* (Winter 2003), 253–64.

2. Paul J. Nyden, "Byrd Challenges Bush's Ideas on War; West Virginia Senator Warns of Another Vietnam," *West Virginia Gazette,* June 29, 2002 (www.truthout.com)

3. James LeMoyne, "Pentagon's Strategy for the Press: Good News or No News," *New York Times,* February 17, 1991. The relationship between the press and the military is scathingly caricatured in the movie *Three Kings.*

4. Anthony Swofford, *Jarhead: A Marine's Chronicle of the Gulf War and Other Battles* (New York: Scribners, 2003), 14–15.

5. Felicity Barringer, " 'Reality TV' About GIs on War Duty," *New York Times,* February 21, 2002.

6. *Ibid.*

7. See Andrew J. Bacevich, *The American Empire* (Cambridge: Harvard University Press, 2002), 192; see 181ff for a succinct critique of U.S. policy in Kosovo.

8. Wolfgang Schivelbusch, *New York Times,* April 22, 2003. In his book on the culture of defeat he asks whether "America's post-September 11 war fever is really a response to an earlier and unresolved defeat?" His alternative suggestion is not much more comforting: "Could if be that the decades of relative American peacefulness and readiness to cooperate that followed the defeat in Vietnam were merely an interim period, akin to the Weimar Republic. . . ." 294.

9. John Dower, *Embracing Defeat: Japan in the Wake of World War II* (New York: W.W. Norton, The New Press, 1999), 40–41.

10. See John Prados's analysis of the speech on www.tompaine.com, May 2, 2003.

11. Transcript of Bush speech www.americanrhetoric.com/wariniraq/gwbushiraq5103. htm (accessed May 8, 2003).

12. Paul G. Pierpaoli, Jr., *Truman and Korea: The Political Culture of the Early Cold War* (Columbia: University of Missouri Press, 1999), 29.

13. Eliot Cohen, "This Is World War IV," *Wall Street Journal,* Nov 20, 2001. In an interview with the online www.insightmag.com, Cohen said he used the phrase *World War IV* "tongue-in-cheek as a way of getting people to think about the current conflict as something bigger than the Afghanistan war." See Stephen Goode, "The Character of Wartime Statesmen," interview with Eliot Cohen, May 27, 2003.

14. Norman Podhoretz, "How to Win World War IV," *Commentary,* 113, no. 2 (February 2002), 19–29; Charles Feldman, Stan Wilson, CNN, "Ex-CIA director: U.S. faces 'World War IV,' " posted April 3, 2003, www.cnn.com.

15. See Paul Rogers, "Permanent Occupation?," OpenDemocracy, April 24, 2003 (www.opendemocracy.com). Rogers writes that the combination of new and old bases marks a "major military investment in . . . the Persian Gulf and Central Asia . . . that are the primary and secondary regions of the world for new oil exploration and development."

16. Carl Hulse and James Dao, "Cold War Long Over, Bush Administration Examines Steps to a Revamped Arsenal," *New York Times,* May 29, 2003, A23. The House of Representatives removed bans on research into "smaller" nuclear weapons; provided funding for the development of "turning existing nuclear warheads into weapons capable of

piercing underground bunkers," paved the way to renewed underground testing, and provided funds for research into "advanced' concepts."

10. Remembrance of Empires Past: 9/11 and the End of the Cold War by Corey Robin

1. Corey Robin, "The Ex-Cons: Right-Wing Thinkers Go Left!" *Lingua Franca,* February 2001, 32–33; Irving Kristol, interview with author (Washington, August 31, 2000).
2. Frank Rich, "The Day Before Tuesday," *New York Times,* September 15, 2001, A23; Maureen Dowd, "From Botox to Botulism," *New York Times,* September 26, 2001, A19; David Brooks, "The Age of Conflict: Politics and Culture after September 11," *Weekly Standard,* November 7, 2001.
3. Francis Fukuyama, "Francis Fukuyama says Tuesday's attack marks the end of 'America's Exceptionalism,' " *Financial Times,* September 15, 2001, 1; Nicholas Lemann, "The Next World Order," *The New Yorker,* April 1, 2002, 48; David Brooks, "Facing Up to Our Fears," *Newsweek,* October 22, 2001.
4. Andrew Sullivan, "High Impact: The Dumb Idea of September 11," *New York Times Magazine,* December 9, 2001; George Packer, "Recapturing the Flag," *New York Times Magazine,* September 30, 2001, 15–16; Brooks, "Facing Up to Our Fears"; Brooks, "The Age of Conflict."
5. Brooks, "Facing Up to Our Fears."
6. Brooks, "The Age of Conflict."
7. On 9/11, trust in government, and the welfare state, see Jacob Weisberg, "Feds Up," *New York Times Magazine,* October 21, 2001, 21–22; Michael Kelly, "The Left's Great Divide," *Washington Post,* November 7, 2001, A29; Robert Putnam, "Bowling Together," *The American Prospect,* January 23, 2002; Bernard Weinraub, "The Moods They Are A 'Changing in Films," *New York Times,* October 10, 2001, E1; Nina Bernstein, "On Pier 94, a Welfare State That Works, and Possible Models for the Future," *New York Times,* September 6, 2001, B8; Michael Kazin, "The Nation: After the Attacks, Which Side Is the Left On?" *New York Times,* October 7, 2001, section 4, 4; Katrina vanden Heuvel and Joel Rogers, "What's Left? A New Life for Progressivism," *Los Angeles Times,* November 25, 2001, M2; Michael Kelly, "A Renaissance of Liberalism," *Atlantic Monthly,* January 2002, 18–19. On 9/11 and the culture wars, see Richard Posner, "Strong Fiber After All," *Atlantic Monthly,* January 2002, 22–23; Rick Lyman, "At Least for the Moment, a Cooling of the Culture Wars," *New York Times,* November 13, 2001, E1; Maureen Dowd, "Hunks and Brutes," *New York Times,* November 28, 2001, A25; Richard Posner, "Reflections on an America Transformed," *New York Times,* September 8, 2002, Week in Review, 15. On 9/11, bipartisanship, and the new presidency, see "George Bush, G.O.P. Moderate," *New York Times,* September 29, 2001, A18; Maureen Dowd, "Autumn of Fears," *New York Times,* November 23, 2001, Week in Review, 17; Richard L. Berke, "Bush 'Is My Commander,' Gore Declares in Call for Unity," *New York Times,* September 30, 2001, A29; Frank Bruni, "For President, a Mission and a Role in History," *New York Times,* September 21, 2001, A1; "Politics Is Adjourned," *New York Times,* September 20, 2001, A30; Adam Clymer, "Disaster Forges a Spirit of Cooperation in a Usually Contentious Congress," *New York Times,* September 20, 2001, B3. For a general statement of these various themes, see "In for the Long Haul," *New York Times,* September 16, 2001, Week in Review, 10.
8. Judy Keen, "Same President, Different Man in Oval Office," *USA Today,* October 29, 2001, 6A.
9. Christopher Hitchens, "Images in a Rearview Mirror," *The Nation,* December 3, 2001, 9.
10. Lemann, "Next World Order," 44; Joseph S. Nye Jr., *The Paradox of American Power:*

Why the World's Only Superpower Can't Go It Alone (New York: Oxford University Press, 2002), 168; Brooks, "The Age of Conflict."

11. George Steiner, *In Bluebeard's Castle: Some Notes Toward the Redefinition of Culture* (New Haven: Yale University Press, 1971), 11.

12. Cheney cited in Donald Kagan and Frederick W. Kagan, *While America Sleeps: Self-Delusion, Military Weakness, and the Threat to Peace Today* (New York: St. Martin's Press, 2000), 294; Condoleezza Rice, "Promoting the National Interest" *Foreign Affairs* (June 2000), 45; Nye, *Paradox of American Power*, 139.

13. *The Clinton Foreign Policy Reader: Presidential Speeches with Commentary*, ed. Alvin Z. Rubinstein, Albina Shayevich, and Boris Zlotnikov (Armonk, NY: M.E. Sharpe, 2000), 9, 20, 22–23. It should be pointed out that after several years of reduced military spending, Clinton, in his second term, steadily began to increase military appropriations. Between 1998 and 2000, military expenditures went from $259 billion to $301 billion. This increase in spending coincided with a reconsideration of the dangers confronting the United States. In his last years in office, Clinton began to sound the alarm more forcefully against the threat of terrorism and rogue states. The contrast between the rhetoric of the early and later years of the Clinton administration is quite significant. See *Clinton Foreign Policy Reader*, 36–42; Paul-Marie de la Gorce, "Offensive New Pentagon Defence Doctrine," *Le Monde Diplomatique*, March 2002.

14. David Halberstam, *War in a Time of Peace* (New York: Scribner, 2001), 22–23, 110–13, 152–53, 160–63, 193, 242.

15. Nye, *Paradox of American Power*, 8–11, 110. On occasion, Clinton even went so far as to suggest that pouring so much money into fighting the Cold War was, if not exactly a waste, then at least an unnecessary strain on the nation's vital resources. "The Cold War," he said at American University in 1993, "was a draining time. We devoted trillions of dollars to it, much more than many of our more visionary leaders thought we should have." *Clinton Foreign Policy Reader*, 9.

16. Brooks, "The Age of Conflict;" Robert D. Kaplan, *The Coming Anarchy: Shattering the Dreams of the Post Cold War* (New York: Vintage, 2000), 23–24, 89. Also see Francis Fukuyama, *The End of History and the Last Man* (New York: HarperCollins, 1992, 2002), 304–5, 311–12.

17. See Robert Putnam, *Bowling Alone: The Collapse and Revival of American Community* (New York: Simon & Schuster, 2000); Dinesh D'Souza *The Virtue of Prosperity: Finding Values in an Age of Techno-Affluence* (New York: Simon & Schuster, 2000); John B. Judis, *The Paradox of American Democracy: Elites, Special Interests, and the Betrayal of the Public Trust* (New York: Pantheon, 2000); Kagan and Kagan, *While America Sleeps.*

18. Indeed, the Clinton administration's many pronouncements on the issue of multi- and unilateralism sound remarkably similar to those of the current Bush administration. In an address to the United Nations in 1993, Clinton stated, "We will often work in partnership with others and through multilateral institutions such as the United Nations. It is in our national interest to do so. But we must not hesitate to act unilaterally when there is a threat to our core interests or to those of our allies." That same year, Anthony Lake, his national security advisor, declared, "We should act multilaterally where doing so advances our interests—and should act unilaterally when that will serve our purpose." In 1994, Clinton affirmed that he sought U.S. "influence over" multilateral decisions and operations. In 1995, he declared, "We will act with others when we can, but alone when we must." More recently, Clinton's assistant secretary of defense has declared, against the counsel and advice of classic balance-of-power realists, that the United States should maintain its monopoly of power as the surest path to peace. As for the debates between realists and humanitarians, internationalists and isolationists, the fact is that many of the neoconservative critics of the Clinton administration are as committed to humanitarian, internationalist intervention as the Clinton administration was. *The Clinton Foreign Policy Reader*, 6, 16–17, 26, 28; Nye, 15; Robert Kagan and William Kristol, "The Present

Danger," *The National Interest* (Spring 2000); "Paul Wolfowitz, velociraptor," *The Economist,* February 9, 2002; Lemann, 42; Robert Kagan, "Fightin' Democrats," *Washington Post,* March 10, 2002.

19. Kagan and Kagan, *While America Sleeps,* 1–2, 4; Kaplan, *The Coming Anarchy,* 157, 172, 176.

20. Brooks, "The Age of Conflict"; Steven Mufson, "The Way Bush Sees the World," *Washington Post,* February 17, 2002, B1; "Paul Wolfowitz, velociraptor."

21. Lemann, "Next World Order," 43, 47–48; Seymour M. Hersh, "The Iraq Hawks," *The New Yorker* (December 24 and 31, 2001), 61; Robert Kagan, "Fightin' Democrats"; Kagan and Kagan, *While America Sleeps,* 293, 295.

22. Emily Eakin, "All Roads Lead to D.C.," *New York Times,* March 31, 2002, Week in Review, 4; Lemann, "Next World Order," 44. Also see Alexander Stille, "What Is America's Place in the World Now?" *New York Times,* January 12, 2002, B7; Michael Ignatieff, "The American Empire (Get Used to It.)," *New York Times Magazine,* January 5, 2003, 22ff; Bill Keller, "The I-Can't-Believe-I'm-a-Hawk Club," *New York Times,* February 8, 2003, A17; Lawrence Kaplan, "Regime Change," *The New Republic,* March 3, 2003.

23. Lemann, "Next World Order," 43–44; Hersh, "The Iraq Hawks," 61; George W. Bush, "State of the Union Address," *New York Times,* January 30, 2002, A22; Mufson, "The Way Bush Sees the World," B1.

24. Michael Howard, "Stumbling into Battle," *Harper's,* January 2002, 13–18; Paul Kennedy, "Has the US Lost Its Way?" *The Guardian,* March 2, 2002; Stanley Hoffman, "On the War," *New York Review of Books,* November 1, 2001, 4–6; Tony Judt, "America and the War," *New York Review of Books,* November 15, 2001, 4–6; Tony Judt, " 'The War on Terror,' " *New York Review of Books,* December 20, 2001, 102–3. Also see Benjamin Schwarz and Christopher Layne, "A New Grand Strategy," *The Atlantic,* January 2002, 36–42.

25. Chalmers Johnson, *Blowback: The Costs and Consequences of American Empire* (New York: Henry Holt, 2000), 9.

26. As a 1970 report to a Senate Foreign Relations subcommittee noted, "Overseas bases, the presence of elements of United States armed forces, joint planning, joint exercises, or excessive military assistant programs . . . all but guarantee some involvement by the United States in the internal affairs of the host government." Cited in "U.S. Military Bases and Empire," *Monthly Review,* March 2002.

27. Elaine Sciolino with Eric Schmitt, "U.S. Rethinks Its Role in Saudi Arabia," *New York Times,* March 10, 2002, A24; Howard W. French, "Airman's Rape Conviction Fans Okinawa's Ire Over U.S. Bases," *New York Times,* March 29, 2002, A3; "U.S. Military Bases and Empire;" Johnson, 34–64.

28. Hersh, "The Iraq Hawks," 61–63; Lemann, "Next World Order," 47.

29. Eric Schmitt and Steve Lee Myers, "U.S. Steps Up Air Attack, While Defending Results of Campaign," *New York Times,* October 26, 2001, B1; Susan Sachs, "U.S. Appears to Be Losing Public Relations War So Far," *New York Times,* October 28, 2001, B8; Warren Hoge, "Public Apprehension Felt in Europe Over the Goals of Afghanistan Bombings," *New York Times,* November 1, 2001, B2; Dana Canedy, "Vietnam-Era G.I.'s Watch New War Warily," *New York Times,* November 12, 2001, B9.

30. Suzanne Daley, "Many in Europe Voice Worry U.S. Will Not Consult Them," *New York Times,* January 31, 2002, A12; Suzanne Daley, "French Minister Calls U.S. Policy 'Simplistic,' " *New York Times,* February 7, 2002, A14; Karen De Young, "War's Black and White Phase Turns to Gray," *Los Angeles Times,* February 12, 2002, A1; Robert Kuttner, "Bush Blunder Shows It's Time for Dissent," *Boston Globe,* February 13, 2002; David E. Sanger, "Allies Hear Sour Notes in 'Axis of Evil' Chorus," *New York Times,* February 17, 2002, A18; Chris Matthews, "A Wayward Crusade," MSNBC (February 14, 2002); Todd S. Purdum, "Democrats Starting to Fault President on the War's Fu-

ture," *New York Times,* March 1, 2002, A1; Elisabeth Bumiller, "Out of the Shadows, but Lawmakers Complain They Are Still in the Dark," *New York Times,* March 11, 2002, A16; Sheryl Gay Stolberg, "Daschle Wants President to Tell Congress More About His Plans for War," *New York Times,* March 4, 2002, A10; Robert C. Byrd, "Why Congress Has to Ask Questions," *New York Times,* March 12, 2002, A27.

31. Robin Wright, "Urgent Calls for Peace in Mideast Ring Hollow as Prospects Dwindle," *Los Angeles Times,* March 31, 2002.

32. Wright, "Urgent Calls for Peace."

33. James Traub, "Questions for Richard C. Holbrooke," *New York Times Magazine,* March 24, 2002, 20; Paul Krugman, "Conquest and Neglect," *New York Times,* April 11, 2003, A25. Also see Anton Ferreira, "Confusion Reigns in Afghanistan, U.S. Says," Reuters News Service, February 11, 2002; Michael Evans, "Marines to Face Guerilla War as Taliban Fighters Change Tactics," *The Times,* March 21, 2002; Andrew Buncombe, "British Forces Caught in Attack by Taliban," *The Independent,* March 22, 2002; Ben Fenton, "General Warns of Unwinnable Guerilla War," *Daily Telegraph,* March 22, 2002; Jeffrey Gettleman, "Empty American Promises Embitter an Afghan Village," *Los Angeles Times,* March 26, 2002; Medeleine Bunting, "Western Intervention Has Done Little for the Afghans and Less to Beat Terrorism," *The Guardian,* May 20, 2002; Phil Reeves, "Living in Poverty and Fear of Abandonment, the Barely Functioning State That Trusted Its Saviours," *The Independent,* February 24, 2003; Carlotta Gall, "U.N. Representative Warns That Afghan Peace Is Fragile," *New York Times,* February 24, 2003, A8; Judith Huber, "Afghanistan: The Taliban's Smiling Face," *Le Monde Diplomatique,* March 2003; Robert Evans, " 'Climate of fear' Rules Afghanistan," Reuters, April 22, 2003; Mark Shoofs, "Russian Drug Official Criticizes U.S. for Afghan Heroin Surge," *Wall Street Journal,* August 11, 2002; Ahmed Rashid, "Who's Winning the War on Terror?" *Yale Global Online,* September 5, 2003; David Rohde, "Taliban Officials Tell of Plans to Grind Down the Americans," *New York Times,* September 12, 2003, A27.

34. According to a national poll conducted by Putnam and his colleagues during the months preceding and following September 11, 51 percent of Americans claimed that their trust in the national government had increased following the terrorist attacks, while only 7 percent said that it had decreased. At the same time, Putnam admits that this changed attitude has not produced any concrete action. "Generally speaking, attitudes (such as trust and concern) have shifted more than behavior has." Putnam, "Bowling Together."

35. David E. Rosenbaum, "Senate Deletes Higher Mileage Standard in Energy Bill," *New York Times,* March 14, 2002, A28.

36. Diana B. Henriques and David Barstow, "Victim's Fund Likely to Pay Average of $1.6 Million Each," *New York Times,* December 21, 2001, A1. For an excellent critique, see Eve Weinbaum and Max Page, "Compensate All 9/11 Families Equally," *Christian Science Monitor,* January 4, 2002, 11.

37. Tara Copp and Jessica Wehrman, "Troops Dig into Own Pockets to Pay for Gear," Scripps Howard News Service, September 11, 2003.

38. Tim Jones, "Military Sees No Rush to Enlist," *Chicago Tribune,* March 24, 2002; David W. Chen, "Armed Forces Stress Careers, Not Current War," *New York Times,* October 20, 2001, B10.

39. Andrew Gumbel, "Pentagon Targets Latinos and Mexicans to Man the Front Lines in War on Terror," *The Independent,* September 10, 2003.

40. R.W. Apple Jr., "Nature of Foe Is Obstacle in Appealing for Sacrifice," *New York Times,* October 15, 2001, B2; Frank Rich, "War Is Heck," *New York Times,* November 10, 2001, A23; Alison Mitchell, "After Asking for Volunteers, Government Tries to Determine What They Will Do," *New York Times,* November 10, 2001, B7. Also see Michael Lipsky, "The War at Home: Wartime Used to Entail National Unity and Sacrifice," *The American Prospect,* January 28, 2002, 15–16.

41. *The NewsHour* (October 29, 2001).

42. Elisabeth Bumiller, "Bush Asks Volunteers to Join Fight on Terrorism," *New York Times,* January 31, 2002, A20; Mitchell, "After Asking for Volunteers," B7. Also see David Brooks, "Love the Service Around Here," *New York Times Magazine,* November 25, 2001, 34.

43. My discussion here is indebted to conversations with Steve Fraser.

44. This corporate abdication of government power applies even to those cases—like the first Gulf War or the signing of NAFTA—where many had thought they'd seen the heavy footprints of corporate America. According to the best accounts of the Gulf War and NAFTA, it was political officials, particularly the first President Bush, who pressed these policies, often persuading a reluctant business and military community to follow along. John R. MacArthur, *The Selling of "Free Trade": NAFTA, Washington, and the Subversion of American Democracy* (Berkeley: University of California Press, 2000), 137, 170, 174–75, 194; Halberstam, *Peace in Time of War,* 69–70; Kagan and Kagan, *While America Sleeps,* 244–50.

45. Thomas Friedman, *The Lexus and the Olive Tree: Understanding Globalization* (New York: Farrar, Straus, Giroux, 1999), 373.

46. Cf. Dan Baum, "Big Oil Fears War, Too," *Salon,* February 24, 2003. Also see the widely circulated e-mail from Pulitzer-Prize–winning *Newsday* reporter Laurie Garrett, "Report from Davos" (March 2003).

CONTRIBUTORS

Michael A. Bernstein is Professor of History and Associated Faculty-Member in Economics at the University of California, San Diego. The author of numerous articles on the economic and political history of the United States, his most recent book is *A Perilous Progress: Economists and Public Purpose in Twentieth Century America.*

Bruce Cumings is the Norman and Edna Freehling Professor of History at the University of Chicago. He has written extensively on East Asian history and international affairs and is the author of, among other publications, the two-volume study, *The Origins of the Korean War, Parallax Visions: Making Sense of American-East Asian Relations, North Korea: Another Country,* and is the editor of the forthcoming modern volume of the *Cambridge History of Korea.*

Carolyn Eisenberg is Professor of History at Hofstra University. She is the author of *Drawing the Line: the American Decision to Divide Germany, 1944–49,* which won the 1996 Stuart Bernath Book Prize and the 1996 Herbert Hoover Library Association Prize. She is presently writing a new book on Kissinger and Nixon and the politics of national security.

Maurice Isserman is Professor of History at Hamilton College in Clinton, New York. He is the author of, among other works, *Which Side Were You On? The American Communist Party During the Second World War, If I Had a Hammer: The Death of the Old Left and the Birth of the New Left,* and *The Other American: The Life of Michael Harrington.* He is currently writing a history of Himalayan mountaineering.

Chalmers Johnson, President of the Japan Policy Research Institute, held endowed chairs in Asian politics at both the Berkeley and San Diego campuses of the University of California. Among his fifteen books are *Peasant Nationalism and Communist Power in the Chinese Revolution, MITI and the Japanese Miracle, Blowback: The Costs and Consequences of American Empire,* and, most recently, *The Sorrows of Empire: Militarism, Secrecy, and the End of the Republic.*

Nelson Lichtenstein is Professor of History at the University of California, Santa Barbara. He is the author of *Walter Reuther: The Most Dangerous Man in Detroit* and, most recently, *State of the Union: A Century of American Labor.* His edited collection, *Imagining Capitalism: Social Thought and Political Economy in 20th Century America,* will appear in 2005.

Leo P. Ribuffo is Society of the Cincinnati George Washington Distinguished Professor of History at George Washington University. He is author of *The Old Christian Right: The Protestant Far Right from the Great Depression to the Cold War* and *Right Center Left: Essays in American History.*

Corey Robin is Assistant Professor of Political Science at Brooklyn College, City University of New York. His articles have appeared in *The New York Times Magazine, The Times Literary Supplement, Washington Post Book World, American Political Science Review,* and other newspapers, magazines, and journals. His first book, *Fear: The History of a Political Idea,* is forthcoming from Oxford University Press.

Ellen Schrecker is Professor of History at Yeshiva University and has written extensively on the red scare of the early Cold War. Among her books are *No Ivory Tower: McCarthyism and the Universities* and *Many Are the Crimes: McCarthyism in America.* Her current project is a comparison of the McCarthy era with the contemporary assault on civil liberties.

Jessica Wang is Associate Professor of History at the University of California, Los Angeles, and the author of *American Science in an Age of Anxiety: Scientists, Anticommunism, and the Cold War* (1999). Her current research focuses on the New Deal and technocratic politics in the 1930s.

Marilyn B. Young is Professor of History at New York University and currently Director of the International Center for Advanced Studies Project on the Cold War as Global Conflict. She is the author of *The Vietnam Wars, 1945–1990* and co-editor of two books of documents on the Vietnam War. Her next project is on the Korean War.

ACKNOWLEDGMENTS

It is customary for authors and editors to make obligatory noises about the collective effort that went into their books. This volume, however, really was a collective project—and not just because it contains the contributions of nine other scholars. It got its start sometime in the late 1990s during a casual conversation with Nelson Lichtenstein about the need for an intellectual intervention in the debate about the meaning of the Cold War. We were worried about the contemporary implications of the triumphalism that had developed after the fall of the Soviet Union and wanted to offer an alternative interpretation. Other people shared our concerns and, within a few months, we were talking about a conference and a book; a few of us even held an informal planning session at the 1999 meeting of the Society for Historians of American Foreign Relations. But it was only after André Schiffrin suggested that Maurice Isserman and I put together a collection of essays taking off from our article on Soviet espionage in *The Nation* in the summer of 2000 that all these conversations jelled into a tangible project. The next step was yet another planning session as well as a panel discussion at the January 2001 annual meeting of the American Historical Association. Though I ultimately took on the responsibility for editing this book, I could not have conceptualized it without the help of many others—Michael Bernstein, Kai Bird, Carolyn Eisenberg, Maurice Isserman, Nelson Lichtenstein, Leo Ribuffo, and Marilyn Young in particular.

This volume owes a very special debt to Marilyn Young and Allen Hunter, who, as the director and co-director of the Project on the Cold War as Global Conflict of the International Center for Advanced Studies at New York University, organized a conference with the financial assistance of NYU and an Andrew Mellon Foundation

Sawyer Seminar grant in the spring of 2002 that allowed the authors of the essays to test out their ideas and benefit from the comments of each other and of Csaba Bekes, Michael Cox, Melinda Kalmar, Christopher Simpson, Anders Stephanson, and Odd Arne Westad. Among the others who also contributed to this volume in one way or another are Michael Kazin, Jeryl Martin-Hannibal, Stuart Schaar, Martin Sherwin, Carole Silver, Judith Stein, and the participants in the ICAS conference.

It is an honor to work with André Schiffrin at The New Press and to have a publisher who not only understands one's project, but collaborates in it in the best sense of the word. Our editor, Marc Favreau, has been enormously helpful, proffering the kind of intelligent editorial assistance that authors dream of but rarely get. I am also indebted to Sarah Fan at the New Press, Rich Klin, and to Ronald Goldfarb, the most supportive of agents. And, finally, my husband and chief colleague, Marvin Gettleman, has, as always, done more for me and my work than he can ever imagine or than I have any right to expect. I am awed and sustained by his generosity and love.

INDEX